SECRET
FALKIRK

Jack Gillon

AMBERLEY

First published 2018

Amberley Publishing
The Hill, Stroud, Gloucestershire, GL5 4EP
www.amberley-books.com

Copyright © Jack Gillon, 2018

The right of Jack Gillon to be identified as the Author
of this work has been asserted in accordance with the
Copyrights, Designs and Patents Act 1988.

ISBN 978 1 4456 8083 5 (print)
ISBN 978 1 4456 8084 2 (ebook)

British Library Cataloguing in Publication Data.
A catalogue record for this book is available from the
British Library.

Origination by Amberley Publishing.
Printed in Great Britain.

Contents

Acknowledgements   5
Introduction   6

1. The Falkirk Bairns   7
2. First and Second Battles of Falkirk   9
3. Falkirk Old and St Modan's Parish Church   11
4. Falkirk's Town Walls   13
5. Falkirk Steeple   14
6. Falkirk Steeple Crash   15
7. Robert Buchanan – Falkirk's Bard   17
8. Falkirk's Old Market Place   21
9. Burns in Falkirk   24
10. Carron Iron Works   26
11. The Tattie Kirk, Cow Wynd   30
12. Falkirk and District Tramway   31
13. Falkirk High Street   35
14. Newmarket Street   36
15. Princes Street and Falkirk's Cinemas   41
16. The Grand Theatre and Opera House   44
17. The Emperor of Jiu-jitsu in Falkirk   46
18. The Temperance Hotel, Lint Riggs – A Beneficence of a Bairn   48
19. Aitken's Brewery, Newmarket Street   51
20. Falkirk Public Library, Hope Street   53
21. Robert Dollar and Dollar Park   56
22. Falkirk Infirmary, Thornhill Road   58
23. Barr's   59
24. The Gentleman Fountain   62
25. Callendar House and the Dark Tunnel   63
26. Marion's and Greenhorn's Wells   66
27. Falkirk Railway Stations   69
28. Vicar Street Post Office   70
29. Grahamston Iron Co. Gates   71
30. The Canals, Burke and Hare, and the Union Inn   73
31. Camelon Brass Band   77
32. Westerglen Radio Transmitter   79
33. Alfred Nobel in Falkirk   80
34. Redding Pit Disaster   82
35. King Kenny   85
36. Arthur's O'on   85

37. Larbert Railway Station and the Dobbie Hall   87
38. Larbert Railway Station and the Quintinshill Rail Disaster   89
39. Larbert Railway Bridge   90
40. First Scottish Senior Football under Floodlights at Stenhousemuir   91
41. Jimmy Finlayson, Larbert-born Hollywood Funny Man   95

Acknowledgements

I am hugely indebted to all the Bairns of Falkirk for their kindness and assistance on my visits to the town.

My brother Alastair suggested some topics for the book and provided invaluable help with additional photographs.

The people at A. G. Barr allowed the use of the old photos of Barr's. Sandy Reid provided the image of the football match at Ochilview.

As ever, massive thanks to my wife, Emma Jane, for her patience and support.

The book is dedicated to my brother Norman, who sadly passed away during the course of compiling this book. Norman knew Falkirk well. He served his apprenticeship as a joiner, building buses for Walter Alexander's. He was a bit of an enthusiast for the dancing and, like so many other couples in the 1950s, met his future wife, Margaret, at Doak's Dance hall in Falkirk.

View of Falkirk in 1824.

Introduction

Falkirk is a small town with a big history. Its strategic location, midway between Edinburgh and Glasgow at the crossroads of lowland Scotland, was the main influence on the town's development and contributed to its key role in Scotland's history. The Romans were the first to make a significant mark on the district, William Wallace and Bonnie Prince Charlie fought the English nearby, cattle were driven from all over Scotland to the great trysts in the area, Central Scotland's canals came together at Camelon, and local foundries fuelled the Industrial Revolution.

Many of the stories in this book have been told before by accomplished local historians. However, it is hoped that the book has perhaps uncovered some fresh aspects of the long and colourful history of the 'dear auld toon, wi' grey spire crown'd', even for people that know it well.

Falkirk High Street.

1. The Falkirk Bairns

Following a major drought, the Livingstons of Callendar House arranged for a piped supply of water to be taken into the centre of Falkirk. The first water was drawn from the well in 1681. Legend has it that the Livingstons donated the well 'To the Wives and the Bairns o' Fa'kirk', and natives of the town have been known as Bairns ever since.

The Bairns of Falkirk have been described as a mixture of Glasgow and Edinburgh: 'Neither so ready and demonstrative with their friendship as the one, nor so reserved as the other. They have a warm-heartedness which lies deep; they are patient, tolerant, cautious, but kindly and generous, and when they do give their friendship, staunch and loyal.' (*Third Statistical Account*, Rev. Wilson S. Leslie, 1951)

A number of these traits of the Falkirk Bairns are described in this report of a royal visit to the town: 'The people of Falkirk are usually emotionally restrained, and resistant to political stunts and religious revivalism. This emotional restraint was strikingly illustrated on the occasion when King George VI, Queen Elizabeth and the two princesses visited the town. The citizens were gratified and elated. In the heart of industrial Falkirk there is a warm loyalty to the crown, and an affectionate interest in the royal family; and in homes with a strong leftist tendency one often hears an appreciation of their exacting duties and the emphatic remark, I would not have their job for anything. Now the point is that as the royal party drove from the station towards the centre of the town, their approach was heralded only by a scattered burst of cheering. As they left their cars and went up the steps

Falkirk's coat of arms on the frontage of the former Burgh Buildings.

Above: Illustration of the coat of arms.

Left: The official Falkirk coat of arms.

to enter the Burgh Buildings there was no demonstration. When later they made their appearance again and stood chatting with members of the council, while thousands of eyes watched intently, the crowd stood in the grip of a hypnotic silence as if they were beholding a holy ritual; and still in silence the royal party entered their cars and drove away. This was an amazing and revealing incident. An isolated cheer raised by someone bold enough to shatter the silence would have sounded like brawling in church. This combination of emotional reserve and generosity was experienced by a minister who had come from a more spontaneously expressive community, and was perturbed by the lack of any outward sign that he was winning the favour of his congregation, when they casually raised his stipend by twenty per cent.' (*Third Statistical Account*, Rev. Wilson S. Leslie, 1951)

The famous town mottoes, 'Better Meddle wi' the De'il than the Bairns o' Fa'kirk' and 'Touch ane, touch a' ('Tangite Unum Tangite Omnes'), are a clear indication that the people of Falkirk will join together to defend themselves, and if one is troubled the others will provide support. They are included on scrolls in a version of the Falkirk coat of arms inscribed on the upper levels of the Glebe Street frontage of the former Burgh Buildings – although the word devil is obscured due to an old superstition that claims that it is unlucky to have satanic references on a building. The inscribed stone depicts a phoenix, Carron Co.'s crest, over a shield held by two boys brandishing clubs. The shield includes figures representing the two Battles of Falkirk and three Scottish claymores. This version of the coat of arms dates from the 1880s and was never formally approved.

The more official coat of arms provides a symbolic history of the town. It includes a lion rampant holding a shield with a representation of the Church of Falkirk between two crossed swords, symbolising the first Battle of Falkirk. A targe and two claymores represent the second Battle of Falkirk. These are framed by an indented line to denote the Antonine Wall.

2. First and Second Battles of Falkirk

The First Battle of Falkirk took place on 22 July 1298. The Scottish army under William Wallace was defeated by Edward I's English forces, who were determined to revenge their routing by the Scots at the Battle of Stirling Bridge. It was the first battle in which the English longbow was used to deadly effect. The battle took place between Falkirk and Carron, and is commemorated by a memorial presented by William Dollar on the edge of Victoria Park.

The Second Battle of Falkirk, or the Battle of Falkirk Muir, at which Bonnie Prince Charlie's Jacobite army defeated government forces under General Hawley, took place on 17 January 1746. The English suffered serious losses, while the Jacobites only lost about forty men. It is reputed that locals viewed the battle from the steeple. The Jacobite army would go on to be defeated three months later at Culloden. The site of the battle is marked by an obelisk to the south-west of the town.

Above left: First Battle of Falkirk Memorial.

Above right: Second Battle of Falkirk Memorial.

Below: Stained-glass windows depicting Prince Charles and his generals.

'After the battle Charles was conducted by torchlight to a lodging which had been provided for him in the house of a Mrs Graham, the widow of a physician, a Jacobite, and a woman of superior intelligence and manners. This house, which stands opposite to the steeple, was then the best in the town.' (*Round About Falkirk*, Robert Gillespie, 1879)

The stained-glass windows in the Howgate shopping centre portray Prince Charles Edward Stuart and his generals – Lord George Murray and Sir John Drummond. They were first installed in South Bantaskine House around 1860 by the Wilson family, whose ancestors had been involved in the battle.

3. Falkirk Old and St Modan's Parish Church

The present Falkirk Old Parish Church is only the latest religious building on the site. St Modan, the patron saint of the town, is said to have established an ecclesiastical building in the area in the sixth century and Malcolm III is thought to have built a church here in 1057. The church was radically altered in 1811 when much of an earlier medieval building

Falkirk Parish Church.

Above left: The grave of Sir John de Graeme.

Above right: Memorial to the men of Bute.

was demolished, and the church was rebuilt with only the medieval square-plan tower surviving from the previous building of around 1450.

Early references to 'Faukirke' date from the thirteenth century and there are different theories about the derivation of the name. The one that is most often repeated relates to the early establishment of a church, which was known as the Fawe Kirk (the speckled church or the church built of mottled stone). This is just one theory on the origin of the name. Another suggests that the church fell into disuse and became known as the Fallen or Fall Kirk. Falkirk has a name in Gaelic (Ecchlesbreach), Welsh, Norman, French, Latin, Lowland Scots and English, which reflects the turbulent history of the town.

Most of the memorials in the parish church graveyard were removed in the 1960s and only the most historically significant remain. The grave of Sir John de Graeme, a Scottish knight who was a casualty at the first Battle of Falkirk fighting alongside Sir William Wallace, is enclosed by a decorative iron structure that dates from 1860. Grahamston takes its name from Sir John – 'Ane better knight not to the world was lent'. The prominent Celtic cross, erected by the Marquess of Bute in 1877, commemorates the 'gallant men of Bute' who were killed at the first Battle of Falkirk. Other memorials commemorate both Jacobite and government casualties of the second Battle of Falkirk.

4. Falkirk's Town Walls

In 1647, the town was strengthened with a wall for keeping out strangers, with five ports or gates, at either end of the High Street and in Kirk Wynd, Cow Wynd and Robert's Wynd. The last named, sometimes called Bantaskine Port, was on the south side of the High Street (at today's access to the Howgate Centre) and led to the Pleasance. It was through this port that Lord George Murray entered the town with his troops in January 1746, following the Jacobite victory at the second Battle of Falkirk. The gates and wall were later removed, possibly in the late 18th century, as the town started to expand.

Third Statistical Account, Revd Wilson S. Leslie, 1951

Falkirk High Street developed along the natural ridge running east to west with a number of narrow wynds and closes to the north and south – a typical medieval layout known as the 'fish-bone' pattern. The narrow Woo'er (Weaver) Street, to the east of the steeple, is a remaining example of a typical close. The Howgate Centre was developed with its entrance following the line of the historic Robert's Wynd, one of the five gates in the town wall.

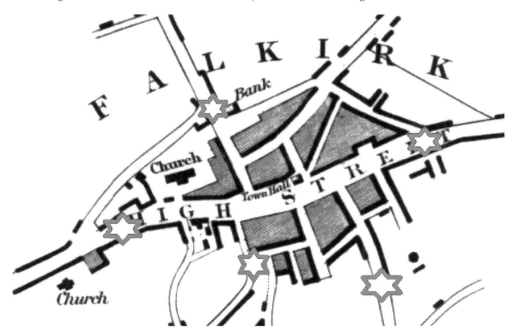

Plan showing the approximate location of Falkirk's town ports.

5. Falkirk Steeple

The iconic symbol of Falkirk and the dominating feature of the High Street is the 43-metre- (141-foot-) high steeple with its octagonal stone spire and clock. The current steeple dates from 1814 and is the third incarnation of the famous Falkirk landmark.

Falkirk's first steeple was built in the late sixteenth century. Its precise location is unknown, but it is suggested that it stood at the junction of Manor Street and Kirk Wynd. It is recorded that it was demolished in 1697 due to its ruinous and unsafe condition. In the same year, a new steeple attached to the front of the tolbooth was built.

In 1801, William Glen, a local businessman, was given permission to demolish the old tolbooth to the east of the steeple and rebuild on the site. The new building shared a wall with the steeple and a few years later, in 1803, the steeple started to subside and cracks appeared in the stone – demolition was the only option.

There ensued a long legal conflict and it was ten years before the architect David Hamilton was commissioned to design a new steeple. In 1812, the Falkirk Stentmasters launched an appeal to raise the funds required for the work to replace the ruinous old steeple with the outstanding structure that graces the town centre today.

From the early seventeenth century, the Stentmasters or Stint-masters (in Old Scots, Stent means an assessment of property for taxation and derives from the Old French *estente* – valuation) were responsible for collecting rates according to the 'means and substance' of

Above left: Falkirk's Old Steeple (1697–1804).

Above right: Falkirk Steeple.

the individuals and maintaining the infrastructure of the town. They were also responsible for the fire engines, paying someone to ring the town bell and appointing a town drummer. The Feuars of Falkirk were involved with many municipal projects. The establishment of the town council, under the Municipal Reform Act of 1833, which was followed by the Police and Improvement Act of 1859, finally removed the powers of the Stentmasters and Feuars.

The foundation stone of the new steeple was laid on 24 March 1813, and by June 1814 the grand new building was complete. In 1815, a local watchmaker fitted the clock, an essential feature at a time when few people owned watches.

6. Falkirk Steeple Crash

Falkirk Town Steeple, which has been a familiar and popular landmark with the people of the locality for more than a century was partially destroyed yesterday afternoon through being struck by lightning in the course of a short, sharp thunderstorm. Located as the building is in a central position on the High Street and surrounded by shops and tenement properties, the occurrence naturally created considerable alarm and excitement, but, fortunately, it was unattended by any loss of human life. This circumstance is all the more remarkable when regard is had to the fact that something like forty feet, representing the major portion of the fifty feet Ionic spire, collapsed and crashed into the street and through the roofs of adjoining tenement dwellings. The outstanding feature, indeed, apart from the highly alarming

The steeple following the lightning strike.

nature of the occurrence, was the positively miraculous escapes from serious injury
or death of the tenants occupying the premises struck by the falling masonry.

Falkirk Herald, 18 June 1927

On Friday 17 June 1927 at 2.10 p.m., a large part of the upper part of the Falkirk steeple was brought down by a lightning strike. There were reports of a blinding flash of lightning, followed by a reverberating clap of thunder and the almost simultaneous crash of the falling steeple. Massive blocks of stone fell with a deafening roar to the street, windows in the locality were shattered and fragments of the fallen masonry ricocheted over housetops into streets a hundred yards from the steeple. The weather vane was discovered in a court on the north side of the High Street. Fortunately, there was a torrential downpour of rain immediately before the thunderbolt struck, which sent pedestrians on the street running for shelter.

Eyewitnesses described being blinded by an enormous flash and looking up at the clock just as the lightning struck near the top of the steeple, a great cloud engulfed the building and, when the cloud cleared, the steeple was in a 'beheaded state'.

John McOrnish of Sunnyside, Camelon, had a miraculous escape. He was delivering Barr's aerated waters, with his horse-drawn lorry, to a shop on the north side of the steeple when plaster rained down on him. He was stunned by 'an awful boom', but managed to run to the west side of the steeple. He noted that he had served in France and had never heard a shell burst like it. He just missed being struck by a block of stone, which sadly killed his unfortunate horse, Carnaver.

Stones fell through the roof of the Steeple Land, a tenement next to the steeple. A Mrs Barr, who was in the top flat with her two children (Andrew and Jamie), had a particularly terrifying experience. They were practically buried under the falling masonry and were rescued when neighbours forced open the door of the flat. Mrs Barr described being blinded by a flash of light and thunder shaking the house. They were fortunate to escape with only minor injuries and only six or seven people required the attention of a doctor after the incident. A number of other buildings were damaged and the Falkirk Fire Brigade had to deal with a fire at the Universal Bar caused by fused electrics.

The news of the event travelled fast and thousands of people gathered on the High Street to view the scene. They were kept at a safe distance by the police until barricades were erected later in the day. Steeplejacks were employed to remove loose stone down to the level of the clock, and the crowd watched them with bated breath as they removed masonry and threw it down to the street. While they were working, a collie dog wandered into the danger zone and the hush of the huge crowd was broken by whistles and calls to the dog. However, one of the steeplejacks threw down some small stones to scare it off. By 10 p.m. most of the dangerous masonry had been removed and one of the steeplejacks 30 metres (100 feet) above the ground was noted as stunning the crowd of onlookers by, 'as cool as the proverbial cucumber, dusting his hands and kicking away a small stone, as he would have a banana peel on the pavement'.

A special meeting of the town council was held in the Burgh Buildings the following day to agree steps to have the area made safe as quickly as possible and accommodate the five families from the severely damaged Steeple Land until 'all cause for anxiety and danger has been removed'. It was noted that every true Bairn felt as though 'grievous bodily harm had been done to an intimate personal friend'. In the aftermath of the event many locals were said to be suffering from 'kink-in-the-neck', due to the constant habit of looking up to view the damage to the steeple. There was also many a call of 'hunt the gowk', when people looked up to check the time on the missing clock.

It seems that money could not be taken from the rates for the restoration work and a subscription fund, with a target of £2,500, was set up to restore the steeple. Falkirk Bairns from home and abroad donated to the fund and by March 1929 the restored 'Cock o' the Steeple was once again sitting proudly on its perch at the pinnacle of the rebuilt spire'. It was noted that Mr Robert Dollar of San Francisco had donated £200 towards the provision of a new clock (the old clock and two of the faces were restored and are now in the care of the National Museum of Scotland in Edinburgh).

7. Robert Buchanan – Falkirk's Bard

Robert Buchanan was born in Falkirk's Steeple Land on 22 June 1835. His father was a baker who worked in and later owned the Pie Office at the steeple. Robert attended Falkirk Parish School where he was 'not noteworthy for either his regular attendance or overwhelming love of his studies'. On leaving school he was apprenticed as a currier in his uncle John Gillespie's business at the foot of Bell's Wynd. However, his 'constitution was delicate' and

Robert Buchanan.

ROBERT BUCHANAN:

The Pie Office, High Street.

The unveiling of the monument to Robert Buchanan.

The Cock o' the Steeple.

he did not have the 'bodily strength necessary for such laborious employment'. At the age of twenty-two Robert was nominated to Her Majesty's Customs and was appointed to a position at the port of Grangemouth.

During his time at Grangemouth, Robert was noted as being esteemed and respected by his work colleagues and the general public. He served as a gunner in the local volunteer corps and took an active part as a freemason in Lodge Zetland 391. He also excelled as a vocalist and flute player.

After ten years at Grangemouth, Robert was promoted to a position in Dublin and later to Londonderry. Although Robert's career prospered in Ireland, he was homesick for Falkirk – his 'dear auld toon wi' grey spire crowned'. His wife, Margaret Rankine, a fellow Bairn of Falkirk, passed away from consumption in July 1874 and her remains were returned to Falkirk for internment. The loss of Margaret was a severe blow to Robert and, despite plans to return to his native town, he passed away in Londonderry on 31 December 1875.

Robert was known at school as a 'ready rhymer' and, from 1856, contributed poems to the *Falkirk Herald* on a regular basis. His poetry is noted as being distinguished for its 'light, fanciful grace and airy turn of thought and rhythm'. A collection of his poems was published in 1901. These feature a number of works dedicated to Falkirk and the 'Glories of Grangemeouth'.

His poem 'The Dear Auld Hame (Falkirk Town)' was written for a reunion of the Bairns of Falkirk living in Glasgow. It was set to music composed by John Fulcher, and was first performed by the local singer Michael Rennie at the Glasgow Trades Hall on 26 January 1866, where it was 'warmly applauded by the assembled Bairns of Falkirk'. The tune was arranged for the Falkirk Iron Works Band and played at most of their public appearances. It was for a time Falkirk's anthem (the 'Auld Lang Syne' of the Falkirk Bairns); for many years it was sung at 'all convivial gatherings held in the "dear auld toon"' and wherever the Bairns of Falkirk congregated. It was even introduced into the curriculum of Falkirk board schools.

'The Dear Auld Hame (Falkirk Town)':

The dear auld toon, wi' grey spire crown'd
In happy langsyne days,
We wandered, sun and tempest browned,
Amang they glens and braes;
We were bairns then, we're bairns yet,
Our hearts beat aye the same,
And time can never memory flit
Frae thee, our dear auld hame.

CHORUS
For we canna forget the dear auld hame,
Gae wander where we will;
Like the sunny beam o' a simmer's dream
That lingers near us still.

We mind where Carron silvery flings
Her white spray o'er the linn,
And dashing doon the woodland sings,
Wi' bubbling, brattling din;
And love blinks o' a bonnie e'e
We won by Marion's Well,
Twines every round life's stormy sea,
A fairy plaited spell.

Wha wadna lo'e thee? Dear auld hame!
Wha round thee hasna shared
That sacred fire that laid De Graeme
Within the auld kirkyaird?
And strewed thy field wi' horse brave,
Wha focht in Freedom's name,
And bleeding won an honoured grave
In building Scotia's fame.

Oh, dear auld hame! tho' toiling years
Hae left us sere and grey,
A glimpse o' langsyne 'mid our tears
Turns dark'ning nicht to day.
We were bairns then, we're bairns yet,
Our hearts beat aye the same,
And time can never mem'ry flit
Frae thee, oor dear auld hame.

In 1899, a proposal to erect a monument to Buchanan to 'perpetuate his memory' was suggested in the columns of the *Falkirk Herald*. In less than three months, £38 and 10*s* was raised by subscription for the proposed monument. The subscriptions were donated by those that 'had the privilege of personal acquaintance with Buchanan, and who admired him for his poetic gifts and his qualities of head and heart' and 'those of a later generation who were happy to support one who had sang so sweetly of the dear auld toon'. Robert Barr of Arnotdale, a personal friend of Buchanan, was one of the main subscribers and made up the shortfall of just over £6 in the cost of the monument.

The 'chaste and imposing' monument to Buchanan was unveiled in Falkirk Cemetery on 30 September 1899. Despite torrential rain a large crowd gathered for the ceremony, including one of Buchanan's daughters, who had travelled from Liverpool to attend the event. The unveiling ceremony ended with a rendition of the 'The Dear Auld Hame (Falkirk Town)', which it was reported 'touched the hearts of everyone that attended'.

Buchanan also wrote humouros articles, in which he imagined the Cock of the Steeple writing to the Bairns of Falkirk. In one, published in October 1869, the Steeple Cock gives thanks for some recent repairs to the steeple:

Thank ye, 'Bairns'! I fin' kinna firmer on my perch noo, and I can turn my neb to a nor'-easter wi' a feeling o' security I haena kent for a ling time. Mony a nicht, when the wind whistled, and roared, my tap swithered whether it would tak' a fleeing leap to Maggie Wood's Loan or stick still, and the steeple under my feet rock'd and rowed like a ship in a storm, hae I contemplated the awfu' possibeelity o' yer wauk'ning in the morning and finding me, or rather my remains, a wing here an' a leg there, a ' the way along the street as far as Hill's tobacco shop. [Councillor Hill's tobacco shop was at No. 51 High Street.]

Perhaps a recital of 'The Dear Auld Hame (Falkirk Town)' should be revived for present-day events in the town.

8. Falkirk's Old Market Place

Falkirk was made a Burgh of Barony by James IV in 1600 and in 1646, in the reign of Charles I, a Burgh of Regality. Burgh of Barony status conferred on the landowner, the Livingstons of Callendar House, the right to hold weekly markets. Burgh of Regality granted the leading noblemen powers to try criminals for all offences except treason.

Falkirk's former marketplace was the widened area of the High Street to the west of the steeple. The mercat cross was erected in the early 1600s to mark the site of the agricultural markets (the site of the old mercat cross is now commemorated by contrasting cobbles on the carriageway). Mercat crosses were a symbol of a town's right to hold a market –

Left: The Market Place.

Below: The Cross Well.

Right: The repositioned Cross Well.

Below: Tolbooth Street plaque.

TOLBOOTH STREET

THE SHORTEST STREET IN GREAT BRITAIN

AT A LENGTH OF 17·67 METRES - (58 FEET)

an important privilege. It was where public proclamations were made and punishments carried out. The last public hanging in Falkirk was in 1828. The tolbooth prison was handily located in a building to the east of the steeple and the town tron (weighing machine) stood nearby.

Falkirk remained principally a market town with mainly agricultural trades: tanners, saddlers and blacksmiths during the early part of the nineteenth century. An old rhyme of the time alludes to its agricultural basis – 'Glasgow for bells, Linlithgow for wells, and Falkirk for beans and pease'. The marketplace was where agricultural workers would gather on feeing days, to be hired by farmers for the season.

'The old Cross Well, which was built by the Earl of Callendar, must have been a somewhat imposing ornament. A lion, from whose throat ran a plentiful supply of good water, faced the street; while another, on the apex, bore a shield with the family arms.' (*Round About Falkirk*, Robert Gillespie, 1879). The Cross Well originally dated from 1681. The well head was replaced in 1817 with a near replica of the original. It consists of a 3.8-metre (12-feet 6-inches) stone column topped by a lion with the Livingston arms. After an absence of around a decade, the well was reinstated in a more central position on the High Street.

The statue of Wellington, by sculptor Robert Forrest, was purchased for £130 by public subscription when Falkirk provost Robert Adam took a liking to it when he visited an exhibition of Forrest's work. It was erected at the steeple in 1854. Robert Forrest (1790–1852) was a self-taught, Lanark-based sculptor, who began his career as a stonemason. His first patron, Colonel Gordon, found him carving figures out of a quarry face. Gordon commissioned works by Forrest and promoted his skills as a sculptor. In 1830, Forrest exhibited various statues in Edinburgh. Before his death in 1852, he had executed thirty groups and statues for the exhibition – the Wellington statue may have been one. The statue was moved to Newmarket Street in 1905.

A plaque on Tolbooth Street, just behind the steeple, claims that it is Britain's shortest street.

9. Burns in Falkirk

A plaque on the building at No. 189 High Street commemorates the stay of Robert Burns, the national bard, at the Cross Keys Inn in Falkirk on 25 August 1787. Burns is said to have carved the following lines on a window pane at the inn with a diamond-tipped stylus:

> Sound be his sleep and blythe his morn,
> That never did a lassie wrang;
> Who poverty ne'er held in scorn,
> For misery ever tholed a pang.

Plaque commemorating Burns' stay at the Crosss Keys Inn.

Burns visited the grave of Sir John de Graeme before proceeding to Carron Iron Works to have a look at what must have been a new wonder of the time. Unfortunately it was a Sunday and he was refused entry. Resorting to the nearby Carron Inn, he vented his disappointment by inscribing the following verse:

> We cam na here to view your works
> In hopes to be mair wise,
> But only, lest we gang to Hell,
> It may be nae surprise;
> But when we tirl'd at your door,
> Your porter dought na hear us;
> Sae may, should we to Hell's yetts come,
> Your billy Satan sair us.

To which, at some time later, William Benson, a clerk at Carron Works, is said to have penned the following response:

> If you came here to view our works
> You should have been more civil
> Than to give a fictitious name,
> In hopes to cheat the devil,
> Six days a week to you and all,

We think it very well;
The other if you go to church,
May keep you out of hell.

It seems that Burns did return for a visit to Carron Iron Works, which he likened to the mythological blacksmithing skills of the Cyclops.

10. Carron Iron Works

Scotland's first major iron foundry was established on the north bank of the River Carron in 1759. The site had a convenient water supply and a local source of iron ore from Bo'ness. Carron Co. was at the forefront of the Industrial Revolution and was the engineering showpiece of Scotland. It was to become the largest ironworks in Europe with over 2,000 workers and was immensely important in the fortunes of Falkirk. The ironworks attracted thousands of skilled workers to the area – so many from England that it became known as the 'English Foundry'. The company was renowned for its armaments; but also manufactured stoves, kitchen ranges, garden and kitchen implements, baths, grates, and the famous red telephone boxes. The worldwide influence of the company is reflected in the continued use of a cast-iron cooking pot in parts of Africa, which is still known as the Falkirk pot.

The scale of the business was huge. The company had its own network of railway lines connecting its mines to its foundries and the Carron Shipping Line was established in 1772

The Carron Iron Works.

Above: The blast furnaces at Carron Iron Works.

Right: Advert for a Carron Iron Works fire grate.

A ship's carronade.

A cast of iron running out from a blast furnace at Carron Iron Works.

to ensure dependable delivery of the company's goods. Falkirk developed as a hub for iron casting with over twenty foundries setting up adjacent to either the canal or the railway.

Carron Works' Carronade was a small-barrelled naval cannon that was shorter and lighter than standard. It meant that it was easier to load, manoeuvrable, and more could be carried on ships. It was used to great effect in numerous naval and military campaigns. It was originally known as the Gasconade after Charles Gascoigne, a partner

The remaining clock tower at Carron Iron Works.

in the company, but was better known by its later name, the Carronade. The Carronade remained in production from 1778 through to the 1850s and established Carron Co.'s worldwide fame and reputation for quality. Lord Nelson and the Duke of Wellington both insisted on using cannon cast at Carron. Carron Works continued to produce munitions in both world wars.

Working conditions in the foundries were hard, with boys as young as nine working at the furnaces. It was scorching and grimy work. Heavy ladles of boiling molten iron were carried from the furnace to sand moulds by pairs of men known as 'neebours' – it was said that you could tell which side of the mould that they carried by the way they leaned to one side or the other when walking home.

The central gabled clock tower is all that remains of the long range of buildings that formed Carron Co.'s offices on Stenhouse Road following the demolition in 1990. The tower forms a curious local landmark and acts as a reminder of the important contribution that Carron Co. made to the Industrial Revolution. The gated area on the ground floor of the tower displays examples of Carron Co.'s ordnance production: two heavy cannon, which were used at the Battle of Waterloo, and two Carronades. The frontage of the tower also includes an iron lintel from the first blast furnace on the site, dated 1760, and a cylinder cast dated 1766 for James Watt's steam engine. The upper level stone carving shows the company's crest with crossed cannons and a phoenix rising from the flames with the company motto above – 'Esto Perpetua' ('Let it Endure Forever').

11. The Tattie Kirk, Cow Wynd

One of the most distinctive buildings in Falkirk is the octagonal-shaped Tattie Kirk, which is slightly hidden away off the Cow Wynd. It was built in 1806 for the Anti-Burgher congregation, a breakaway religious group, which, in the eighteenth century, refused to take the Burghal Oath, requiring support for the established church. The new congregation occupied a number of temporary buildings until the Tattie Kirk was built.

It is said that the octagonal shape was to ensure that 'there was no corner for the Devil to hide in'. The reason for the name Tattie Kirk is unclear – there are a number of theories all related to the humble potato. In 1879, the congregation, by this time known as the South United Presbyterian (UP), moved to a church in Grahams Road and the building has since been put to a variety of uses.

The Tattie Kirk.

12. Falkirk and District Tramway

For passenger traffic a tramway system was constructed by the Falkirk and District
Tramway Company under their order of 1901. This served the burgh and the
adjoining villages of Larbert, Stenhousemuir and the village of Laurieston. In 1924,
the Laurieston service was abandoned, chiefly because of the advent of the buses,
while the circular route serving the burgh and the other villages was reconstructed
and the rolling stock was renewed. The trams on this route were abandoned in 1936
and replaced by a bus service.

Third Statistical Account, Revd Wilson S. Leslie, 1951

The first trams ran in Falkirk on 21 October 1905 to a rapturous reception from the
thousands of Falkirk Bairns that crowded the route. The Falkirk and District Tramway Co.
had started laying the 7 miles of 4-foot gauge track in January 1905 from Larbert Cross.
The erection of the overhead power lines, supplied by electricity from Bonnybridge Power
Station, started in May 1905.

The old bridges at Bainsford and Camelon crossing the Forth & Clyde Canal had to be
replaced for the tram network. The bridge at Bainsford was a bascule (French meaning
see-saw) bridge that worked on drawbridge principles, with counterweights below
ground that were moved up and down to raise and lower the bridge to allow the passage
of ships. The wooden bridge was removed in 1905 and replaced by an upgraded, more
robust structure to allow trams to cross the canal. A signalling system was required to let
tram drivers know if the bridge was open and the tram lines were single track on each
side of the bridge, so that they could be isolated from the system, if there was a problem

Falkirk tram at Larbert Cross outside the Wheat Sheaf Bar.

Falkirk special trams at Carron Works.

The old Bainsford Bridge.

Bainsford Bridge.

Camelon Bridge.

Tram generating station.

View towards Skew Bridge, Laurieston.

with the bridge. The gantries carrying the tram wires over the bridge were originally hard-up against the bridge, but those on the towpath side blocked the tow ropes of the barges. Trams had to stop on each side of the bridge and passengers had to disembark to change trams until 1906, when the necessary alterations to the gantries were made. As at Bainsford, the bascule bridge at Camelon was replaced by a steel swing bridge in 1905 to accommodate the tram service.

The trams normally ran both ways round a circular route from Falkirk through Bainsford, Stenhousemuir, Larbert and Camelon. At peak times, the service was increased to a part route between Larbert and Camelon Station via Grahamston, Bainsford and the Carron Works. The opening of the branch line to Laurieston in 1909 required the lowering of the road below the Skew Bridge, which carried the rail line from Polmont to Larbert.

The trams were cheap, fast, convenient, regular – there was a tram every 7.5 minutes at peak times – and hugely popular – over 3 million passengers used the service in the first year of operation.

The original Falkirk tramcars were all single-truck double deckers without roof covers, which were replaced in 1929–30 by ten single-deck enclosed Pullman cars. With their electric heating and red moquette upholstered seats, rather than wood, the new cars were very popular.

Drivers were paid 6d an hour, with fines for heavy power consumption. During the First World War, with so many men in the armed forces, women were employed as 'lady conductors' from June 1915 and as drivers from June 1916.

The Laurieston tram service was abandoned in 1924, mainly due to the introduction of buses, which were more flexible in their routes. In 1935, the Falkirk trams were taken over by Scottish Midland Transport Group, in which Walter Alexander & Sons had a major share. Alexander's bus empire had its origins in Camelon, in 1913, when the enterprising Walter Alexander, who had a bicycle repair shop in the town, bought a second-hand charabanc and started to run a bus service. The Falkirk tramway service was replaced by buses, with the last tram running on 21 July 1936.

13. Falkirk High Street

The High Street has long been the main thoroughfare of Falkirk. It was first laid with causey setts in 1851 and was pedestrianised in the mid-1980s. It seems that the Falkirk Bairns had previously imposed their own form of pedestrian priority, one account of Falkirk noting that, 'pedestrians in Falkirk, local and visiting, accept the fact that High Street pavements are narrow and meet the difficulty by walking unconcernedly in the street, to the visible alarm and bewilderment of motorists passing through the town, who have not elsewhere encountered this phenomenon'. (*Third Statistical Account*, Revd Wilson S. Leslie, 1951)

Falkirk High Street.

At one time there were dozens of pubs on the High Street and Falkirk had the unfortunate reputation of being one of the most drunken towns in Scotland. This may have accounted to some extent for the Bairns habit of walking on the street, rather than the pavement.

Falkirk was the first town in Britain to have a fully automated method of street lighting. Lamp posts were installed in the main streets of the town in 1903, after the opening of Falkirk Power Station. The lamp posts had two sets of lights – at midnight, the top lamp was switched off and the lower one switched on.

Mathieson's were a ubiquitous feature of the Falkirk area for over 100 years from the company's foundation in 1872 by Robert and Sarah Mathieson.

A sign for a Jaeger shop is prominent on the right of the image of the High Street. The Jaeger Co. was established in 1884 and initially specialised in the sale of woollen underwear. This was based on the theories of Dr Gustav Jaeger (1832–1917), the founder of the company, who believed that it was better to wear wool rather than cotton next to the skin.

14. Newmarket Street

Newmarket Street at the end of the eighteenth century was little more than a rough track. Road widening improvements were made in 1815 and the terracing was not completed until nearer the end of the nineteenth century. The street is named Market Road on the 1860 Ordnance Survey map of Falkirk. It takes its name from the Corn Exchange, which was built on the south side of the street in 1858.

An early view looking west on Newmarket Street.

Looking west on Newmarket Street after the arrival of the trams.

An early view looking east on Newmarket Street.

The Wellington Statue and Town Hall.

The Town Hall.

The South African War Memorial.

The second half of the nineteenth century was a boom period for Falkirk, and many new public buildings were erected, including banks, schools, the town jail, the municipal chambers and a new Town Hall. The massive Town Hall building, which had seating for 1,700 people, occupied a site on the south side of Newmarket Street. It was opened in 1879 and was a reconstruction of the earlier Corn Exchange. The Corn Exchange was let out 'for the purpose of Lectures, Concerts, Dancing, Public Exhibitions, Sale-Room purposes and all Public Entertainments, with the exception of Thursdays which the Feuars reserve for a Grain Market till Three o'clock in the afternoon'. Admission to the Saturday dances at the Town Hall was free for women and there were many complaints of domestic servants coming back late and not always being fit for work. Grain was still being sold in part of the Town Hall until 1907 and it was for many years known as the Town Hall and Corn Exchange.

The Town Hall's clock tower was a prominent landmark in the town, and the building was at the centre of many of Falkirk's social and civic events. The building was demolished in 1968, due to structural problems, with the aim of constructing new halls for the parish church. However, part of the wall of the church collapsed during demolition and the site was left as a landscaped area.

Falkirk's memorial to local soldiers killed in the South African War was officially unveiled by Field Marshal Earl Roberts on 19 October 1906. The bronze statue depicts a soldier of the Argyll and Sutherland Highlanders in a kilt and slouch hat, defending a wounded comrade with his rifle and bayonet. The names of soldiers are inscribed on a panel on the granite plinth. The design for the statue was the result of a competition, which was won by John Campbell, a teacher at the Falkirk Science and Arts School. The Second Boer War (1899–1902) was fought by Britain against South African Boer farmers.

The original iron railings, which are prominent in the early images of Newmarket Street, would have been removed for the war effort in the 1940s. Railings and gates were removed throughout the country during the Second World War following a direction by Lord Beaverbrook, the wartime Minister of Supply. There is some debate about what happened to them after they were removed. It is claimed that the metal was unsuitable for reprocessing and that they were dumped at sea. There are stories that there was so much offloaded in parts of the Thames that the vast quantity of iron disrupted ships' compasses. It is also claimed that they were used as ballast in ships – with many houses in African seaports being festooned with fine Georgian railings salvaged in the destination ports. The removal of so much ornamental cast iron was a great architectural loss. However, even if they never became guns and tanks it was seen as a morale-boosting exercise.

The statue of the Duke of Wellington was moved from Market Place to Newmarket Street in 1905. The statue shows the 'renowned warrior' Field Marshal Arthur Wellesley, 1st Duke of Wellington – the Iron Duke – with his war horse Copenhagen. The Duke was the hero of Waterloo and twice British Prime Minister. The statue is perhaps appropriately located in Falkirk, as many of the cannons that served at the Battle of Waterloo were manufactured at Carron. In July 2014, vandals smashed off the head of the Duke; it was retrieved and has been returned to the Duke's shoulders.

15. Princes Street and Falkirk's Cinemas

The buildings (including the Argyll Bar) that terminated Newmarket Street at its east end were demolished to make way for Princes Street. The new street was officially opened in March 1933 by the Prince of Wales, who was to become Edward VIII and the Duke of Windsor, following his abdication.

The mock half-timbered façade of the former Tudor House Restaurant always seems slightly out of place in Falkirk – it is certainly a distinctive landmark. The Tudor House opened on New Year's Eve 1935 with a gala fundraising evening for the local Girl Guides. The building was substantially reconstructed after a fire in 2001, and now operates as a hotel. The art deco Regal Cinema opened in 1934 on the new street. The cinema was converted for triple screens in 1973 and went through a number of changes of name – ABC and Cannon – until its final closure as a cinema in 2001. It has since been converted into a bar/nightclub.

Cinema going reached its peak in the years immediately after the Second World War. Most people would have made a weekly visit to the pictures and they were also the venue of choice for a first date. The main feature and the 'B' film would be viewed through a haze of hanging cigarette smoke caught in the beam of the back projection.

Looking south on Vicar Street. The buildings in the left mid-ground of the image were demolished for the extension of Newmarket Street.

The Tudor House Restaurant and the Regal Cinema on Princes Street.

Falkirk Cinema listings from 1926.

Falkirk had its fair share of establishments in which to enjoy a night in front of the silver screen: the Bank Street picture house, which opened in 1934 in a converted church; the upmarket Salon/Photo Playhouse at the corner of Newmarket Street and Vicar Street, which opened in 1921 and closed in 1960; the Electric Theatre in Silver Row; and the Picturedrome in Melville Street. The Pavilion (the 'Pivvie' for short) on Newmarket Street opened in August 1914. It was a purpose-built hall with seating for 950. It was enlarged to seat 1,337 in 1933, rebranded as the Gaumont in 1950 and later the Odeon in 1962. It was demolished in 1973 and redeveloped as shops and offices.

The introduction of television in Scotland in 1952 brought the little screen into the home, and for many it was no longer necessary to leave the fireside for a night's entertainment. Hollywood recognised this and made a desperate attempt to make cinema going more interesting by reintroducing 3D movies in 1952. 3D had been around as far back as 1922, but had fallen out of favour. The 1952 film *Bwana Devil*, with man-eating lions jumping out of the screen, started the 3D craze of the fifties and they were very popular for a time. The problem was that if the film wasn't projected accurately the result was blurry and people complained that they caused headaches. Sitting in the cinema in funny specs must have also put many people off and, when widescreen Cinemascope was introduced, the 3D craze fizzled out for a time.

16. The Grand Theatre and Opera House

The Grand Theatre and Opera House, which has just been erected in Falkirk, was opened on Thursday by a reception and private view. The Grand Theatre and Opera House is now an accomplished fact in the town, and a more handsome and more up-to-date building one could not wish to see. The theatre has been erected on the latest principles, at a cost of upwards of £11,000, and 2,000 people can find accommodation within its walls, the seating capacity comprising dress circle, family circle, orchestra stalls, pit, amphitheatre and gallery, together with fourteen private boxes. The building is surmounted by a large dome, beautifully decorated, and centred by a group of seven gasoliers, which throw a brilliant light beneath. The theatre is up to date in every way, and the safety of the public would seem to be amply provided for. The people of Falkirk had every right to be proud of their new theatre.

The Falkirk Herald and Midland Counties Journal, 26 December 1903

The Grand Theatre and Opera House opened on 24 December 1903. The new art nouveau building on Vicar Street, known as Vicar Chambers, contained shops, offices and flats with an entrance corridor to the theatre.

There had been some delays in the construction of the building and 'a large crowd of workmen in the various branches of the building trade had worked night and day so that the building might be completed by the advertised time'.

Mr R. C. BUCHANAN, Managing Director.

Above left: The Grand Theatre and Opera House.

Above right: Mr R. C. Buchanan, first general manager of the Grand Theatre and Opera House.

Below: Roller skating.

James Aitken, of the Falkirk brewery, was the main director of the theatre company and the building was designed by the architect Alexander Cullen. An original scheme to build a theatre on the site, also backed by Aitken, in 1899, failed due to funding difficulties.

The opening reception was attended by several hundred of the principal ladies and gentlemen of the town and surrounding district. They assembled in the theatre and were given the opportunity of visiting the various parts of the building. Refreshments were provided by Messrs Mathieson & Sons. The formal opening ceremony commenced at 5.30 p.m. The chair was occupied by Major Howard, chairman of the theatre company. Bailie Bogle performed the opening ceremony in the absence of Provost Weir through illness. The chairman presented Bailie Bogle with a pair of mother-of-pearl silver-mounted opera glasses as a souvenir of the occasion and Mr James Aitken proposed a vote of thanks to the architect Mr Alex Cullen.

On the day that details of the theatre opening were published, the local newspaper also carried an item that reported its vociferous condemnation by members of the clergy of the town. Mr Buchanan, the general manager of the Grand, responded by stating that the theatre would be a 'good tonic for people suffering from the wear and tear of the ever increasing struggle for existence, would help to reduce drunkenness by taking people from the street corners, and provide mental recreation and wholesome pleasure'. The theatre had five bars, which perhaps casts some doubt on the likely reduction of drunkenness following its opening.

The Grand originally presented drama, musicals, opera, pantomime, revues and variety. Films were added to the programme within a few years and it became a full-time picture house when it was taken over by the ABC cinema group in 1929. The Grand was closed in April 1932, demolished in 1933 and was replaced by the art deco-inspired Regal Cinema, with its frontage on the newly created Princes Street, in 1934.

Falkirk's other theatre, the Roxy on Silver Row, started life as the Erskine Church and was used for a time as a roller-skating rink. There was a craze for roller skating in the 1900s, when almost every town in the country had a rink devoted to the pastime. A reduction in petty crime was attributed to the 'elevating moral influence of skating in diminishing drinking in public houses and providing healthy recreation for people who might otherwise be employing their time to less advantage'. Hordes of people flocked to the rinks for a while. However, by the end of 1910 there was 'a universal decline in the interest in roller skating and the fleeting nature of the craze was exposed with numerous ventures coming to grief'. This is reflected in the conversion of Falkirk's rink to the Electric Theatre in 1910. The venue was enlarged in 1921 and the name changed to the Empire. It was refurbished in 1938 as the Roxy, closed in 1958 and was demolished in 1961.

17. The Emperor of Jiu-jitsu in Falkirk

In October 1908, there was a departure from the normal bill of fare at the Grand Theatre when Yukio Tani (1881–1950) appeared for six nights. Tani was a jiu-jitsu master and a hugely popular act in theatres during the 1900s. He learned his craft in Japan and travelled

GRAND THEATRE AND OPERA HOUSE, FALKIRK.

Managing Director............Mr R. C. BUCHANAN.
Resident Manager...............Mr H. W. EBBUTT.
Telephone—No. 0315 (Nat.).

TIMES AND PRICES AS USUAL.
SMOKING ALLOWED IN ALL PARTS.

MONDAY, Oct. 26th (for Six Nights Only), Important and Expensive Engagement of the Great

YUKIO TANI.

The Emperor of all Ju-Jitsu Wrestlers and Light-Weight Champion Catch-as-Catch-Can Wrestler of the World,

Supported by Powerful Company of
VAUDEVILLE ARTISTES.

Above: Advert for appearance of Yukio Tani at the Grand Theatre and Opera House.

Right: Yukio Tani in action.

to London at the invitation of Edward William Barton-Wright, the founder of baritsu (a self-defence system that was made famous when it was name checked in the Sherlock Holmes story *The Adventure of the Empty House*).

Tani started to perform in music halls, where he was billed as 'The Emperor of Jiu-jitsu'. He would give demonstrations of jiu-jitsu and challenge all-comers with the offer of a purse of £100 to anyone that could defeat him and £20 to anyone that could last ten minutes in the ring with him. There was no doubt many locals that were tempted by the prizes – a £100 was the equivalent of a year's wages for many at the time and Tani, the 'Pocket Hercules', at a diminutive 5 feet 6 inches (1.68 metres), perhaps looked like an easy challenge. However, few collected the prize: larger men were overcome in seconds by Tani's lightning holds and during one six-month tour, he defeated an average of twenty men a week, a total of over 500 challengers, including professional wrestlers. During his career, Tani apparently lost only one match to another Japanese martial arts expert.

18. The Temperance Hotel, Lint Riggs –
A Beneficence of a Bairn

The Lint Riggs was originally a notoriously rat-infested narrow lane linking the High Street and New Market Street. It was 2.4 metres (8 feet) wide – just enough for a horse and cart – and was closed with an iron gate at the High Street end. The crumbling buildings

The Lint Riggs.

Right: Advert for the temperance movement.

Below: A humorous look at the temperance movement.

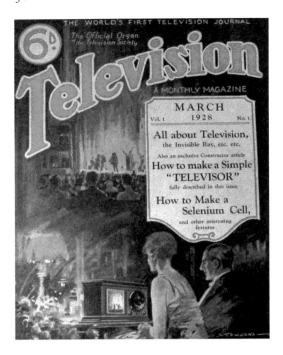

The first edition of *Television* magazine from March 1928 with instructions on how to build a televisor.

were removed and the elegant new street was formed in 1903 as part of a town council improvement scheme. The street name, meaning flax fields, is a link to Falkirk's historic linen industry.

The Temperance Hotel on the Lint Riggs was opened in the former Crown Hotel premises in March 1923. At the time, Falkirk had the unfortunate reputation of being one of the most drunken towns in Scotland, but also had an active temperance movement, which promoted abstinence from alcohol consumption.

The hotel was funded by a legacy in the will of Dr John Aitken, who left £20,000 for a temperance establishment. Dr Aitken was a local scientific researcher who passed away at the age of eighty in November 1919 at his home, Ardenlea, in Falkirk. He was a Fellow of the Royal Society and a friend of Lord Kelvin. The Aitken Trust purchased the Crown Hotel for £8,500 and local architect J. G. Callander drew up plans for its reconstruction and conversion into the new Temperance Hotel. It was intended as a 'direct counter-attraction to the public house and a place where people could meet for simple recreation and where social parties could be convened free from the menace of alcohol'.

It was noted at the time that the facilities provided were the best in the country outside of London.

Entering from the Lint Riggs, a well-balanced lounge hall is reached, around which are placed the luncheon room and tea room, a ladies' lounge and smoke room. The tea room, which has accommodation for nearly one hundred persons, has also a direct access from the High Street, and is exquisitely and tastefully designed. A special feature of this apartment is the electric crystal fittings, which give the necessary lighting effect to a well-thought-out colour scheme, while the furnishings have also been carefully selected, and are of a high-class standard. The smoke room, which will accommodate about 40 individuals, has been beautifully furnished, and the decorations therein are of a very restful character. A well-appointed staircase leads to the first and second floors, and the first floor comprises a large lecture or dance hall and a well-equipped recreation room. The second floor is devoted to four visitors' bedrooms. The basement floor, access to which is from Newmarket Street, has a billiard room, and six separately enclosed slipper baths. Ample lavatory accommodation has been provided, and the principal apartments are heated on the low pressure hot water heating system. No effort has been spared to provide for the comfort of the patronising public. (*The Falkirk Herald*, 31 March 1923)

The opening ceremony was attended by a large crowd and 'after a tour of inspection of the premises, an enjoyable tea was served by daintily garbed waitresses'. One of the speakers noted that the hotel would 'raise the moral tone of the burgh of Falkirk' and hoped that the term 'Dirty Falkirk', which was familiar in previous times, would never be heard again in the future. The formal opening ceremony was followed by a musical and dramatic programme by Mrs Greta Watson, James Veitch, Duncan Clark and Fitzpatrick's Orchestra. Ices were served and exhibition games of billiards were played.

The Temperance was a much used venue in Falkirk. The chess club, the philatelic society, the horticultural society, the table tennis association, the orchestral union, the operatic society and the chamber of commerce were just some of the local groups that held meetings at the premises.

The Temperance also has some claim to being the location of the first public demonstration of television in Scotland. John Logie Baird's grandfather and great-grandfather were tenant farmers in the Falkirk area. Baird was a frequent visitor to the town and in the early 1920s he struck up a working relationship with engineer John Hart, who ran a radio supply shop in Falkirk's Pleasance. This led to the demonstration of the prototype television system in the Temperance Café in December 1925. The Falkirk 'Televisor', the earliest surviving authenticated piece of Baird's equipment, was displayed in the window of Hart's Falkirk shop in the 1920s. It was then kept by the Royal Scottish Museum, and is now in the possession of Falkirk Museum.

19. Aitken's Brewery, Newmarket Street

The brewery of the county is situated in Falkirk, and belongs to Messrs. James Aitken & Co. The business, which has been conducted for four generations by the same family, has, from first to last, been very successful on account of the superior quality of the brew; and year by year Aitken's Ale continues to gain wider ground as a favourite beverage.

The History of Stirlingshire, William Nimmo, 1880

Aitken's Brewery.

Aitken's advert.

James Aitken's brewery was first established in 1723 on a site on the north side of Newmarket Street to the west of Lint Riggs. In 1757, it relocated to a new site at the west end of Newmarket Street. Aitken's ale was a prize-winning brew and an internationally known brand. It helped to quench the thirst of generations of thirsty foundry workers and there is a tradition that many of Bonnie Prince Charlie's Highlanders lingered a little too long in Falkirk after the second Battle of Falkirk due to the quality of Aitken's ales.

Until 1830, when artesian wells were sunk on the site, the brewery used water brought by carts from a local well. The brewery was rebuilt in 1900, and its 55-metre (180-feet) chimney was a local landmark and dominated the centre of the town. In 1960, the firm became part of Caledonian United Breweries, later to be swallowed up by Tennent's. Brewing at Falkirk ended in 1968 and the site was sold off. The brewery was demolished in 1970 to make way for a supermarket.

20. Falkirk Public Library, Hope Street

The red-sandstone library was designed by architects McArthy and Watson in a finely detailed Gothic style with large leaded glass windows. The building included a reading room, reference library and large recreation room. The frontage is embellished by carved figures holding books and the inscriptions 'Let there be light' and 'tangite unum, tangite omnes' (Falkirk's motto).

The foundation stone of the library was laid on 12 October 1901 by Bailie Christie, chair of the Library Committee, in the presence of a 'large and influential gathering'. Bailie Christie paid tribute to Andrew Carnegie who had provided funds towards the costs of the building and pointed out that the contribution of Robert Dollar should be acknowledged. Falkirk had a library as far back as 1836, but it was Dollar's gift of £1,000 for the purchase of books for the YMCA library that resulted in Falkirk adopting the Free Libraries Act.

In 1884, there were only eighty-four official free libraries in Britain, which rose to 400 by the end of the nineteenth century. Much of the growth was due to the generosity of Andrew Carnegie, 'whose faith in libraries for the people as agencies for good was so strong'.

Carnegie and his wife visited Falkirk on 9 October 1902 for the official opening ceremony. He was 'wildly cheered' by the massive crowd that had gathered when he opened the door of the library for the first time with a golden key. In his speech, Carnegie noted that 'a public library was the most democratic place in the world'. Provost Weir considered that the event would be long remembered as a red-letter day in the history of Falkirk.

Immediately after leaving the library at the end of the opening ceremony, the celebrations moved to the Town Hall for lunch and more speeches. However, Carnegie was taken on a slight detour to the High Street shop of Mr H. B. Watson, boot merchant. Mr Watson had a number of relics of Prince Charlie and the Jacobite rebellion, which Carnegie was noted as examining with the keenest interest.

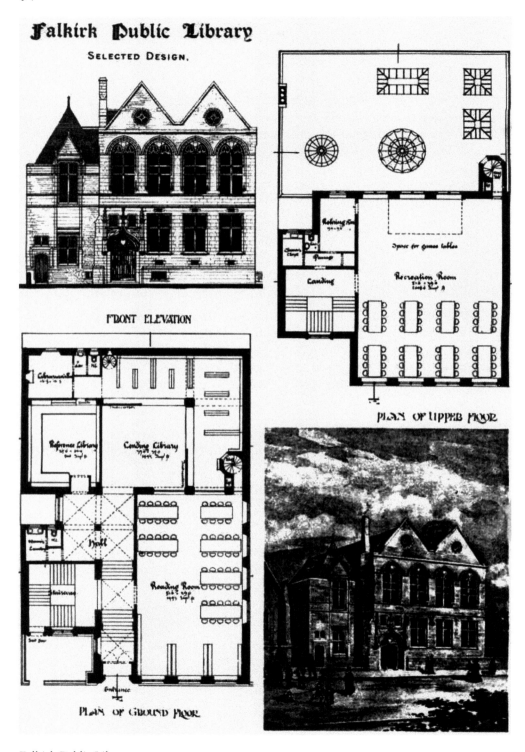

Falkirk Public Library.

Right: Falkirk Public Library.

Below: Mr and Mrs Carnegie.

MR ANDREW CARNEGIE.

MRS CARNEGIE.

21. Robert Dollar and Dollar Park

Robert Dollar was a Falkirk Bairn who, from humble beginnings, went on to become one of the richest men in the world. Dollar was born in Bainsford in 1844. He left school at the age of twelve and worked in various jobs in the Falkirk area. In 1857, the family moved to Canada where Robert found work as a lumberjack and logger.

Left: Robert Dollar.

Below: Dollar Park.

Falkirk War Memorial.

He later moved to Michigan and established his own logging company, which at first sustained losses. Following his marriage to Margaret Proudfoot in 1874, to which he attributed his success in business, his skills as an entrepreneur resulted in a huge expansion in his lumber interests and his wealth. In 1888, the Dollar family moved to San Rafael, California, and in 1906 Robert bought a house in the city and named it Falkirk. San Rafael and Falkirk are now twin towns.

In 1895, Dollar moved into the shipping industry with the purchase of a vessel to move his timber. This was the first of many; as he went on to develop the biggest shipping empire in the world, including a round-the-world passenger service. After his entry into the shipping business he was given the honorary title of captain. His fame was such that he featured on the cover of *Time* magazine in March 1928 and one observer noted that 'he was all but a god in the Orient'.

Robert Dollar died on 16 May 1932 at his home in San Rafael, California. Over 3,000 people attended his internment and the US government arranged for flowers to be dropped from the sky over the funeral. His house in San Rafael is now a cultural centre complete with Falkirk burgh lamp standards, which were presented to San Rafael in 1989.

Dollar Park is a pleasant area of landscaped grounds five minutes from Falkirk town centre on the road to Camelon. The park was a gift to the people of Falkirk from Robert Dollar. Dollar's philanthropy was based on a belief that he should leave the world better than he found it. He contributed generously to many religious, social and community causes. He was particularly benevolent to his hometown. Dollar made his first trip home to Falkirk in 1884 when he gave £1,000 to purchase books for the town library. He donated Arnotdale House, which stands at the centre of the park that bears his name, to the town. He also paid for the carillon of thirteen bells that hang in the parish church and the monument in Victoria Park in memory of Sir John de Graeme. Arnotdale was a museum from the 1920s to the 1960s. His generous gifts to Falkirk were recognised in 1926, when he was made a freeman of the town.

The Falkirk War Memorial is a simple stone cenotaph that stands in Dollar Park adjoining the road from Camelon to Falkirk. The original inscription on a bronze plaque reads: 'Over Eleven Hundred Bairns Died for their King and Country and in the Cause of Freedom, 1914–1919. They died that we might live.' On the north side a similar panel reads: 'In proud and grateful remembrance of those who fell and those who carried on in the Great War. Let us forget them not.' The memorial was unveiled on 13 June 1926 by the Duke of Montrose in front of a crowd estimated at 10,000. The guard of honour was provided by a party from the 7th Territorial Battalion, Argyll and Sutherland Highlanders. The unveiling ceremony opened with the singing of the 124th psalm and a prayer by the Revd J. B. Johnston. Buglers then sounded the 'Last Post', pipers played a lament and the Falkirk and District Choral Union choir sang 'Heroes Departed'.

22. Falkirk Infirmary, Thornhill Road

Falkirk Cottage Hospital was opened on Thornhill Road on 27 July 1889. The hospital was funded by public subscription and demand was such that further publicly funded extensions were made to the building in the 1900s. In 1904, the name was changed to Falkirk Infirmary. By the 1920s, it was clear that a new hospital was required. A massive five-year campaign was launched in April 1925, in which the Falkirk Bairns employed every possible means of fundraising. The new hospital at Gartcows started treating patients in the early months of 1931 and the facility was officially opened by Prince George on 18 January 1932. There were originally eighty-five beds and forty-five nurses, which had increased to 200 beds and seventy-five nurses within five years. By 2011, the new Forth Valley Royal Hospital was completed on the site of the old Royal Scottish National Hospital in Larbert.

Falkirk Infirmary.

23. Barr's

Robert Barr, the fourth son of a farming family from Beith in Ayrshire, started a cork-cutting business in Callendar Riggs in 1830. In 1875, his son, also called Robert Barr, began to produce aerated waters (the name given to fizzy drinks at the time) at a factory on Burnfoot Lane in Falkirk.

Barr's Factory. The number of horse-drawn carts indicates a flourishing operation.

Barr's staff in 1901.

Barr's advert.

Aerated water was hugely popular at this time, as the quality of the piped water in towns was often poor. Soft drinks were not only a treat, but they were also safe and pure, combined with a sugar boost. Iron founding, a major employer in the Falkirk area, was also thirsty work.

The range of products developed rapidly, including 'Wee Macgregor Brew', 'Japanese Plum' and 'Raspberry Cider'. Many of the drinks were still brewed with the fermentation stopped at the point below the maximum alcohol level for sale as a non-alcoholic beverage – in those days 1.1 per cent alcohol.

The company's most renowned product, Barr's original recipe Iron Brew – 'Scotland's other National Drink' – was launched on 15 April 1901. The name Iron Brew was changed to Irn-Bru on 18 July 1946 in order to meet the requirements of new food labelling regulations, which required the brand name to be accurate. Although Iron Brew contained a small amount of iron (0.002% ammonium ferric citrate), it wasn't actually brewed.

Barr's original adverts for Iron Brew featured testimonials from famous athletes of the day. The company's advertising was, and remains, innovative, eccentric and sometimes controversial. The fondly remembered, although perhaps now considered less than politically correct, 'Adventures of Ba-Bru and Sandy' appeared in newspapers for five decades and was the longest running advertising cartoon campaign in history. More recent adverts have featured Irn-Bru drinkers becoming unusually strong, durable or magnetic. The brand has always made the most of its Scottish roots and, in 2007, its 'Made in Scotland from Girders' campaign won a major advertising award.

In its early years, Barr's used horse-drawn carts for deliveries, which were restricted to a 10-mile round trip each day – the distance a horse could comfortably travel. One of these horses became a tragic footnote in the town's history when the spire of Falkirk steeple was badly damaged by a lightning strike in 1927; the only fatality was an unfortunate Barr's lemonade delivery horse that was crushed by the falling masonry.

Another of Barr's horses, Carnera, was the company's most famous equine. Carnera was bought in Perthshire in 1930, was over nineteen hands (2 metres) tall and was said to be the largest working horse in the world. Sadly, Carnera slipped on Falkirk's Cow Wynd in January 1937 and had to be killed.

Irn-Bru wasn't available during Second World War due to the shortages of raw materials, which went towards the production of 'standard' drinks such as lemonade.

The restorative powers of Irn-Bru as a hangover cure are legendary and are praised by Billy Connolly for saving his life on many Sunday mornings in his song 'The afternoon after the morning after the night before'.

An alliance of two great producers of sweet treats from the Falkirk area came together when the McCowan's confectionery company, famed for their Highland Cream Toffee, produced the popular Irn-Bru bar, which has several Facebook pages dedicated to campaigns for its return.

Irn-Bru has been the most popular soft drink in Scotland for decades and is the third biggest selling soft drink in the UK. It is now made in Cumbernauld by A. G. Barr and its appeal is not just national; Irn-Bru is also sold in more than forty-five countries worldwide. There are five factories in Russia producing the fluorescent brew where it has been available since 1998 and is particularly popular.

24. The Gentleman Fountain

Patrick Gentleman was a successful and well-respected Falkirk merchant who was a partner, along with his brother, in the long-established Falkirk drapers firm of P. & J. Gentleman. He had a particular interest in the welfare of the people of Falkirk and was a member of the town council. Patrick died in 1865 and bequeathed a legacy for the erection of an ornamental drinking fountain in the town.

There was some delay in finding an appropriate site. In October 1868, the new custom-built Sheriff Court House opened in a fine baronial building at the corner of Hope Street and West Bridge Street. The new court house also contained prison cells and an extension for the police station. It was a significant improvement in facilities for the organisation of law in Falkirk. In the first half of the nineteenth century, court sittings had taken place in assorted locations such as the Red Lion Inn on the High Street and Wilson's Building opposite the Steeple. The building continued as the court house until it was replaced in late 1990, and is in use as funeral directors at the time of writing.

The construction of the new court house suggested the vacant space, the approximate site of the old West Port, in front of the building was an appropriate location for the fountain. The 6.4-metre- (21-feet-) high cast-iron fountain consisted of an octagonal design dome supported on eight pillars standing on a granite plinth. It was made by the Sun Foundry in Glasgow and cost £200. Baillie Gentleman, Patrick's brother, formally handed the fountain over to Provost Russel, on behalf of the town, on 21 June 1871. The provost drank a toast with water from the well and trusted that it would long continue to flow for the benefit

The Gentleman Fountain.

of the Bairns of Falkirk. The fountain was described as a 'singularly fine specimen of iron moulding' and a 'valuable addition to the stock of burgh embellishmemts'. The fountain was removed in 1923 to allow for road widening.

25. Callendar House and the Dark Tunnel

Callendar House, with its 91-metre- (300-foot-) long frontage, is the most noteworthy historic structure in Falkirk. The Callendar estate was granted to the Livingston family in 1345, and it was the family seat of the Earls of Callendar and Linlithgow for nearly 400 years. The Livingstons were close to Mary Queen of Scots, and the queen was a guest a number of times at the house. In July 1651, Cromwell's forces laid siege to the garrison at Callendar House, which attempted without success to hold the building in the name of the king. The Livingstons lost the estate in 1715 due to their allegiance to the Jacobite cause.

In 1783, the estate was bought by William Forbes, who had made a fortune copper bottoming the keels of ships – hence his nickname 'Copperbottom'. Forbes made a number of changes to the estate that upset the locals. In August 1797, there was a boisterous demonstration near the estate, which Forbes thought was the Falkirk mob advancing on the house with ill intent. He took flight and mistook the flames of Carron Iron Works for a torched Callendar House. His actions were savagely lampooned in a contemporary caricature.

Callendar House.

Callendar House now.

Copperbottom's Retreat.

Entrance to the Dark Tunnel.

The Forbes family considered that the construction of the Union Canal would spoil their view and disturb their privacy. Their objections were vociferous and the canal builders were forced to run the canal in a 631-metre (690-yard) tunnel in the vicinity of Callendar House. Known as the Dark Tunnel, it remains an impressive monument to the technical skill of the engineers and the back-breaking toil of the navvies, who came mainly from the Highlands and Ireland to work on the canal.

The Forbes family were responsible for the remodelling of the house into the outstanding French Renaissance-style building that exists today. The Callendar estate remained in the ownership of the Forbes family until it was sold to the local authority in 1963. High-rise flats and the short-lived (1964–81) Callendar Park College of Education were built in part of the grounds.

The house remained disused and in a semi-derelict condition until it was fittingly restored as an excellent museum in 1997. The huge landscaped gardens are now a fine public park incorporating a boating lake and children's play area.

A section of the Antonine Wall runs through the grounds of Callendar House. The Romans were the first to make a significant mark in the Falkirk area when Emperor Antoninus Pius ordered the construction of the Antonine Wall, the Vallum Antoninior, spanning the 63 kilometres (39 miles) from the Forth to the Clyde in around AD 142. The plan was to keep the troublesome Caledonian tribes north of the wall. The wall marked the most northerly frontier of the Roman Empire and was an outstanding monument to the engineering prowess of the Roman army. Its construction over a twelve-year period involved the building of a turf rampart on a stone base, which was protected by a broad V-shaped defensive ditch and a low mound.

The Antonine Wall was abandoned in AD 164 when the Roman army withdrew from Scotland, pulling the northern frontier back down to Hadrian's Wall. After invasions from the north in AD 197, the Emperor Septimius Severus arrived in AD 208 to restore order along the Scottish borders. However, after only a few years the Antonine Wall was abandoned permanently and the main Roman defensive line reverted south to Hadrian's Wall. Its turf construction meant that little of the wall remains. In 2008, the wall's international importance was recognised by its designation by UNESCO as part of the Frontiers of the Roman Empire World Heritage Site.

26. Marion's and Greenhorn's Wells

Of Marion's Well there is scant record. According to tradition, it got its name from Marion Livingston – a nun of the house of Callendar, who, in the performance of the sacerdotal vow which kept her from the world, visited the well at intervals, and used its soft waters as a pediluvium. The original well which was built round with stone, stood at the bottom of the Cladden's Brae, on the bank of the East Burn. It was further protected by a circle of upright slabs – the great resting-place of the water maids, and the scene of many a happy 'touzle' as the stoups or pitchers were sent rolling and rattling down into the brawling brook. And ever since little Rachel at the well of Haran met her suitor Jacob, who there and then opened an interesting courtship by assisting the fair one to water her fleecy flock, the public fountain, strange to say, has been a favourite trysting-place with the world's Romeos and Juliets.

Round About Falkirk, Robert Gillespie, 1879

Marion's Well.

Greenhorn's Well.

Marion's Well stood on the south side of Callendar Road, at what is now a roundabout at the north end of Corporation Street. It was an important local water source and supplied a washhouse on the north side of Callendar Road. The well, which it seems was popular with courting couples meeting up for a 'touzle', has been completely lost to road improvements.

'Christ's Well, or what is now called Greenhorn's Well, to which flocks of invalids in the olden times were wont to resort for the virtue of its medicinal waters. And its situation, before utilitarian demands bereft it of its sylvan shade, was exceedingly picturesque. The well lay in a little nook, thickly covered with bushes and wild-flowers; while the streamlet which flowed from its copious fountain sported and sang down a miniature glen'. (*Round About Falkirk*, Robert Gillespie, 1879)

Greenhorn's Well is set into the stone wall at the junction of Windsor Road and Gartcows Road. The wall was the boundary of Falkirk's Poor House, which dated from 1905. The inscription on the well reads:

Greenhorn's Well. Surrounded by the bleak and barren moor along the south of Falkirk, the stranger was at one time agreeably surprised to find in a sequestered vale a small delightful stream trickling from a moss covered fountain and on its way mingling its waters with a sister stream flowing from a cave which of yore gave shelter to Sir William Wallace. This interesting spot, immediately to the south hereof, was for many generations a favourite haunt of the inhabitants of Falkirk, who were also attracted thither by the salubrity of the waters, about 80 years ago the well had fallen into such a dilapidated state that with the view of repairing it and the roads thereto a few of the Bairns o' Fa'kirk formed themselves into a club the members of which were J. Melville, Rob Ronald Rod Keir, Archibald Wyse, Robert Cowie, John Graham, Adam Cowie, Mat. Middlehurst, William Crawford, James Hume, Alex Reid. The young men with a laudable and patriotic zeal began about mid-summer 1824 to improve and ornament the well and its surroundings, and on 10 September 1824, the stone and basin gratuitously furnished by James Hume, apprentice mason, were laid in an appropriate manner and these gifts are preserved therein. The Falkirk Town Council imbued with the same commendable spirit as the former Bairns ordered the further restoration to be made for the benefit of the inhabitants, to whom they now entrust this erection for preservation.

27. Falkirk Railway Stations

The first railway station at Falkirk, which was renamed Falkirk High in 1903, opened on 21 February 1842 on the Edinburgh–Glasgow line. The tunnel to the east of the station was of such interest that it was opened for inspection by the public for a small charge for three nights before the first train ran. The station was inconveniently located to the south of the town and horse buses were required to transport commuters to and from the town centre. When it opened, connection by the canals to Edinburgh and Glasgow at Lock 16 almost surpassed the rail service in terms of popularity.

The Cow Wynd, which links Falkirk High to the town centre, takes its name from the fact that the road provided access to the main grazing grounds to the south of the town. It was previously known as Coalhill Road, from its use as the route for coal carts from Shieldhill to Carron Iron Works. In 1888, Falkirk council resolved to rename the street in what was considered the more tasteful High Station Road. However, public pressure resulted in it reverting to the traditional name in 1906.

The more convenient Grahamston station, on the line between the Edinburgh and Glasgow Railway at Polmont and Larbert, was opened by the Stirlingshire Midland Junction Railway on 1 October 1850.

Grahamston station.

Grahams Road.

The bridge over the railway line at Grahamston station was a narrow iron structure, which was only able to accommodate pedestrians, until 1902 when it was upgraded for traffic; prior to that, the main route into town required a detour around McFarlane Crescent to the east of Grahams Road.

28. Vicar Street Post Office

The Gothic-inspired post office building by W. T. Oldrieve was opened in 1893 and was followed by the adjoining British Linen Company Bank in 1899. The pair of buildings form an impressive architectural grouping. A post office is recorded in Falkirk as early as 1689, and immediately prior to the opening of the Vicar Street premises, the town had a number of post offices based in small shops.

Vicar Street post office.

29. Grahamston Iron Co. Gates

The exceptional cast-iron entrance gates of the Grahamston Iron Co. were originally made to demonstrate the quality of Falkirk iron work for the International Exhibition of Industry, Science and Art held in Edinburgh's Meadows in 1886.

Thirty thousand people passed through the gates on 6 May 1886 when Prince Albert Victor opened the International Exhibition. The exhibition building was an imposing structure comprising a Grand Hall, which could hold 10,000 people. Over 20,000 exhibits illustrated the 'material progress of the age' and there were 1,725 works of art in the fine art galleries. The grounds were laid out with walks, rockery, fountains and a bandstand. The principal open-air attractions were the electric railway, which ran between the main Brougham Place entrance and Middle Meadow Walk; the working man's model dwelling house, which included the most modern appliances for sanitation and convenience; and the refreshment rooms, both temperance and otherwise. The exhibition buildings and grounds were lit by 3,200 electric lamps in the largest illumination scheme ever attempted in Scotland.

Grahamston Iron Co. gates.

The gates are 8 metres (26 feet) high, 6 metres (20 feet) wide, weigh over 20 tons and were said to be the largest set of iron gates in the world when they were first made. The royal arms of Scotland are centred on the arch with the arms of the city of Edinburgh on each side.

After the exhibition, the gates were moved to the Grahamston Iron Co.'s foundry at the end of Gowan Avenue, which branches off from Grahams Road. The Grahamston Iron Co. closed in 1994, after 126 years of producing iron goods. In 2002, the gates were restored and re-erected at Carronshore, near to the site of the Carron Iron Works, where they stand as testimony to the skills of generations of local iron workers.

The International Exhibition of Industry, Science and Art.

30. The Canals, Burke and Hare, and the Union Inn

The Forth & Clyde Canal, originally known as the Great Canal, the oldest and longest canal in Scotland, was authorised by an Act of Parliament in 1768. The idea of linking the east and west coasts of Scotland by a waterway was to avoid the difficult sea route and was first considered in the reign of Charles II (1660–85). It was a remarkable feat of engineering at 62 kilometres (39 miles) long. Construction began at the east coast in June 1768, but stalled a number of times before it finally opened in July 1790, linking Falkirk to Port Dundas in Glasgow.

The Edinburgh & Glasgow Union Canal was approved by an Act of Parliament in 1817. Construction began at the Edinburgh end in 1818 and it was opened in 1822. The canal originally ran 50 kilometres (31 miles) from the Port Hopetoun basin in Edinburgh to Falkirk. It was 1.5 metres (5 feet) deep, followed a land contour throughout its length and required no locks – this involved significant engineering works such as the massive Avon Aqueduct. The canals were connected at the Port Downie Basin, beside Lock 16, by a series of eleven locks that climbed 33.5 metres (110 feet).

William Burke, of the infamous Burke and Hare, was a navvy on the Union Canal and lived for a time in Maddiston. When the work on the canal was complete, Burke moved to Edinburgh

Above: Lock 16 and the Union Inn.

Left: William Burke.

The Falkirk Wheel.

The Kelpies.

where he teamed up with William Hare. The pair took advantage of the shortage of bodies available for anatomical dissections in the medical schools. Before the Anatomy Act of 1832, which expanded the legal supply of medical cadavers, executed criminals were the main source, but this had been reduced due to a decrease in executions in the early nineteenth century.

The medical schools came to rely on bodies that had been acquired by nefarious means and grave robbing by 'resurrectionists' became one of the main sources. This gave rise to particular public fear, and watchtowers were set up in graveyards so that families could watch over the graves of their relatives for such time that the bodies would no longer be of use for dissection.

Burke and Hare saw the potential profit in this, but rather than going to the hard work of grave robbing, they simply murdered their victims and sold the bodies to the Edinburgh Medical School for dissection. Over a period of a few months in 1828, they were responsible for the murders of seventeen victims, which shocked and terrified Edinburgh. On their apprehension and trial, William Burke was publicly hanged on the morning of 28 January 1829 in front of a crowd estimated at between 20,000 and 25,000 and, on the following day, his body was dissected in the anatomy theatre of the University's Old College. Hare, who had been granted immunity from prosecution by giving evidence against Burke, was released in February 1829 and assisted in leaving Edinburgh.

Canal transport had distinct advantages – a horse could pull 50 tons on the canal, but only 2 tons on the road – and industry boomed along the canal. Before the arrival of the railways, a flourishing passenger service also ran on the canals between Edinburgh and Glasgow. From 1831, it was possible to take a bunk on the night boat passenger service – known as hoolits (from owls) – for the journey. By 1836, around 200,000 passengers were using the canals every year for journeys between the two cities. The journey between Edinburgh and Glasgow originally took six and a half hours. The introduction of swift boats, drawn by two horses that were changed every 2 miles, reduced the journey time to three and a half hours. In 1841, it cost 6s (cabin fare) or 4s (steerage) to travel by swift passage boat between the cities. The years 1840–41 marked the peak of the passenger traffic, with five boats leaving Glasgow for Edinburgh every weekday, supplemented by three night boats.

The large Port Downie Basin was a busy interchange, where goods were offloaded for road transport to neighbouring towns and villages. The Union Inn at Port Downie is a fine example of an early nineteenth-century trading post inn. It dates from the time of the completion of the Union Canal in 1822. Its location, at what was a pivotal trade point where the Forth & Clyde and Union Canal joined, made it one of the best-known hostelries in Scotland in its heyday. Travellers could disembark and take refreshments at the inn, while barges passed through the chain of locks that linked the two canals, or catch a stagecoach for their onward journey to other parts of Scotland.

The Forth & Clyde and Union Canals suffered, like most canals, from railway competition. In 1842, the opening of the Edinburgh & Glasgow Railway drastically reduced their importance and they fell into a slow decline. The ambitious Millennium Link project in the 1990s involved the renovation and reopening of the two canals. The solution to the restoration of the connection between the two canals, originally linked by eleven locks, which were removed in 1933, was the Falkirk Wheel. Opened in 2002, the revolutionary Wheel is a spectacular engineering marvel and the only boat-lifting device of its kind in the world.

The 350-hectare Helix Park opened in the summer of 2014 with the two strikingly beautiful 30-metre- (98-foot-) high steel sculptures of the Kelpies as its centrepiece. The Kelpies link the mythical Scottish water spirit with the heavy horses that were the historic source of power for industry, agriculture and the canals.

31. Camelon Brass Band

There's Auld Camelon Band they're aye tae the fore;
They started wi' flutes in the year '34,
If you had only heard them their music you'd adore,
For always their number was less than a score,
Their auld flutes ha'e been turned into brass
Three cheers tae the friends that gave them the cash,
For we've all joined together to gi'e them a hand,
and try and make good members tae the auld Camelon Band.

(The Camelon Brass Band, 1907)

Camelon.

Nineteenth-century brass band.

In the nineteenth century, there was a profusion of brass bands in Britain. The bands were closely associated with the rise of industrialisation and many of them had links with foundries, mills or collieries. The Falkirk area was no exception, and there were a dozen or so bands in the district.

Camelon Brass band, which evolved from an original flute band formed in 1834, was one of the earliest and best known in the area. Robert Smith was a founding member and his sons served in the band for decades.

The development of Camelon is closely associated with the fast and reliable transport links provided by the canals. William Cadell, who had been involved in establishing the Carron Co., brought workers from England and started a nail-making business at Camelon in 1790, which encouraged development in the area. The work was hard, involved working up to sixteen-hour days, and wages were low – 15s per week out of which the nailer had to pay for the iron. Apprentices began a six-year training from as early as nine years old and worked for their lodging, food and clothing. The introduction of machine-based nail making in the middle of the nineteenth century resulted in a rapid decline in the hand-made nail industry.

It is likely that members of the brass band would have been employed in nail making and playing in the band would have provided a pleasant pastime away from the grind of the hard work involved in the industry.

The band would have provided entertainment at community events, but contests between bands, with the added incentive of the prize money on offer, were an important part of brass band life. The Camelon Band was first recorded as winning a contest in Perth in 1863 and its last documented competitive contest was in 1950.

32. Westerglen Radio Transmitter

The BBC's Westerglen radio transmitter must have looked remarkably futuristic when it opened on 2 May 1932, a few miles to the south-west of Falkirk. It was the first high-powered transmitting station in Scotland. Westerglen was selected as the best site after survey work using a portable transmitter on a lorry. Its location, at 152 metres (500 feet) above sea level, and its proximity to the population of Central Scotland meant that it could radiate a signal approximately 112–128 kilometres (70–80 miles) in all directions from Falkirk and reach a substantial number of households. The main hall was lit by a dome in the roof to reduce dazzle and eye strain for the engineers when reading the many dials.

Westerglen radio transmitter.

Main hall at the Westerglen radio transmitter.

33. Alfred Nobel in Falkirk

Dynamite is manufactured at Redding, near Falkirk, by the British Dynamite
Company (Limited). This substance is a most valuable agent in mining and
quarrying. It is not affected by damp, and it requires far less labour in boring blast
holes than gunpowder, besides being about eight times more powerful.

The History of Stirlingshire, William Nimmo, 1880

Laurieston was feued in 1756 by Francis Lord Napier as a planned model village. It was
first known as Langtown, then as New Merchiston, after Napier's Merchiston estate in
Edinburgh. In 1762, it was purchased by Sir Laurence Dundas, the mastermind behind
the Forth & Clyde Canal, and became known as Lawrencetown, which became Laurieston.
Laurieston was a centre for William Cadell's nail-making business in the 1770s. Cadell was
the son of Carron Co.'s founder, who bought out the right to make nails from the company
and had a thriving business in Laurieston, Camelon and other parts of the country.

Hawthorn Cottage in Laurieston was the Scottish home of Alfred Nobel. The Nobel
family business was in explosives and Nobel, who was a brilliant chemist, was a great
innovator in the field. His invention of the relatively stable dynamite was groundbreaking.

Nobel's business interests were worldwide. In 1871, he established the British Dynamite
Factory on the remote Ardeer peninsula, which was developed as the largest explosives
factory in the world. The company obtained chemicals from the Westquarter Chemical
Co. Nobel bought shares in the company and in 1874 its director, Mr George McRoberts,

Photo Bolas and Co., Ludgate Hill.

THE LATE MR. ALFRED NOBEL.

Alfred Nobel.

Hawthorn Cottage, Laurieston.

became the chief chemist and the factory manager at Ardeer. Nobel converted the factory at Westquarter to manufacture explosives and detonators, and, at its peak, the factory employed 1,700 people. When McRoberts moved to Ardeer, he sold his house, Hawthorn Cottage in Laurieston, to Nobel to serve as his Scottish home. Nobel spent a considerable amount of time in the area during the 1870s and it is the only building in Scotland associated with him.

Nobel left the bulk of his immense fortune to establish the Nobel Prize, shortly before his death in 1896. He was prompted to do this when a French newspaper mistakenly published his obituary before his death. It condemned him as: 'Dr. Alfred Nobel, who became rich by finding ways to kill more people faster than ever before.' Nobel was shocked by what he read and concerned about how he would be remembered.

34. Redding Pit Disaster

On 25 September 1923, the No. 23 Redding Colliery suffered one of the worst disasters in the history of Scottish mining when a sudden inrush of water from old and disused coal workings at an upper level flooded the pit.

Redding pit.

Relatives await news of the missing miners.

An anxious crowd watch the rescue efforts at Redding.

Seventy-two miners were working on the night shift at that time. Six escaped during the initial flood, but sixty-six were trapped underground. A further twenty-one men were rescued through an old airshaft on the day of the disaster. A massive effort was mounted to find the other missing miners: pumps were requisitioned from other pits to drain the water, divers searched for survivors and the rescuers worked tirelessly to save their workmates. However, the rescue work was impeded by heavy falls within the workings and the risk of fire from black damp. There was jubilation when another five men were rescued nine days after the initial flood. One of the survivors said that the men ate matchboxes and sucked coal for sustenance during the time that they were trapped, and that there was much discussion about the results of the football.

Tragically, no other men were brought to the surface alive. Most were killed instantly; eleven had survived underground for almost two weeks, but could not be rescued. These men had left poignant notes for their loved ones, which were initially optimistic and later accepting of their fate. The body of the fortieth man was finally recovered in early December.

A relief fund raised £60,000 for the bereaved families and the disaster resulted in changes to pit safety procedures. The pit closed in 1958 and a memorial to the forty men that lost their lives in the disaster was erected near Redding Cross in 1980.

35. King Kenny

On 16 December 1933 local character King Kenny, who will be remembered by Falkirk Bairns of a certain vintage, was arrested for causing trouble due to a speech he made to a large crowd at Falkirk's Market Place, which functioned as the town's Speakers' Corner.

King Kenny, Kenneth Mackenzie, was a well-known character around the Falkirk area for many years. He would entertain cinema queues with his banjo and write long discursive tracts in chalk on the pavements. Despite being somewhat eccentric, he also boasted of having a certificate from Bellsdyke Hospital, which confirmed that he was sane.

On this particular December day in 1933, Kenny was holding forth to his audience on the controversial subject of the Edinburgh Kosmo Dance club prosecution – a case in which a number of men had been arrested for living off the immoral earnings of prostitutes. It seems that this created a degree of unrest among his audience and, when he declined to stop speaking on the subject, he was arrested by the police for conducting himself in a disorderly manner.

He was described as a youth when he appeared at a sitting of Falkirk Police Court on a charge of breach of the peace following the incident. Wearing silver covered shoes, he bowed to Bailie Flanagan when he entered the court and is described as being undecided whether to sit, stoop or stand in the dock. The charge was read out to him and he informed the court that he was pleading not guilty, although he rapidly changed his mind to a plea of guilty.

The case against him was that he was standing on a small box, bawling and shouting at the pitch of his voice and making rude remarks about certain people. In his defence Kenny claimed that he was simply letting his public hear his views on a subject that had been widely covered in the news. He described himself as a 'bit of a Christian' and wanted the public to be told about morality. He then apologised for the trouble he had caused and said that it 'was a terrible thing to run against the law'. Kenny assured the court that he now considered it healthier to refrain from public speaking. Bailie Flanagan, who seemed amused by the proceedings, was satisfied that Kenny would refrain from public speaking and he was dismissed with an admonition.

36. Arthur's O'on

The name Stenhousemuir is derived from 'Stenhus', an anachronistic form of Stone House. The stone house in question was Arthur's O'on, which was located to the north of the River Carron. It was a circular beehive-shaped Roman temple or shrine, dating to the period of the garrisoning of the Antonine Wall, and took its name from its resemblance to historic

Arthur's O'on.

Sir Michael Bruce in a yoke forever having to carry stones from Arthur's O'on.

bread ovens. From the twelfth century it was recognised as one of the 'Wonders of Britain'. In the eighteenth century, it was described as 'the best and most entire old building in Britain' and 'the grandest Roman monument in Britain'.

It was a remarkable survival from the times of the Roman occupation. However, the building was demolished on the instruction of Sir Michael Bruce of Stenhouse in 1743 to line a mill dam on the River Carron. It seems that the dam was swept away by floods shortly after. The destruction of Arthur's O'on enraged antiquarians – Sir Michael Bruce was described by one as a 'villain and sordid rascal'. Sir James Clerk was so appalled by the loss of Arthur's O'on that, in 1760, he had an exact replica of the building constructed at Penicuik House.

Ordnance Survey maps place the site of Arthur's O'on in the proximity of Adam Crescent in Stenhousemuir. Its name has fuelled conjecture that it is linked to the legends of King Arthur and the Knights of the Round Table. The name of Camelon is also believed by some to relate to Camelot of Arthurian legend.

37. Larbert Railway Station and the Dobbie Hall

Larbert railway station was opened in 1848 by the Scottish Central Railway and was modernised in 1892. The opening of the station resulted in the economic growth of the village. The original station buildings were removed in 1976.

Larbert station.

The Dobbie Hall.

The Station Hotel in the background of the image of the station is in a distinctive Tudor style. There has been a hostelry on this site for as long as there has been a railway station at Larbert. The hotel is on Foundry Loan. The street name references the iron-casting industries, which were once prominent in Larbert. Dobbie, Forbes & Co. opened a foundry in 1872. This was followed by James Jones' sawmill, which supplied the wood for Scott of the Antarctic's boat *Discovery*, and later the Jones and Campbell foundry.

The Dobbie Hall in Larbert was opened in August 1901 by the Duchess of Montrose, when she unclipped a jewelled bracelet from the handles on the main door. The new building replaced an earlier meeting hall in Tryst Road at a cost of around £12,000. The hall was a gift to the town from Major Robert Dobbie. Robert Dobbie was a self-made man. He started work as a moulder and opened a foundry in Larbert in 1872. His company exported cast-iron goods all over the world. Robert's son had been killed in the Boer War and the Dobbie Hall was intended as a tangible memorial to his lost son. The opening night concert was for the benefit of the wives of the soldiers in the Boer War. Robert was an honorary major from his involvement with the local volunteers. Gene Vincent and Marty Wilde played at the Dobbie in the 1950s, and in the 1960s it hosted some of the major pop acts of the day. The infamous 'Dobbie Shuffle' was a unique form of intimate dancing popular at the venue, which now has a locally produced beer named after it.

38. Larbert Railway Station and the Quintinshill Rail Disaster

The most appalling disaster in the history of British railways occurred early on Saturday morning on the Caledonian Railway near Gretna Green on the Border. At Quinton's Hill Cabin, which is about a mile and a half from Gretna, a local train was being shunted across the up main line so as to allow the Euston express from Glasgow to pass. At this moment a Caledonian train conveying about 500 of the Royal Scots (Territorials) to the south, which was travelling at the rate of 60 miles an hour, came up, and dashed into the local train. To add to the horror of the scene, the Euston express collided almost immediately afterwards with the wrecked trains. Many of the passengers were killed outright by the tremendous impact which converted the trains into heaps of debris, but the casualty list was enormously swollen by an outbreak of fire which it was impossible to subdue. With few

Plaque commemorating the Quintinshill Rail Disaster at Larbert station.

exceptions, the killed, misssing and injured belonged to the Territorial battalion which has its headquarters in Leith.

Aberdeen Weekly Journal, 28 May 1914

The Station Hotel is reflected in the plaque at Larbert station commemorating the Quintinshill Rail Disaster. Five hundred men of the Leith Battalion of the Royal Scots embarked on a train at Larbert station on the morning of 22 May 1915, after camping overnight on the Tryst. The train was bound for Liverpool, where a boat was waiting to transport the soldiers to Gallipoli.

Tragically, they only made it as far as the Quintinshill Siding, near Gretna, where a catastrophic multiple train collision occured due to a serious signalling error. Rescue efforts were hampered by a fire that swept through the wooden carriages of the troop train. There were a total of 227 fatalities, the greatest ever loss of life for a rail crash in Britain. Two hundred and fifteen of the dead were soldiers and hundreds more were seriously injured. Most of the sixty soldiers that survived with no injuries were so traumatised by the incident that they were sent home.

39. Larbert Railway Bridge

From the time of the Romans, Larbert has been an important crossing point of the River Carron. The old road bridge at Larbert dates from 1782. At one time a toll, which went towards its maintenance, was charged for crossing it. A new bridge now carries the main A9 from Larbert to Falkirk.

The fifteen arches of the railway viaduct were constructed in 1848. On the night of 29 April 1867, a train, consisting of fifty-three carriages, travelling from Perth to Edinburgh was derailed when the rear axle of one of the wagons snapped while crossing the railway viaduct at Larbert. Most of the carriages careered off the viaduct and fell into the River Carron. The train was carrying livestock, and many cattle and sheep were killed – although hundreds were also rescued alive. The crew of the train, a cattleman and a shepherd travelling in the guard's van made a remarkable escape with only minor injuries.

The noise that the crash produced was heard for a considerable distance, and 'excited the wildest alarm in the community of Larbert'. Nearly all of the villagers rushed to the scene and 'exerted themselves in a highly praiseworthy manner to render whatever assistance was necessary in the emergency'.

The 'huge accumulation of ruin in the valley below the bridge' was described as a 'scene which would appal the beholder with broken and smashed wagons piled up in a grotesque manner and hundreds of dead or injured animals'.

The Larbert Railway Viaduct.

40. First Scottish Senior Football under Floodlights at Stenhousemuir

The Falkirk area's three local senior football teams all have a long history.

Falkirk Football and Athletic Club (The Bairns) was formed in 1876. Falkirk FC joined the Scottish League in 1902, was promoted in 1905 and went on to win the Scottish Cup in 1913 and 1957. Between 1885 and the end of 2002/03 Scottish football season, the club was based at Brockville Park. After the creation of the Scottish Premier League in 1998, the terraces at Brockville did not meet new safety standards for Premier League matches and Falkirk FC was refused promotion. The site was sold to a supermarket chain, which built a new branch in place of Brockville Park. The club's present home ground, since the 2004/05 season, is the Falkirk Stadium, an 8,750 all-seated venue on the outskirts of Falkirk. East Stirlingshire FC can trace its history back to 1880, and the team first played league football in 1900.

Ochilview Park has been the home of Stenhousemuir Football Club (The Warriors) since 1890. On Wednesday 7 November 1951, the ground was the venue for a historic moment in Scottish football when the first senior game under floodlights in Scotland was played

FALKIRK

The Bairns

Falkirk Football Club – The Bairns.

Stenhousemuir Football Club – The Warriors.

Match between Stenhousemuir and Clyde in the 1950s with the original floodlights in the background.

The Highland Cattle statues at Stenhousemuir.

McCowan's Highland toffee.

between Stenhousemuir and Hibernian. A trial game was played on the night before the main event, to test the floodlights, and four additional lights were added, bringing the total to eight. The floodlights were paid for by Tommy Douglas, a local Stenhousemuir butcher.

An early fog cleared for a prompt 7 p.m. start in front of an attendance of 6,000. Stenhousemuir opened the scoring after twenty-four minutes with a goal from Kerr. Goals from Mulkerrin and Turnbull gave Hibs a 2-1 lead by half-time. Another goal from Mulkerrin sent Hibs further ahead after the interval, but Stenhousemuir then scored from a penalty. Johnstone scored the fourth for Hibs and Jimmy Allan kept the game alive with another goal for Stenhousemuir twelve minutes later; however, with ten minutes to go Souness converted a cross from Willie Ormond.

Ormond (1927–84) was born in Falkirk and played for the Warriors at the start of his career, before going on to become one of Hib's Famous Five. The final score was 5-3 to Hibernian, although the Hibs team had to fight all the way. It sounds like attractive football and the white ball under the floodlights was noted as making the game appear much faster than normal.

Reports at the time noted that from the spectator's point of view, every move on the field under the lights was observed without the slightest problem and it was deemed a great success. Most of the players thought that the floodlights were useful and that they were able to play with little difficulty. Hibs goalkeeper, Jimmy Kerr, had some minor reservations, due to problems with corner kicks and high crosses under the lights.

All of the leading Scottish club officials had been invited to the game and were impressed by the initiative of Stenhousemuir. It was expected that they would report back to their clubs and that there would be a 'feverish installing of lights at many grounds'.

After the game, tributes were paid to the enterprise of the Ochilview officials for showing what could be done with floodlight football and Harry Swan, Hib's chairman, thanked the Stenhousemuir board for showing Scotland the potential for floodlight football. Mr Swan also kindly asked Stenhousemuir to keep the whole receipts from the game.

Ochilview stood next to McCowan's factory on Tryst Road and the delightful smell of toffee and other sweet treats being made pervaded this part of Stenhousemuir for many years. McCowan's, famous for its Highland cream toffee, was established in Stenhousemuir in 1922. Andrew McCowan had a lemonade business in the village, but it was his wife's toffee that proved more successful. The Tryst Road factory opened in 1924 and was a major employer in the village. The Highland cow statues at Stenhousemuir commemorate the town's link with the great cattle sales at the Tryst; they also bring to mind the packaging for McCowan's famous Highland toffee.

41. Jimmy Finlayson, Larbert-born Hollywood Funny Man

James Henderson 'Jimmy' Finlayson was born in Larbert, Stirlingshire, on the 27 August 1887. He was an apprentice in his father's iron foundry before entering the University of Edinburgh to study business. During his time in Edinburgh, he met and became friends with John Clyde, a well-known Scottish actor of the time. This fuelled Finlayson's interest in the stage and by 1910 he had abandoned his studies to tread the boards, performing in venues around Britain.

In 1912, following the death of both his parents, Finlayson went to New York to act in a play that ended up on Broadway for a long run. Finlayson also toured in vaudeville with Alec Lauder, brother of the legendary Sir Harry. In 1916, one of his stage tours stopped in Hollywood, where he decided to quit the show and try his luck in films.

He found work in numerous Mack Sennett-produced comedies, most notably as one of the original Keystone Kops or paired with cross-eyed Ben Turpin. However, he is best remembered for his work at the Hal Roach Studios. In the mid-1920s, Roach attempted to make Finlayson a top-billed star and gave him his own series of two-reelers, but he was destined not to achieve great success as a solo artist.

In 1927, the *All-Star Comedy* series gave Finlayson equal billing with his new co-stars Stan Laurel and Oliver Hardy, with some studio publicity even referring to the three as a 'famous comedy trio'. However, Laurel and Hardy were on the ascendancy and, despite Finlayson's diminished billing, he remained an indispensable part of the Laurel and Hardy team. He played supporting parts in thirty-three of Laurel and Hardy's films, usually as some kind of comedy villain, and was their best-known comic foil. Stan Laurel said that Jimmy Finlayson helped establish the success of the films as much as he or Hardy.

Jimmy Finlayson with Laurel and Hardy.

Finlayson had a range of trademark mannerisms, which were favourites with moviegoers at the time. He was famous for his bald head, fake handlebar moustache, double-take reaction, an askance look and a long drawn-out 'Dohhhhhhh', which is said to have directly influenced Homer's 'D'oh!' in *The Simpsons*.

Finlayson was forced to retire from regular film-making in 1937 due to ill health shortly after appearing with Laurel and Hardy in *Way Out West*. However, he continued to make the occasional appearance in movies right up to just before his death from a heart attack on 9 October 1953 in Los Angeles.

The life and work of 'Fin', as he is known to his many fans, is still celebrated by the Sons of Finlay, an offshoot of the Laurel and Hardy Fan club, the Sons of the Desert.

Taylor & Francis Books Ltd
Taylor & Francis Group plc

P O Box 6329 , Basingstoke , RG24 8DR

For a full list of Taylor & Francis imprints plea
v.tandf.co.u
>mer Service Contact:
ie - 01264 343070 , Direct
ccounts Contacts.
813000 , Fax : 01256 35

INVOICE TO

ECONOMIC HISTOR\
DEPT ECONOMIC SO
UNIVERSITY OF LEIC
LEICESTER
LE1 7RH

:VIEW EDITOF
:ONOMIC HIST
:PT ECONOMI
UNIVERSITY OF
LEICESTER
LE1 7RH

Shipper -

Line	Order Reference	ISBN	QTY	Title / Author Details
1	S TILLBROOK	0415267323	1	REVIEW COPY - WE HAVE MUCH PLEASURE IN SENDING YOU THE ACCOMPANYING BOOK FOR REVIEW. THE PUBLISHER REQUESTS THAT NO REVIEW SHOULD APPEAR BEFORE PUBLICATION DATE. A COPY OF THE REVIEW WOULD BE GREATLY APPRECIATED. FURTHER INFORMATION AVAILABLE FROM THE PUBLICITY DEPT. Back-Order released, Our Document Ref 1' MONETARY STABILITY IN EUROPE/COLLIGNON :

Order Lines - **1**   Net Weight - **0.623**   Total Quantity - **1**

OP POR Batch 66314 /351 Document Type - **GRR**   Entered Date 27JUN03

Despatch Method - **LETTER 2ND CLASS**   Site - **Andover - T&F**

All claims for shortages and damages must be made within 14 days from

PAYMENT METHODS (Please ensure you quote your account number.)   **Account Numbe**

CHEQUE
Please make payable to **Taylor & Francis** and attach to this slip.

CREDIT or CHARGECARD - (MA:

GIROBANK
Sterling Account Number - 2904748.

CREDIT TRANSFER
Please Quote Taylor & Francis and your Invoice Number.
Bankers - National Westminster Bank PLC, Old Market Square, 3 London Street, Basingstoke, Hampshire, RG21 7NS.
STERLING Sort Code: 60-02-49 , Account Number: 80772048   , Our **IBAN** number is :- GB88NWBK60024980772048

Expiry Date _____   Am(

Please send your payment to - Taylor & Francis, P O Box 6329, Basingstoke, Hampshire, RG24 8DR, UK.
All Orders,Claims and Returns should be addressed to - Thomson Publishing Services, Cheriton House, North Way, Andover, Hants, SP1

Monetary Stability in Europe

The European Monetary Union (EMU) was created to overcome the economic difficulties that Europe experienced in the last part of the twentieth century. Like the European Community itself, EMU reflects the fact that European countries have learned that they have much to gain by working together as a whole.

EMU, however, is also a challenge to economic theory. Its success will depend on how it is managed, yet, the full economic and political ramifications of the monetary union cannot be predicted. A large number of theoretical models and empirical facts have been scrutinised by economists, yet, inevitably, explaining why past policy actions or institutions have failed and how the future could be improved sometimes requires questioning of well-established, familiar principles. Too often, new facts are interpreted in the light of conventional wisdom.

In this book, the author presents fresh perspectives on the theories surrounding EMU. Urging the reader to examine conventional ideas from new viewpoints, he discusses the events which led to EMU, analysing the current situation, and projecting possible futures.

Essential reading for academics and professionals concerned with the background and implications of EMU, this book will also be of considerable interest to scholars in the fields of European studies, monetary economics, international economics and economic history.

Stefan Collignon is Professor of European Political Economy at the London School of Economics and Political Science (LSE). Previously, he served as Deputy Director General for Europe in the Federal Ministry of Finance, Berlin; he also teaches at the College d'Europe (Bruge).

Routledge International Studies in Money and Banking

1 **Private Banking in Europe**
   Lynn Bicker

2 **Bank Deregulation and Monetary Order**
   George Selgin

3 **Money in Islam**
   A study in Islamic political economy
   Masudul Alam Choudhury

4 **The Future of European Financial Centres**
   Kirsten Bindemann

5 **Payment Systems in Global Perspective**
   Maxwell J. Fry, Isaak Kilato, Sandra Roger, Krzysztof Senderowicz,
   David Sheppard, Francisco Solis and John Trundle

6 **What Is Money?**
   John Smithin

7 **Finance**
   A characteristics approach
   Edited by David Blake

8 **Organisational Change and Retail Finance**
   An ethnographic perspective
   Richard Harper, Dave Randall and Mark Rouncefield

9 **The History of the Bundesbank**
   Lessons for the European Central Bank
   Jakob de Haan

10 **The Euro**
   A challenge and opportunity for financial markets
   Published on behalf of *Société Universitaire Européenne de Recherches Financières (SUERF)*
   Edited by Michael Artis, Axel Weber and Elizabeth Hennessy

11 **Central Banking in Eastern Europe**
   Nigel Healey

12 **Money, Credit and Prices Stability**
   Paul Dalziel

13 **Monetary Policy, Capital Flows and Exchange Rates**
   Essays in memory of Maxwell Fry
   Edited by William Allen and David Dickinson

14 **Adapting to Financial Globalisation**
   Edited by Morten Balling, Eduard H. Hochreiter and Elizabeth Hennessy

15 **Monetary Macroeconomics**
   A new approach
   Alvaro Cencini

16 **Monetary Stability in Europe**
   Stefan Collignon

Monetary Stability in Europe

Stefan Collignon

London and New York

First published 2002
by Routledge
11 New Fetter Lane, London EC4P 4EE

Simultaneously published in the USA and Canada
by Routledge
29 West 35th Street, New York, NY 10001

Routledge is an imprint of the Taylor & Francis Group

Typeset in 10/12 pt Garamond by
Newgen Imaging Systems (P) Ltd, Chennai, India
Printed and bound in Great Britain by Biddles Ltd, Guildford and King's Lynn

British Library Cataloguing in Publication Data
A catalogue record for this book is available
from the British Library

Library of Congress Cataloging in Publication Data
Collignon, Stefan, 1951–
    Monetary stability in Europe – Stefan Collignon.
        p. cm.
    Includes bibliographical references and index.
    1. Economic and Monetary Union. 2. Monetary policy – European Union
    Countries. I. Title

    HG925 .C656 2002
    332.4′494–dc21   2001048668

ISBN 0-415-26732-3

Contents

List of illustrations   vi
Preface   viii

1   Why stable money matters or 'the loss of paradise'   1

2   After Bretton Woods: the world of bloc floating   27

3   International consequences of bloc floating   55

4   The instability of the bloc floating regime   75

5   A fresh look at Optimum Currency Area theory   93

6   Is EMU sustainable?   113

7   Sustaining price stability   129

8   Monetary policy and structural unemployment   143

Notes   195
Bibliography   211
Index   226

Illustrations

Figures

1.1	The structure of collective intentionality	5
1.2	Unit labour cost	14
1.3	Misery index: (a) inflation + unemployment rates; (b) inflation − growth rate	17
1.4	(a) US inflation rate; (b) inflation differential to USA	24
2.1	Interest rates (a) USA; (b) Germany; (c) France	30
2.2	(a) Real short-term interest rate; (b) real interest rates on government bonds	31
2.3	Variation of foreign exchange reserve	35
2.4	(a) Share of currency zones in world exports; (b) export share of currency zones as per cent of world exports	37
2.5	Investment decision under risk	49
2.6	Risk premia and portfolio shares	50
2.7	(a) France's marginal q; (b) Germany's marginal q	53
3.1	Fundamental equilibrium	62
3.2	US dollar/DM exchange rate	69
3.3	NEERs	70
3.4	NEER volatility (USA versus Germany)	70
3.5	NEER Germany	71
3.6	REER Germany	71
5.1	Temporary and permanent shocks	101
5.2	Size and import share	107
5.3	Net benefit of a single currency for country i	109
6.1	Marginal cost−benefit analysis of EMU	116
6.2	Country contribution to aggregate net benefit from EMU	117
6.3	Total net benefits in a Benthamite OCA	117
6.4	Voting weights in the EU	118
7.1	Convergence of inflation rates	132
7.2	Convergence of interest rates	132
7.3	Optimal conservativeness before and after EMU	142
8.1	(a) Unemployment rates; (b) employment rates	145

8.2	Job creating growth in (a) Europe; (b) USA; (c) Japan	154
8.3	(a) Total factor productivity; (b) total factor productivity change	158
8.4	(a) Capital intensity; (b) annual variation in capital intensity	159
8.5	(a) Real wage position; (b) profitability; (c) real wage pressure	165
8.6	Convergence of capital intensity	166
8.7	Investment share and unemployment rate: (a) EU 15; (b) Spain; (c) Portugal	168
8.8	NAIRU as labour market equilibrium	175
8.9	The effect of an interest rate increase in a contract economy	177
8.A1	Wage pressure and cap intensity: (a) EU 15; (b) Germany; (c) USA	193

Tables

1.1	European growth, 1890–1992	8
1.2	Nominal unit labour costs relative to 19 industrialised countries	11
2.1	Exchange rate regimes of the IMF-members	36
2.2	Exchange rate management and orientation of trade in 1991	38
2.3	Volatility under bloc floating and basket pegs	48
2.4	Risk premia under different pegging regimes	48
3.1	Trade matrix in a three-country world	57
3.2	Import shares and change of slope	60
3.3	Volatility of German NEER	72
4.1	Response of monetary variables to shocks	88
4.2	Growth of macroeconomic variables with respect to Germany	91
5.1	Size and degree of openness of European Union member states – 1997	97
5.2	Weight in Euro-GDP	99
8.1	Aggregate growth rates	147
8.2	A comparison of NAIRU estimates from cross-country studies	151
8.3	Economic growth and unemployment	153
8.4	Ratio of number of years with positive to negative output gaps	167
8.A1	Unit root tests	191
8.A2	Unit root test in presence of a structural break in 1989	192
8.A3	Regression results	194

Preface

This book describes a vision of Europe's history and future and of economic theory. The twentieth century has seen the best and worst of humankind. The advances of science, knowledge and education, as well as material progress, have been unparalleled. People are richer, healthier and are living longer at the beginning of this century than at the beginning of the last one. Karl Marx never saw an airplane, but his great-grandchildren fly to the Seychelles for a holiday, communicate by e-mail in the Global Village and watch a football match or a Royal funeral with three billion other people via satellite TV. While the nineteenth century seemed to be a period of almost unbroken material, intellectual and moral progress, this century was without doubt the most murderous by scale, frequency and length of warfare, famine and genocide in history (Hobsbawm 1994).

For Europe, the contrast is also stunning: convinced of its centrality as the cradle of (western) civilization, it was the centre of two world wars, lost its power to the United States and saw the share of its population dwindle to 6.5 per cent in the world. In the eighteenth century Europeans formulated fundamental human values like *Liberté*, *Egalité*, *Fraternité*. In the twentieth century the spirit of human kindness was represented by leaders such as Mahatma Gandhi, Martin Luther King, Jr. or the Dalai Lama while Europeans were ruled by Stalin, Hitler and Chamberlain. The World War I was followed by the Age of Catastrophe (Hobsbawm 1994), a world economic crisis of unprecedented depth, hyperinflation, and mass unemployment. After the World War II, the western part of Europe lived through an unprecedented Golden Age, based on institutional stability and political and economic cooperation under American hegemony. However, once US power had passed its zenith and the international monetary system of Bretton Woods had been abolished, the old strains of capitalism – low growth, severe cyclical slumps, mass unemployment, and social inequality – that seemed to have disappeared during the Golden Age returned.

European Monetary Union (EMU) is the attempt to overcome some of the difficulties that Europe has experienced during the last quarter of the century. Like the European Community itself, EMU reflects the lesson learned that Europe has had much to gain by working together as a whole. This cooperation went far beyond the diplomatic games of the nineteenth or the first part of the twentieth century. As Jean Monnet put it: '*Nous ne coalisons pas les Etats, nous unissons des hommes.*'[1] Given the evidence of volatile human volitions, European integration after the Second World War proceeded by creating cooperative institutions which tried to preserve the more precious part of the European heritage. A whole generation of Europeans must have felt what Keynes has lucidly described: '. . . that civilisation was a thin and precarious crust erected by the personality and the will of a very few, and only maintained by rules and conventions skilfully put across and guilefully preserved.' (Keynes 1938). Obviously, abolishing all national currencies and replacing them with the euro did not happen without resistance, but there were a few which had the will and the personality to push EMU through.

The next step is to ensure that EMU will help to preserve the thin and precarious crust of civilisation in Europe. In view of past experience, this requires, more than anything, the return of full employment and the preservation of certain standards of social safety. For nothing is more likely to excite the beast in humans than insecurity and threats to their livelihood.

EMU's success will depend on how it is managed. But action without understanding cannot produce desired results. 'Practical men', wrote Keynes, 'who believe themselves to be quite exempt from any intellectual influences, are usually the slaves of some defunct economist' (1936: 383). Today, Keynes is himself a defunct economist, but our practical men and women seem to have fallen for the intellectual answers of the 1920s, draped in the fashionable cloth of New Classical Economics and styled in the language of mathematics and econometrics. Karaoke-economists keep singing the old song that wages are too high, social services too generous, and that government spending needs to be cut to balance budgets. Not surprisingly, similar causes produce similar effects and the thin crust of civilisation becomes brittle. Not only is public enthusiasm for European integration receding, but the consent to the system of liberal democracy is questioned as extreme right wing parties emerge.

The parallel to the 1920s is striking. Analysing the disintegration of the Weimar Republic, Childers (1982: 414) wrote:

> The political importance of the inflation has, of course, been readily acknowledged in most studies of electoral realignment in pre-Hitler Germany. Contemporary analyses were quick to point out the profound social, economic, and psychological dislocations associated with the inflation, and subsequent treatments have concluded that the inflation certainly contributed to the radicalization of important elements in the middle class electorate. Yet, while the political ramifications of the inflation have drawn comment, surprisingly little attention has been focused on the politically disruptive effects of stabilisation. This is particularly striking since the manner in which the Reich government liquidated the inflation in late 1923

---

1   Jean Monnet, *Discours Washington* (30 April 1952); in Monnet (1996).

and early 1924 shaped the contours of public debate on economic issues until the onset of the depression. Indeed, it was the government's stabilization program that provoked the most persistent and programmatic political response of the pre-depression period.

In a similar manner, the Great Inflation of the 1970s was followed in the 1980s and 1990s by stabilisation policies which have fundamentally structured the economic and political debate in Europe.

This is why EMU is also a challenge to economic theory. A new age needs new ideas. Discussing EMU has become a growth industry for economists. A large number of theoretical models and empirical facts have been scrutinised. Inevitably, explaining why past policy actions or institutions have failed, and how the future could be improved, may require at times to question well-established, familiar principles. In my view, this is what economic theory building is about. However, only too often, new facts are interpreted in the light of conventional wisdom. If every reader of this book, after working his way to the end, looks at least at one previously held idea from a new perspective, I will have fulfilled my task. This preface is not scientific: that starts at Chapter 1. But intellectual integrity commands that I reveal the normative context in which the theoretical ideas of the following chapters evolve.

This book grew out of my work at the *Association for the Monetary Union* during the 1990s. I have benefited from the wisdom of Europe's leading industrialists and from the frequent dialogue with political decision-makers and over 15,000 citizens I have met to discuss EMU in big cities and small villages all over Europe. Of course, the views presented here are mine alone, and so are all possible errors. But I would like to express my gratitude for stimulating discussions with Bertrand de Maigret, Hajo Riese, Manfred Nitsch, Charles Goodhart, Jean Pisani-Ferry, Peter Bofinger, Heiner Flassbeck, Hans-Peter Fröhlich, Niels Tygesen, Martin Weale, Andrew Hughes-Hallet, Pier-Carlo Padoan, Angel Torres, Willem Buiter, Hans-Jürgen Krupp, Reimut Jochimsen, Pierre Jaillet, Francesco Papadia, Marc-Olivier Strauss-Kahn, Ludwing Schubert, Christa Randzio-Plath, Karl Lamers (who inadvertently inspired Chapter 4), David Croughan, Agnes Bénassy-Quéré, Andreas Worms, Julian von Landesberger, Franco Modigliani, Rudi Dornbusch, Allan Meltzer and many more. This book would not have been possible without the total support, critical feedback and permanent dialogue with Susanne Mundschenk and the devoted secretarial backup by Menuka Scetbon-Didi. Sebastian Dullien saved me from some embarrassing mistakes and Allison Zinder checked my English. Finally, the greatest burden was on my wife, Judith, who saw less of me than she deserved. I only hope that the sacrifice was not in vain.

Stefan Collignon
Paris 2001

1 Why stable money matters or 'the loss of paradise'

Europe has a new currency, the euro. It has been the fruit of a long evolution of European monetary co-operation. But despite this apparently irresistible historic process, many observers have been puzzled: was it inevitable or merely an arbitrary political decision without economic foundation? Was there no alternative to old nations of Europe giving up the symbol of national sovereignty? In Europe, changes in monetary arrangements have usually reflected the chaotic ups and downs of its history. This is nowhere more obvious than in Austria which, by the end of the twentieth century, has had its sixth currency in less than 100 years. Thus, even such a fundamental institution as money can be short-lived and volatile. Will the adventure of European Monetary Union (EMU) succeed – or will it disappear as many other regimes in the past? Of course, impermanence is the essence of the world. Even though nothing lasts forever, some things last longer than others. How long will the euro last?

As far as the Treaty on European Union (TEU) is concerned, the single currency will last forever. In the public debate Eurosceptic warnings about impending disaster (e.g. Feldstein 1997; Congdon 1997) were not infrequent, but few (Lascelles 1997) have spelt out how EMU could become undone. Others, like the Bundesbank (Tietmeyer 1995; Jochimsen 1998), have insisted that 'ultimately a monetary union is an undisolvable community of solidarity' and, therefore, only countries with a sufficient degree of convergence ought to join. This argument implicitly assumes that joining EMU without sufficient convergence could create difficulties for premature qualified members, and that they would have to be bailed out by the others. But what would happen if this solidarity and loyalty to each other did not exist? Would countries wish to leave? Ultimately, EMU's sustainability begs the question: Why do some international monetary regimes fail while others succeed? Which domestic or international conditions bind nations together in economic agreements, and which break them apart? (McNamara 1998).

For the neoclassical economic theorist, the question of the sustainability of monetary institutions is odd: Why should it matter? If economic agents were free of money illusion, they would distinguish monetary from real magnitudes, at least in the long term. Economic value is derived from utility. In general equilibrium, markets would determine relative prices, that is, the ratios at which goods are exchanged, in proportion to their respective utilities. The money market would determine the stock of money and money prices (Grandmont 1983). Yet this implies that the value of money in relation to goods is zero. Thus, it cannot serve a purpose at all (Duffie 1990). Consequently, why would one bother with making money last? This question is related to a second one: how can money, an intrinsically worthless means of exchange, acquire value? Traditional explanations centred around the functions of money, such as means of exchange, payment, unit of account or store of value. In overlapping generations models, money has value if it either facilitates existing trades or allows for new ones. But as Blanchard and Fischer (1989: 159) show, trust in the value of money is necessary for money to have value. If at a period zero the young do not believe that money will be valued at time 1, they will not buy money, and money will never be valued. Modern theories emphasise the role of money under conditions of uncertainty and asymmetric information (Goodhart 1989; Brunner and Meltzer 1971). For Riese (1986a, 1990, 1995) the value of money derives from the fact that it serves as a means of payment – and not just a means of exchange – and this requires that money is kept 'scarce' by the central bank. We will return to this argument in Chapter 8. What matters here, is that we can assign utility to the use of money which is derived from the functions it serves. If for some reason, money does not fulfil these functions correctly, its functions are transferred to different carriers or assets and money loses its value and ultimately becomes 'useless'. In an international context this process is explained by currency substitution models (Mizen and Pentecost 1996) or by models of monetary hierarchy (Nitsch 1995; Herr 1992). What all these explanations have in common is that for money to be used, it needs to have a positive value. Therefore, sustaining money as an institution requires maintaining this value.

Over the course of history, money has taken all kinds of forms, from metal coins (copper, silver, gold) to bank notes and deposits, although the unit of accounts (pound, franc, dollar . . .) have normally covered longer periods than their material support. For centuries, economists have sought to explain the origin of money (Menger 1892). Early theories linked it to a commodity. A modern look reveals it to be a more effusive concept with a variety of assets and means of payment covering a range of instruments from bank notes to electronic transfers and credit cards (Collignon 1998). Money's characteristics as an asset became apparent at the end of the eighteenth century, when money was related to the monopoly of note issue by the central bank and no longer to the coinage of precious metals. Ever since, monetary management has been a matter of credibility. Money has become a promise to pay – if it ever has been anything else. Trust in honouring the promise is essential for the sustainability of money as an institution.

However, it is not only the institution of money itself that is of uncertain durability, but also the organisations that manage it. Sweden is the country with the longest tradition (since 1668) of central banking; the Bank of England was founded in 1694; the Banque de France in 1800 and the Deutsche Reichbank in 1875. But the Bundesbank only appeared in 1957. On an international level, the Bretton Woods Agreement in 1944 set up an international monetary system with rules which were abolished in 1971, but IMF as an organisation continued to exist with new objectives. With the birth of a new currency, the euro and the European

System of Central Banks (ESCB) as its organisation, one may ask how long this newcomer is going to last. In fact the question has even been raised whether central banks are a necessary institution at all (Smith 1936). I will not discuss these arguments here. Instead, I will show in the next section that money is an institution that matters and, therefore, deserves to be sustained. In the rest of the chapter, we will then look at the historical background against which we can explain not only the emergence of EMU, but also the expectations that it implicitly raises.

Money as an institution

The human mind is of a fickle nature – a fact well known to philosophers and literary artists, but less to economists. Usually, economic theory works with utility maximising economic agents who have fairly constant preference structures or tastes. This might be a perfectly justified assumption – over the short run. However, over time, preferences are not stable. For example, public consensus on international monetary arrangements has shifted five times in one century. From the Gold Standard the world moved to flexible exchange rates after World War I; from the Bretton Woods fixed system again to a flexible rate regime in the 1970s; and now EMU reverts to monetary stability in Europe. These oscillations are puzzling. Each time flexible exchange rate regimes have been coincidental with macroeconomic instability and low growth, and fixed rates with welfare improvements. Does every generation have to learn the same lessons anew? It might well be that the Golden Age only appears golden after it is over. We live, after all, as Hirschman put it,

> ... in a world in which men think they want one thing and then upon getting it, find out to their dismay that they don't want it nearly as much as they thought or don't want it at all and that something else, of which they were hardly aware, is what they really want ...

> (Hirschman 1982: 21)

It may also be that once we have experienced disappointment, the 'rebound effect' makes for an exaggeration of the benefits and an underestimate of the costs of the action that provides a counterpoint to what has been done previously. We will deal with volatile policy preferences in the case of EMU in Chapter 6. Yet, the history of monetary arrangements of Europe in the twentieth century implicitly poses a normative question: are fixed rates preferable over flexible ones or is it the other way round? And if preferences are not stable, then why may social phenomena have any durability at all?

A short philosophical digression on institutional norms

Part of the answer is that society consists of more than a set of utility maximising individuals with given preferences. Of course, individuals *have* preferences, however, they also share mutual beliefs. Methodological individualism, the philosophical tenet of economics, usually abstracts from these shared values and thereby reduces collective intentionality to individual intentionality.[1] However, the reproductive processes of society are determined by individuals as much as by institutions and organisations that fix patterns of human actions, supply information to other agents and enable regular and predictable behaviour in an uncertain, highly complex world with limited information. Thus, institutions are constraints that structure human interaction in order to reduce uncertainty. Society is held together by contracts that oblige or bind individual players to some correlated strategy. The content of these contracts is determined by institutions, that is, rules of the game, and by organisations which are the players (North 1993).[2]

We will call the institution of EMU the set of rules, fixed by the Maastricht Treaty (TEU), that are designed to structure monetary relations in the Union and give sense and purpose to monetary policy. Similarly, the Stability and Growth Pact is an institution to guide and direct fiscal policy in EMU. However, these rules are all derived from the primary norm of maintaining price stability.[3] On the other hand, the ESCB, the Euro group, the European Commission or national governments are the players of the game; they are organisations. A functional society requires that contracts, whether explicit or implicit, reflect a credible commitment by the players. When creating a new currency, like the euro, *ex ovo*, the interesting question is how such a social contract comes into being and what sustains it. The question is not how Maastricht was negotiated[4] or what games individual players played, but rather what the consensual foundations are which make such a treaty possible.

Money is one of the most fundamental institutions in a liberal society with a market economy (Collignon 1995). This is because money is assigned its status by collective intentionality. Money thereby acquires a normative character, and this fact structures the whole of society. A long-standing philosophical tradition, going back to Hume (1740), maintains that normative statements cannot be derived from objective, scientific statements. Some economists have drawn the conclusion from this axiom, that 'positive economics is in principle independent of any particular ethical position or normative judgements . . . ' (Friedman 1953). This implies that once the economist has described economic facts, any evaluation is still left absolutely open. Against this view, Searle (1969: 263) has argued that 'in the case of certain institutional facts, the evaluations involving obligations, commitments and responsibilities are no longer left completely open because the statement of the institutional fact involves these notions.' Consequently, when we are dealing with the institutional fact of money, we cannot dissociate our analysis from the normative context which gives money its legitimacy, that is, that which creates the belief in its validity. For example, it would be senseless to argue that it is a *fact* that one of the functions of money is to have purchasing power, but the objective of maintaining price stability is a normative value *judgement* independent of this fact. Therefore, when we analyse the sustainability of institutions like EMU, we have to do two things: we need to state the rules of the 'social contract' which sets up the institution of money (constitutive rules) and then assess the likelihood that the related organisations will behave in such a way that the credibility (legitimate validity) of the institution will be maintained.

Searle (1995: 43–5) has shown with respect to the evolution of paper money how constitutive rules create institutional facts. There is, as he put it, 'an element of magic, a conjuring trick, a sleigh of hand in the creation of institutional facts'. It results from the collective intentionality assigning a new status to some phenomenon which cannot be performed solely by virtue of its intrinsic physical features. For example, the material support of money, such as coins, paper, electronic data, is intrinsically rather worthless, but it obtains value because society uses it with a commonly shared, collective intentionality. Without some underlying norms, or constitutive rules, individuals would not be able to communicate their intentions, nor could they behave accordingly. This explains why the persistence and sustainability of institutions is so dependent on credible commitments, for they alone will keep the collective agreement alive and the institution legitimate. Nowhere is this more obvious than in the field of monetary policy in a large sense. Sustaining EMU means maintaining the credibility and legitimacy of monetary institutions of Europe.

North (1993) distinguishes between *motivational* and *imperative* credibility. Motivational credibility applies, if the players want to continue to honour their commitment at the time of performance (i.e. time consistent behaviour). In this case, institutions are self-enforcing and the success of the institutions sustains their success. Alternatively, the credibility is 'imperative' when the performance of the players (i.e. the application of the constitutive rule by the related organisations) is coerced or at least discretion is disabled. This requires *regulative rules* (Searle 1995: 27). However, both forms of credibility derive naturally from the normative status of *constitutive rules*, for any rule implies the possibility of abuse. Therefore, imperative credibility is necessary to protect motivational credibility. Regulative rules, which can only work on the background of the related constitutive rules, are necessary to maintain the 'imperative credibility' of the institutions. Figure 1.1

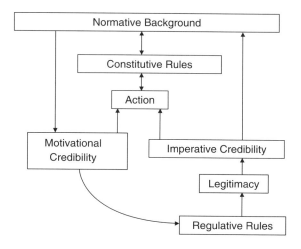

Figure 1.1 The structure of collective intentionality.

shows the inter-relatedness of norms, rules and motivations as the structure of collective intentionality (arrows indicate the direction of influence).

This model of social institutions could explain why the political process towards EMU, notably during the negotiations of the Maastricht Treaty (see Bini-Smaghi *et al.* 1994), has focused on institutional 'stability conditions' as the normative constitutive rules. The norm of maintaining price stability is at the core of the collective European monetary agreement. Once EMU had started, monetary policy rules, such as targeting the growth of money supply aggregates or the level of inflation rates became regulative rules to serve the Treaty objectives.

Collective intentionality is necessary to create the institutional fact of money. But if it requires a norm, such as maintaining the purchasing power of money to make the system functional, this is not a one-way street. If the constitutional rules that establish money are credible, then they also create an environment of certainty which will feed back into the anticipations and behaviour of the players. This creates a degree of moral cohesiveness in society[5] and gives rise to very different behaviours than if the legitimacy of the monetary system is under doubt.

This interdependence between constitutive and regulative rules has been a central preoccupation in the theories of the German ordo-liberals who laid the intellectual foundations of Germany's post-war economic model (Bernholz 1989). Röpke made the point that

> a sophisticated economic system which involves a widely developed division of labour and hence a considerable mutual dependence of the individuals concerned, can only be developed and maintained if an important assumption is made. This is that those who have entered this kind of dependence must feel safe enough in their moral, legal and institutional surroundings to continue to accept the risks involved in such interaction.
>
> (Röpke 1951)

To achieve this, two prerequisites are required, according to this school of thought: 'a free, stable and internationally convertible currency' and a 'stable legal order'. One does not have to share all aspects of 'ordo-liberalism' to see that the monetary constitution influences the daily economic process (Eucken 1989: 122). Clearly, money matters for these thinkers.

Sustaining institutions

According to our analysis, institutions are necessary to make human behaviour predictable in the social realm, that is, when actions are not determined by the physical characteristics or utility of objects. But, this does not exclude that institutions may change when new skills and knowledge lead to revised evaluations of opportunities. Organisations can gradually modify informal constraints and formally alter the rules on which the institutions are based. However, shifts in individual preferences are not enough to change institutions. Institutions oblige individuals to act occasionally (even frequently) against their individual, volatile preferences. From an individual point of view this may appear annoying, but the obligation is an indispensable feature in making society sustainable. This does not mean that institutions can prevail or be sustained against the collective intentionality. It means that personal preferences may occasionally be at odds with collective ones. But in the long run, many individual preferences are shaped and structured by institutions. European integration since World War II has effectively been based on such a conception of institutions.[6]

Our approach to institutions and money is quite different from the neoclassical postulate of 'instrumental rationality' where institutions are unnecessary, ideas and ideologies do not matter and markets are efficient. Neoclassical economics operates in the framework of individual intentionality, which is justified when we can assume that the collectively shared set of values is constant. However, even with given tastes but bounded or 'intended' rationality, when actors have incomplete information and limited mental capacity, institutions are critical for the long-run performance of economies and policies and their duration will depend on their credibility (North 1993). If however, the sustainability of monetary institutions is the object of our research, we have to include the wider framework of shared convictions and values[7] and allow for the possibility that even collective intentionality may be volatile. As an institution, money may stabilise individual preferences. But in order to fulfil this function, it needs to be sustained. Thus, money matters in the long-run. It can not be neutral. This claim is not to be confused with the familiar Phillips curve trade-off: my thesis is that the stability of money has long-run effects on output and on society as a whole.

There is plenty of evidence that monetary institutions matter. One does not have to go back as far as to German hyperinflation which obliterated the life savings of millions and pushed hundreds of thousands into poverty (Hughes 1982).[8] It is enough to look at the international monetary system of Bretton Woods which was a foundation of keeping nations together in peaceful economic co-operation. Bretton Woods was an institution that established monetary and economic rules for the (western) world. As we will see in the next section, it was grounded in the collective intentionality so well described by Nurkse (1944). The system broke down when the US, as a principal player, persistently violated the regulative rules by which the dollar served as the system's anchor and was supposed to be kept convertible into gold. With rising inflation and doubtful gold convertibility, the anchor currency lost its motivational credibility. Collective intentionality in the world and national policy motivations changed. The norm of a 'stable' monetary system was replaced by a 'flexible' system.

EMU is, to use the language developed by North, a new institution (a set of rules) which will be run by an organisation (the ESCB) in concert with other organisations (the European Commission, national governments, etc.). Each organisation has its particular, independent task. The sustainability of the new monetary institution will be determined by the perceived effectiveness of the organisations that run it, for this is an important element in the durability of the collective intentionality. If EMU were perceived as ineffective, then the support for the institutional structure of the European Union (EU) would weaken and wane. Thus, the sustainability of EMU – just as any other previous monetary regime in Europe – will depend on what people expect and the ability of the organisations to provide it. Consequently, the organisations of the new institutions will also have to communicate the sense and purpose of their policy actions. In doing so, they also change peoples' expectations and transform the relations among the people and peoples of Europe. This, at least, is the motive that underlies the collective intentions behind the EMU-agreement.[9]

This book will trace the logic behind the shifts in collective intentionality that led to the creation of the euro, and it will assess the likelihood that EMU can deliver. However, before we analyse specific features in this arrangement, it is useful to recall the economic context which has shaped the experiences and expectations of the European people as they will shape the actions of the new European institutional players. In this context, three questions emerge: Why did pre-EMU monetary arrangements not survive? Under what conditions will EMU be sustainable? What can be done to improve the euro's chances of becoming a lasting currency? We will focus in our analysis on the medium to long-term perspectives of European Monetary Integration (EMI).

The search for European monetary stability

Monetary Union is Europe's response to the lessons of the twentieth century. The interwar period with hyperinflation, unsustainable public finances and mass unemployment was at the root of the political instability in the first half of the century which was marked by wars, revolutions and dictatorships, culminating in the concentration camps of Auschwitz. The second half saw a period of unknown prosperity, peace and renewed co-operation, despite the underlying tensions of the cold war and increasing difficulties after the early 1970s. Western Europe experienced a Golden Age for a quarter of a century that represents for many today a Paradise Lost (Eichengreen 1993, 1996, 1997a). Table 1.1 shows the average annual growth performance over a long-time horizon.

Real GDP per capita grew 1.9 per cent over the long-term period 1890–1992, but the subperiods diverged significantly from this trend. The Dark Age between (and including) the two world wars is not surprisingly a time of stagnation, while the Golden Age (1950–73) is characterised by exceptional growth rates for GDP and productivity. Post-1973 growth appears low in light of expectations created

Table 1.1 European growth, 1890–1992

	Real GDP	Population	Real GDP per capita	Real GDP per person-hour
1890–1913	2.6	0.8	1.7	1.6
1913–1950	1.4	0.5	1.0	1.9
1950–1973	4.6	0.7	3.8	4.7
1973–1992	2.0	0.3	1.7	2.7
1890–1992	2.5	0.6	1.9	2.6

Source: N. Crafts and G. Toniolo (1996).

during the previous quarter of a century, but when compared with the long-run trends, per capita output is still close to average, and productivity is even higher. Nevertheless, real GDP growth after 1973 is clearly closer to the period of stagnation than the Golden Age and this explains a part of Europe's high unemployment (see Chapter 8). In addition to growth, the subperiods are also marked by distinct monetary characteristics. The Golden Age was an era of great monetary and macroeconomic stability. Inflation was low and exchange rates stable. The Dark Age was marked by monetary instability and fluctuating exchange rate arrangements. The 1920s were the years of high inflation (in Germany and Austria even of hyper-inflation). The imposition of deflationary policies in pursuit of financial ortho-doxy, and the return of leading economies to the gold standard forced world trade into a vicious downward spiral leading to the Great Depression. Real wages increased (except in Germany) and unemployment rose. Although very different in their quantitative extent (Feinstein *et al.* 1997), these features are not without qualitative resemblance to the period following the Golden Age after 1973.

The Bretton Woods Agreement for monetary stability

The architects of the Bretton Woods Agreement of 1944 had tried to draw the les-sons from the dramatic instability in interwar monetary relations. This was resumed by Nurkse (1944) who saw 'free and flexible exchange rates' as important culprits in the economic crisis in the Dark Age between the wars. They increased risk and discouraged trade, created unemployment and invited speculative capital flows. In many ways his analysis is reminiscent of the monetary experience after the collapse of the Bretton Woods System and the public debate which preceded the creation of EMU:

> Freely fluctuating exchanges involve three serious disadvantages. In the first place, they create an element of risk which tends to discourage international trade. The risk may be covered by 'hedging' operations where a forward exchange market exists; but such insurance, if obtainable at all, is obtainable only at a price and therefore generally adds to the cost of trading . . .
>
> Secondly, as a means of adjusting the balance of payments, exchange fluctua-tions involve constant shifts of labour and other resources between produc-tion for the home market and production for export. Such shifts may be costly and disturbing; they tend to create frictional unemployment, and are obviously wasteful if the exchange-market conditions that call for them are temporary . . .
>
> Thirdly, experience has shown that fluctuating exchanges cannot always be relied upon to promote adjustment. Any considerable or continuous move-ment of the exchange rate is liable to generate anticipations of a further move-ment in the same direction, thus giving rise to speculative capital transfer of disequilibrating kind . . . Self-aggravating movements of this kind, instead of promoting adjustment in the balance of payments, are apt to intensify any initial disequilibrium and to produce what may be called 'explosive conditions of instability'.

(Nurkse 1944: 210–11)

The monetary system of Bretton Woods was the answer to the lessons learned from the Dark Age interwar experience. It created new international institutions, but its principal achievement was the maintenance of a stable macroeconomic environment. The post-war economic institutions were to a large extent influenced by Keynes's General Theory or rather, by how the theory was interpreted (Kenen 1985). Their purpose was to maintain internal (full employment) and external (current account) equilibrium. By manipulating the fiscal-monetary mix, discretionary policy actions were to prevent unemployment from exceeding certain target levels or excess demand from overheating the economy, and to develop inflationary pressures which would show up in balance of payment difficulties.

The Bretton Woods System worked effectively as a gold–dollar exchange standard. The US-currency served as the system's anchor. Other countries would declare the par value of their currencies either in terms of dollar or gold alone, but the value of the dollar was exclusively fixed in terms of gold at \$35 an ounce. This solved the $n-1$ country problem which meant that in a system of n currencies there exist only $n-1$ degrees of freedom. Once $n-1$ countries have adopted policies to determine their payment position, the payment outcome in the nth country is determined as a residual (Williamson 1983). Since the US as the nth country pegged to gold as a reserve asset, it was the only country obliged to hold its reserves in gold. This exerted domestic discipline against excessive money creation and kept inflation down (Gilbert 1997). The other countries could only keep their exchange rates fixed as long as they possessed sufficient foreign exchange reserves. When monetary gold reserves would not grow rapidly enough to keep up with the accelerated growth in the Golden Age, the reserve deficiency in the rest of the world was filled by US dollars. This implied a balance of payment deficit for the US and a surplus in the rest of the world. At first, the dollar gap was closed by a mix of capital exports from the US (aid and the Marshall Plan) and dramatic devaluations of most currencies against the dollar in 1949 (Bordo 1993). Once the effects of these measures had worn off, the constraints of the system became more apparent. Table 1.2 shows, however, that the degree of undervaluation of European currencies was corrected only very slowly before the regime of fixed rates came to an end. Once nominal exchange rates had been allowed to float, the dollar depreciated rapidly and by 1980 many European currencies were actually overvalued.

Nevertheless, for most of the 1950s and 1960s the dollar maintained a position of structural overvaluation (Friedman and Schwartz 1982: 290–3) which also contributed to keeping domestic US-inflation under control. Together with the gold link, the strong dollar helped to stabilise the domestic purchasing power in the world's anchor currency in the early years of the Golden Age. Given the fixed exchange rate, this stability extended to the rest of the world. But when prices increased more rapidly in the periphery due to the differential impact of productivity increases in catch-up growth (Balassa effect), the dollar overvaluation slowly eroded and the current account balance became a permanent concern outside the USA (Obstfeld 1993). Fast growing countries were hitting the exchange reserve constraint. Cooper (1968) records that in 1962 all major industrial countries were simultaneously wishing to increase their current account surpluses,

Table 1.2 Nominal unit labour costs relative to 19 industrialised countries

	Index 1991 = 100				In per cent of USA			
	1960	1970	1980	1990	1960	1970	1980	1990
B	111.0	104.7	117.2	98.9	66.5	64.7	117.9	97.7
DK	82.4	84.9	105.6	105.4	49.4	52.5	106.2	104.2
D	91.6	98.6	112.5	103.0	54.9	60.9	113.2	101.8
EL	178.4	161.8	101.8	108.7	107.0	100.0	102.4	107.4
E	66.6	64.9	99.2	98.4	39.9	40.1	99.8	97.2
F	127.7	128.9	123.9	103.8	76.6	79.7	124.6	102.6
IRL	106.2	105.1	111.2	104.3	63.7	65.0	111.9	103.1
I	81.0	77.7	76.0	98.4	48.6	48.0	76.5	97.2
NL	83.7	88.1	126.8	102.0	50.2	54.4	127.6	100.8
A	82.9	83.9	92.1	100.5	49.7	51.9	92.7	99.3
P	102.5	99.9	83.3	86.8	61.5	61.7	83.8	85.8
FIN	87.3	85.2	78.9	101.6	52.3	52.7	79.4	100.4
S	101.3	100.1	102.4	98.8	60.7	61.9	103.0	97.6
UK	99.2	100.6	100.3	96.8	59.5	62.2	100.9	95.7
EUR 15+	88.6	92.6	118.3	103.1	53.1	57.2	119.0	101.9
USA	166.8	161.8	99.4	101.2	100.0	100.0	100.0	100.0
JAP	54.4	54.3	80.3	93.9	32.6	33.6	80.8	92.8

Source: *European Economy* 63 (1997) and own calculations.

or decrease their deficits (Williamson 1983: 383–4). Thus, either internal or external balance had to be sacrificed, unless an additional policy tool could be found to solve the inconsistency. In the policy debates of the 1960s, Germany insisted on price stability as the primary objective of its economic policy and it was more readily prepared to abandon full employment. Most other countries, under Keynesian influence, focused more on the external balance aspects. The search for new policy tools produced two findings: income policies and more flexible exchange rates.

One important tenet in the General Theory was that 'a stable general level of money-wages is, on balance of considerations, the most advisable policy for a closed system' (Keynes 1936: 270). The emerging economies after World War II were essentially closed, domestic economies. The autarkic policies of the 1930s and the controls on trade and capital movements imposed during the war left countries less exposed to international flows than in the 1920s. At the end of World War II, western economies were even less open than before World War I (Eichengreen and Kenen 1994). Thus, the idea of stable money wages corresponded to some degree with the structural reality of post-war Europe. However, the success of economic development in Europe was going to undermine this structure gradually. With stable money wages and fixed exchange rates, adjustment to achieve external balance was not possible. The Bretton Woods Agreement recognised this fact by allowing the adjustment of exchange rates in cases of a 'fundamental disequilibrium'. The impact of flexible exchange rates on wages was not explicitly mentioned by Keynes (1936). With respect to stable money wages in an open economy he simply stated, '. . . the same conclusion will hold good for an open system, provided that equilibrium with the rest of the world can be secured by the means of fluctuating exchanges' (1936: 270). The post-Keynesian approach in the post-war period always emphasised the *adjustment* aspect of exchange rates and not the *fluctuation* aspect. This led economists to become forgetful about the lessons learned by Nurske. The collective intentionality changed. As we will see, this one-sidedness also overshadowed later the debate on the utility of EMU in the context of optimum currency area theory.

From an adjustment point of view, nominal wage flexibility was necessary to operate a successful gold-standard mechanism. If prices remained stable in terms of gold, adjustment required a reduction in nominal wages. If both prices and money-wages were stable, the exchange rate had to be adjusted in order to re-establish a fundamental equilibrium after a disturbance. With stable money wages, as Keynes had claimed, this meant that prices would increase, and real wages would fall. Therefore, fluctuating exchange rates required real wage flexibility, as Meade pointed out (1951, quoted in Kenen 1985). Even Friedman's famous 'Case for Flexible Exchange Rates' was founded on the assumption that

> wage rates tend to be among the less flexible prices. In consequence, an incipient deficit that is countered by a policy permitting or forcing prices to decline is likely to produce unemployment rather than, or in addition to, wage decreases. [. . .] This is clearly an inefficient method of adjusting to external changes.
>
> (Friedman 1953a: 467)

We will see in Chapter 8, Table 8.1 that, at least for Europe and Japan, the assumption that wages are less volatile than good prices is not in accordance with the facts. What was missing from theory in those years was a rational micro-foundation of nominal or real wage rigidity. Most importantly, the adjustment theory of exchange rates assumed 'money illusion', whereby money wages were divorced from the cost of living. This might have appeared reasonable, as long as general price stability was taken for granted and inflation was a surprise. But with flexible (in particular with depreciating) exchange rates and increasingly open economies, prices will not stay stable.[10] Once inflationary expectations were integrated into wage bargaining, money illusion became itself an illusion. Nominal wages had become upward flexible and downward sticky. With fluctuating exchange rates the price level also had to become more volatile, particularly for small countries. We will return to this argument in later chapters. As we will see, it meant also that flexible exchange rates led to the development of nominal inertia in a way that was not anticipated by the 'adjustment' theory. Consequently, the fundamental pillar of the successful post-war growth performance, namely stable money wages, was no longer sustainable when and after the Bretton Woods stable exchange rate regime broke down.

Golden Age versus Dark Age: lessons to be learned

The extraordinary performance of the post-war period requires an explanation. Crafts and Toniolo (1996) have shown that war damage and reconstruction can account for only a part of the rapid growth in the Golden Age, since most of the recovery was already completed by 1950. There may have been some scope for catch-up growth with the US thereafter, but the essential characteristics emphasised by these authors are:

1   High per capita income growth was a distinctly European phenomenon.
2   High growth rates characterised almost all European economies, regardless of their social, political and economic institutions.
3   Initially poorer countries tended to grow faster than richer ones, so that by the early 1970s, the dispersion in *levels* of per capita income was much less pronounced than in 1950 (catch-up growth).
4   Full employment prevailed, cyclical fluctuations were mild, and inflation rates were at socially acceptable low levels.

Explaining the causes for the high growth performance between 1950 and 1973 requires a book on its own. However, there is one dominating feature: investment. Neoclassical growth accounting reveals capital accumulation and total factor productivity as principal sources of European growth (see Chapter 8). Levine and Renelt (1992) report evidence whereby the acceleration in growth in the Golden Age came from increased investment in both physical and human capital.[11] Eichengreen (1996) reckons that net investment rates in Europe were nearly twice as high in the 1950s and 1960s than before or since, rising from 9.6 per cent in 1920–38 to 16.8 per cent in 1950–70. In most countries investment rates after World War II exceeded by 50 per cent those between 1914 and 1945 (Eichengreen and Kenen 1994: 22). Eichengreen (1996) also suggests that increasing the gross investment share of GDP from 20 to 30 per cent may have raised the growth rate by as much as 2 percentage points. As we will see, this has had important consequences for European employment.

Yet, investment was not the only factor. The high rate of European growth can best be explained by the triptych of high investment, high exports and considerable wage moderation (i.e. the real world equivalent of Keynes's stable money-wages). In several European countries wage demands were linked to productivity increases. In the 1950s, they were even at times lagging behind in return for an agreement by industry to modernise and expand productive capacity. This applied in particular to Germany, Austria, Benelux and Norway. The UK, Ireland, France and Italy were less successful in building such social consensus (Eichengreen 1996). In the early 1960s, nominal unit labour cost increased in the European aggregate more than in the US, but real wages still lagged behind the rapid productivity increases, so that the profit share increased. (See Figure 1.2 and Figure 8.6(a) and (b).)[12]

Together with fixed exchange rates under the Bretton Woods Agreement, relative wage moderation allowed the reaping of efficiency and productivity gains from international trade, and in particular from intra-European trade, by specialising on comparative advantages. The volume of exports expanded by more than 8 per cent per annum in Europe, compared to 5.3 per cent in the US and 16.5 per cent in Japan.

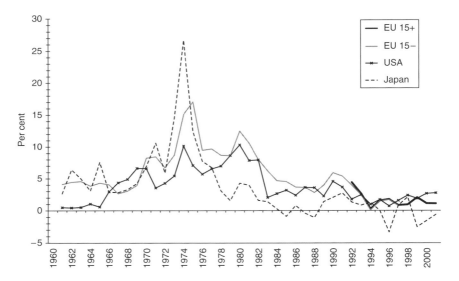

Figure 1.2 Unit labour cost (annual variation in per cent).
Source: AMECO (1999).

This rapid export growth concentrated investment in sectors with high productivity growth and this facilitated the relative stability of unit labour costs. The exceptional performance was helped by the institutional framework of the Bretton Woods era: stable exchange rates and trade liberalisation under GATT in the world economy; Marshall Plan and European integration on the old continent. Wage restraint, however, was crucial for this strategy. The stability of money-wages was supported by stable exchange rates. We will show in Chapter 3 that the abolition of fixed exchange rates in 1971–3 created large distributional conflicts which were exacerbated by the oil price shock. During the Golden Age, however, wage moderation reduced the danger that excessive inflation would create competitiveness problems large enough to call into question the exchange rate peg (Eichengreen 1997). However, most European countries also started from a position of undervaluation relative to the US dollar which allowed them some leeway with unit labour cost increases.[13] Nominal unit labour costs in the 1960s relative to 19 industrialised countries were significantly lower than in the US, as Table 1.2 shows.

After the war, Europe developed institutions (commitment mechanisms) that bound capitalists to invest profits and workers to exercise wage restraint. These institutions solved commitment and co-ordination problems. Without them neither wage moderation nor the expansion of international trade could have taken place (Eichengreen 1996: 41). These domestic institutions have become the basis for what may be called the European social model (Bercusson *et al*. 1996). It was based on three pillars:

1   private property rights and a market price system;
2   a distributional settlement between capital and labour that included tax and transfer payments and more or less balanced budgets;
3   achievement of full employment and development of the welfare state as a foundation for political stability (Eichengreen and Kenen 1994).

Only the first pillar survived the Bretton Woods System.

One should add a fourth element that was indispensable to the maintenance of this domestic consensus: price stability. Only if workers were confident about the future purchasing power of their money-wages would they be willing to agree to wage settlements not in excess of general productivity increases. Only then would relative income shares stay roughly constant. It is doubtful that the domestic institutions of wage moderation on which the European model was built could have worked without the regime of fixed exchange rates.

The breakdown of Bretton Woods

If support for flexible exchange rates grew over time, it was partially due to some other disenchantment with the Bretton Woods regime (Kenen 1985). In fact, the decision to adjust exchange rates was eminently political and the way the system worked was rightly described as 'government-led' (Padoa-Schioppa and Saccomanni 1994). Governments would often attempt to postpone an inevitable devaluation for fear of losing face. Possibly more important was the need to achieve current account convertibility for local currencies in order to facilitate trade and cross-border investment. But with the increasing mobility of capital, sustaining a system of pegged exchange rates became increasingly difficult. At the first sign of an impending devaluation, investors would withdraw their capital in order to avoid capital losses. This could quickly exhaust a country's foreign exchange reserves, if it attempted to defend its peg. For Friedman (1953a: 476) the advantage of flexible rates was that they offered 'no definite sticking point' for speculators and this idea became a tempting option for policy makers.

In the mid-1960s, the value of US short-term liabilities started to exceed the value of US gold holdings. Holders of dollar assets became alarmed, the 'confidence premium' on dollar interest rates disappeared, and after 1967 speculation against the dollar increasingly sought the Deutschmark as an alternative reserve asset. The DM was one of the few currencies which showed good economic fundamentals and was free of restrictions on capital flows. High interest rates also added to its attractiveness at the time. Furthermore, traditional key currencies like pound sterling and the French franc had already lost their reputation after the sterling devaluation of 15 per cent in November 1967, and the franc devaluation (11.1 per cent) in August 1969. At the same time, Germany had acquired a solid surplus on current account, adding quickly to its external net asset position. This situation attracted a massive flow of speculative funds from abroad into the DM. In May 1971, the DM and the Dutch guilder were allowed to float temporarily, after the French and Italian authorities had rejected a joint float because of concerns about competitiveness. In August 1971 President Nixon announced unilaterally the suspension of dollar–gold convertibility. The Smithsonian Agreement of December 1971 finally tripled the margins of all participating currencies fluctuating, *vis-à-vis* the dollar to 2.25 per cent.

This new monetary rule urgently required a mechanism for reducing intra-EC exchange rate fluctuations, otherwise any two EC currencies could have moved by up to 9 per cent against each other. Consequently the Basle Agreement of April 1973 between the six founding EC countries, joined by Denmark, the UK and Ireland, halved their margins of fluctuation later to 4.5 per cent (±2.25 on either side). This arrangement was called the 'snake in the tunnel'. When the Smithsonian Agreement broke down in 1973, 'the snake left the tunnel', and floated freely against all other currencies. It was the beginning of a long and twisted march to EMU.

The New Dark Age

The end of the Golden Age is normally assumed to coincide with the first oil shock in 1973. But it might be more appropriate to take as the decisive point the 1971 decision to abandon the gold peg of the US dollar, even if the general free float only followed in 1973. The persistent balance of payment deficit of the US, that had allowed to fill the 'dollar gap', had raised the ratio of foreign-held dollars to US gold reserves over time. The gold convertibility of the dollar became increasingly doubtful and ultimately a run on US gold did occur, which forced the suspension of the gold link of the US currency (Little *et al.* 1993). This was a violation of the system's constitutive rule and led to the loss of motivational credibility. After that, prices no longer had a nominal anchor and monetary discipline ceased until it was regained painfully in the early 1980s. Price shocks from raw material markets now had permanent effects on the price level. This was a structural change compared to previous incidents like the raw material boom after the Korean war (Friedman and Schwartz 1982: 569–72).

The 25 years that followed were marked by significantly lower economic growth. Although productivity growth only fell to its secular trend, per capita income grew only at the rate of the pre-World War I *belle époque* when technological progress and productivity improvements were much lower. Most importantly, European real GDP growth more than halved in comparison to the previous era (see also Table 8.1). These developments paralleled with high inflation in the 1970s, dramatic disinflation in the 1980s, persistent lower investment, rising structural unemployment and increasing public indebtedness. Real convergence in income levels also slowed, while the variance of output and unanticipated monetary aggregates increased. In short, the Golden Age was followed by a period of macroeconomic instability, which we might well call the New Dark Age. This is apparent from a look at the two misery indices in Figure 1.3: The first index (a) shows the sum of inflation and unemployment. It was low in the 1960s and shot

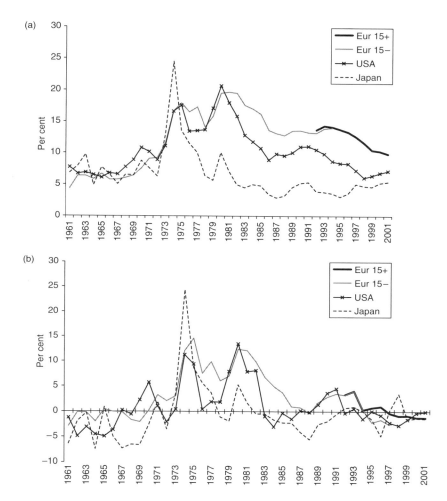

Figure 1.3 Misery index: (a) inflation + unemployment rates; (b) inflation − growth rate.
Source: AMECO (1999) and own calculations.

up after the first and second oil price shocks. Although it decreased rather rapidly in Japan and in the 1980s in the USA, the index remained persistently high in Europe reflecting high and rising levels of unemployment. The second index (b) calculates misery as the difference between inflation and economic growth. Again, the 1960s reflect a relatively blissful period, although less in Europe than in Japan and the US.

After the two oil shocks, it took Europe much longer to eliminate misery – and it did so only for a short time. Europe seems to have much greater difficulties in keeping economic growth above inflation than the two other leading world economies. Not surprisingly, a sense of crisis ('Eurosclerosis') started to prevail. I will argue in Chapter 8 that the described developments – high inflation, low growth and high unemployment – are intrinsically linked. Europe's answer has been twofold: with the completion of the Single Market Programme by 1992, it had sought to re-invigour its industrial strength and competitiveness (Economie Européenne 1994); with the creation of economic and monetary union, it has returned to the basic lesson that monetary stability is a necessary condition for economic growth.

The case for price stability

What has caused the decline of the Golden Age? Many theories have been asserted. For some it is just a return to normal, 'the explanadum in post-war European history being not the slowdown of the 1970s but the growth spurt of the previous two decades' (Crafts and Toniolo 1996: 25). Olson (1996) explains Eurosclerosis by the development of special-interest legislation and monopolistic practices that make an economy less productive. However, both labour productivity and total factor productivity have remained consistently higher in Europe than in the USA (see Table 8.1). Eichengreen (1996) suggests that the increasingly prominent role of governments and welfare state programmes were not able to adjust efficiently and rapidly to the new circumstances after the catch-up phase of economic growth had passed. This is the labour market rigidity argument with which we will deal more comprehensively in Chapter 8.

However, even if these explanations are able to explain partial aspects of European post-war development, they remain unsatisfying as they either abstract from an extremely complex and diverse economic, social and political reality or assume a metaphysical force or law that consumes itself over time. This is particularly evident in the hypothesis of 'the end of catch-up'. For example, the regressions by Levine and Renelt (1992), reported by Crafts and Toniolo (1996),[14] can be interpreted as 'reflecting lower scope for catch-up'; but the fact that the negative coefficient for the initial per capita GDP in the regressions explaining growth of output per head increased from the period 1950–73 to 1973–89 could also mean that rich countries were simply harder hit by the growth reduction than others.[15] We will deal with this argument more extensively in Chapters 4 and 8.

What could be the unifying event that explains Europe's disappointing performance after the end of Bretton Woods? Two answers spring to mind: the oil shock and flexible exchange rates. As Eichengreen (1996) points out, the former worsened the inter-temporal terms of trade for workers offering wage moderation in return for higher investment. The latter removed the exchange rate as a nominal anchor, so that Keynesian stabilisation policy lost its powers. However, the problem with both of these explanations is timing: European wage explosion had taken place already before the oil price shock at the end of 1960. In fact it might be argued that the dramatic increase in raw materials in the early 1970s was a response to an earlier deterioration of purchasing power in dollar terms by the oil suppliers (James 1996).[16] Similarly, the change in labour market behaviour seems to have been the consequence, rather than the cause of the breakdown of the Bretton Woods Agreement on fixed exchange rates. Thus, it is likely that the end of the Golden Age and the failure of Bretton Woods have the same roots.

The collapse of Bretton Woods has been attributed to flaws in the structure of the system and to policy mistakes. It is certainly true that a system that cannot deal with policy imbalances is doomed. But one has to be careful not to make what Ryle (1990) called a 'category mistake'. Such a mistake mixes logical categories. For example, the statement: 'the glass broke because a stone hit it' attributes falsely a cause to an event. The proper statement is, 'the glass broke when a stone hit it, because the glass was brittle'. The increasingly inflationary monetary policy in the US was the event which violated the regulative rules of the Bretton Woods System and undermined the legitimacy and, ultimately, the constitutive rules of the system. But the structure of fixed exchange rate regimes always has a 'brittleness' which makes it vulnerable, as we will show in Chapter 4. A monetary union with a single currency is more robust. However, it is possible that Bretton Woods could have been sustained as long as the anchor country would have continued to play by the rules.

Once the inflationary spirit was out of the bottle, disintegration followed rapidly. With a drifting anchor, the normative foundations of money were shaken. Thus, my explanation for the end of the Golden Age is that inflation destabilised the economic system. This argument concentrates on the long-run relationship between inflation and growth and not the short-term Phillips curve trade-off.[17] In fact, empirical evidence points strongly to a predominantly negative long-term relationship between growth and inflation (Fischer 1993, 1994). Under this hypothesis, the Golden Age came to an end because of the inflationary pressures that developed in the US from the mid-1960s on as a consequence of the monetary expansion associated with the Vietnam War. Bordo (1993) has shown that US authorities were expanding domestic credit at a rapid rate through most of the 1960s and early 1970s. Inflation began accelerating in 1964 and exceeded that of the GNP-weighted inflation rate in the G7 (excluding US) in 1968. Eichengreen (1993) compares US-aggregates with other industrial countries and argues that the US expansion had stronger inflationary effects because the US was growing more slowly than Europe or Japan. Inflation was exported from the anchor currency in the Bretton Woods System via fixed exchange rates into the rest of the international monetary system. This then undermined the commitment mechanisms of wage restraint on which the system was based. Inflation led to compensating wage demands. The resulting misalignment in real exchange rates caused the break-up of the fixed exchange rate system and removed the stable nominal anchor for the international monetary system. From that moment on, the effects of shocks persisted, nominal inertia became a dominant feature, and monetary policy had to take a quasi-permanent restrictive stance. The virtuous circle which had allowed high investment, high returns and high productivity growth with low unemployment in the previous decade was destroyed. We will return to the mechanisms behind these developments in subsequent chapters.

Here, I wish to emphasise the disruptive effect of inflation on the wage moderation consensus.

The fundamental thesis underlying all chapters of this book is that Europe's Golden Age was destroyed by the Great Inflation of the 1970s. High real interest rates, rising unemployment and deteriorating public finance in the 1980s and 1990s were unavoidable side effects of the inevitable disinflation policies required to restore price stability. The creation of the European Monetary System (EMS) in 1979 was the attempt to return to monetary stability. But for structural reasons, discussed in the following chapters, currency blocs with regional exchange rate pegging were not able to re-ignite the previous growth dynamics. If EMU succeeds in eradicating inflationary expectations, it will contribute to an economic environment that will stimulate growth, create employment and reduce public debt ratios.

A formal model

The logic of our argument that inflation undermined the stable wage consensus in Europe can be demonstrated by a simple model. Let us assume that the rate of inflation evolves as a random walk, so that the current rate is equal to last period's plus a white noise term. In this case, the rate of inflation is expected to remain constant:

$$\pi_t = \pi_{t-1} + \varepsilon_t, \tag{1.1}$$

where π is the rate of inflation and ε the white noise term. The model could be augmented by a drift and a moving average error term, but this would not add much to our argument. For reasons that will become obvious in Chapter 8, Equation (1.1) may be overly pessimistic. More realistic models, like Alogoskoufis and Smith (1991), show Equation (1.1) as an AR(1) process, so that:

$$\pi_t = \pi^*(1 - \theta) + \theta\pi_{t-1} + \varepsilon_t. \tag{1.1a}$$

Here π^* is the steady state inflation rate and θ is the autoregressive coefficient or the indicator for inflation persistence. Obstfeld (1993) estimates a similar coefficient that can be derived from a sluggish (log) price level. π^* is then a forward-looking equilibrium rate of inflation that depends exclusively on exogenous fundamentals. In this case θ measures the degree of persistence of price equilibria and $\theta = 0$ corresponds to perfect price flexibility, that is, inflation is always in long-run equilibrium. Equation (1.1a) can also be interpreted in terms of our model of institutional credibility. A low θ would reflect high motivational credibility of the monetary institutions. A low value for π^* is implied by imperative credibility.

Alogoskoufis and Smith (1991) present evidence, supported by Eichengreen (1993) that θ is regime-dependent and increases when the commitment of authorities to maintain price stability is low. This is not surprising for Equation (1.1a) explains current expected inflation as a weighted average of steady state inflation and the past realised rate. If θ rises, price setters give less weight to a steady state inflation rate that they do not expect to prevail much longer. Obstfeld (1993) has estimated price equations for G7-countries and shows that his parameters for nominal price flexibility have been close to 1 in the period 1952–71 for most countries except France (0.232), Japan (0.327) and UK (1.363). Eichengreen (1993) has estimated coefficients for lagged price inflation that are less than 1, but they are larger after World War II, and they also show a tendency for inflation persistence to rise between 1970 and 1973. Thus the assumption that $\theta = 1$ can be justified by uncertain inflationary expectations and low imperative credibility of monetary institutions and this assumption does not remove generality from our argument. For the illustrative logic of our argument here it is acceptable to assume that inflation follows a random walk.

The general solution to the first-order difference Equation (1.1) is

$$\pi_t = \pi_0 + \sum_{i=1}^{t} \varepsilon_i, \tag{1.2}$$

where π_0 is the initial rate of inflation. Next we assume that wages are set in nominal terms, but workers seek to protect their living standards. Hence, the wage equation is:

$$\dot{w}_t = \xi_1 \pi_t + \xi_2 x_t + \eta_t. \tag{1.3}$$

$\dot{w}_t$ is the rate of nominal wage increase, ξ_1 is a coefficient for the degree of *nominal wage indexation*. If $\xi_1 = 0$, we have no indexation or perfect nominal wage rigidity, that is, perfectly stable money wages. If $\xi_1 = 1$ nominal wages are perfectly indexed and flexible. Wage increases will then completely compensate for the loss of purchasing power and the rate of wage growth becomes a random walk plus noise process. Nominal inertia arises from staggered wage and price setting, from the cost of changing wages and prices, and from adaptive expectations. However, adaptive expectations imply that wage earners are consistently proved wrong in their expectations. With rational expectations, workers would use all available information including the expected rate of inflation and, therefore, $\xi_1 = 1$ with respect to $E(\pi_t)$. Under rational expectations $E(\pi) = \pi^*(1 - \theta) + \theta\pi_{t-1}$ because of Equation (1.1a), so that Equation (1.3) is transformed into:

$$\dot{w}_t = \xi_1[\pi^*(1 - \theta) + \theta\pi_{t-1}] + \xi_2 x_t + \eta_t. \tag{1.3'}$$

The difference between Equation (1.3) and Equation (1.3') is ε_t which is white noise. With low confidence in price stability $\theta = 1$ we can assume that wages are perfectly indexed on past inflation. But with high motivational and imperative credibility (θ is low and π^* are low) wages remain stable – just as Keynes had claimed.

Another way to describe ξ_1 is simply to call it the elasticity or flexibility by which nominal wages respond to price changes. Wages are rigid or price-inelastic when $\xi_1 = 0$ and perfectly elastic or flexible when $\xi_1 = 1$. The concept of nominal wage flexibility is related, but not identical with, real wage resistance. Nominal wage flexibility in our sense describes the degree by which workers seek recompensation for an erosion in their real wages by higher money wages. Real wage rigidity arises when the real wage responds to factors other than changes in the price level. In Equation (1.3), x_t is a vector of labour market factors, which may have influence on the wage bargaining process and ξ_2 is a related structural coefficient vector for real wage rigidity. One of these factors may be short-term Phillips curve dynamics so that ξ_2 reflects the response of real wages to unemployment.[18] As will be discussed in Chapter 8, $\xi_2 = 0$ implies perfect real wage rigidity, that is, wages do not respond to factors other than inflation. We will make this assumption here to show that even under extreme conditions of labour market rigidity the extent of wage inflation depends more on price shocks than on labour market conditions. η_t is a white noise process.

By inserting Equation (1.2) into Equation (1.3) and assuming that prices and wages in period zero are stable, we get

$$\dot{w}_t = \dot{w}_0 - \eta_0 + \xi_1 \sum_{i=1}^{t} \varepsilon_i + \eta_t. \tag{1.4}$$

The rate of wage increases has a stochastic trend because the inflation rate follows a random walk. In other words, successive inflation shocks $\sum_{i=1}^{t} \varepsilon_i$ have permanent effects on the rate of wage increases. High inflation shocks raise the rate of wage increases permanently; negative shocks lower it. Thus, if inflationary shocks are imported from the world anchor currency, as it was the case in the late 1960s, then wage increases in Europe have become permanently higher. If the European growth model was based on wage moderation, imported inflation has undermined it.

Why did negative price shocks not make the system return to stability? Equation (1.4) can also be written as the rate of change of wage inflation:

$$\Delta \dot{w}_t = \dot{w}_t - \dot{w}_{t-1} = \xi_1 \varepsilon_t + \Delta \eta_t. \tag{1.5}$$

This shows that the rate of wage increases will stay constant only if $\xi_1 \varepsilon_t = -\Delta \eta_t$, where η_t is the irregular (white noise) term in the wage equation. Non-acceleration in wage inflation requires that in any given period inflationary impulses must be exactly compensated by a negative variation in the wage-setting disturbance. This is rather unlikely, given that workers will hardly be convinced to lower their pay increases when inflation is accelerating. On the other hand, ε_t is the unanticipated variation in the inflation rate, and $\xi_1 \varepsilon_t$ is the mean of the wage acceleration, so that $\Delta \eta_t$ is the unanticipated or surprise acceleration of wage inflation. If price deflation is not fully credible, then wage reductions may be less than price surprises and $\Delta \dot{w}_t - \xi_1 \varepsilon_t = \Delta \eta_t > 0$. Especially in the early periods of disinflation, or when the mean inflation rate is still high, it is likely that $\Delta \eta_t$ would exhibit a tendency to be positive. Thus, wage inflation would come down, but only slowly.[19] Furthermore, if ξ_1 is not constant but rises with inflationary expectations – as one would expect with Lucas (1973, 1976)[20] – then nominal wages become more volatile in periods of rising and falling inflation. This can be observed in Europe during the 1970s and the 1980s – but less so in the USA (see Table 8.1). This is not surprising in view of the fact that price stability in Europe was undermined by flexible exchange rates and a large degree of openness (see section *On the usefulness of adjusting the nominal exchange rate* in Chapter 5). On the other hand, if a regime of stable prices prevails and imperative credibility of the institutions is high, ε and $\Delta\eta$ are likely to be small, as well as ξ_1. Wage moderation is then sustainable, even if structural parameters are very rigid.[21] What this demonstrates is that the rate of inflation is decisive for wage increases, and not the structural parameters which affect wage bargaining only marginally.[22]

Alogskoufis and Smith (1991) show price and wage equations for the UK and the USA to be very similar to Equations (1.1) and (1.2). They find that the hypothesis cannot be rejected that consumer price inflation in both countries follows on AR(1) process and that the log of the price level has a unit root. Their equivalent of our coefficient ξ_1 is 0.947 (with s.e. 0.066) for the UK and 0.636 (s.e. 0.084) for the USA. The unemployment level is insignificant and its rate of change enters in the first lag with a coefficient (ξ_2) -0.695 (0.189) and -0.954 (0.144) respectively (second lags are -0.149 (0.106) and -0.018 (0.084)). We may take this as evidence that our assumptions are not too far removed from reality, although reality is less rigid. However, Alogoskoufis and Smith produce important evidence that there are dramatic shifts in the degree of persistence of consumer price inflation (θ). These shifts are related in their timing to fundamental monetary policy regime changes in the international monetary system: the end of the classical gold standard after World War I and the end of the dollar–gold standard with the break-down of Bretton Woods. They explain the observed parameter change by the incorporation of the monetary policy regime into price and wage setting. The nature of the regime depends on whether authorities are willing to accommodate inflationary demand for money or not. Accommodation implies higher expected future wages than otherwise, and these higher future wages are partly reflected in the path of prices from today onward, with the net result of higher inflation persistence. Similarly, the authors find that flexible exchange rate regimes will result in more persistent inflation *differentials* between countries than in fixed exchange rate regimes. We will find in subsequent chapters that this is highly plausible and relevant for Europe, given the differences in the degree of openness of European economies. They, therefore, conclude: 'What is required for low inflation persistence is credible lack of accommodation'.

This explanation would allow the conclusion that Europe's Golden Age was not so much terminated by insufficient labour market flexibility due to the European social model, but rather by the Great Inflation of the 1970s. In fact, econometric evidence indicates that structural rigidities in European wage equations (other than inflation persistence) have been relatively stable except for the price expectations process (Artis and Ormerod 1994). This is not to deny that more 'flexible', that

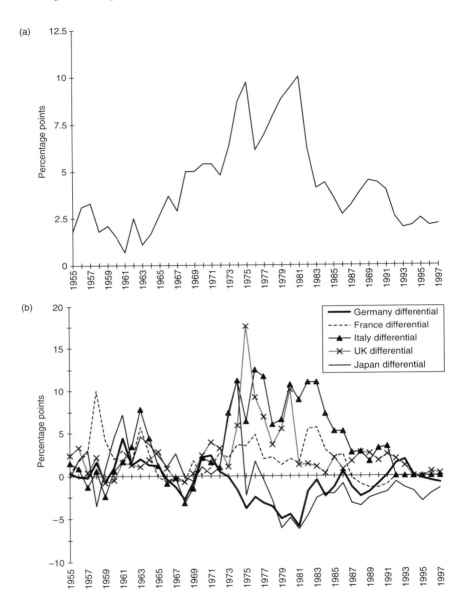

Figure 1.4 (a) US inflation rate; (b) inflation differential to USA.

Source: European Commission.

is, higher structural coefficients ξ_2, would have helped to prevent the persistence of the great inflation.[23] But it would not necessarily have eased disinflation. Thus, changing structures in labour markets are not only a difficult and long-winded task, but also have uncertain outcomes. More important is our conclusion that price stability matters: if inflation is credibly low, wage moderation is likely to hold.[24] Money-wages will remain stable, just as Keynes had postulated. Figure 1.4(a,b) shows some support for our hypothesis that inflation in the international anchor currency caused the subsequent inflationary pressures in other economies.

It shows the inflation *rate* in the US and the relative inflation *differential* for some major industrial countries. From the mid-1950s to the mid-1960s the US inflation rate remained stable around 2.5 per cent and the price increases in Europe remained close to this rate. Although slightly higher in the first half of the 1960s, this phenomenon might be explained by the Balassa-effect. This is what one would expect in a fixed exchange rate system. By 1965/6, inflation accelerated in the USA, while inflation remained behind in the partner countries: the European inflation differential became negative. However, given their fixed peg, European inflation was pulled up: the negative inflation differential of maximal 2.5 per cent was less than the US-inflation rate of 5 per cent.[25] That ignited a catch-up wage inflation in the late 1960s that could only be contained in Germany – not least because the DM was revalued in 1969 and again after 1971 and 1973. From 1972 until 1991, with the minor exception of 1986, inflation was lower in Germany than in the US. Under these circumstances it is not surprising to have seen the DM emerge as the new nominal anchor for the European economy.[26]

In the next chapter we will analyse why smaller European countries pegged their currency to the Deutschmark. But one lesson can already be anticipated: if Europe's exceptional growth performance after the war was based on stable exchange rates, moderate wage increases, high investment and exports, and if imported inflation has destroyed it, then it was tempting to fix exchange rates to a European currency with stable prices. We will see in Chapter 4, however, that this was not the optimal solution to Europe's difficulties after 1973. Ultimately a more promising route was an EMU with a strong commitment to price stability. This could then possibly pave the way to a mode of development based on wage moderation and high investment that has proven so successful in the Golden Age.

Summary and conclusion

This analysis leads us to a number of conclusions and open questions. First, it has been made clear that the sustainability of any monetary institution will depend on the application and credibility of certain constitutive rules. With respect to money this fundamental norm is the preservation of purchasing power, that is, price stability. This constitutive rule is of particular importance because the norms of a monetary economy matter for the whole of a market economy. Second, monetary regimes have changed several times during this century. The Golden Age after World War II was the most successful period with respect to economic growth, employment and monetary stability. It ended when the leading anchor currency gave up its commitment to price stability. Inflationary shocks then had persistent effects on wage bargaining. This led to the collapse of the social model on which the European post-war period was built and became a major cause of high unemployment in the 1980s and 1990s.

From these two propositions one may draw the conclusion that monetary stability, and more specifically price stability, are necessary conditions for the sustainability of a monetary regime. We will further specify this claim in Chapter 6. EMU, Europe's newest monetary regime, makes price stability explicitly the 'primary objective' of monetary policy. In Chapters 7 and 8 we will analyse the conditions necessary for maintaining the credibility of the stability commitment. However, before looking at these issues, two questions still remain open:

1   Why is it that the regime of floating exchange rates has only lasted for a short time in Europe?
2   Why is it that the regime of fixed, but adjustable exchange rates that prevailed under EMS did not last either?

In short, what was the inner logic that pushed Europe to the complete unification of its monetary institutions?

2 After Bretton Woods

The world of bloc floating

In the years after 1973, the world economy went through a period of turbulence before it started to restructure in the 1980s. Under the impact of the two oil shocks of 1973 and 1979, volatility of exchange rates increased markedly. This was partly a result of diverging policies in response to shocks and partly due to instability following the development of international financial markets, which outgrew the real economy. In the general climate of uncertainty, smaller countries sought to better control their environment by pegging their exchange rate to some larger currency or to a basket. A consequence was the emergence of monetary blocs around regional anchor currencies.

This chapter will look at the underlying causes of increased exchange-rate volatility, show the emergence of regional currency blocs and formulate a model, which explains exchange rate pegging as a rational policy option.

The unstable regime of flexible exchange rates

It is commonly believed that the collapse of Bretton Woods meant a regime shift from fixed (but adjustable) exchange rates to generally floating exchange rates in 1973. But this is not entirely correct. A variety of exchange rate regimes were adopted by countries at different times (Argy 1990). It is true that officially the world passed to a regime of generalised floating exchange rates in 1973 when simple adjustments of exchange rates within the framework of the Smithonian Agreement of 1971 were no longer sustainable.

During the transition, foreign exchange markets had only little confidence in the pegging commitment during 1971–3. Free floating looked attractive because it was supposed to insulate domestic economies and particularly monetary policies from external shocks. By 1973, the regime changed: the original Bretton Woods System was terminated when the dollar lost its anchor currency function by severing its fixed price link to gold. The international monetary system then went adrift. In the words of Eichengreen and Kenen (1994: 36), 'the nth country problem would henceforth be solved by foreign exchange traders'. International monetary relations turned into a market-led system (Padoa-Schioppa and Saccomanni 1994). In theory, this meant that the foreign reserve constraint had disappeared. Under a fixed exchange rate system a country could adopt only those economic and monetary policies that were consistent with maintaining foreign exchange reserves sufficient for the stabilisation of exchange rates. Generally, with a flexible arrangement, any domestic policy mix is possible because exchange rate fluctuations adjust and reserves remain stable. However, this requires that monetary authorities choose their own internal nominal anchor for monetary policy.

A monetary anchor is a nominal variable that is the target for monetary policy (Flood and Mussa 1994). Broadly, three types of anchors can be distinguished.

1   *Fixed nominal anchors* or commodity standards consist of a fixed currency price for a standardised metallic unit like gold. Such standards exhibit the tendency for the nominal price *level* to remain stationary over time so that periods of inflation are followed by periods of deflation.
2   *With moving nominal anchors* monetary authorities attempt to hit a moving nominal target such as monetary aggregates, inflation or nominal income targets. They are moving because they aim at the growth rate of a nominal variable which is based on a determined past. Under these standards the *inflation rate* is stationary over time, and the rates of change of other nominal variables return to some long-term baseline.
3   *An exchange rate anchor* exists when countries share a nominal anchor, which is targeted by the anchor country, while other countries target the exchange rate to that anchor currency. The nature of this peg can be fixed or moving (permanently fixed, adjustable, crawling, etc.), just as the exchange anchor can itself follow a fixed (Bretton Woods) or moving European Monetary System (EMS) nominal anchor.

We have seen in the previous chapter that Keynes emphasised stable purchasing power of money-wages in his General Theory. This would assimilate his wage standard to a commodity standard. But the Golden Age with its moderate wage claims was closer to a moving wage standard where the rate of productivity growth was the benchmark. After the break-up of Bretton Woods, monetarist policies targeting money supply aggregates were intended to be the constraint on wage growth. As Friedman (1953a: 479) put it: 'A general wage rise becomes possible only if the monetary authorities create the additional money to finance the higher level of prices'. After 1973, Germany seems to have operated a monetary policy, which worked as a *de facto* wage standard (Streeck 1994).[1]

In a fixed exchange rate regime, the stability of the anchor is crucial for the sustainability of the system. A stable anchor, that is, a currency whose rate of inflation is low or zero, exerts discipline on monetary policy in the pegging country. Thus, the objective to bring down inflation can be an incentive to peg to a stable currency as we have seen in Europe in the 1980s. Yet, a stable fixed nominal anchor can also become a deflationary constraint, as we have learned from the Gold Standard. On the other hand, when an anchor becomes unstable, the fixed exchange rate system unravels quite rapidly as demonstrated by the experience of Bretton Woods or the EMS.

With the regime shift in 1971, the nominal anchor in the international monetary system became indeterminate. International capital flows achieved proportions that were unimaginable in the 1960s (Collignon 1994), external disequilibria persisted longer and to a larger extent than the advocates of flexible rates had expected. Exchange rates between major international currencies became highly volatile in the short run and followed megaswings in the long run that were unprecedented in history. We will discuss the evidence in the next chapter. However, large variations in real exchange rates had an important impact on output and employment. Furthermore, inflation-fighting tactics increasingly dominated domestic policies, and interest rates rose to very high nominal and real levels.

Figure 2.1(a–c) show the evolution of interest rates for USA, Germany and France. Nominal interest rates were low in the 1960s, and high throughout most of the 1970s, the early 1980s and 1990s.

However, while the rise of interest rates in the 1970s can be explained by increasing inflation, nominal rates remained high even after inflation had fallen, notably in France. This is clear from Figure 2.2(a) and (b) which show real interest rates. Alternative stances in monetary policy are expressed by real short-term interest rates (Bofinger *et al.* 1996: 346). In the Golden Age real short-term interest rates were low, below 2 per cent. In the early 1980s, they rose dramatically in order to stop inflation. However, while American monetary policy became less restrictive with regained price stability, it remained excessively tight in Europe. German real short-term rates fluctuated between 2 and 5 per cent between 1980 and 1995. In France price stability was achieved by 1987, when the 'Franc fort' policy became dominant, but real short-term interest rates rose to 11 per cent. These development trends are also evident for real long-term rates, although less pronounced. In the late 1960s, when Germany resisted US inflation, real government bond yields reached 5 per cent. They hovered above 3 per cent through most of the 1980s, peaking twice above 6 per cent. Only in the late 1990s did real interest rate finally come down. The 11-month centred moving average is generally higher in Germany after 1980, with the exception of the reunification years with relatively high inflation. Thus, the post-Bretton Woods macroeconomic environment had changed significantly. After the Great Inflation followed a period of severe monetary tightness. Both were inter-related and related to the exchange rate regime.

Immediately after the breakdown of Bretton Woods, governments attempted unsuccessfully to find new ways to return to exchange rate stability. This failure was in part a consequence of the oil price shock. It aggravated inflationary divergences and contributed to the emergence of internationally integrated capital markets that were incompatible with the 'insular' post-war economies and the related capital controls.

The emerging global capital market

The decision by OPEC to raise oil prices from $3.70 to $11.65 a barrel, effective from 1 January 1974, was probably the largest shock the world economy has ever experienced. More than 10 per cent of world payments for trade were redirected in a

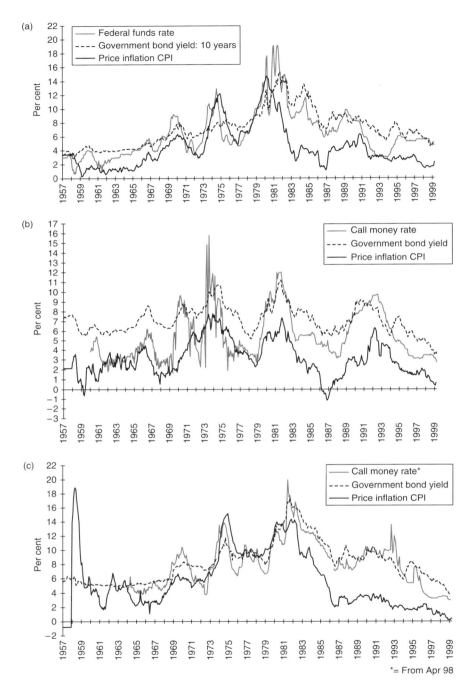

Figure 2.1 Interest rates (a) USA; (b) Germany; (c) France.
Source: IMF (1999).

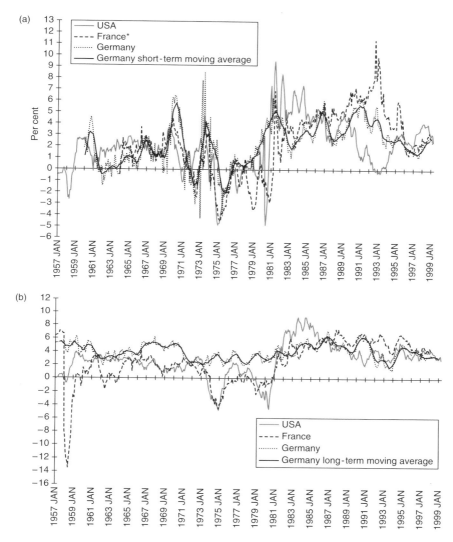

Figure 2.2 (a) Real short-term interest rate; (b) real interest rates on government bonds.
Source: IMF (1999).

single quarter (Little *et al.* 1993). This caused not only a sharp increase in inflation, but also a drastic reduction in output. Some countries, especially Germany, the USA and to some degree Japan, reacted by fighting inflation and adjusting fully to higher oil prices. Others preferred to borrow in order to cover their increased import bills and to smoothen their output losses over time. Not surprisingly, inflation rates diverged significantly between countries and this required continued adjustments in exchange rates. In addition, the borrowing requirements for cyclical smoothing contributed significantly to the emergence in the early 1970 of an integrated world money and capital market, as in the 1920s. The Eurodollar market had already started in the late 1950s in London and was fuelled by US capital restrictions. In the 1970s it became necessary to recycle the bulging current account surpluses by oil producing countries. This opened the gates for large international capital flows. By the late 1960, Eurocurrency credits to developing countries had reached a volume of about half a billion dollars a year; by 1981 they had increased to $44 billion. The international bond market also rebounded (Little *et al.* 1993: 14). These large capital flows increased the volatility in foreign exchange markets and ultimately inhibited a return to the 'fixed but adjustable' exchange rate regime of the post-war era.

The recession that followed the first oil price shock and the contractionary policies in major industrial countries resulted in two key outcomes: it increased borrowing requirements in developing countries that attempted to maintain economic growth; and it laid the ground for the debt crisis in 1982. Thus, while balance of payment difficulties during the fixed exchange rate era had imposed early adjustment and thereby avoided major crisis, the new world of higher capital mobility with markets recycling petro-dollars created a more flexible, yet more vulnerable, financial system. The multilateral management of international reserves that had marked the government-led Bretton Woods System became increasingly impossible. In conjunction with the communications technology, domestic and offshore financial markets were opened and integrated into a single global market (Goldstein and Mussa 1993). Financial liberalisation, lower transaction costs, and increasing speed of transferring funds worldwide also made other currencies than the US dollar increasingly attractive. This led to a multi-currency reserve system, where international liquidity expanded at a much more rapid pace than under the previous Bretton Woods System. Consequently, inflation remained high. But the Eurocurrency market also enabled countries to sustain deficit positions, which were much larger and more persistent than if countries had still been constrained to mobilise their own reserves (Padoa-Schioppa and Saccomanni 1994). Once US monetary policy shifted and interest rates rose to historic highs in the early 1980s, the adjustment was harsh and took crisis proportions in many countries.

These developments also have had important consequences for the micro-structure of financial markets.

- The internationalisation of portfolios by investors looking for attractive short-term investment opportunities has increased the volume of short-term capital movements.
- Institutionalised financial investment management has concentrated market activity in a few financial institutions, which are operating simultaneously in foreign exchange, money and bond markets, often with highly leveraged positions.

- Securitisation has reduced banks' roles as intermediaries. The traditional exclusive direct relationship between lenders and borrowers as a vehicle for transmitting information has been increasingly replaced by price signals in financial markets.
- At the institutional level, the territorial correspondence between financial markets and central banks' jurisdiction has been weakened. Simultaneously, financial liberalisation and innovation have blurred the distinction between banks and non-banks.

This new environment has transformed the framework for monetary policy. The effectiveness of central banks in the conduct of monetary policy has increasingly been eroded. Several factors have been at work. First, the rapid liquidity expansion fuelled rising inflation in the 1970s and contributed, as we have seen in the last chapter, to rising nominal inertia in price and wage setting. Second, exchange rate volatility increased dramatically with the rising volumes and mobility in capital markets. The growing role of financial markets meant that, in the short term, exchange rates were no longer determined by fundamental data from the real economy: foreign exchange transactions related to financial operations have outgrown trade transactions at the ratio 25 : 1 (Collignon 1994). In today's market-led international monetary system, exchange rates are determined as asset prices that react to changes in expectations, news, and interest rate differentials. As a consequence, they can deviate quite substantially from fundamental equilibria (De Grauwe 1989). Thirdly, the high capital mobility allowed the financing of these disequilibria and thereby contributed to their longer persistence. Fourthly, as we will see in Chapter 3, the emerging structure of currency blocs in the world economy has made fundamental equilibrium exchange rates themselves more volatile and, therefore, less suited for policy orientations. As a consequence, exchange rate policies, and to some degree also monetary policy, seemed to escape increasingly from the control of monetary authorities.

A European response: the EMS

These developments were cause for concern in Europe, and they took place on a world scale. Nevertheless, they affected Europe more than other countries. European economies were more open and therefore more vulnerable to exchange rate variations (see Table 5.1). The uncoordinated approach to the revaluations and devaluations of European currencies caused distortions in the common market and threatened the functioning of the common agricultural policy. These considerations led to the creation of the EMS in 1979. It established a fixed exchange rate system between participating countries with institutional rules for realignments and the backing of finance facilities for exchange market interventions. In theory the $n - 1$ country problem was solved by the creation of the ECU as a unit of account, but effectively the DM became the anchor currency in the system (Giavazzi and Giovannini 1989; Collignon 1994). The reason for this is found in the relative stability and size of the DM currency zone as a nominal anchor.

For Germany's partners in the European Union (EU), the disappearance of the fixed exchange rate system of Bretton Woods posed a dilemma: in principle, flexible exchange rates increase the degree of autonomy in their conduct of monetary policy. However, in an extremely open economy, exchange rate variations affect *all* relative prices: not only export competitiveness, but also the cost of imported production inputs, which become volatile. Therefore, the information content of prices was blurred and the outcome of investment decisions became more uncertain. This affected each producer and every company as long as their production techniques were not identical. By adopting fully flexible exchange rates and following strict monetary policies, European economies should have improved domestic control of monetary aggregates. But they also would have put the benefits from integration into jeopardy, for every exchange rate shock would have distorted the relative price structure. Yet, fixing exchange rates to the DM meant giving up the capacity to conduct autonomous monetary policies. Therefore, the EMS tried to square this circle by leaving some margins of flexibility in the form of a 'fixed, but adjustable' exchange rate system with narrow and large bands around central parities.[2] However, for reasons that we will analyse in the next two chapters, the system proved unsustainable. Ultimately, the political choice was between full surrender to the Bundesbank or sharing responsibility for monetary policy in European Monetary Union (EMU).

The DM-bloc emerged only gradually, both in size and with respect to the fixity of exchange rate commitments: small open economies like the Benelux, Austria and Denmark preferred to stabilise their macroeconomic environment by adhering to a fairly fixed currency peg with the DM as the nominal anchor. Larger countries with a lesser degree of openness such as France, Italy and Spain also saw the need to reduce disturbing currency volatility, but at first they gave greater weight to the microeconomic aspects of competitiveness over stability. Their DM peg, therefore, was adjusted more frequently until it became increasingly clear in the mid-1980s that this prevented full macroeconomic stabilisation. Only then did countries like France and others opt for a 'hard currency' policy. It is also true that capital controls at first maintained some margins for national monetary policy (Giavazzi and Giovannini 1989; Eichengreen and Wyplosz 1993). But the increasing international capital mobility did not stop at Europe's borders.

The growth and hardening of the EMS also made it more brittle. With the creation of the internal market, financial liberalisation in Europe and the removal of all capital controls, it was also evident that there existed an 'inconsistent quartet' (Padoa-Schioppa 1992) between the policy objectives of free trade, free movement of labour and capital, fixed exchange rates and autonomous national monetary policies. Ultimately, the single market required the EMU to act as an instrument to co-ordinate monetary policies.

Bloc floating as an international monetary system

Europe was not the only case where small countries pegged to an anchor currency. The post-Bretton Woods world increasingly became one where only leading international currencies floated freely against each other. Most smaller regional currencies linked their currencies for macro- or microeconomic reasons to regional anchor currencies. They kept the volatility with respect to the anchor in exchange rate movements as low as possible and accepted exposure to the full impact of fluctuations from other currencies. This stabilisation could be managed by more rigid systems of fixed (but adjustable) exchange rates (like the EMS in the 1980s or East Asia to the dollar until the mid-1990s) or by some kind of crawling peg (like Portugal in the early 1980s, Greece until 1998 and Central Europe today). As a consequence, currency blocs have emerged that float as a whole with respect to other blocs, while they maintain relatively high monetary and exchange rate stability within each region.

Bloc floating became the dominant feature in the world economy during the 1980s. In theory, flexible exchange rates imply that foreign exchange reserves become more stable because exchange rates adjust to supply and demand in the foreign market. However, as Figure 2.3 shows, no clear structural break is apparent in the reserve volatility of USA, France or Germany.

As a rule, periods of exchange rate instability seem to be positively correlated to periods of foreign reserve volatility. This contradicts the theory. But it is easily understandable in light of bloc floating: if authorities attempt to reduce the volatility of exchange rates, they have to intervene in the market and that creates reserve volatility. After abandoning their link to the US dollar in the 1970s, an increasing number of countries have pegged their exchange rates to regional anchor currencies. In 1992, only 26 currencies out of 178 followed a fixed exchange

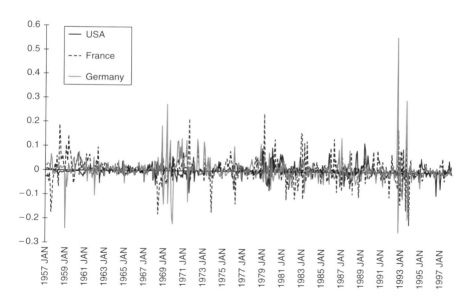

Figure 2.3 Variation of foreign exchange reserve.
Source: IMF (1998).

rate to the dollar (see Table 2.1). However, more important than the number of currencies is a currency zone for international trade.

Empirical evidence for the emergence of monetary blocs has been provided by Frankel and Wei (1992) and Bénassy-Quéré (1995, 1997 and 1999). A country is defined as belonging to a currency bloc when the relative exchange rate variability is significantly lower within a group of countries than across groups.[3] This definition permits some flexibility in the pegging rule but emphasises the reduction in exchange rate volatility. The size of the currency bloc can be measured by the share of foreign trade between countries belonging to the bloc compared to total world trade. It appears that the dominant characteristic of the last twenty years was the emergence of the DM-bloc, while Asia, with the exception of Japan, belongs to the dollar zone.

The share in world trade of countries without an exchange anchor has fallen from 27 per cent in 1978 to 6 per cent in 1992 (see Figure 2.4(a)). Over the same period, the DM-zone has continuously expanded. While it covered only Germany, Benelux and Denmark in the 1970s, it has nearly doubled in weight, progressing from 26 per cent to 47 per cent in world trade and linking most of (Western) Europe in the early 1990s. Only after the ERM crisis in 1992–3 did it slightly lose ground (Figure 2.4(b)). The dollar-zone has lost ground in Africa and the Middle East, but it increased in Asia, where it covered nearly all countries with the exception of Japan until 1997. It keeps its share in world trade

Table 2.1 Exchange rate regimes of the IMF-members

Number of countries	1978	1983	1988	1992
Fixity to a currency				
US dollar	43	34	39	26
French franc	14	13	14	14
Pound Sterling	4	1	0	0
Rouble	–	–	–	9
Deutschmark	0	0	0	2
Other currency	3	4	5	6
Fixity to a currency basket				
SDR	15	13	8	3
ECU	–	1	1	2
Other basket	21	26	30	26
Limited flexibility				
Snake, then EMS	4	7	7	8
Other fixed exchange rates with narrow margins	–	9	4	4
High flexibility				
Crawling peg and managed float	7	29	27	30
Free floating	27	9	17	48
Total	138	146	152	178

Source: IMF, exchange arrangements and exchange restrictions, various numbers; in Bénassy-Quéré (1995).

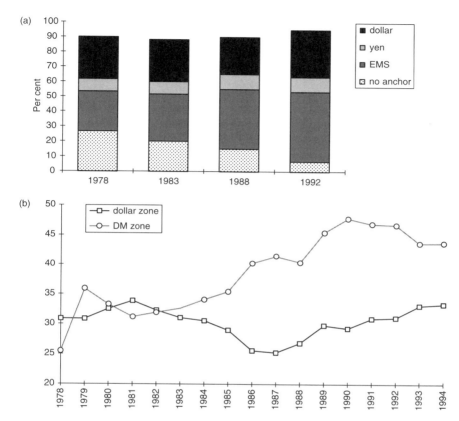

Figure 2.4 (a) Share of currency zones in world exports; (b) export share of currency zones as
per cent of world exports.

Source: (a) Bénassy-Quéré in CEPII 63 (1995); (b) CHELEM and own calculations.

around 30 per cent. The Japanese Yen, on the other hand, does not serve as an
anchor for any currency.

The strength of an anchor currency cannot be deducted from the size of
its monetary zone alone. The DM-zone is the largest currency bloc in world
trade, but the dollar remains the dominant world currency. The relative weakness
of the DM is apparent from the fact that it is much more difficult for the
DM to impose itself as an anchor currency than for the dollar. The DM never
becomes an anchor for a country when its trade share with the EU is below
50 per cent. The USA, by contrast, does not have to be a country's most important
trading partner for the dollar to become a country's anchor (see Table 2.2).

Table 2.2 Exchange rate management and orientation of trade in 1991

Countries or zones	Nominal anchorage	Main partners	
		For imports	For exports
Europe			
Non-meridian, EU and Austria	EMS	**EU**	**EU**
Italy, Spain, Greece	EMS	**EU**	**EU**
Scandinavia (except Denmark)	EMS	**EU**	**EU**
Switzerland	EMS	**EU**	**EU**
Other OECD			
Turkey	None	**EU**	**EU**
Canada	Dollar	**USA**	**USA**
Australia	Dollar	*USA*	*Japan*
Latin America			
Argentina	None	*EU*	*EU*
Brazil	None	*EU/USA*	*EU/USA*
Chile	Dollar	*EU/USA*	*EU*
Colombia	Dollar	*EU/USA*	*EU/USA*
Mexico	Dollar	**USA**	**USA**
Peru	None	*EU/USA*	*EU/USA*
Ecuador	None	*USA*	*USA*
Venezuela	None	*USA*	**USA**
Asia			
India	None	*EU*	*EU*
Indonesia	Dollar	*Japan*	*Japan*
Pakistan	Dollar	*EU*	*EU*
China	Dollar	*Japan*	*USA*
Malaysia, Philippines, Thailand	Dollar	*Japan*	*EU/Japan/ USA*
Korea, Singapore	Dollar	*Japan*	*USA*
Africa			
Morocco	EMS	**EU**	**EU**
Tunisia	EMS	**EU**	**EU**
Algeria	None	**EU**	**EU**
Middle East			
Egypt	None	*EU/USA*	**EU**
Israel	None	*USA*	*EU/USA*
Gulf	Dollar	*EU*	*EU/Japan*
Central and Western Europe			
Hungary	None	**EU**	**EU**
Poland, Romania	None	**EU**	**EU**

Sources: CEPII Data bank CHELEM and author Agnes Bénassy-Quéré (1995, 1997).

In bold: Trading partners of minimum 50%.

In italics: Partners of 20% to 50%.

This emergence of currency blocs demands an explanation. Neither the optimum currency area literature (see Chapter 5) nor nominal anchor theories about imported disinflation credibility provide a satisfying answer.

Why currency blocs emerge: a model

The accumulation of productive assets is the foundation of economic growth. It should, therefore, be of concern to economic policy makers. As we have seen, Europe's economic success after the war was based on unusually high rates of private investment and rapid export growth. Both were the motors of income creation (Riese 1986), which is measured by the growth rate. In this section we focus on the link between exchange rates and growth. We will abstract from other factors such as monetary, fiscal or income policies, or technical progress as far as possible. Our hypothesis is that income growth is a result of investment, which is a function of profitability. The exchange rate affects profitability in foreign trade via the level of competitiveness and via the uncertainty created by exchange rate volatility. The rest of this chapter will focus on the volatility impact, given that the role of real exchange rate is clearly established in the literature.

The investment function

Our argument can be modelled by a simple mean–variance portfolio model linked to a standard investment demand function in a three-country world. Private investors are assumed to be risk-averse, maximising their expected utility subject to their portfolio wealth constraint. Public authorities are to maximise the aggregate capital stock subject to private investor behaviour. Firms invest as long as risk-adjusted returns on capital exceed alternative yields. They can choose among four assets:

1 domestic monetary assets (securities) in country A, that are assumed to be riskless with their yield i_A determined by monetary authorities and financial markets;
2 foreign real assets yielding nominal $i_{B,C,j}$;
3 domestic real assets are assumed to yield a return on non-tradable goods which are perfectly foreseeable;
4 real assets related to tradables derive their return from trading goods in foreign currency of country B or C; and whose yields are subject to exchange risk. The yields of monetary assets set limits on the acceptable return on domestic real assets. In an economy with capital controls, monetary yields between countries may differ, while they would be identical with perfect capital mobility. We will assume the yield on monetary assets ($i_{A,B,C}$) as exogenously given, irrespective of whether they are determined by country A, B or C. In an open economy with increasing or perfect capital mobility, expectations about profit rates may converge,[4] but exchange rate volatility will rise. This adds a risk premium to foreign trade related investment and pushes up required returns.

Formalising these ideas, we assume a three-country world, and divide total output in country A (Y_A) into non-tradables (N) and tradables related to B and C, requiring different amounts of capital (K) and effective labour (L):

$$Y_A = \sum_i Y_i = F(K_i, L_i), \qquad i = N, B, C, \quad F_{K_i}, F_{L_i} > 0,$$

$$F_{KK}, F_{LL} < 0. \tag{2.1}$$

To make things easy, we assume that the production function is identical for all three markets. Investment related to trading in each of these three markets depends on expected profits. In the exchange-risk-free domestic market, the investment decision at firm level – and in aggregate – can be modelled by Tobin's q. This relation is defined as the ratio of the market value of the enterprise to capital replacement cost (Tobin and Brainard 1977), or simply the ratio of the internal rate of return to the risk-free money market interest rate (Bofinger *et al.* 1996: 556). We may then calculate different qs, relating to investment in the three markets.

Let us start with the domestic market. The net present value (PV_N) of expected cash flow (CF) for a firm operating in the non-tradable market is

$$PV_N = \sum_{t=1}^n CF_{N_t} \times \frac{1}{(1 + i_N)^t}, \tag{2.2}$$

where CF_N is the difference between expected revenue and expenditure and i_N the discount rate. The internal rate of return or profit rate of a given investment project is the rate i_N at which the net present value of future cash flows is exactly equal to the cost of investment in the present period, so that

$$PV_N - I_{N_0} = 0 \quad \text{and} \quad \frac{\sum_{t=1}^n CF_{N_t}}{I_{N_0}} = (1 + i_N)^t. \tag{2.2a}$$

Keynes (1936: 135) has called this rate the marginal efficiency of capital. If we assume a constant rate of expected inflation $E(\pi_A)$, the real return on capital is

$$\frac{\sum_{t=1}^n CF_{N_t}}{[1 + E(\pi)]^t I_{N_0}} \approx [1 + i_N - E(\pi_A)]^t = (1 + r_N)^t. \tag{2.2b}$$

Entrepreneurs compare this rate of return from productive investment to alternative investment opportunities in risk-free domestic monetary assets, which yield the interest rate i_A or real return r_A. Unless the investment yields at least as much as monetary assets, there is no incentive to increase the capital stock. Therefore i_A is the minimal rate of return or the required rate of profit. The q-ratio is

$$q_N = \frac{1 + i_N}{1 + i_A} = \frac{1 + i_N - E(\pi_A)}{(1 + i_A - \pi_A)} \approx \frac{r_N}{r_A}, \tag{2.3}$$

where r_N is the internal real rate of return on non-tradable investment and $r_A = i_A - \pi_A$ the real short-term interest rate prevailing in A.[5] q reflects the excess return or economic profit that productive investment would earn over and above the placing of funds in risk-free securities. As r_N and r_A are not easily measured, empirical studies prefer the formulation whereby q is the ratio of the market value of an investment project to the replacement cost. Under certain assumptions the two formulations are identical, but what matters for investment is the q ratio on the margin, that is, the increment of market valuation for the cost of the associated investment. Average q values for existing capital stock may be quite different from the supposed equilibrium value 1. But at the margin, q should be close to unity (Tobin and Golub 1998). In reality, investment may already stop at an earlier rate, say $\bar{q}$ if a minimum profit rate is required for investment. As we will see, risk premia may explain such minimum requirements.

In our simplified model, q is a function of the interest rate; it will fall, if interest rates on monetary assets rise. In more complex models, q is also related to the real exchange rate and fiscal policy. One advantage of using q is that we do not need to distinguish between real or nominal rates of return. In models with neoclassical production functions r_N is equivalent to the marginal product of capital (F_K), a technical variable dependent on the size of the capital stock.[6] Investment will then be determined by the growth of the capital stock to the point where the marginal product of capital is equal to r_A and $q = 1$. Therefore, q reflects a transitory quasi-rent.[7] We have taken i_A (and hence r_A) as exogenously given by conditions in financial markets and monetary policy. This implies that the marginal product of capital will adjust to r_N – and not the other way round (Riese 1986). In a Keynesian environment, r_N must itself be a function of r_A, because an increase in real interest rates would have negative consequences for effective demand, which in turn would affect the future cash flow of the firm as well as the internal rate of return.[8] A formal description of the impact of a change of monetary interest rates (i_A) on q is given in Chapter 8.

The higher the q *ex ante*, the higher profit opportunities are and the higher the incentive is for firms to invest. By aggregating firm investment, we obtain the aggregate investment function (Tobin and Brainard 1977) for the domestic market,[9] and this reflects the increase in the capital stock at the given prices:

$$I_N = P_0 \cdot \Delta K = \varphi_N(q_N - \bar{q}) + a_0, \qquad (2.4)$$

where $\bar{q}$ is the 'normal' value of q, with $\varphi(+) = +$, $\varphi(\bar{0}) = \bar{0}$, $\varphi(-) = -$ and a_0 some autonomous investment ('animal spirits').

Exchange risk

All this is standard theory. Next we look at investment related to tradables. For simplicity we will formulate the argument only in terms of investment for exports, although imports would also require domestic investment. For example, the import of cars would require investment in sales offices, petrol stations, repair shops, etc.

However, given that the value-added of exports is in general larger than the secondary value-added to imports, it is justified to concentrate on the (net) impact of exports for investment. We assume that all cash flow is realised in foreign currency, which has to be converted into domestic currency in order to make it comparable with investment expenditure, which itself is assumed to be exclusively in domestic currency. Therefore, the expected profitability of this foreign trade related investment would depend on the level of the exchange rate and its expected variation.

If, at first, we take prices at home and abroad and the exchange rate as fixed, the internal rate of return on exports to B is given as

$$PV_B = \frac{\sum_{t=1}^{n} CF_{B_t}}{e_{A/B} I_{B_0}} = 1 + i_B = 1 + r_B + \pi_B, \tag{2.5}$$

where CF_{B_t} is the cash flow denominated in B-currency, and $e_{A/B}$ is the nominal exchange rate defined as the price of foreign (B) currency in terms of domestic (A) currency. I_{B_0} is the investment expenditure that firms undertake *at home* in order to trade with country B. It is not direct foreign investment, which would show up in the calculation of cash flow in B-currency. A low level in $e_{A/B}$ implies a 'competitive' exchange rate, which makes domestic investment cheap relative to the earnings in foreign currency and, therefore, yields a high nominal profit rate i_B. In a stable monetary environment, this rate also depends on the local profit conditions in B that determine the cash flow in foreign currency. It is, of course, dependent on expectations relating to future market opportunities.[10] In order to focus on the exchange rate effects, we will, however, assume that agents have perfect foresight with respect to the market evaluation of their profit expectations. Thus, the only risk we analyse in this chapter is the exchange risk since we assume inflation to be forecasted correctly.[11] This will make our model more manageable without subtracting from its main feature.

If we admit different rates of inflation for both countries and flexible exchange rates, then Equation (2.5) must be transformed into:

$$\frac{\sum_{t=1}^{n} CF_{B_t}}{e_{A/B} I_{B_0}} = [1 + r_B + E(\pi_B - \pi_A - \delta_1)]^t = [1 + r_B + E(dp_1)]^t. \tag{2.5a}$$

Here δ_1 is the rate of the *nominal appreciation* of A's currency with respect to B's. p_1 is the log of the real exchange rate between currency A and B and therefore dp_1 is the *rate of real depreciation of currency* A (i.e. a real *appreciation of currency* B).[12] The total expected real return in A from exports to B is the sum of gross profits calculated at today's prices plus the expected rate of real depreciation. Thus, $R_B = r_B + dp_1$ is the (*ex post*) rate of the total real return on investment related to trading with country B. This return has two elements: r_B, which can be perfectly forecasted, possibly because its risk has been hedged away; and a stochastic element, $E(dp_1)$, which is risky. We assume rational expectations with respect to the latter. In analogy we define $R_C = r_C + dp_2$ for future use. The realised (*ex post*) return from foreign trade with B is random, due to the variation in the real exchange rate dp_B. The risk of being hit by exchange rate variations can be measured by its variance. With rational expectations, the expected return is:

$$E[R_B] = r_B + E[dp_1],$$

with the variance $\text{var}(R_B) = \text{var}(dp_1) = \sigma_1^2$.
    Similarly for trade with C it is:

$$E[R_C] = r_C + E[dp_2] \quad \text{and} \quad \text{var}(R_C) = \text{var}(dp_2) = \sigma_2^2.$$

Again, entrepreneurs will compare this expected (real) return with the alternative of placing funds in local (risk free) securities, so that

$$q_B = \frac{1 + r_B + E(dp_1)}{1 + r_A} \approx \frac{E(R_B)}{r_A}. \tag{2.3a}$$

Investment will be high, if expected profits from exporting are high. Its volume depends on the competitive *level* of the exchange rate, which determines r_B, and on the country's capacity to achieve a *real depreciation* with respect to its partner (dp_1).[13] In an open economy, q is therefore not only a function of the interest rate, but also the real exchange rate.[14] However, given that the exchange rate movements go in the same direction as interest rates (an increase of interest rates causes an appreciation), we will only refer to interest rates when discussing the impact of monetary policy on q. In more sophisticated formulations, one should also include fiscal policy.
    The aggregate investment function can now be formulated for our three markets N, B, C as:

$$I_A = P_0 \Delta K_A = \varphi_N(q_N - \bar{q}_N) + \varphi_B(q_B - \bar{q}_B) + \varphi_C(q_C - \bar{q}_C) + a_0. \tag{2.4a}$$

If all qs are equal to their normal values $\bar{q}$, the investor's (firm's) portfolio is in equilibrium, meaning each of the four assets yields the same return and there is no reason to re-allocate wealth. If wealth increases by an exogenous rate (a_0), it is allocated to the four assets in the determined proportions and the capital stock grows autonomously. If $q > \bar{q}$ real capital is accumulated at a more rapid rate and investment is higher. As we have seen, q represents profits as entrepreneurial quasi-rents, which tend to disappear over time due to diminishing returns on capital. However, if A is small with respect to B and possesses unused capacities of effective labour,[15] it will be able to keep q_B quasi-permanently above the equilibrium level (i.e. $\bar{q} = 1$), as long as the exchange rate is pegged at a competitive level and a real appreciation is avoided. Investment is then targeted at exports and growth will be export-led. This gives us a possible theoretical explanation for European economic growth in the Golden Age – or for the rapid development in newly industrialising countries in Asia in the 1980s. Under Bretton Woods (or in the dollar zone later on) exchange rates were fixed at a competitive rate after the initial post-war devaluations.[16] The dollar, as a stable anchor currency, also constrained inflation. Therefore, a rapid real appreciation of European currencies could be avoided in the post-war era[17] and long periods of high investment were possible.

Neglecting a_0, investment will be forthcoming as long as the rate of return is higher than some 'normal' relation between the profit from productive investment and the yield on some riskless security. Thus, $q > \bar{q}$ implies that investors wish to increase the share of the capital stock, which yields a higher return, until this return has fallen to the normal level. Thus, $\bar{q}$ is called the *equilibrium q*. It allows us to derive the *required rate of return*, $\bar{q}_B i_A = \bar{R}_B$ and $\bar{q}_C i_A = \bar{R}_C$, indicating the minimum profit rate required for an expansion of the capital stock, given prevailing conditions in financial markets.

Under the simplified assumptions of perfect foresight at home, the required profit rate on non-tradables is equal to the monetary interest rate so that:

$$\bar{q}_N = (r_N/r_A) = 1.$$

But in foreign trade, firms are confronted with exchange risk and will require profits to cover potential exchange losses. Therefore, the required return includes a risk premium (ρ) related to the volatility of the real exchange p_1. We have:

$$\bar{R}_B = r_A(1 + \rho_1) \quad \text{and} \quad \bar{q}_B = \frac{\bar{R}_B}{r_A} = (1 + \rho_1). \tag{2.3b}$$

The profitability in tradables has to be higher than for non-tradables in order to cover the risk premium. Consequently, the higher the exchange rate risk, the lower the potential for investment is. The *ex post* excess return in period t earned by firms in their export market B over domestic risk-free securities is:

$$u_{B_t} = R_{B_t} - r_{A_t} = r_{B_t} - r_{A_t} + dp_{1_t}, \tag{2.6}$$

with the mean μ_1 and variance σ_1^2. Under the hypothesis of rational expectations we have:

$$E(\mu_{B_t}) = E(R_{B_t}) - r_{A_t} = \mu_1. \tag{2.6a}$$

The mean forecast error, that is, the difference between the realised excess return and the required risk premium is

$$R_B - E(R_B) = u_B - \mu_B = \varepsilon_B. \tag{2.6b}$$

This would be unforeseeable in efficient markets with $E(\varepsilon) = 0$ and $\text{var}(\varepsilon_B) = \sigma_1^2$.

Referring back to our definition of q in Equation (2.3a), it is obvious that $E(u_B) = q_B - 1$, so that $q_B = 1 + \mu_1$. However, Equation (2.3b) demonstrates that

$\bar{q} = 1 + \rho$. If $q > \bar{q}$, the expected excess profit is higher than the risk premium and the capital stock will increase until excess return falls to the level of the risk premium. When $q = \bar{q}$, we have portfolio equilibrium when the excess return on holding assets related to tradables is just compensating for the exchange risk and the asset allocation in the wealth portfolio remains unchanged.[18] Therefore, when the portfolio is in equilibrium, $\mu_1 = \rho_1$.

Investment and portfolio allocation

Thus, our model shows two ways in which exchange rates influence Tobin's q: the *level* of exchange rates affects the economy's competitiveness and profitability, and that is reflected in q; and the *variance* of the exchange rate movements determines the risk premium and, therefore, the normal or equilibrium $\bar{q}$. Both together determine the volume of investment. Public authorities could accelerate the rate of capital accumulation by improving domestic conditions of competitiveness or by reducing the risk premium required to compensate for exchange risk.[19] Individual investors on the other hand maximise their given wealth by optimally diversifying their asset holdings in terms of expected returns and risk. Exchange risk can be measured as the variance of the rate of depreciation. If the real exchange rate volatility for p_2 exceeds p_1, that is, if $\left(\sigma_2^2 > \sigma_1^2\right)$, then the required excess return μ_2 must be higher than μ_1. Therefore, the typical investor allocates his assets by maximising the utility of his real wealth at the end of the investment period

$$\mathrm{E}[U(\mathcal{W})] = U(\mathcal{W}, \sigma_w^2) \qquad U' > 0; U'' < 0$$

with respect to m_B and m_C and subject to the wealth constraint

$$\mathcal{W} = [m_\mathrm{B} R_\mathrm{B} + m_\mathrm{C} R_\mathrm{C} + (1 - m_\mathrm{B} - m_\mathrm{C}) i_\mathrm{A}] \mathcal{W}_0. \tag{2.7}$$

Here $\mathcal{W}$ is a real wealth index with $\mathcal{W}_0$ as base, and m_B and m_C are the shares of real assets related to the respective countries B and C in the portfolio of investors in A. In order to simplify our analysis, we will assume them to be identical to trade shares.

It can be shown that the solution of this maximisation yields the following equations for the risk premium (Minford 1992: 189–91):

$$\rho_1 \equiv \mathrm{E}[\bar{R}_\mathrm{B}] - r_\mathrm{A} = \vartheta\left(m_\mathrm{B}\sigma_1^2 + m_\mathrm{C}\sigma_{1,2}\right) = \vartheta m\left(\alpha_1\sigma_1^2 + \alpha_2\sigma_{1,2}\right)$$
$$= \vartheta m\left(\alpha_1[\sigma_1^2 - \sigma_{1,2}] + \sigma_{1,2}\right), \tag{2.7a}$$

$$\rho_2 \equiv \mathrm{E}[\bar{R}_\mathrm{C}] - r_\mathrm{A} = \vartheta\left(m_\mathrm{C}\sigma_2^2 + m_\mathrm{B}\sigma_{1,2}\right) = \vartheta m\left(\alpha_2\sigma_1^2 + \alpha_2\sigma_{1,2}\right)$$
$$= \vartheta m\left(\alpha_2[\sigma_2^2 - \sigma_{1,2}] + \sigma_{1,2}\right). \tag{2.7b}$$

The risk premium depends on the degree of risk aversion $\vartheta = -(U''/U') > 0$, the share of tradables, that is, risky assets in the economy (m) and the variances (σ_1^2, σ_2^2)

and covariance $(\sigma_{1,2})$ of the exchange rate.[20] We have assimilated $m = m_B + m_C$ to the degree of openness of the economy. α_1 and α_2 are the regional trade shares, whereby $\alpha_1 + \alpha_2 = 1$ and $m\alpha_1 = m_B$. Thus, the larger the degree of openness, the larger the required excess returns are on top of the domestic discount rate (*ceteris paribus*). Given that the degree of openness is normally larger for small countries than for larger ones,[21] small countries could only improve their rate of capital accumulation by reducing the variance of their returns on tradables, that is, exchange rate volatility.[22]

Furthermore, because of Equation (2.7), the expected return on the total wealth in country A is

$$E[R_A] = m_B E[R_B] + m_C E[R_C] + (1 - m)r_A, \tag{2.8a}$$

with the variance

$$\sigma_{R_A}^2 = m^2 \left[\alpha_1^2 \sigma_1^2 + \alpha_2^2 \sigma_2 + 2\alpha_1 \alpha_2 \sigma_{1,2}\right] = m^2 \sigma_A^2. \tag{2.8b}$$

The economy's average required excess return is

$$\mu_A = E(R_A) - r_A = m_B \rho_1 + m_C \rho_2 = m[\alpha_1 \rho_1 + \alpha_2 \rho_2].$$

The term in brackets in Equation (2.8b) is an expression for the variance σ_A^2 of the rate of change of the Real Effective Exchange Rate (REER) index.[23] In other words, the volatility of the REER is a measure for the exchange rate-induced uncertainty in the economy's average profit rate.

Our result implies that the average return has to be increased by the risk premium, which is the weighted average of individual risk premia. A shift from fixed to floating exchange rates would require higher rates of profit and a fall in real wages. Therefore, the exchange rate regime must have distributional effects, if the required return and profitability are dependent on real wages. If nominal wages are sticky, a rise in prices would have to do the trick. Thus, our model provides an explanation for the wage-price spiral, which pushed European unit labour costs and inflation up in the 1970s. In addition, nominal inertia has increased in flexible exchange rate regimes, as we have seen in the last chapter. If some degree of nominal wage rigidity prevails, the shift to flexible exchange rates inevitably had to ignite an inflationary process. After the end of Bretton Woods this dynamic was reinforced by the oil price shock, but it also would have occurred if that shock had been less pronounced. This process is more important for small open economies than for larger ones with a lower degree of openness (*m*). Given that most European countries are small, Europe must have suffered more from the move to flexible exchange rates than large unified countries like USA and Japan. This could explain why wage inflation, measured in terms of unit labour costs (Figure 1.2), was more persistent in Europe. Therefore, small countries would have benefited from returning to some kind of fixed exchange rate arrangement, and this explains the emergence of the EMS.[24] By stabilising their exchange rates, small, open economies could also reduce wage-price pressures.

Anchor currency versus basket peg

If authorities in A wish to stabilise investment by lowering the required excess return, they have three options.

- They may reduce the degree of openness m. Such isolationism might improve the scope for domestic investment stimulating policies, but especially small countries might quickly hit market-size constraints. Furthermore, protection- ist measures would create distortions, which could actually increase the excess return and lead to financial repression. However, as we will see below, the redistribution of international trade shares, for example, by the creation of EMU, is a different form of reducing m and could have more beneficial effects on international risk premia.
- They may peg their currency to an anchor and reduce the volatility of one particular exchange rate (say p_1), while the other remains freely floating. This is what I call *bloc floating*.[25] For sake of simplicity, we will assume a perfect peg where $\sigma_1 = 0$ and therefore also $\sigma_{1,2} = 0$. In reality, as Bénassy- Quéré has demonstrated, it is sufficient to postulate that σ_1 is significantly lower than σ_2.[26]
- They may peg to a basket of currencies and aim to stabilise the real effective exchange rate. In Europe, this is a policy that countries like Sweden and Norway followed during the 1980s.[27]

If we discard the isolationist strategy, we wish to know whether bloc floating yields better results, that is, higher investment, than a basket peg. The answer can be derived from Equations (2.7a), (2.7b) and (2.8a). Table 2.3 shows the structural differences between the two regimes.[28]

Under bloc floating, we have eliminated all exchange risk to the anchor cur- rency but are exposed to the exchange risk from the floating rate with the rest of the world. Under a basket peg, we have eliminated volatility in the REER, but this requires the two exchange rates to be negatively correlated. By applying Table 2.3 to Equations (2.7a) and (2.7b), we get the risk premia for our two tradables' assets under the two exchange regimes (Table 2.4).

Thus, under bloc floating, trade relations with the anchor currency country are riskless and similar to domestic conditions,[29] but they are risky with the rest of the world. With a basket peg, trade relations are less clearly determined, because the risk premium for either region can be positive, zero or even negative. Substituting into Equation (2.4a), we obtain aggregate investment under bloc floating:

$$I_A^{BF} = \varphi_N(q_N - 1) + \varphi_B(q_B - 1) + \varphi_C\left[q_C - \left(1 + \vartheta m \alpha_2 \sigma_2^2\right)\right] + a_0$$
$$\text{for } m\alpha_2 \neq \overline{0}. \tag{2.9a}$$

Table 2.3 Volatility under bloc floating and basket pegs

	Bloc floating	Basket peg
Variances		
σ_1^2	0 by definition	$\left(\dfrac{\alpha_2}{\alpha_1}\right)^2 \sigma_2^2 = \alpha_2^2\sigma_3^2$
σ_2^2	$\dfrac{1}{\alpha_2}\sigma_A^2 = \sigma_3^2$	$\left(\dfrac{\alpha_1}{\alpha_2}\right)^2 \sigma_1^2 = \alpha_1^2\sigma_3^2$
σ_A^2	$\alpha_2^2\sigma_2^2 = \alpha_2^2\sigma_3^2$	0 by definition
Covariances		
$\sigma_{1,2}^2$	0 by definition	$-\left[\dfrac{\alpha_1^2}{2\alpha_1\alpha_2}\sigma_1^2 + \dfrac{\alpha_2^2}{2\alpha_1\alpha_2}\sigma_2^2\right] < 0$
$\sigma_{A,1}^2$	0 by definition	0 by definition
$\sigma_{A,2}^2$	$-\left[\dfrac{1}{2\alpha_2^2}\sigma_A^2 + \dfrac{1}{2}\sigma_2^2\right]$	0 by definition
$\sigma_{A,3}^2$	$-\sigma_{A,2}^2 > 0$	0 by definition

Table 2.4 Risk premia under different pegging regimes

	Bloc floating	Basket peg
ρ_1	0	$\dfrac{\vartheta m}{2}\left(\alpha_1^2\sigma_1^2 - \alpha_2^2\sigma_2^2\right)$
ρ_2	$\vartheta m\ \alpha_2\sigma_2^2$	$\dfrac{\vartheta m}{2}\left(\alpha_2^2\sigma_2^2 - \alpha_1^2\sigma_1^2\right)$

Investment into trade with country B is likely to expand faster than with country C. Figure 2.5 can demonstrate this logic.

The horizontal axis measures exchange risk as the standard deviation of the rate of change of the real exchange rate to the right and the quantity of investment to the left. The vertical axis shows the expected rate of return on investment. To simplify matters, we draw separate investments functions for non-tradables and tradables but identical functions for C and B. The amount of investment in non-tradable I_N is determined by the risk-free rate on securities r_A. At that point $q_N = 1$. Hence I_n is an autonomous investment in $I_n = a_0$. Investment in tradables is subject to risk considerations. The higher the exchange-rate volatility, the higher the required risk premium $\rho = E(R) - r_A$ is. The right-hand side in the graph shows the risk pricing line. Its slope reflects the risk sensitivity of inventors. The higher the standard deviation of the change in the exchange rate, the higher the risk premium required to undertake investment is. Yet, given that $\sigma_1 = 0$, investment in trade with country B (I_B) is high, because $\bar{q}_B = 1$ and a good number of profitable investment projects is available. On the other hand, exchange risk with country B is $\sigma_2 > 0$ and the risk premium grows as a quadratic function. Investment (I_C) is consequently reduced. For very high volatility, investment is reduced to the exogenous constant a_0 where C is vertical.[30]

required return on investment or $\bar{q}$

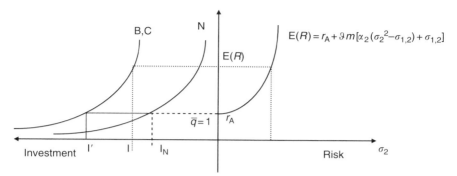

Figure 2.5 Investment decision under risk.

Given our three-country world, the variance in p_2 is equivalent to the volatility in p_3, that is, in the exchange rate between B and C over which A has no control. Therefore, unless A can exert some control over p_2, it is completely at the mercy of exchange policies between B and C (small country case).[31] Thus, a small country A has a strong incentive to concentrate its investment on trading with B and consequently to expand its tradeshare α_1 and reduce α_2. Simultaneously, volatility in the real effective exchange rate σ_A^2 will fall, while the volatility with respect to C (σ_2^2) rises relative to the real effective exchange rate.[32]

This analysis shows that the emergence of currency blocs is the logical consequence when authorities aim to maximise investment and growth while risk-averse private investors maximise profits. Clearly, this logic must have been underlying the emergence of the EMS/DM-Zone in the 1980s, or the choice of a dollar peg for non-Japanese Asian countries apparent in Figure 2.4. But while Asia represents the case of small countries pegging to a large country, Europe reflects a strategy of jointly pegging a small currency (the DM) or a basket (the ECU) in order to gain protection from third currency variations. Obviously, the choice of an anchor currency depends on its initial weight (α_1) as well as on the elasticity of the investment function with respect to risk.

Let us now consider the alternative option of a basket peg. This was the system chosen by Finland, Norway and Sweden in the 1980s (Hörngren and Vredin 1989). Under what conditions is this option preferable over an anchor peg? Pegging a basket implies perfect stability in the effective exchange rate in our model, that is, $\sigma_A^2 = 0$. The bilateral volatilities are independently given. In our three-country model this implies that the exchange rates p_1 and p_2 are negatively correlated. Consequently, at least part of the risk premium could be diversified away and basket pegging would appear superior to bilateral pegging from an aggregate view. However, the impact of uncertainty on investment depends on the nature of the investor. Only companies large enough to diversify their market strategies sufficiently to cover both non-tradables and tradables would benefit from stability in the effective exchange rate. For smaller firms standard hedging instruments in financial markets cannot eliminate this non-diversifiable risk (Huizinga 1994). A small individual firm with constrained access to capital, and which is therefore inhibited in replicating the macro-portfolio, will choose to expand market penetration where risk is lowest, given identical profit expectations. Under a basket peg we get the investment function:

$$I_A^{BP} = \varphi_N(q_N - 1) + \varphi_B \left\{ q_B - \left(1 + \frac{\vartheta m}{2} \left[\alpha_1^2 \sigma_1^2 - \alpha_2^2 \sigma_2^2\right]\right)\right\}$$
$$+ \varphi_C \left\{ q_C \left(1 - \frac{\vartheta m}{2} \left[\alpha_2^2 \sigma_2^2 - \alpha_1^2 \sigma_1^2\right]\right)\right\} + a_0. \tag{2.9b}$$

The actual impact of the basket peg depends on the two-risk premia, as shown in Figure 2.4. The risk premium $\rho = E[R_E] - i_A$ disappears for $\alpha_1 = \sigma_1/(\sigma_1 + \sigma_2)$ and $\rho_2 = E[R_C] - i_A$ if $\alpha_1 = \sigma_2/(\sigma_1 + \sigma_2)$. Above the 45°-line in Figure 2.4 the risk premium is positive, below it is negative.

If we define the exchange rate p_1 with country B by $\sigma_1 > \sigma_2$, we find that investment related to C is subject to a positive risk premium $\rho_2 > 0$ as long as $\rho_1 = 0$, that is, as long as $\alpha_1 = \sigma_1/(\sigma_1 + \sigma_2)$. This is equivalent to the bloc floating situation and shown in Figure 2.6 by point D and E′. However, under a basket peg, if country A continues to extend its economic ties with B, so that α_1 increases

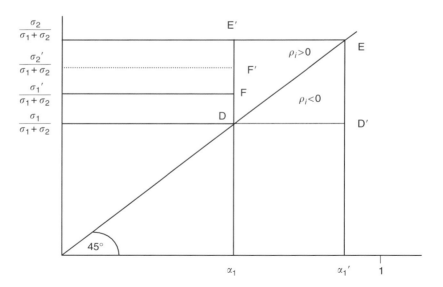

Figure 2.6 Risk premia and portfolio shares.

to α_1', the risk premium on C-investment falls until it reaches zero at E, while simultaneously the premium on B becomes negative up to point D'. The consequence is a further integration of A's and B's economy with expanding investment and growth, and increasing specialisation in trade with the less volatile currency zone. Of course, if the volatility in P_1 exceeds P_2, the processes would be reversed and frequent reversals would reduce the inclination to invest in either of the two currency zones and expand non-tradables.

The assumption of exogenous bilateral exchange-rate volatilities may apply in the case of small countries with fully liberalised capital markets and the absence of central bank intervention. However, to the degree that a shift from bloc floating to basket pegging implies an increase in σ_1 (authorities intervene less to keep p_1 stable), it is likely to produce reverse effects: a given portfolio share α_1, ρ_1 will become positive as shown by point F. Simultaneously, $\alpha_2/(\sigma_1 + \sigma_2)$ might fall to point F', thereby reducing the risk premium ρ_2. The normal $\bar{q}_B$-ratio required for B-investment rises and $\bar{q}_C$ falls for C. This will reduce investment related to B and expand investment to C, therefore reducing α_1. The net effect on aggregate investment and growth depends on the specific investment functions φ_B and φ_C. It is, however, likely that the switch from a basket peg to a single currency peg might increase growth opportunities, if B is a large country or currency zone while C is (relatively) small. This logic could explain why the growth of the DM-Zone accelerated with its size.

Ultimately, what matters is how exchange rate regimes affect volatility. Under a basket peg the determinants are the correlation coefficients between the two exchange rates and the effective exchange rate. However, in the small country case, where A cannot influence p_3, both bilateral exchange rate volatilities (σ_1^2 and σ_2^2) are a function of the variance of the exchange rate between the two international currencies, σ_3^2 (see Table 2.3). Therefore, exchange rate stability and capital accumulation in a small country will depend ultimately on the volatility of key currencies. Yet, if currency blocs cluster around key currencies, the capacity of anchor-countries to use exchange rates as an adjustment tool in case of fundamental disequilibria will be restrained, since only a small portion of foreign trade and investment is affected by the exchange rate variation. The next chapter will prove that bloc floating will increase the volatility of the equilibrium exchange rate of key currencies as a trade-off to lower volatility within monetary blocs.

Summary and conclusion

This chapter has focused on the international monetary system as it effectively worked after 1971–3. The world did not enter a regime of free floating but clustered into currency blocs around primarily two anchor currencies: the dollar and the DM.

The reasons for this development are found in the rapid development of international financial markets as a result of the oil price shock and the need to recycle petro-dollars. This led to an increase of financial volatility (interest and exchange rates), which had disturbing effects on investment. Even if the role of financial markets increased significantly during this period, governments continued to pursue exchange rate objectives. In fact, this was imperative to keep a check on some of the distortions that developed under unconstrained market activity. Smaller industrialised countries, as well as developing countries, did not really have the option to let their exchange rates float for fear of destabilising their economy. They faced the choice between different pegging modalities: major national currencies versus synthetically created baskets of currencies; fixed versus moving targets. Many countries followed different policy regimes at different times. In the end, a new system emerged which I call *bloc floating*: individual currencies pegged regional anchor currencies, while these reserve currencies floated freely with respect to each other.

We have developed a theoretical model, which showed this connection. It leads us to expect that small countries would peg a larger currency and develop regional investment and trade. Although the dynamic growth of intra-community trade is well known, empirical studies on the impact of exchange-rate volatility are ambivalent. Early studies on the correlation of exchange risk and foreign trade were not conclusive, possibly because they used short-term volatility indicators although companies can hedge this risk. More recent studies using medium-term volatility seem to detect the expected link. Studies on the impact on direct foreign investment also do not find a negative correlation with volatility, but again this might be biased by DFI itself fulfilling a hedging function (Molle and Morsink 1990). The negative impact of exchange-rate volatility on investment and employment, however, may be more evident. According to some studies (Gros 1996; Belke and Gros 1997) a 1 per cent-point increase in the standard deviation of monthly exchange rate variations reduces investment by 4–5 per cent in Germany and employment by 0.6 per cent in the following year.

An alternative research strategy would focus on q. Given that the marginal rate of return over cost is hardly an empirically verifiable magnitude, Tobin's q simulates the relation by comparing the (marginal) market value over replacement costs. Gebauer *et al.* (1994) have tried to build a time series of q for Germany. They notice that the increase in the volatility of financial assets in the 1980s makes the estimate of an investment function based on q unreliable. According to our model, higher volatility should rise, the required return and thus we would not be surprised by Gebauer's results. The higher required return due to higher volatility of exchange rate in the open European economies could also explain why European firms seem to have increased their profit margins as a response to the dollar appreciation in the early 1980s, while American firms seem to have done the opposite (Bean 1994). Given that the European degree of openness is a multiple of the American one, risk premia in Europe must be significantly higher and investment accordingly lower.

Figure 2.7 shows marginal qs for France and Germany on a monthly basis. The French series may be level distorted because the IMF IFS Data bank does not provide a monthly producer price index before 1993, so I used the CPI. It is visually apparent that the amplitude of the q-series changes increases in the 1970s and in the second half of the 1980s.

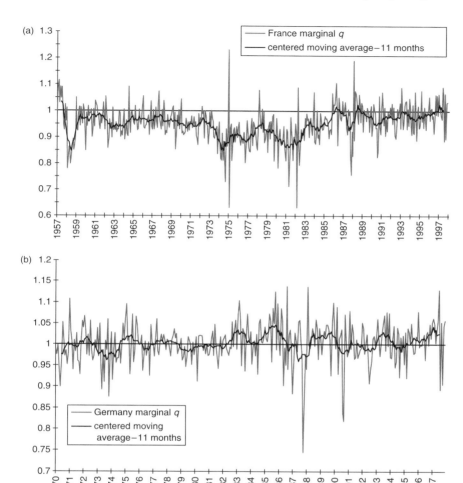

Figure 2.7 (a) France's marginal *q*; (b) Germany's marginal *q*.
Source: IMF and own calculations.

To conclude, we may conveniently divide the phenomenon of bloc floating into four phases of monetary development.

1   *Disintegration of Bretton Woods.* 1973–9 were the years of the Great Inflation and a significant dollar depreciation against the DM and the yen. The external value of the DM rose over 100 per cent and that of the yen over 85 per cent. Old monetary policy rules were no longer applied, but new ones had not yet been established. The international fixed rate system disinteg-rated rapidly. Except for some small countries, which remained tightly

fixed to the dollar, pegging experiments, like in the European Snake, proved unsuccessful.

2   *Emergence of the EMS.* 1979–85 were the years of worldwide disinflation and a dramatic dollar appreciation. Its value increased nearly two thirds against the DM and one quarter against the yen. In the US this was a consequence of the strict monetarist policies pursued by the Fed leading to a long, sustained over-valuation of the US dollar. Developing countries were forced to combat infla-tion and re-establish fundamental equilibria subsequent to the international debt crisis. In Asia, several countries depreciated their fixed exchange rate to the dollar and started their economic miracle. In Europe, disinflation occurred under German leadership within the EMS. With price stability slowly being regained, a tendency for the effective exchange rate of the DM to depreciate in real terms and with stronger institutional arrangements, pegging the DM became more successful in the EMS.

3   *Unsustained stability.* 1986–92 was a period of revival. Inflation came under control. Under the impact of the Plaza (September 1985) and the Louvre Agree-ment (February 1987), the dollar corrected its overvaluation by about three-quarters against the DM and one-half against the yen and then stabilised. The Asian tiger countries leaped forward. The EU reached or exceeded output growth of 3 per cent (the average of the previous decade) for the first time since the late 1970s. Employment also improved. The anchor role of the DM gained weight, since an increasing number of countries pegged the DM officially inside the EMS and unilaterally from outside. The currency bloc around Germany grew rapidly and even exceeded the dollar-bloc in world trade. With the completion of the single market, capital controls were abolished and, as a consequence, the EMS turned increasingly into a non-adjustable system. But when the anchor function of the DM was shaken under the shock of German re-unification, the flexibility of the exchange rate mechanism was broken up. After the Gulf War, the world economy entered a serious recession.

4   *Transition to EMU: 1992–9.* That the EMS turbulences of 1992 and 1993 did not dissolve the system was due largely to the signing of the Maastricht Treaty. Although the widening of the ERM-intervention margins after the 1992 and 1993 turbulences seemed to have some similarity with the Smithonian Agreement, the difference between Germany in the 1990s and the USA in the 1960s and 1970s was the commitment to price stability. It set a clear and achievable target for economic convergence in Europe and obliged govern-ments to comply with the Maastricht criteria. But it also constrained economic growth in Europe.

The emergence of bloc floating has had important consequences for the world economy. In the next chapter we will analyse its impact on the fundamental equi-librium exchange rate between the anchor currencies. In Chapter 4 we will use a simple IS-LM model to show that bloc floating not only had investment-fostering effects in the periphery, but also created a deflationary bias. Ultimately this led to the creation of the EMU.

3 International consequences of bloc floating

In his famous defence of flexible exchange rates, Friedman (1953a) argued that flexibility was not equivalent to instability. If rates were free to vary, they would help to correct any surplus or deficit in the balance of payments and this fact would contribute to making exchange rates 'highly stable'. Thus, instability of exchange rates was a symptom of instability in the underlying economic structure. Speculators in the market were assumed to distinguish between *temporary* balance of payment disequilibria and *fundamental* factors with a likelihood of being permanent. Financial markets would moderate the transitory variation by taking positions against the trend, but they would speed up fundamental adjustment by moving in the direction of the new equilibrium.

The large fluctuations in exchange rates after the end of Bretton Woods contradicted Friedman's theory. Dornbusch (1976) showed that exchange rate variations due to fundamental factors affect the expectations of financial markets in such a way that the exchange rate temporarily 'overshoots' its long-term equilibrium level. Thus, the rationality of financial markets contributes to exchange rate instability. But Dornbusch's model seemed to be more apt to explain short-term volatility than the megaswings among major international exchange rates that dominated the 1980s. This is because, in his model, the exchange rate dynamics result from the difference between short-term and long-term equilibria when prices are sticky. But if prices are flexible in the long run, what is the equilibrium that they adjust to?

In order to explain long run movements of the real exchange rate, one line of research has developed dynamic models with 'bubble' characteristics (Blanchard 1979; Dornbusch 1982). A bubble is an explosive time path of the exchange rate, which brings it progressively further away from the economic fundamentals, but ultimately it will burst. Thus, it leads to an increasing divergence of the actual exchange rate from its equilibrium level. Although speculators may attach low probability to the immediate end of the bubble, and therefore wish to ride it out, this behaviour is inconsistent with perfect foresight rational expectations models. In limited rationality, models where 'small menu costs' disturb the visibility of fundamentals, exchange rate volatility is disconnected from the variability of underlying fundamentals within certain ranges (De Grauwe 1989). Only beyond these ranges will economic fundamentals still operate as an attractor for exchange rate dynamics. These models are compatible with our explanation of currency blocs, for by pegging to an anchor, uncertainty is reduced and visibility is increased. But the models hardly provide a rationale for the large swings between key currencies.

The problem is that all these models assume the equilibrium exchange rate as relatively stable while the market rate deviates from it. However, if the equilibrium rate is itself unstable and volatile, then flexibility in the market rate can no longer be relied upon to correct fundamental disequilibria in the economy, because market participants would have faint ideas in what direction the rate should be moving. We will now demonstrate that one important reason for the increased volatility in the fundamental exchange rate is the emergence of bloc floating.[1] The next section will prove this 'enlarging effect' of bloc floating on the equilibrium exchange rate and the section on Exchange rate dynamics will show how the equilibrium path is affected by policy shifts. Finally, we will look at some empirical evidence.

Enlarging effects of bloc floating on fundamental exchange rate movements

We define the fundamental equilibrium exchange rate as the rate at which external and internal balance is simultaneously achieved. As we saw in the last chapter, most models work with 'the' exchange rate, that is, a single exchange rate. Empirically it is assimilated to the Real Effective Exchange Rate (REER), which is the trade-share weighted average of the bilateral exchange rates. Thus, for a country A, the fundamental equilibrium exchange rate is the (weighted) relative price ratio P_A between domestic and foreign prices, providing the solution to the following simultaneous equation system:

$$Y^* = Y(Y_A, Y_{C+B}, P_A)$$
$$T^* = T(Y_A, Y_{C+B}, P_A)$$

(3.1)

where Y^* and T^* are policy objective parameters for income (output) and the trade balance. Y_A is domestic demand consisting of aggregate spending by domestic residents (private and public consumption and investment) plus net exports (spending by foreign residents). For simplicity we will assume foreign demand (Y_{C+B}) constant. P_A is the REER, defined as $P_A = P_1^{\alpha_1} \cdot P_2^{\alpha_2}$. As in the last chapter we make the heroic assumption that prices remain stable, so that the real exchange rate reflects movements of the nominal rate. In a three-country world we have two exchange rates and two exogenous variables for foreign demand, so that:

$$Y^* = Y(Y_A, Y_B, Y_C, P_1, P_2, \alpha_1, \alpha_2)$$
$$T^* = T(Y_A, Y_B, Y_C, P_1, P_2, \alpha_1, \alpha_2)$$

(3.1′)

where Y^* and T^* are the policy parameters.

When modelling bloc floating, we take P_1, Y_B and Y_C as fixed and α_1, α_2 as structural parameters. Thus, Y_A and P_2 are the endogenous variables. The solution of the system requires, of course, knowledge of the vectors of parameters that specify the behaviour of the $Y(\cdot)$ and $T(\cdot)$ equations. If the equilibrium exchange rate is stable over time, then the parameter vectors have to be stable as well. However, our previous analysis has shown that, in a regime with several exchange rates and different volatilities, the structural parameters will not remain stable because the trade shares α_1 and α_2 will vary as a response to utility maximising portfolio behaviour of investors. Therefore, the stable equilibrium exchange rate is subject to the Lucas critique (Lucas 1976). In order to analyse how the equilibrium exchange rate evolves in an exchange regime with pegged rates, we will return to our three-country bloc floating world. Keeping P_1 fixed, P_2 is flexible, bearing all the thrust of adjustment. In order to keep the mathematics simple we will also assume that the pegging commitment is 100 per cent, that is, the variance of P_1 is zero ($\sigma_1^2 = 0$). We will first determine external, then internal, balance equations and subsequently show how the slopes of the simultaneous equation solution vary with bloc floating.

External balance

Our three-country world has the trade matrix as shown in Table 3.1.

AB (Y_B, P_1) describes the volume of exports (denominated in domestic currency) by country A to country B as a function of income in B (Y_B) and the relative price (P_1) between the two countries. The $+$ or $-$ sign under the variable indicates the sign of the first derivative.

A's trade balance is:

$$T_A = T(Y_A, Y_B, Y_C, P_1, P_2, \alpha_1, \alpha_2) = X_A - M_A$$
$$= AB(Y_B, P_1) + AC(Y_C, P_2) - P_1 \cdot BA(Y_A, P_1) - P_2 \cdot CA(Y_A, P_2).$$

$$(3.1a)$$

Table 3.1 Trade matrix in a three-country world

Exports by	Imports to			Σ
	A	B	C	
A	–	AB (Y_B, P_1) + +	AC (Y_C, P_2) + +	X_A
B	BA (Y_A, P_1) + –	–	BC (Y_C, P_3) + –	X_B
C	CA (Y_A, P_2) + –	CB (Y_B, P_3) + –	–	X_C
Σ	M_A	M_B	M_C	

The relative import shares are

$$\alpha_1 = \frac{P_1 \cdot \text{BA}}{M_A}; \qquad \alpha_2 = \frac{P_2 \cdot \text{CA}}{M_A}; \qquad \alpha_1 + \alpha_2 = 1. \tag{3.2}$$

In the last chapter we made the assumption that these trade shares are identical with the portfolio shares of wealth allocation. Additionally, we now assume that marginal imports are distributed in the same proportion as total imports and the marginal propensity to import is equal to the average propensity and the degree of openness:

$$m = \frac{M_A}{Y_A} = \frac{\partial M_A}{\partial Y_A} = \frac{\alpha_1 M_A + \alpha_2 M_A}{Y_A} = \alpha_1 \frac{\partial M_A}{\partial Y_A} + \alpha_2 \frac{\partial M_A}{\partial Y_A}. \tag{3.2a}$$

Writing for $\partial \text{BA}/\partial Y_A = \text{BA}_Y$, we have

$$P_1 \cdot \text{BA}_Y = \alpha_1 m; \qquad P_2 \cdot \text{CA}_Y = \alpha_2 m. \tag{3.2b}$$

In general, variations in the trade balance depend on two relative price variables and on effective demand in the three countries. We assume Y_B and Y_C as constants. Bloc floating implies that the real exchange rate P_1 between country A and B is fixed, so that relative prices between the two countries are invariant (domestic prices are assumed constant), while the exchange rate to C can move to accomplish the adjustment required to keep fundamental equilibrium. Therefore, A and B form a currency bloc, and the exchange rate P_2 represents the floating rate between two anchor currencies. We will deal with the result of the fixed rate regime within the bloc for the peripheral country B in the next chapter. Here we focus on the consequences for the floating key currencies. Clearly, the impact of a variation of P_2 on the trade balance is small when the share of trade denominated in the flexible exchange rate (α_2) is small. This implies that in order to adjust the real effective exchange rate to the level required by fundamental equilibrium, the flexible exchange rate has to vary by the factor of $1/\alpha_2$.[2] With $0 < \alpha_2 < 1$, P_2 will fluctuate more than the REER or 'the' exchange rate in a two-country floating rate model where $\alpha_2 = 1$. In other words, the larger the regional currency zone (α_1), the larger the required change in the flexible bilateral exchange rate (P_2) will be.

In order to show the impact of bloc floating on the economy's equilibrium, we will now determine the response of the trade balance to a change in relative prices. Differentiating Equation (3.1a) yields:[3]

$$T^A_{P_2} = \frac{\partial T^A}{\partial P_2} = \text{AC}_{P_2} - \text{CA} - P_2 \cdot \text{CA}_{P_2} = \alpha_2 M_A(\varepsilon_{C/A} + \varepsilon_{A/C} - 1). \tag{3.3a}$$

A rise in the relative price of imports from country C, that is, a depreciation of A's currency, will improve the trade balance, provided the Marshall–Lerner condition ($\varepsilon_{C/A} + \varepsilon_{A/C} - 1 > 0$) is fulfilled. However, the impact depends also on the trade weight α_2.

Assuming income in countries B and C constant (no repercussion effects), we have the trade balance effect of a domestic expenditure shift:

$$T_Y^A = \frac{\partial T^A}{\partial Y} = -m. \tag{3.3b}$$

External balance requires a target value. In its simplest form, assuming no foreign assets, external balance implies $T^A = 0$. Williamson (1991) objects to this on the grounds that countries may benefit from exporting or importing capital over long periods. External balance then reflects a target value T^* which may change over time but is constrained by the inter-temporal budget constraint (Frenkel and Razin 1996). Hence, treating Y_B, Y_C and P_1 as constants, we have the external balance in the implicit function form:

$$\text{EB:} \quad T(Y_A, P_2, \alpha_2) - T^* = 0. \tag{3.4}$$

The policy parameter T^* determines the position of the external balance equilibrium curve in the (P_2, Y)-space, not its slope. Under bloc floating, the required adjustment by P_2 to an exogenous demand shock in A is:

$$\left. \frac{\mathrm{d}P_2}{\mathrm{d}Y} \right|_{EB} = -\frac{T_Y^A}{T_{P_2}^A} = \frac{m}{\alpha_2 M_A \left(\varepsilon_{C/A} + \varepsilon_{A/C} - 1 \right)}. \tag{3.4a}$$

As is well known, the external balance curve is upward sloping because higher domestic demand necessitates higher net exports to keep external balance. This requires devaluation. The larger the degree of openness (import propensity), and the lower the Marshall–Lerner effect is, the larger is the depreciation. In addition to these textbook results, the required price adjustment increases with the size of the pegged currency bloc, for the larger the trade bloc α_1, the smaller α_2 will be. A small, open economy that provides the anchor for a large currency bloc will require large changes in the flexible exchange rate in order to achieve external balance. In Chapter 2 we showed that the currency bloc around the DM has continuously increased since the late 1970s and hence the slope in Equation (3.4a) must have risen.

Table 3.2 gives some indication of possible parameter changes. The first two columns show the total import shares (m) for European Union (EU) countries. They have increased in all countries between 1963 and 1992 with the exception of Denmark. Columns 3 and 4 give the share of non-EU imports as a percentage of total imports, that is, the equivalent of α_2. This share has fallen everywhere, again with the exception of Denmark, on average by more than a third. Columns 5 and 6 give the ratio of m/α_2. Thus, assuming $M_A(\varepsilon_{C/A} + \varepsilon_{A/C} - 1)$ as constant, say 1, the slope of Equation (3.4a) would have increased by significant proportions between 1963 and 1992. Only in Denmark would the slope have flattened. One should keep in mind, however, that in a bloc floating regime only the anchor currency

Table 3.2 Import shares and change of slope

	Import share, m		Non-EU imports/ imports, α_2		m/α_2		Increase in percent
	1	*2*	*3*	*4*	*5 (1/3)*	*6 (2/4)*	*7*
	1963	*1997*	*1963*	*1997*	*1963*	*1997*	
B	34.54	59.91	33.33	25.08	1.04	2.39	130.5
DK	25.16	27.23	35.00	31.71	0.72	0.86	19.5
D	14.45	22.58	50.00	44.23	0.29	0.51	76.6
GR	9.63	16.00	37.50	28.69	0.26	0.56	117.2
E	7.53	20.90	50.00	35.26	0.15	0.59	293.5
F	10.10	19.51	52.44	39.14	0.19	0.50	158.7
IRL	30.00	61.79	25.00	43.09	1.20	1.43	19.5
I	11.09	18.90	52.86	42.58	0.21	0.44	111.5
NL	35.62	44.13	33.93	39.54	1.05	1.12	6.3
P	15.19	30.30	50.00	26.86	0.30	1.13	271.2
UK	14.57	22.54	69.84	47.88	0.21	0.47	125.7
EUR 11		12.03		39.11		0.31	
EUR 15	14.85	24.54	49.84	39.79	0.30	0.62	107.0

Source: European Commission and own calculations.

country will determine the external exchange rate (P_2) and not the peripheral countries within the bloc. We will return to this aspect in the next chapter.

Internal balance

Next we turn to the domestic goods market. Internal balance is defined as the equilibrium when aggregate planned spending by domestic residents (absorption) plus net exports (the trade balance) equal the highest level of incomes consistent with continued control of inflation (Williamson 1991). This equilibrium income therefore reflects the NAIRU (non-accelerating-inflation rate of unemployment). We will define the NAIRU and its determinants in greater detail in Chapter 8. Here we may simply state that the NAIRU reflects the equilibrium q in the investment function of the previous chapter.

$$\text{IB:}\quad E(Y_A) + T^A(Y_A, P_2, \alpha_2) - Y^* = 0. \tag{3.5}$$

We assume that aggregate spending by domestic residents (consumption plus investment) depends only on their income and not on relative prices, with the marginal propensity to spend on domestic goods:[4]

$$1 > \frac{\partial E}{\partial Y_A} = 1 - s > 0$$

and the target NAIRU income as Y^*. However, effective income Y_A is determined by monetary and fiscal policies. For example, a cut in interest rates would raise q

and stimulate investment and consumption.[5] Alternatively, budget policy could expand or restrict demand. An increase in the target income Y^* (because of population growth, for example) would require an accommodative fiscal/monetary policy stance. Inversely, if Y^* fell, for instance due to lower productivity or a slow down in population growth, more restrictive expenditure policies would be required to maintain internal balance. The impact of a given policy measure on internal balance depends on whether the initial position of the economy is in equilibrium and on the behaviour of the NAIRU. In this chapter we focus on the anchor country, which is free to set its external exchange rate in accordance with fundamental equilibrium requirements. In the next chapter we will look at peripheral countries, which do not have this option because they peg to the anchor currency.

Under bloc floating, the internal balance has the slope

$$\left.\frac{dP_2}{dY}\right|_{IB} = -\frac{1 - s - m}{\alpha_2 M_A (\varepsilon_{C/A} + \varepsilon_{A/C} - 1)} \tag{3.5a}$$

which takes all the load of adjustment. It is downward sloping as a lower (less competitive) real exchange rate reduces net exports and has to be offset by higher spending to keep output constant. Again bloc floating amplifies the required price adjustment effect, although a high degree of openness (m) mitigates this impact. Thus, *ceteris paribus*, the internal balance curve is flatter when the saving propensity or the degree of openness is high, that is, when the propensity to spend on domestic goods is low. The larger the currency bloc, the steeper it is. Table 3.2 shows the simulated increase in the slope if $s = 0$.

Fundamental equilibrium

Figure 3.1 shows the locus of points compatible with internal balance on the IB-line. Above the IB-line, demand exceeds supply and inflationary pressures prevail; below the line a demand deficiency causes unemployment. External balance is drawn by the EB-line. Above the EB-curve, the trade balance is higher (surplus) than the target rate.

Full macroeconomic balance is achieved at the intersection of both curves, determining the fundamental equilibrium exchange rate $(\bar{P}_2)^6$ at the equilibrium income level $(\bar{Y})$. Below $\bar{P}_2$ the exchange rate is overvalued and if it could not be devalued, the policy choice would be between unemployment or current account deficit. Above $\bar{P}_2$, the real exchange rate is too competitive, and the choice is between inflation or trade surpluses (or a combination of both). By adjusting the real exchange rate, this policy dilemma of demand management can be solved and fundamental equilibrium achieved.[7]

In terms of our discussion in the previous chapter, the FEER is the exchange rate where investors' portfolios are in balance, with $q_i = \bar{q}_i / i = N, B, C$, so that

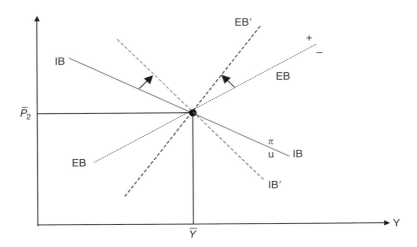

Figure 3.1 Fundamental equilibrium.

neither investment in tradables, nor non-tradables, nor securities are preferred. In Williamson's (1994) interpretation of normative FEERs, the IB-curve would shift with changes in the NAIRU-compatible income level (Y^*), possibly because of labour market developments. The EB-line would shift with a change in terms-of-trade or current account targets (T^*).[8] Either way, FEERs are neither constant nor equal to one, as postulated by purchasing power parity.[9] Assume, for example, that the domestic labour force increases. Output must be raised to maintain full employment and this shifts the IB-curve upwards, because a less restrictive fiscal/monetary policy mix is needed for internal balance. The external balance curve stays in place, however, so that the new equilibrium is found at the new intersection with a higher P_2, that is, after a real depreciation.[10] In a similar fashion, a change in the trade balance objective would shift the EB-curve and therefore the FEER.

It is clear that the size of the real exchange rate adjustment will depend on the slope of the IB and EB curves. But under bloc floating, the steepness of these curves is a function of the size of the currency blocs. Equations (3.4a) and (3.5a) show that the higher these slopes are, the smaller the trade share α_2 is. This is shown in Figure 3.1 by the punctuated IB' and EB' curves. If P_1 is fixed and only P_2 is free to adjust, the latter has to move more in order to produce the same effect. Thus, any change in non-inflationary equilibrium income, terms-of-trade or current account targets will require a higher rate of change in the FEER, that is, a higher fundamental depreciation. Bloc floating increases the movements in the equilibrium exchange rate.

This is formally shown by the simultaneous satisfaction of the internal and external balance equilibrium Equations (3.4) and (3.5). Both equations having continuous derivatives, the system satisfies the conditions of the implicit-function theorem with the Jacobian:[11]

$$J = \begin{vmatrix} 1 - s - m & \alpha_2(\varepsilon_{A/C} + \varepsilon_{C/A} - 1) \\ -m & \alpha_2(\varepsilon_{A/C} + \varepsilon_{C/A} - 1) \end{vmatrix} = \alpha_2(1 - s)(\varepsilon_{A/C} + \varepsilon_{C/A} - 1) > 0 \quad (3.6)$$

After totally differentiating Equations (3.4) and (3.5) and keeping either Y^* or T^* constant we obtain the two sets of solutions:

$$\left.\frac{dP_2}{dT^*}\right|_{Y^*=\text{constant}} = \frac{1 - s - m}{\alpha_2(1 - s)(\varepsilon_{C/A} + \varepsilon_{A/C} - 1)}; \quad \left.\frac{dY}{dT^*}\right|_{Y^*=\text{constant}} = \frac{1}{1 - s}. \quad (3.7)$$

$$\left.\frac{dP_2}{dY^*}\right|_{T^*=\text{constant}} = \frac{m}{\alpha_2(1 - s)(\varepsilon_{A/C} + \varepsilon_{C/A} - 1)}; \quad \left.\frac{dY}{dY^*}\right|_{T^*=\text{constant}} = \frac{1}{1 - s}. \quad (3.8)$$

Thus, not surprisingly, an increase in either of the two target variables Y^* or T^* will raise equilibrium income $(\overline{Y})$ by the multiplier effect $(1/1 - s)$.[12] However, the price-effect depends on the degree of openness (m) and on the size of currency bloc $(\alpha_2 = 1 - \alpha_1)$. *Ceteris paribus*, an increase in the current account target (T^*), requires a higher increase in $\bar{P}_2$ (a higher equilibrium devaluation) if the trade-share with the own currency bloc is high. Given the small volume of foreign trade that is transacted in flexible exchange rates, the price-channel would have to work harder in order to achieve the same numbers. The same applies to an increase in NAIRU-compatible income (Y^*). Furthermore, we have seen in the last chapter that the currency bloc around the DM has grown over time. Our model shows that this must have made the external exchange rate of the DM more volatile. If the size of the currency bloc around P_1 increases, that is, $\Delta\alpha_2 < 0$, the required adjustment in the flexible exchange rate P_2 accelerates at the rate:

$$\left.\frac{\partial_2 \bar{P}_2}{\partial T^* \partial \alpha_2}\right|_{Y^*=\text{constant}} = \frac{-(1 - s - m)}{(1 - s)(\varepsilon_{A/C} + \varepsilon_{C/A} - 1)\alpha_2^2}. \quad (3.9a)$$

$$\left.\frac{\partial_2 \bar{P}_2}{\partial T^* \partial \alpha_2}\right|_{Y^*=\text{constant}} = \frac{-m}{(1 - s)(\varepsilon_{A/C} + \varepsilon_{C/A} - 1)\alpha_2^2}. \quad (3.9b)$$

The size of the required adjustment of the flexible exchange rate grows[13] as a quadratic function of the size of the currency bloc. This proves formally that bloc floating renders the fundamental equilibrium exchange rate more volatile.

We now have an important result: the increased exchange rate stability *within* the currency bloc comes with the trade-off of higher instability *between* the currency blocs. I call this the *enlarging effect* of bloc floating on the equilibrium exchange rate.

Analytically, this is a new phenomenon. The literature on foreign exchange rates has focused on overshooting and magnification effects. *Overshooting*, first formalised by Dornbusch (1976), describes a temporary deviation by the nominal exchange rate from the long-term equilibrium exchange rate, which is due to rapid adjustment in financial markets and sticky goods prices. The *magnification effect* (Bilson 1979) shows that the nominal exchange rate will respond more than proportionately to a change in money supply if today's monetary policy stance creates expectations of further increases in money supply in the future. The *enlarging effect* described here in a bloc floating model is of a different order: it enlarges the effect of the variation in the *equilibrium* exchange rate, rather than the observed exchange rate.

Exchange rate dynamics

So far, our analysis has been conducted in comparative–static terms. We can now also show the dynamic time path of the equilibrium exchange rate. We will continue to assume the trade share α_2 as exogenously given. From Equations (3.7) and (3.8) we obtain the total differential[14]

$$dP_2 = \frac{b_1}{\alpha_2}dT^* + \frac{b_2}{\alpha_2}dY^*,$$ (3.10)

where

$$b_1 = \frac{1 - s - m}{(1 - s)(\varepsilon_{C/A} + \varepsilon_{A/C} - 1)}$$

and

$$b_2 = \frac{m}{(1 - s)(\varepsilon_{C/A} + \varepsilon_{A/C} - 1)}.$$

In discrete time this can be written as:

$$\bar{P}_t = \bar{P}_{t-1} + \frac{b_1}{\alpha_2}\Delta T_t^* + \frac{b_2}{\alpha_2}\Delta Y_t^*.$$ (3.10a)

To solve this first order difference equation we need to specify rules for the variations of the trade balance target (ΔT_t^*) and the non-inflationary income target (ΔY_t^*). Williamson (1994) discusses the basic principle for choosing current account targets, based on savings availability and investment levels, the sustainability of imbalances and international consistency. Current account targets change over time and are determined by short- and long-term considerations. A simple way to model this is to explain the shift in targets by a deterministic (long-term) trend and an irregular term. Similarly, the deterministic trend of internal balance may reflect the rate of growth of the labour force (n) and the irregular term business cycle proxies like output gaps, capacity utilisation or simply a difference between q and $\bar{q}$.[15] Thus:

$$\Delta T_t^* = T_0 + \varepsilon_{Tt} \quad \text{with Var}(\Delta Y_t^*) = \sigma_T^2, \tag{3.11a}$$

$$\Delta Y_t^* = n + \varepsilon_{Yt} \quad \text{with Var}(\Delta Y_t^*) = \sigma_Y^2. \tag{3.11b}$$

with T_0 as the deterministic rate of change of the trade balance and n the growth of labour force. We assume that ε_{Tt} and ε_{Yt} are two uncorrelated white noise processes. T_0 would be equal to zero when long-term policy objectives remain invariant, say a zero trade balance. If the foreign debt service is growing, the trade balance has to rise ($T_0 > 0$) in order to ensure sustainability of the external debt. When it is falling, T_0 may become negative, but there is no need. ε_{T_t} and ε_{Y_t} can also be interpreted as policy fine-tuning.

Inserting Equations (3.11a) and (3.11b) into (3.10a) yields the equilibrium exchange rate as a random walk plus drift:

$$\bar{P}_{2_t} = \bar{P}_{2_{t-1}} + \frac{b_1}{\alpha_2} T_0 + \frac{b_2}{\alpha_2} n + \frac{b_1}{\alpha_2} \varepsilon_{T_t} + \frac{b_2}{\alpha_2} \varepsilon_{Y_t}. \tag{3.10b}$$

The variance of the shifts in the equilibrium exchange rate is:

$$\text{Var}(\overline{dP_2}) = \text{E}\left[\overline{dP_2} - \text{E}(\overline{dP_2})\right]^2 = \frac{b_1^2}{\alpha_2^2}\sigma_T^2 + \frac{b_2^2}{\alpha_2^2}\sigma_Y^2 = \overline{\sigma_2^2}. \tag{3.10'}$$

Thus, the variance of the shifts in the equilibrium rate of depreciation is highly dependant on the size of the currency bloc. The larger the bloc (α_1), the higher is the uncertainty about the 'right' equilibrium rate, *ceteris paribus*. If its size changes over time, the variance is not constant, although we have assumed σ_T^2 and σ_Y^2 as constant (white noise). This analysis provides us with a testable link to observed exchange rate variations. When the trade share α_2 falls, then we may observe an increase not only in $\overline{\sigma_2^2}$, but also in σ_2^2. In other words, not only the volatility of the equilibrium exchange rate increases, but also the variance of the observable real exchange rate rises, because the risk measure of market rates cannot permanently remain below the risk measure of the equilibrium rate. But given that the reduction in α_2 is a result of a previous increase in the volatility of the exchange rate, today's variance becomes conditional on past variances. Therefore, a GARCH model should pick up our theory, as we will recall in the next section.

Given the initial condition $\bar{P}_0$, the general solution for the time-path of the equilibrium exchange rate is:

$$\bar{P}_2(t) = \bar{P}_0 + \frac{b_1 T_0 + b_2 n}{\alpha_2} t + \frac{b_1}{\alpha_2} \sum_{i=1}^{t} \varepsilon_{T_t} + \frac{b_2}{\alpha_2} \sum_{i=1}^{t} \varepsilon_{Y_t}. \tag{3.10c}$$

Hence, the behaviour of the equilibrium exchange rate is partly determined by the linear deterministic trend, partly by two stochastic trends. The linear time trend depends not only on the two policy objectives T_0 and n, but also on the trade share α_2. The smaller this structural parameter, that is, the larger the currency bloc, the larger the time drift of the equilibrium exchange rate is. Thus, if a country with a growing labour force needs to improve its trade balance in the long run (T_0, $n > 0$), there is not only a deterministic trend for the equilibrium exchange rate to depreciate, but the depreciation will also be more rapid for a country that provides the anchor for a currency bloc. This may have been the case for the US over the last ten years. On the other hand, if intra-bloc trade balances yield a surplus, say because the anchor currency is undervalued within the bloc, then $T_0 < 0$ in order to achieve external balance. The flexible equilibrium exchange rate will have a tendency to appreciate, if labour force growth is low. This could explain the long-term behaviour of the DM–dollar rate under the European Monetary System (EMS).

If it is clear that the deterministic time trend dominates the time path in the long run, it is also true that it can be clouded by the stochastic trend (Enders 1995: 170). Each short-term policy shock, whether related to internal or external balance objectives, has permanent effects on the mean of $\overline{P}_2(t)$. However, the impact of these accumulated white noise policy shocks on the equilibrium exchange rate are amplified by bloc floating because of the structural parameters b_1/α_2 and b_2/α_2 which are higher, the larger the currency bloc.

A number of empirical studies have found that a simple random walk predicts flexible exchange rates better than structural models (Frankel 1993: 111–15). Our model is consistent with such findings, even if we have included a drift, because the deterministic part may itself change at discretionary intervals. We could, for example, explain the dollar strength of the early 1980s by the fact that US policy seemed to have had an implicit current account target (induced by the high budget deficits) that was considerably lower than in the previous years: the current account fell from a surplus of 0.3 per cent of GNP in 1981 to a deficit of 2.9 per cent in 1985. Such a development would have implied a negative T_0 for this period. After the Plaza Agreement in 1985 it became clear that objectives had changed and the dollar started to depreciate again ($T_0 > 0$).

Our Equation (3.10c) also explains the poor performance of models where a stable fundamental exchange rate is supposed to work as an attractor. This can be shown by looking at conditional forecasts. The forecast function of our equilibrium exchange rate s periods ahead is:

$$\overline{P}_{2_{t+s}} = \overline{P}_{2_t} + \frac{b_1 T_0 + b_2 n}{\alpha_2} s + \frac{b_1}{\alpha_2} \sum_{i=1}^{s} \varepsilon_{T_{t+i}} + \frac{b_2}{\alpha_2} \sum_{i=1}^{s} \varepsilon_{Y_{t+i}}. \tag{3.12}$$

Under rational expectations when $\mathrm{E}(\varepsilon_{T_t}) = \mathrm{E}(\varepsilon_{Y_t}) = 0$, the equilibrium rate after s periods would be:

$$\mathrm{E}(\overline{P}_{2_{t+s}}) = \overline{P}_{2_t} + \frac{b_1 T_0 + b_2 n}{\alpha_2} s,$$

however, the forecast error is[16]

$$e_s = \overline{P}_{2_{t+s}} - E(\overline{P}_{2_{t+s}}) = \frac{b_1}{\alpha_2} \sum_{i=0}^{s} \varepsilon_{T_{t+i}} + \frac{b_2}{\alpha_2} \sum_{i=0}^{s} \varepsilon_{Y_{t+i}}$$

(3.13)

and its variance

$$\sigma_e^2 \equiv E(e_s^2) = s \left[\left(\frac{b_1}{\alpha_2} \right)^2 \sigma_T^2 + \left(\frac{b_2}{\alpha_2} \right)^2 \sigma_Y^2 \right] = s\overline{\sigma}_2^2.$$

(3.13a)

Thus, the standard error for the forecast

$$\sigma_e = \sqrt{s} \left(\frac{b_1}{\alpha_2} \cdot \sigma_T + \frac{b_2}{\alpha_2} \sigma_Y \right)$$

(3.13b)

is not constant but increases with the square root of the forecast period. The longer the future time horizon, the less certain the level of the equilibrium exchange rate is. However, this uncertainty is amplified by bloc floating which enlarges the variance of the equilibrium depreciations/appreciations due to the impact of the standard deviations related to policy changes. Thus, our model provides both a rational explanation for opacity ranges around the fundamental equilibrium that De Grauwe (1989) explained by limited rationality, and for megaswings between key currencies as a consequence of the enlarging impact of short- and long-term policy adjustments. One important policy conclusion must be that the volatility of flexible exchange rates will depend crucially on the steadiness of internal and external policy objectives. The smaller σ_T^2 and σ_Y^2 are, the better the forseeability of the fundamental equilibrium exchange rate will be. This is a strong argument in favour of international policy co-ordination.

We can now also refer back to Chapter 2 and observe the impact of bloc floating on trade and investment. We have seen that investment in tradables requires a risk premium ρ to cover for exchange rate uncertainty. In Table 2.5 this risk premium for the flexible exchange rate was defined as $\rho_2 = \vartheta m \alpha_2 \sigma_2^2$. If economic agents had perfect knowledge, they would be able to derive the equilibrium exchange rate $\overline{P}_2$ and deduct the required appreciation/depreciation. However, they would also take into account the short-term policy adjustments and conclude that the volatility of the equilibrium exchange rate needs to be covered by a minimum or equilibrium risk premium:

$$\overline{\rho_{2_s}} = \vartheta m \alpha_2 \overline{\sigma}_2^2 = \frac{\vartheta m}{\alpha_2} s (b_1^2 \sigma_T^2 + b_2^2 \sigma_Y^2).$$

(3.14)

Thus, investment is biased towards short-term projects because the risk premium is lower for shorter forecast periods (s). *Ceteris paribus*, the larger the currency zone, the higher the minimal risk premium is. But given that the intra-bloc risk premium

ρ_1 is zero, a high ρ_2 must put a break on long-term investment and trade between country A and C. Thus, bloc floating does not only increase the volatility among key-currencies, but it also makes the blocs increasingly insular.[17]

We may conclude that the phenomenon of bloc floating has negative repercussions all over the world by raising required returns due to greater exchange rate uncertainty, and that it leads to lower investment and reduced growth. The paradox is that the larger the uncertainty, the larger the incentive is to reduce risk by choosing to peg one's currency to an anchor – which will further increase uncertainty in the world.

Empirical evidence

What evidence can we find for our model? Economic development in the world has been dominated by two large currency blocs around the dollar and the DM, while the Japanese yen did not attract smaller currencies as a pegging anchor.[18] Empirical confirmation for the theoretical considerations in the section on enlarging effects of blocfloating and the section on Exchange rate dynamics focuses on the questions: is there evidence of currency blocs and can we find indicators for increased exchange rate risk and volatility?

As we pointed out in the first section of Chapter 2, the emergence of currency blocs has been well documented (Frankel and Wei 1992, 1993, 1995 and Bénassy-Quéré 1995, 1997, 1999). It is not only clear that exchange rate variability is lower within regional groupings than across groups, but also that the trade-weighted share of currency blocs has changed. In particular the DM-bloc has doubled in size during the existence of the EMS. Frankel and Wei have shown that international trade is biased toward intra-regional partners, which is consistent with our model. However, based on their cross-country studies, they detected only a limited and diminishing impact of exchange rate variability on trade volume (1995). Rana (1981) found that volatility had negative effects on import volumes in the case of South Korea, Taiwan and the Philippines. Kenen and Rodrik (1986) used time series to find that in seven of eleven industrialised countries, volatility terms had the expected negative impact on imports, with statistically significant values for the United States, Canada, Germany and the UK, that is, four currencies that were freely floating. Furthermore, their volatility coefficients were substantially higher than those for domestic activity and in most cases higher than the log of the real effective exchange rate index. The evidence indicates that exchange rate volatility matters to trade, although it is not clear how much. However, a methodological handicap of many studies on trade and exchange risk might be their level of aggregation.[19] In order to get a clearer picture, one could regress time series of intra-bloc trade on the intra-bloc effective exchange rate and its volatility and trade-flows with the rest of the world on the external exchange rate. This remains a research project for the future.

Ideally, one would also look at investment and growth rather than trade as the relevant macroeconomic variables. Furthermore, the relevant group of goods are tradables and not trade itself. Given the complexities of determining these variables, one may focus on exchange rate volatility directly. Can we detect confirmation of bloc floating effects in indicators of volatility?

Figure 3.2 shows the dollar/DM exchange rate and Figure 3.3 the evolution of the Nominal Effective Exchange Rates (NEERs) for the three main economies. The dramatic shift in the exchange rate regime in the early 1970s is evident with respect to the dollar. The dollar depreciated after the end of Bretton Woods in 1971 until the early 1980s. It then appreciated again excessively, until this was corrected after the Plaza Agreement in 1985. The US-NEER only stabilised after the Louvre accord in 1987 (see Dominquez and Frankel 1993). The Japanese yen appreciated with high volatility until it reached its peak in 1995. Compared to these two currencies Germany's NEER is remarkably stable: it exhibits a long-term trend to revalue, but it is less volatile both in the short term and the long term. This is supported by Figure 3.4, which compares US and German NEER volatility. It is visually obvious, that German exchange rate volatility (here measured as the monthly rate of change of the NEER) exceeded the American before the creation of the EMS. Thereafter, Germany's NEER stabilised as expected. Similar results are obtained if one compares the real effective exchange rates of these three countries (see Collignon 1999 for details).

We may also compare Germany's overall performance with that of its effective exchange rate within the currency bloc. As a proxy we can use the index for the external value of the DM as published by the Bundesbank.

Figure 3.5 shows the nominal effective exchange rate with respect to eighteen industrialised countries, fourteen EU members and the participants of the ERM. It is interesting that through all of the 1970s, that is, before the EMS-era, Germany's nominal effective exchange rate with respect to eighteen industrialised countries

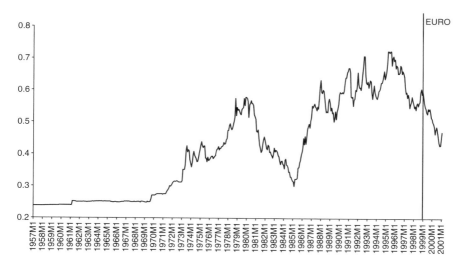

Figure 3.2 US dollar/DM exchange rate.
Source: IMF (1999).

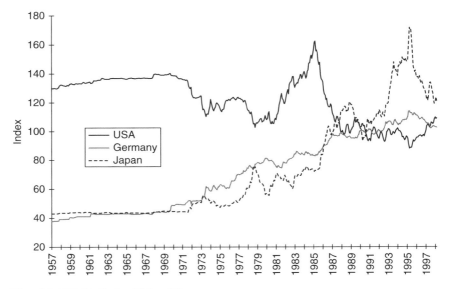

Figure 3.3 NEERs (Index 1985 = 100).

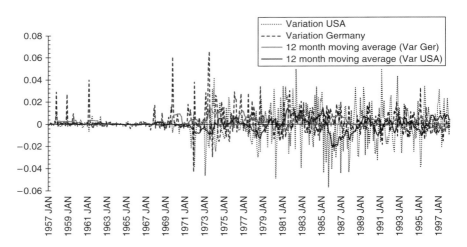

Figure 3.4 NEER volatility (USA versus Germany).

was qualitatively not distinct from its intra-European exchange rate. However, with the creation of the EMS in 1979–80, the external value indicators diverge. As expected, the NEER for eighteen countries follows more closely, although not exactly, the pattern of the dollar–DM exchange rate. It is also evident that, at least

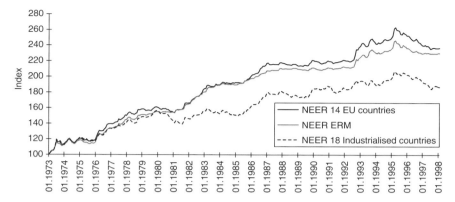

Figure 3.5 NEER Germany (Index 1973 = 100).
Source: Bundesbank.

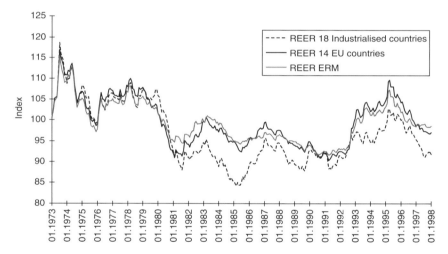

Figure 3.6 REER Germany (Index 1973 = 100).
Source: Bundesbank.

until the EMS-crisis in 1992–3, the intra-bloc rate was less volatile than the larger NEER for eighteen countries. The appreciation of the DM against European currencies has been larger than against other currencies, reflecting the continuing inflation differentials in Europe, which required more (early 1980s) or less (1987–92) frequent realignments. However, in terms of competitiveness, the DM-strength was not a handicap within Europe.

The real exchange rate (Figure 3.6) indicates for most of the EMS-period (i.e. after 1983) an improvement of German competitiveness compared to its partners and a fairly stable range with respect to its international competitors. These trends have only changed after German unification and the EMS-crisis (1992–3). However, since the REER for all industrialised countries includes Europe, the line *understates* the volatility and trends of the external exchange rate outside the bloc. Thus, the stability of the intra-European rate in the second half of the 1980s has protected German industry against the rapid depreciation of the dollar (compare Germany against Japan in Figure 3.3). The time series reveal a significant shift in volatility after the creation of the EMS. In Collignon (1999), I have measured volatility of the REER for Germany, USA and Japan by the standard deviation of the monthly rate of change and by the excess kurtosis of the deviation from the mean. Both are valid measures for exchange risk, the first giving an average deviation, the second estimating the probability of outliers. I have repeated this exercise here for Germany's NEER over the same periods (Table 3.3). It is obvious that the volatility within the currency bloc is significantly lower after 1978 than with respect to all trading partners. The ERM-crisis in 1992–3 does disturb this relative tranquillity temporarily. While the standard deviation of the monthly variation in the exchange rate was approximately equal over the three series before 1978 and fell only marginally thereafter for the German overall-REER, it fell significantly with respect to other ERM-members and was less than half of total REER volatility in the second half of the 1980s. However, in the early 1990s, after the breakdown of the ERM, volatility picked up again (see Table 3.3).

I have put forward the hypothesis that bloc floating increases the volatility in the fundamental equilibrium of the bilateral floating exchange rate and simultaneously reduces the volatility of the effective exchange rate. The problem with empirical verification is that we are unable to observe the equilibrium rate directly. Furthermore, as Barrel *et al.* (1998) show, deviations of observable spot rates from

Table 3.3 Volatility of German NEER

	Δln all	Δln EU	Δln ERM		
Average					
03/1974–10/1978	−0.000662	−0.000667	−0.000942		
11/1978–02/1985	−0.002939	−0.001719	−0.001342		
03/1985–04/1990	0.001386	−0.000292	−0.000413		
05/1990–05/1995	0.001509	0.002484	−0.002169		
Standard deviation				*EU/all*	*ERM/all*
01/03/1974–10/1978	0.012574	0.011988	0.012201	0.95340	0.97034
11/1978–02/1985	0.010407	0.008335	0.006434	0.80090	0.61824
03/1985–04/1990	0.008358	0.005766	0.003796	0.68988	0.45418
05/1990–05/1995	0.009575	0.009269	0.007518	0.96804	0.78517
Excess kurtosis					
01/03/1974–10/1978	−0.431606	−0.015956	0.405638		
11/1978–02/1985	0.446112	1.356002	2.303170		
03/1985–04/1990	−0.341735	−0.201509	1.029385		
05/1990–05/1995	0.407971	2.529915	2.592452		

Source: Bundesbank data.

calculated FEERs persist. The previous section has developed a theory explaining the link between observable exchange rates and FEERs. In Collignon (1999), I have tested a GARCH-model of the REER for Germany, USA and Japan for the period from January 1973 to April 1996. It implies that the mean forecasting error in the effective exchange rate is zero in the long run, but its variance is conditional on the past. If the regional currency bloc is large, the forecasting error in the effective exchange rate for a given period should be lower if the bloc is small, given that the peg conditions expectations. However, if the size of the bloc varies, the conditional variance should rise with rising bloc size. The results are consistent with our theory: the coefficient by which forecasting errors affect the variance of real effective exchange rates are lowest for Germany (0.026), highest for Japan (0.104), and in between for the USA (0.0889). Inversely, the coefficients for the conditional volatility are 0.948 for Germany, 0.7643 for Japan and 0.841 for USA. This conforms to the fact that the currency bloc is largest for Germany, non-existent for Japan, and in between for USA.

These observations are consistent with the hypothesis derived from bloc floating theory, although they are not sufficient to 'prove' positively a bloc floating effect. Further research could be done by directly regressing the change in currency bloc shares on volatility indicators.[20]

Summary and conclusion

Chapter 2 showed that the emergence of regional currency blocs could be explained by the combination of risk-averse private investors maximising their wealth, and public authorities maximising aggregate investment. By pegging their currency to an anchor, they reduce exchange rate risk within the currency bloc and with respect to their effective exchange rate. This will stimulate private investment. However, this chapter has revealed that the conscious policies of *reducing* national exchange rate volatility pursued by many small countries may have produced the 'undesigned' result of *increasing* exchange rate risk between the floating key currencies in the world.[21] Our model showed the mechanism that creates the trade-off between intra-bloc stability and inter-bloc volatility. Although 'hard' statistical proof is difficult to obtain given the lack of counterfactual evidence, empirical evidence does concur with the hypotheses derived from theory.

One important conclusion from our analysis is that European Monetary Union (EMU) will transform the fundamental structure of the international monetary system, which has prevailed over the last quarter of a century. First of all, EMU is not a currency bloc: the Euro is a new and large currency, managed by a single, unified monetary authority. This eliminates exchange risk within Europe. Consequently, the size of the European currency bloc will fall: by integrating intra-European trade under one currency, relative world trade shares change. Intra-EU trade becomes domestic trade, thereby reducing the degree of openness of European economies. While on an average this degree was 24.8 per cent in 1997, the non-EU trade share was only 9.2 per cent of EU-11 GDP. Thus, the parameter m in Equations (3.7) and (3.8) would be more than halved for the EU. From

Equation (3.14) we also know that a reduction in the degree of openness would reduce excess returns required to compensate for the exchange risk impact. This would lower $\bar{q}$ in our investment function. In addition, one should expect that the larger and deeper financial euro-market will also structurally lower interest rates.[22] Both effects taken together will stimulate investment, launching a new growth process.

Secondly, with the subtraction of intra-EU trade from world trade, total recorded world trade will fall and European relative trade shares will get redistributed. Even if it is likely that other European countries, not participating in EMU, will peg their currencies to the euro, the euro-bloc will certainly be smaller than the previous DM-bloc. Therefore α_2 for EMU should be substantially higher (α_1 lower) than it used to be for Germany. As a consequence, the price effect for EMU's flexible exchange rate – especially the euro/dollar rate – should be lower and international exchange rate volatility should fall. However, for other countries nothing changes: Japan or the USA will still export the same volumes to the different regions in the world, although their relative shares in total world trade will increase. But now they deal with an integrated α_{EU} instead of separate portfolio shares for each European country. This will further reduce exchange rate risk for them and open opportunities for increased returns from trade with Europe. Thus, the structural effects from EMU are unambiguously positive for trade and investment. They will cause a structural reduction of exchange risk in the world economy.

What about shock-induced exchange rate volatility? Fundamental exchange rate volatility between the US dollar, the yen and the euro will depend on the net effect of internal and external balance shocks (see Equations (3.10) and (3.10c)). Their outcome is by nature uncertain. Due to the definition of b_1 and b_2, a reduction in Europe's degree of openness (m) will require *larger* exchange rate variations for the Euro-exchange rate in response to changing current account targets, but *less* variations because of changes in income and growth objectives. Thus, Europe may regain a degree of domestic policy autonomy, which it has presently lost. In other words, Europe becomes more autonomous from exchange rate movements and monetary policy will focus more on domestic interest rates. This will have important consequences for the domestic efficiency of monetary policy, as we will see in Chapter 5. But it could also lead to higher volatility between leading world currencies, and notably the dollar–euro exchange rate, if current account targets remain unco-ordinated. Therefore, a stable world economy would also require greater international co-operation after the start of EMU. 'Benign neglect' might be tempting from a domestic point of view, but it would be counterproductive internationally (see also Bergsten and Henning 1996).

4　The instability of the bloc
　　floating regime

Our analysis has so far focused on the tendency for increased volatility among currency blocs as a trade-off for lower volatility within the blocs. According to our model in Chapter 2, this tendency should logically lead to the complete bloc-regionalisation of the world economy. But this is not what we observe. The question therefore is: how far will the process of bloc clustering go? Or rather, what are the forces pulling in the opposite direction?

In a comment to a previous paper on bloc floating (Collignon 1999), Dornbusch raised the issue of the cost of giving away the exchange rate as a key adjustment instrument. This is of particular relevance for the small peripheral countries, and has been important in Optimum Currency Area (OCA) theory. In Chapter 3, we conducted the analysis in terms of the anchor countries, which did have control over the flexible exchange rate as an adjustment tool. Thus, P_2 could be used to achieve fundamental equilibrium, even if bloc floating required larger adjustment shifts. However, from the perspective of the peripheral country B, say Austria or France, the pegging strategy has a disadvantage: by fixing its exchange rate P_1 with A, country B reduces volatility and risk, thereby encouraging investment; but given that P_2 is determined between the two anchor countries A and C (say Germany and USA), the peripheral country has no control at all over the exchange rate as an adjustment tool, because the 'external' exchange rate between B and C is determined by the cross-rate of the two other exchange rates: $P_3 = P_1/P_2$.[1] This means that the adjustment in the exchange rate is dependent on the fundamental equilibrium in the anchor, not the peripheral, country. Thus, under bloc floating, there are three options available for country B:

1　to achieve a real depreciation by a lower rate of inflation, that is, by 'competitive disinflation';[2]
2　to cut the fixed peg and allow regular or irregular exchange-rate adjustments within the bloc;
3　not to adjust and pay the price of increasing fiscal deficits and rising unemployment. Obviously, combinations of these alternatives are possible.

Thus, the question is justified whether nothing is lost in signing away an exchange rate. We will return to this issue in subsequent chapters, especially to Dornbusch's suggestion that wage-price flexibility may make up for the loss in exchange flexibility. However, in this chapter we will look at the issues resulting from inflexible exchange rates for peripheral countries. We will demonstrate that under certain conditions, this inflexibility leads to a deflationary bias within the currency bloc. As a consequence, occasional adjustments are avoidable only under very special conditions and the inner consistency of a currency bloc is never as perfect as we assumed in our model. We will also show that a monetary union – as distinct from a currency bloc – will be able to overcome this dilemma.

The model

In order to present the logic of the argument, we will use a standard open economy model (McCallum 1989) for two countries (A and B) with a non-specified 'outside world' (C). The anchor-country (A), for example Germany, is free to conduct its monetary policy with the goal of stabilising domestic prices. As in previous chapters, the external exchange rate $(p_2)^3$ with respect to the outside world is flexible and adjusts endogenously. The peripheral country (B) pegs its exchange rate (p_1) to A's currency and subordinates its monetary policy to this purpose. Its 'external' exchange rate (p_3) is, therefore, exogenously determined between A and C. While we took the nominal interest rate in our previous model as exogenously given, we now determine it in the context of a standard IS-LM model. Furthermore, we will assume that A's long-term productive capacity is growing at a lower rate than B's, or, in order to simplify the mathematics, we will assume A's potential income to be constant, unless otherwise specified.[4]

We have the following set of equations:

$$y_{A_t} = a_{10} + a_{11}r_{A_t} + a_{12}p_{\alpha_t} + a_{13}g_A + \nu_{A_t},$$
$$a_{11} < 0, \quad a_{12} > 0, \quad a_{13} > 0, \tag{4.1a}$$

$$m_{A_t} - p_{A_t} = a_{20} + a_{21}y_{A_t} + a_{22}i_{A_t} + \varepsilon_{A_t}, \qquad a_{21} > 0, \quad a_{22} < 0, \tag{4.2a}$$

$$r_{A_t} = i_{A_t} - E_t(p_{A_{t+1}} - p_{A_t}) = i_{A_t} - E_t(\pi_A). \tag{4.3a}$$

$$p_{\alpha_t} = \alpha_1 p_1 + \alpha_2 p_2 = \alpha_1(p_{B_t} - p_{A_t} - e_{1_t}) + \alpha_2(p_{C_t} - p_{A_t} - e_{2_t}),$$
$$\alpha_1 + \alpha_2 = 1. \tag{4.4a}$$

$$i_{A_t} = i_{C_t} - E_t(e_{2_{t+1}} - e_{2_t}) = i_{C_t} - E_t(\delta_2). \tag{4.5a}$$

Equation (4.1a) shows effective demand in log terms in a slightly more sophisticated version than in Chapter 3. While we previously reduced all demand factors into Tobin's q, we now introduce separate determinants. Output is a function of real interest rates, 'the' real exchange rate and g_A stands for government net expenditure. ν_t reflects random movements in government spending and 'foreign' income as well as shocks in A's saving and investment behaviour.[5] We assume that A is small compared to C, so that C sets exogenously the nominal 'world' interest rate i_C, assumed to be constant. Thus, Equation (4.5a) is the interest parity relationship. r_{A_t} in

Equation (4.4a) is the real interest rate, dependent on the nominal interest rate i_A, and expected inflation (π_A).

Equation (4.4a) defines the real effective exchange rate, that is, the relative price of foreign goods. As before it is the trade-weighted average of the fixed and flexible real exchange rates, with p_A as the log of domestic money prices and p_B, p_C the foreign price levels. We assume p_C to be exogenously given. An increase in p_α, reflects improved international competitiveness for A (i.e. a depreciation of its real effective exchange rate). e_1, is the log of the nominal exchange rate ($e_{A/B}$) between country A and B and it is constant under a fixed peg. e_2, is the log of the flexible exchange rate between A and C ($e_{A/C}$). An increase in e_1 or e_2 (i.e. δ_1 or δ_2) reflects an appreciation in A's currency. Consequently the expected appreciation is deducted from the world interest rate in Equation (4.5a).

Equation (4.2) specifies the LM relationship with money demand (real money balances) as a function of transactions (y_A) and the nominal interest rate. Money supply is treated as being determined by the central bank. ε_t reflects random monetary shocks.

In addition to these definitions we will specify the supply side by A's full-employment long-term productive capacity $\bar{y}_A$, a constant. This is a normative definition, which could be derived from non-inflation-accelerating full employment of all productive capacities. It is not a supply function, which would describe the actual behaviour of economic agents.[6] Hence, we have the full employment equilibrium:

$$y_{A_t} = \bar{y}_{A_t}, \quad \text{with } \Delta\bar{y}_A = \bar{\gamma}_A = 0. \tag{4.6a}$$

By inserting Equations (4.3a), (4.4a) and (4.5a) into Equation (4.1a) and assuming Equation (4.6a) we obtain the equilibrium in A's goods market:

$$\bar{y}_A = a_{10} + a_{11}\left[i_C - E_t(e_{2_{t+1}} - e_{2_t}) - E_t(p_{A_{t+1}} - p_{A_t})\right]$$
$$+ a_{12}\left[\alpha_1(p_{B_t} - p_{A_t} - e_{1_t}) + \alpha_2(p_{C_t} - p_{A_t} - e_{2_t})\right] + a_{13}g_{A_t} + \nu_{A_t}. \tag{4.7a}$$

Similarly we obtain for the LM-function:

$$m_{A_t} - p_{A_t} = a_{20} + a_{21}\bar{y}_{A_t} + a_{22}\left[i_C - E_t(e_{2_{t+1}} - e_{2_t})\right] + \varepsilon_{A_t}. \tag{4.8a}$$

Given that $\bar{y}_A$, i_C, p_C, e_1, are set exogenously and that the policy variable m_A, is determined by A's central bank, Equations (4.7a) and (4.8a) describe a compact model for the two endogenous variables p_A, and e_2, that is, price-level behaviour and the dynamic exchange rate in country A.

In analogy we obtain for country B the following equations:

$$y_{B_t} = b_{10} + b_{11}r_{B_t} + b_{12}p_{\beta_t} + b_{13}g_{B_t} + \nu_{B_t}, \qquad b_{11} < 0, \quad b_{12} > 0, \quad b_{13} > 0, \tag{4.1b}$$

$$m_{B_t} - p_{B_t} = b_{20} + b_{21}y_{B_t} + b_{22}i_{B_t} + \varepsilon_{B_t}, \qquad b_{21} > 0, \quad b_{22} < 0, \tag{4.2b}$$

$$r_{B_t} = i_{B_t} - E_t(p_{B_{t+1}} - p_{B_t}) = i_{B_t} - E_t(\pi_{B_{t+1}}). \tag{4.3b}$$

However, the exchange rate dynamics are different. In our three-polar world, B has two exchange rates: e_{1_t} is the exchange rate by which B pegs to A's currency, which is a constant under bloc floating. The external exchange rate, e_{2_t}, with the rest of the world (C) is flexible, although exogenously given as the cross-rate of C's exchange rate with the anchor-currency A. Therefore in country B's system, it is not the exchange rate, but money supply, which is endogenously determined. This is the well-known phenomenon that monetary policy cannot be set 'exogenously' under fixed exchange rates.

However, financial markets may occasionally doubt the pegging commitment and expect a devaluation of B's currency. Therefore, the interest rate in B will have to carry a premium ρ_{B_t} to compensate for an expected devaluation – even if it never occurs. Hence:

$$i_{B_t} = i_{A_t} + \rho_{B_t}, \tag{4.5b}$$

and inserting Equation (4.5a) yields

$$i_{B_t} = i_C - E_t(\delta_2) + \rho_{B_t}. \tag{4.5b'}$$

$\delta_1 = e_{1_{t+1}} - e_{1_t}$ and $\delta_2 = e_{2_{t+1}} - e_{2_t}$ are the rate of nominal appreciation of A's currency. Therefore, $\delta_1 > 0$ reflects a depreciation of B's currency with respect to A, but under bloc floating e_{1_t} is a constant and $\delta_1 = 0$. Of course, if the pegging commitment is fully credible, $E_t(\delta_1) = \rho_{B_t} = 0$. Also $\delta_2 > 0$ would reflect an appreciation of B's currency with respect to C if it is pegged to A's currency.

The real effective exchange rate in B now depends on the trade-weighted average of the relative prices with respect to A and C. But the exchange rate with C is determined as the cross rate of p_1 and p_2, that is, the exchange rates between our peripheral country B with the anchor A and the inter-bloc rate between A and C ($p_3 = p_1 - p_2$). Hence:

$$\begin{aligned} p_{\beta_t} &= \beta_1(e_{1_t} + p_{A_t} - p_{B_t}) + \beta_2(e_{1_t} - e_{2_t} + p_{C_t} - p_{B_t}) \\ &= e_{1_t} - p_{B_t} + p_{A_t} + \beta_2(p_{C_t} - p_{A_t} - e_{2_t}) = \beta_2 p_{2_t} - p_{1_t}, \end{aligned} \tag{4.4b}$$

where β_1 is the import share of B from A and β_2 from C, and $\beta_1 + \beta_2 = 1$ as in the previous chapter. Furthermore, we assume that contrary to A, B's productive capacity increases over time with a constant growth rate $\bar{\gamma}_B$ according to

$$\Delta\bar{y}_{B_t} = \bar{\gamma}_B > \bar{\gamma}_A. \tag{4.6b}$$

Thus, $\bar{\gamma}_B$ is the rate of growth of productive capacity at full employment. We then obtain the two equilibrium equations:

$$\begin{aligned} \bar{\gamma}_B + \bar{y}_{B_{t-1}} &= b_{10} + b_{11}\left[i_C - E(e_{2_{t+1}} - e_{2_t}) + \rho_{B_t} - E_t(p_{B_{t+1}} - p_{B_t})\right] \\ &\quad + b_{12}[+e_{1_t} - p_{B_t} + p_{A_t} + \beta_2(p_{C_t} - p_{A_t} - e_{2_t})] \\ &\quad + b_{13}g_{B_t} + \nu_{B_t}, \end{aligned} \tag{4.7b}$$

$$m_{B_t} - p_{B_t} = b_{20} + b_{21}\bar{y}_{B_t} + b_{22}\left[i_{C_t} - E_t(e_{2_{t+1}} - e_{2_t}) + \rho_{B_t}\right] + \varepsilon_{B_t}. \tag{4.8b}$$

Given that monetary policy is determined by B's objective to stabilise its exchange rate with A, the monetary policy rule in B is

Rule B: $\delta_1 = e_{1_{t+1}} - e_{1_t} = 0.$

Since e_{2_t} is dependent on monetary policy in A, while i_C and p_C are exogenous, this system has the two endogenous variables: p_{B_t} and m_{B_t}. This reflects the structural asymmetry of bloc floating where the anchor country maintains its capacity to conduct national monetary policy, while the peripheral country must surrender its freedom to conduct an independent monetary policy for the sake of exchange rate stability.[7] In discussing the dynamics in the two countries, it is convenient to consider first, steady-state anticipated movements in p_{A_t}, p_{B_t}, e_{2_t}, m_{b_t} and then responses to random shocks.

The steady state

In order to demonstrate the consequences of a regime shift to monetary union, we will first analyse the steady-state dynamics under bloc floating and then under a unified monetary policy.

Steady state under bloc floating

Under steady-state assumptions we have: $\nu_{A,B_t} = 0$, $\varepsilon_{A,B_t} = 0$ and $E_t(\delta_1) = e_{1_{t+1}} - e_{1_t} = 0$. Capacity output in A grows at the rate $\Delta\bar{y}_A = \gamma_A = 0$ and in B at $\Delta\bar{y}_B = \bar{\gamma}_B > 0$. The money stock in A increases at the rate $\Delta m_{A_t} = \mu_A$, in B at $\Delta m_{B_t} = \mu_B$ and if world inflation proceeds at the constant rate $\Delta p_{C_t} = \mu_C$, then we also have $i_C = r_C + \mu_C$. Finally, the steady state implies correct anticipations, hence $E_t(e_{2_{t+1}} - e_{2_t}) = e_{2_{t+1}} - e_{2_t} = \delta_2$ and no accelerations in inflation or of exchange rate movements ($\Delta\pi = \Delta\delta = 0$). Also, the pegging commitment is credible: $\rho_B = 0$. For simplicity of notation we have here renamed the inflation rates $\Delta p_n = \pi_n$, $n = $ A, B, C and skip the time index.

By first differencing the two equilibrium Equations (4.7) and (4.8), we obtain:

$$\bar{\gamma}_A = a_{12}\left[\alpha_1(\pi_B - \pi_A - \delta_1) + \alpha_2(\pi_C - \pi_A - \delta_2)\right] + a_{13}\Delta g_A = 0, \qquad (4.9a)$$

$$\mu_A - \pi_A = a_{21}\bar{\gamma}_A = 0, \qquad (4.10a)$$

$$\bar{\gamma}_B = b_{12}\left[\delta_1 + \pi_A - \pi_B + \beta_2(\pi_C - \pi_A - \delta_2)\right] + b_{13}\Delta g_B > 0, \qquad (4.9b)$$

$$\mu_B - \pi_B = b_{21}\bar{\gamma}_B > 0. \qquad (4.10b)$$

Comparing Equations (4.9a) and (4.9b) reveals that the real exchange rate with the world outside the currency bloc has a similar effect on demand in the two countries; the precise impact depends on the relative trade share. However, the relative price structure between the two countries (P_1) is always of greater importance in the peripheral than in the anchor country. We will now make the fundamental assumption that the anchor country is committed to price stability. Therefore, we obtain from Equation (4.10a) the monetary policy rule:

Rule A: $\pi_A = \mu_A - \alpha_{21}\bar{\gamma}_A = 0,$

which implies $\mu_A = 0$ because $\bar{\gamma}_A = 0$.

This is the classic monetarist result in which inflation in A depends on the rate of money supply relative to potential output growth. In terms of our previous discussion, this means A has chosen a domestic nominal anchor. Given that $\gamma_A = 0$, money growth would be set to zero by A's central bank in order to retain price stability. As a consequence, the flexible exchange rate has to adjust to keep the economy in equilibrium. From Equation (4.9a) we derive:

$$\delta_2 = \pi_C + \frac{\alpha_1}{\alpha_2}\pi_B - \frac{1}{\alpha_2}\pi_A - \frac{\alpha_1}{\alpha_2}\delta_1 + \frac{a_{13}}{\alpha_2 a_{12}}\Delta g_A, \tag{4.11a}$$

which simplifies under steady-state bloc floating ($\delta_1 = 0$) with stable prices in A ($\pi_A = 0$) to:

$$\delta_2 = \pi_C + \frac{\alpha_1}{\alpha_2}\pi_B + \frac{a_{13}}{\alpha_2 a_{12}}\Delta g_A. \tag{4.11a'}$$

If A's commitment to price stability is higher than in the world economy (corrected by the impact of inflation from bloc neighbours), the value of its currency must appreciate.[8] The same is true for a loosening of the fiscal policy stance, since the currency appreciation must compensate for excess demand.

These are standard results. But bloc floating has a similar enlarging effect on the nominal equilibrium exchange rate, as we have analysed in the previous chapter with respect to fundamental equilibrium. The impact of public expenditure on the exchange rate increases with the size of intra-bloc integration as α_2 tends toward zero. Thus, under bloc floating fiscal policy, changes contribute to higher equilibrium exchange rate volatility than in a free-floating world. In addition, the rate of inflation in the peripheral bloc country (B) appreciates A's external exchange rate with the rest of the world (C). This effect is even stronger than the fiscal effect when the weight of the currency bloc grows, that is, as α_1 rises and α_2 falls. The reason is that a larger part of intra-bloc transactions require a larger external exchange rate appreciation if the internal real exchange rate depreciates because of higher inflation in neighbouring bloc-countries. This interesting result implies that the exchange rate dynamics between key currencies (say DM and USD) depend partly on inflation in non-key currency countries. Or, to put it differently, under bloc floating Italy's inflation caused an appreciation of the DM with respect to the dollar. For the peripheral (B), say Italy, this implies that a positive inflation differential above the anchor country (A) *appreciates* its own nominal effective exchange rate.[9] This is the opposite of what a two-country model would conclude.

Next we look at the steady-state dynamics in the peripheral country B. The endogenous variables in the system (4.9b) and (4.10b) are B's rate of inflation and money supply growth. The monetary policy rule in B is $\delta_1 = 0$.

From Equation (4.10b) we know that the endogenous steady-state rate of money supply in B is

$$\mu_B = b_{21}\overline{\gamma}_B + \pi_B. \tag{4.10b'}$$

The equilibrium rate of change in the price level is derived from Equation (4.9b) after inserting (4.11a)

$$\pi_B = \delta_1 - \pi_A - \frac{\beta_2 a_{13}}{a_{12}(\alpha_2 + \beta_2 - \alpha_2\beta_2)}\Delta g_A$$

$$+ \frac{\alpha_2}{b_{12}(\alpha_2 + \beta_2 - \alpha_2\beta_2)}(b_{13}\Delta g_B - \overline{\gamma}_B). \tag{4.11b}$$

Under bloc floating and assuming price stability in the anchor country we obtain:

$$\pi_B = \frac{\alpha_2 b_{13}}{b_{12}(\alpha_2 + \beta_2 - \alpha_2\beta_2)}\Delta g_B - \frac{\beta_2 a_{13}}{a_{12}(\alpha_2 + \beta_2 - \alpha_2\beta_2)}\Delta g_A$$

$$- \frac{\alpha_2}{b_{12}(\alpha_2 + \beta_2 - \alpha_2\beta_2)}\overline{\gamma}_B. \tag{4.11b'}$$

This equation shows a deflationary bias in the peripheral country. If we abstract from fiscal policies ($\Delta g_B = \Delta g_A = 0$) and assume α_2, $\beta_2 > 0$, it is immediately obvious that prices in B have to fall (relative to A) when its potential output growth ($\overline{\gamma}_B$) exceeds capacity growth in A. The reason is that with a fixed exchange rate, the price level in the peripheral country is determined by the anchor country.[10] But nominal income is a function of 'the' real exchange rate. Given that B has control over neither the intra-bloc exchange rate nor the external rate, and given that money supply adjusts endogenously, the only policy variable available is the price level. In order to create the demand necessary to absorb the increasing potential output, real money balances have to increase. But this can only be achieved by a fall of the domestic price level in B, that is, the real effective exchange rate has to become more competitive. This is what France tried to achieve by its policy of 'competitive disinflation' (Fitoussi *et al.* 1993), or what has been at the root of the Dutch employment miracle in the 1990s.

If prices in B are stable or sticky, either because B also aims to maintain price stability, or – more realistically – because nominal rigidities prevent downward price adjustment from being instantaneous, then realised GDP-growth (γ_B) will become the endogenous variable and remain below the potential rate $\overline{\gamma}_B$, because the required real depreciation cannot be obtained. This is obvious from Equation (4.11b) which yields:

$$\gamma_B = \frac{1 - \alpha_1\beta_1}{1 - \alpha_1}b_{12}(\delta_1 - \pi_B - \pi_A) - \beta_2 b_{12} a_{13}\Delta g_A + b_{13}\Delta g_B. \tag{4.11b''}$$

The growth rate γ_B is a function of the real exchange rate with respect to A, the impact depending on the size parameters of regional integration. In a textbook world of fixed exchange rates, B is totally integrated with A ($\beta_2 = 0$) and A totally independent, that is, exogenously given to B ($\alpha_1 = 0$). Therefore, the growth rate in B depends only on the demand elasticity (b_{12}) with respect to the real exchange rate with A and domestic fiscal policies. It is independent of fiscal policies in A because we have assumed external demand to remain constant. However, under bloc floating the real exchange rate effect is enlarged and a fiscal expansion in the anchor country causes a contraction in the periphery. The bilateral exchange rate (P_1) matters more if α_1 increases because that reinforces the potential competitive effects with the rest of the world that result from bloc floating (see Chapter 3). It matters less if β_1 increases, because B's competitiveness depends more on intra-bloc trade and less on the rest of the world. Furthermore, if B's tradeshare with A is small but its exchange rate is fixed to A, a fiscal expansion in A will reduce demand in B because it causes an appreciation of A's exchange rate with the rest of the world.[11] This means that a fixed exchange rate regime is more easily sustainable if the currency bloc around the anchor country (α_1) is small and the peripheral country specialises in trade with the anchor (β_1).[12] These conditions seem to have been better fulfilled in dollar-bloc than the European Monetary System (EMS), because α_1 is high for Germany. On the other hand β_1 is higher for small European countries.[13] Thus, regular realignments in the DM-bloc have been a condition for its sustainability.

If $\delta_1 = 0$, and prices in A are stable, only a fall in the price level in B can produce a positive growth effect. If nominal prices and wages are rigid – and there are good theoretical and empirical reasons to assume so, especially since this is the logic implied in a fixed exchange rate regime – then realised growth will remain below potential growth ($\overline{\gamma}_B > \gamma_B$), and unemployment will rise. The growth benefit of keeping the bloc-exchange rate fixed ($\delta_1 = 0$) in order to reduce volatility and encourage investment will be lost due to the lack of external competitiveness. Yet, if B is small in relation to A (β_1 is large), downward price rigidity in B would require less frequent exchange rate re-adjustments to keep resources fully employed. This might explain the better performance of small countries in the DM-bloc like Austria or the Netherlands or even the relatively long stability of the US dollar-peg by South-East Asian countries. However, when the currency bloc around the anchor country becomes large, as in the Deutschmark case, the coefficient in Equation (4.11b″) increases. This makes a competitive deflation strategy more effective. But if prices are sticky, the pressure to devalue will increase with the rise in unemployment. The more rigid the price system in B, the more flexible the exchange rate must be, although this will have negative effects on the investment function.

Fiscal policy can play a compensating role against deflation in B. In fact, price stability in the peripheral ($\pi_B = 0$) is only possible, if the increase in government deficits would exactly compensate the growth of productive capacity. However, this is rather unlikely, given that sooner or later the accelerating public debt would become unsustainable. The deflationary impact of bloc floating becomes even worse when the anchor country attempts to maintain price stability, but relaxes fiscal policy – as after the German unification shock. Not surprisingly, several European countries opted for an exit from bloc floating (Eichengreen and Wyplosz 1990): they adjusted the intra-bloc peg ($\delta_1 > 0$). In fact, in a bloc-floating regime, the anchor country dominates both the peripheral's monetary policy and its fiscal policy if B's prices are sticky. With $\pi_B = \gamma_B = 0$, we obtain $\Delta g_B = (\beta_2 a_{13} b_{12} / \alpha_2 a_{12} b_{13}) \Delta g_A$, where the coefficient rises, the larger the integration of A into the currency bloc. However, if B also increases its trade share with its bloc partners, it can offset this effect by also extending its integration into the bloc. Thus, we obtain the curious[14] result that dependency leads to more dependency: in order to counterbalance the deflationary bias of bloc floating, peripheral countries must extend their integration into the currency bloc in order to regain fiscal policy margins, although this reinforces the deflationary dynamics.

This leads to a dilemma: while fixed exchange rates are a necessary condition for deeper regional integration, the more successful this integration, the harder it is to maintain fixed exchange rates. In the context of separate currencies, peripheral countries have the option to devalue at irregular intervals or to let their deficits increase, although the latter option is unsustainable. The only alternative is a regime shift: unifying monetary policy within the bloc under a single currency will eliminate the deflationary bias of bloc floating, as we will show in the next section.

We may summarise the logic of bloc floating in the steady state as follows:

1   Creating a currency bloc is unambiguously favourable *to the anchor* country: it reduces exchange risk within the bloc, while all policy options for an optimal policy mix remain available.
2   For *peripheral* countries the situation is more ambivalent: low exchange rate volatility would support investment, but if the periphery needs to grow faster than the anchor, the deflationary bias becomes counter-productive. The deflationary bias manifests itself in the dreadful policy triangle of rising deficits, unemployment and falling prices. More or less frequent exchange rate adjustments are then required in order to regain some policy control. In the context of the EMS, these exchange rate realignments were built into the system. When they were no longer applied and the policy mix in Germany reinforced the deflationary bias for the other countries, the system broke down – at least for those large countries where downward price flexibility was least pronounced, such as for Italy and UK.
3   For small peripheral countries in a floating bloc, less price flexibility is required and, therefore, the sustainability of the peg is more easily achieved than for large countries. However, the break-up of the dollar-bloc in South-East Asia shows that even for small countries a rapid appreciation of the anchor currency makes the system unsustainable.

The steady state in monetary union

Under European Monetary Union (EMU) a regime change is taking place. Monetary policy of country A and B is unified under a new European Central Bank (ECB) which must maintain price stability for the whole union, but it can use the unified external exchange rate as an adjustment tool. In terms of our model, an optimal monetary policy is a policy that achieves full capacity utilisation at stable prices.[15]

Steady-state aggregate supply will be the weighted average of the productive capacities of the two countries.

$$\bar{y}_{U_t} = (1 - \eta)\bar{y}_{A_t} + \eta\bar{y}_{B_t}, \tag{4.6c}$$

$$\Delta\bar{y}_U = (1 - \eta)\bar{\gamma}_A + \eta\bar{\gamma}_B. \tag{4.6c'}$$

The other equations become:

$$
\begin{aligned}
y_{U_t} &= (1 - \eta)y_{A_t} + \eta y_{B_t} \\
&= u_{10} + u_{11}r_{U_t} + u_{12}p_{EU_t} + (1 - \eta)a_{13}g_{A_t} + \eta b_{13}g_{B_t} + (1 - \eta)\nu_A + \eta\nu_B,
\end{aligned}
\tag{4.1c}
$$

where η is the GDP-weight of country B and the parameters:

$$u_{10} = (1 - \eta)a_{10} + \eta b_{10},$$

$$u_{11} = (1 - \eta)a_{11} + \eta b_{11} < 0,$$

$$u_{12} = (1 - \eta)a_{12} + \eta b_{12} > 0.$$

Given that there is practically no federal fiscal authority, fiscal policy reflects the weighted average of national budgetary positions. Similarly, demand shocks are weighted by the size of regional GDPs. Monetary policy is unified for all countries. Therefore, money supply and the nominal interest rate are identical in both countries, and a unified price level prevails in the two countries.[16] Hence:

$$m_{U_t} - p_{U_t} = u_{20} + u_{21}y_{U_t} + u_{22}i_{U_t} + \varepsilon_{U_t}, \qquad u_{21} > 0, \quad u_{22} < 0, \tag{4.2c}$$

$$r_{U_t} = i_{U_t} - E_t(p_{U_{t+1}} - p_{U_t}) = i_{U_t} - E(\pi_U), \tag{4.3c}$$

$$p_{EU_t} = p_{C_t} - p_{U_t} - e_{U_t}, \tag{4.4c}$$

$$i_{U_t} = i_C - E_t(e_{U_{t+1}} - e_{U_t}) = i_C - E_t(\delta_u). \tag{4.5c}$$

The monetary union has one single flexible exchange rate (e_{U_t}) with the rest of the world (C).[17] In order to be able to compare monetary union with bloc floating, we continue to assume that the world interest rate (i_C) is exogenously given. p_{EU_t} is the real effective exchange rate and p_{U_t} the price level in the union. The equilibrium equations become:

$$
\begin{aligned}
\bar{y}_{U_t} &= u_{10} + u_{11}\big[i_c - E_t(e_{U_{t+1}} - e_{U_t}) - E_t(p_{t+1} - p_t)\big] + u_{12}\big[(p_{C_t} - p_{U_t} - e_{U_t})\big] \\
&\quad + (1 - \eta)a_{13}g_{A_t} + \eta b_{13}g_{B_t} + (1 - \eta)\nu_A + \eta\nu_B,
\end{aligned}
\tag{4.7c}
$$

$$m_{U_t} - p_{U_t} = u_{20} + u_{21}\bar{y}_{U_t} + u_{22}\big[i_C - E_t(e_{U_{t+1}} - e_{U_t})\big] + \varepsilon_{U_t}. \tag{4.8c}$$

This system has the textbook characteristics of one policy variable (m_U) and two endogenous variables e_U, p_U. Steady state in monetary union implies: $\nu_{A,B} = 0$, $\varepsilon_U = 0$, $E_t(e_{U_{t+1}} - e_{U_t}) = e_{U_{t+1}} - e_{U_t} = \delta_U$, $\Delta\delta_n = \Delta\pi_n = 0$. We have world inflation and interest rates exogenously given as before. Capacity output in the union grows at the weighted average (Equation 4.6c') and the new central bank supplies money at the rate $\Delta m_U = \mu_U$.

After differentiating Equations (4.7c) and (4.8c), we obtain the steady-state equilibrium for monetary union.

$$(1 - \eta)\gamma_A + \eta\gamma_B = u_{12}(\pi_C - \pi_U - \delta_U) + (1 - \eta)a_{13}\Delta g_{A,} + \eta b_{13}\Delta g_{B,} \tag{4.9c}$$

$$\mu_U - \pi_U = u_{21}[(1 - \eta)\gamma_A + \eta\gamma_B]. \tag{4.10c}$$

In monetary union, the money supply rule which keeps prices stable ($\pi_U = 0$) is a weighted average of the respective growth potentials (from Equation 4.10c):

Rule MU: $\mu_U = u_{21}[(1 + \eta)\gamma_A + \eta\gamma_B]$.

This rule shows that money supply in the monetary union can be more expansionary than in the previous bloc-floating regime *without endangering price stability*.[18] Assuming $\gamma_A = 0$ and price stability ($\pi_U = 0$), the central bank should accommodate transaction demand for money in a growing economy, but not inflation:

$$\mu_U = u_{21}\eta\gamma_B > \mu_A = a_{21}\gamma_A = 0.$$

From Equation (4.9c) we know that the external exchange rate appreciates or depreciates according to

$$\delta_U = \pi_C - \pi_U + \frac{1}{u_{12}}[(1 - \eta)\Delta g_A + \eta\Delta g_B - (1 - \eta)\gamma_A - \eta\gamma_B]. \tag{4.11c}$$

Given that η, γ_B, u_{12} and π_C are all exogenous variables and monetary policy ensures that $\pi_U = 0$, it is unlikely that the external exchange rate of the monetary union will be stable. A 'strong', that is, steadily appreciating currency ($\delta_U > 0$), will be the result of a positive price differential between the rest of the world and the union, which is larger than the union's potential growth effect after adjustment for fiscal policy. However, assuming a stable fiscal policy stance and price stability in EMU, in line with the Maastricht Treaty, the external exchange rate of the monetary union will be more stable (less appreciating) than the anchor currency (DM) in the previous bloc-floating regime. However, what matters for the union and especially for country B in the union, is whether it can improve economic growth. The answer is unequivocally yes, because the nominal exchange rate can adjust to produce the real exchange level, at which the increasing productive capacity can be absorbed by effective demand.[19]

This implies that the deflationary bias of the currency bloc regime has been eliminated. The reason is that in a monetary union, the central bank has full control over domestic monetary policy and the external exchange rate, and this allows keeping effective demand consistent with capacity output. In this respect, the monetary union has a similar policy autonomy as previously enjoyed by country A, but this also applies now to country B.[20] Thus, B has gained an additional degree of freedom in pursuing its economic policy objectives.

Thus, monetary union unambiguously improves welfare conditions in a real world with some degree of wage and price rigidity. The logic is simple: in a currency bloc with fixed exchange rates, a dependent country with faster capacity growth than the anchor country cannot achieve stable exchange rates, stable prices and stable deficits and simultaneously remain on the steady-state growth path. If monetary policy is used to keep nominal exchange rates fixed, it has no capacity to stimulate demand by reducing interest rates or depreciating the external exchange rate. Thus, domestic prices (and wages) must fall in order to increase the real money supply necessary to accommodate the transaction demand resulting from real growth. In a monetary union, however, the abolition of the intra-bloc exchange rate (e_1) provides the additional degree of freedom whereby unified money supply accommodates growth for the whole union.

Our analysis has so far focused on long-term equilibrium conditions and demonstrated that a fixed-exchange rate currency bloc is fundamentally unsustainable, unless nominal wages and prices actually fall (relative to A) in countries with high potential output growth.[21] In this respect, our argument differs from earlier arguments, which emphasised the *recessive dynamics* of inflation convergence (Driffil and Miller 1992). In our model it is the fixed currency bloc, which is unsustainable in the presence of nominal price and wage rigidities, while a monetary union is sustainable, even if these rigidities exist, given the additional degree of freedom through exchange policies.

We will now look at the impact of shocks on the system.

Short-term dynamics

Our model has specified three sorts of random shocks: demand shocks $\nu_{A,B,U}$, money supply shocks $\varepsilon_{A,B,U}$ and credibility shocks related to the exchange rate peg within the regional currency bloc ρ_B. To simplify things, we will assume that the stochastic processes generating the shocks are white noise, hence $\nu_{A,B,U}$, $\varepsilon_{A,B,U}$ and ρ_B are uncorrelated. We will also continue to assume that the *external* parameters p_{C_t}, p_{A_t}, p_{B_t}, i_{C_t} remain constant. Similarly, the steady-state rates of money supply $\mu_{A,U}$ do not change, nor does fiscal policy $g_{A,B}$. Consequently, the domestic price level (P_A, P_B, P_C) are endogenous in all three cases. However, the second endogenous variable depends on the exchange regime: it is e_{2_t} for the anchor currency, e_{U_t} for monetary union, and μ_B for the periphery under bloc floating. If we regroup all unchanging variables and parameters into the composite constant AR and AF, we obtain for country A the system equations:

$$AR = a_{11}\left[-E(e_{2_{t+1}} - e_{2_t}) - E(p_{A_{t+1}} - p_{A_t})\right] - a_{12}(p_{A_t} + \alpha_2 e_{2_t}) + \nu_{A_t},$$

$$-p_{A_t} = AF - a_{22}\left[E(e_{2_{t+1}} - e_{2_t})\right] + \varepsilon_{A_t}, \tag{4.8a'}$$

with the composite constants

$$AR = \bar{y}_{A_{t-1}} + \bar{\gamma}_A - a_{10} - a_{11}i_C - a_{12}\left[\alpha_1(p_{B_t} - e_{1_t}) + \alpha_2 p_{C_t}\right] - a_{13}g_{A_t},$$

$$AF = a_{20} - \mu_A - m_{A_{t-1}} + a_{21}(\bar{y}_{A_{t-1}} + \bar{\gamma}_A) + a_{22}i_C.$$

Similarly, we obtain the system equations for monetary union:

$$UR = u_{11}\left[-E(e_{U_{t+1}} - e_{U_t}) - E(p_{U_{t+1}} - p_{U_t})\right]$$
$$- u_{12}(p_{U_t} + e_{U_t}) + \nu_{U_t}, \tag{4.7c'}$$

$$-p_{U_t} = UF - u_{22}\left[E(e_{U_{t+1}} - e_{U_t})\right] + \varepsilon_{U_t} \tag{4.8c'}$$

with the constants

$$UR = \bar{y}_{U_{t-1}} + \bar{\gamma}_U - u_{10} - u_{11}i_C - u_{12}p_{C_t} - (1-\eta)a_{13}\Delta g_A - \eta b_{13}g_B,$$

$$UF = u_{20} - \mu_U - m_{U_{t-1}} + u_{21}(\bar{y}_{U_{t-1}} + \bar{\gamma}_U) + u_{22}i_C$$

and

$$\nu_U = (1-\eta)\nu_A + \eta\nu_B.$$

Finally, in country B it is not the exchange rate, but money supply and prices, that adjust endogenously. Hence we have:

$$BR = b_{11}\left[\rho_{B_t} - E(p_{B_{t+1}} - p_{B_t})\right] - b_{12}(p_{B_t}) + \nu_{B_t}, \tag{4.7b'}$$

$$m_{B_t} - p_{B_t} = BF + b_{22}\rho_{B_t} + \varepsilon_{B_t} \tag{4.8b'}$$

with the two constants:

$$BR = \bar{y}_{B_{t-1}} + \bar{\gamma}_B - b_{10} - b_{11}i_C + b_{11}\delta_2$$
$$- b_{12}[e_{1_t} + \beta_1 p_{A_t} + \beta_2 p_{C_t} - \beta_2 e_{2_t}] - b_{13}g_{B_t},$$

$$BF = b_{20} + b_{21}(\bar{y}_{B_{t-1}} + \bar{\gamma}_B) + b_{22}(i_C - \delta_2).$$

Using the method of undetermined coefficients, we surmise that the solutions for P_t, e_t, and m_{B_t} are:

$$p_{A,B,U_t} = \phi_{10} + \phi_{11}\nu_{A,B,U_t} + \phi_{12}\varepsilon_{A,B,U_t} + \phi_{13}\rho_{B_t}, \tag{4.12}$$

$$e_{2,U_t} = \phi_{20} + \phi_{21}\nu_{A,C_t} + \phi_{22}\varepsilon_{A,C_t}, \tag{4.13}$$

$$m_{B_t} = \phi_{30} + \phi_{31}\nu_{B_t} + \phi_{32}\varepsilon_{B_t} + \phi_{33}\rho_{B_t}. \tag{4.14}$$

Assuming rational expectations, we also have $E(p_{t+1}) = \phi_{10}$, $E(e_{2_{t+1}}) = \phi_{20}$ and $E(m_{B_{t+1}}) = \phi_{30}$.

As the 'external' exchange rate e_2 between the anchor country and the rest of the world is exogenously given in B, real or monetary shocks or a pegging credibility shock ρ_B affect here prices and money supply and not exchange rates. The solution for the undetermined coefficients is given by Table 4.1 (we ignore the constant terms ϕ_{10}, ϕ_{20} which depend on the initial values of the constant parameters).

Table 4.1 Response of monetary variables to shocks

		A	B	U
P_t	$\phi_{11} : \nu$	$\dfrac{a_{22}}{(1 - a_{22})a_{11} - (\alpha_2 - a_{22})a_{12}} > 0$	$\dfrac{-1}{(b_{11} - b_{12})} > 0$	$\dfrac{u_{22}}{(1 - u_{22})(u_{11} - u_{12})} > 0$
	$\phi_{12} : \varepsilon$	$\dfrac{\alpha_2 a_{12} - a_{11}}{(1 - a_{22})a_{11} - (\alpha_2 - a_{22})a_{12}} < 0$	0	$\dfrac{-1}{(1 - u_{22})} < 0$
	$\phi_{13} : \rho_B$	—	$\dfrac{-b_{11}}{(b_{11} - b_{12})} < 0$	—
e_t	$\phi_{21} : \nu$	$\dfrac{-1}{(1 - a_{22})a_{11} - (\alpha_2 - a_{22})a_{12}} > 0$	—	$\dfrac{-1}{(1 - u_{22})(u_{11} - u_{12})} > 0$
	$\phi_{22} : \varepsilon$	$\dfrac{a_{11} - a_{12}}{(1 - a_{22})a_{11} - (\alpha_2 - a_{22})a_{12}} > 0$	—	$\dfrac{1}{(1 - u_{22})} > 0$
m	$\phi_{31} : \nu$	—	$\dfrac{-1}{(b_{11} - b_{12})} > 0$	—
	$\phi_{32} : \varepsilon$	—	1	—
	$\phi_{33} : \rho$	—	$b_{22} - \dfrac{b_{11}}{(b_{11} - b_{12})} < 0$	—

In evaluating the different monetary regimes we will assume that all structural parameters are identical in the three countries ($a_i = b_i = u_i$). It is then immediately clear that a stochastic shock (ν) affecting the investment–saving relation always raises prices. But this effect will be lower in the monetary union than under bloc floating in A or B, because the denominator of the coefficient is higher under U than under A and B. Thus, there is a clear benefit for both anchor and peripheral, from moving to a single currency as prices become more stable. Similarly, the impact of a demand shock on the nominal exchange rate is reduced for A. This implies that, *ceteris paribus*, the dollar–euro nominal exchange rate would be more stable than the dollar–DM rate. In the peripheral B, IS-shocks have a significantly higher impact on prices under bloc floating than in the anchor country A or in the monetary union, although these shocks have no consequences for (real) money demand. Therefore, moving to monetary union will stabilise price movements in these countries as well and eliminate the deflationary bias.

Secondly, shocks to money-demand behaviour (ε) lower prices and appreciate the exchange rate in A and U, while they leave prices unaffected in B and translate into variations of money supply. Comparing the impact in A and U, we find that the price-effect of a monetary shock increases. The exchange rate effect, however, is reduced, again indicating greater transatlantic exchange rate stability. This implies that in monetary union, monetary policy becomes more effective: with greater international exchange rate stability, small monetary policy changes have larger consequences for price stability. Furthermore, it implies that Germany will potentially be a net gainer from monetary union, provided the integrated monetary policy does not commit major errors. Finally, under bloc floating LM-shocks are entirely ineffective in bringing changes to domestic income in B, a fact well established for fixed exchange rate regimes, although they would alter the level of real money balances. By moving to EMU, the peripheral countries will regain control over monetary policy at the union level.

Thirdly, the existence of credibility shocks under bloc floating has detrimental effects for the peripheral country. This is because the appearance of risk premia in the interest rate has a deflationary effect. Money demand will fall. This deflationary effect is eliminated in monetary union.

Fourthly, these shock-effects are independent of whether the IS-disturbances are symmetric ($\nu_A = \nu_B$) or asymmetric ($\nu_A \neq \nu_B$). Asymmetric shocks in EMU therefore require less adjustment than under a bloc-floating regime. This means that in a short-term perspective, giving up the exchange rate as an adjustment tool is less costly in a monetary union than under a fixed exchange rate regime. This distinction has often been overlooked by critics of EMU.

Finally, it is of course possible that the national IS-elasticities deviate from their weighted average, so that shocks do not have a uniform impact in all countries. Nevertheless, the regime shift must lead into the direction of the consequences described here. The same would be true if we took a more realistic specification, by abandoning the white noise assumption for our stochastic shocks. We may, therefore, conclude that a monetary union is a clear improvement over bloc floating.

Summary and conclusions

This chapter has assessed the cost of giving away the exchange rate as an adjustment tool in the periphery of a currency bloc. We have seen that this cost appears in the form of a deflationary bias for countries with higher growth potential than the anchor. It is due to the fact that faster growth requires lower interest or exchange rates than are compatible with the fixed link to the anchor. In a monetary union the problem is overcome because the exchange rate can adjust in order to achieve balance for the whole union economy. Our argument has some similarity with the logic of the classical gold standard adjustment mechanism and the famous debate between Keynes and Ohlin about the transfer problem. In the classical model, a rapidly growing country would develop a balance of payment deficit; the resulting loss of gold would force an internal deflation and cause a real devaluation (McKinnon 1996: Chapter 4). Against this theory, one can hold the 'revisionist view' according to which capital transfers would balance the payment deficit without relative price adjustment, provided capital and goods market are fully integrated.[22] The accumulation of debt would then fuel the growth process.[22] However, this revisionist theory has no endogenous explanation for the initial incentive for firms to invest (Riese 1986a). The growth stimulus must come from 'outside'. But in a market economy the propensity to invest depends on profit expectations and hence on relative prices.[23] Therefore, the balance of payment constraint imposes a deflationary bias under fixed exchange rates. However, in a monetary union, the revisionist view becomes valid because the balance of payment constraint is lifted *within the union*. The unified capital market will allocate investment where and as long as it is profitable. As we have seen, this process can be modelled by Tobin's q and depends on the usual macroeconomic policy mix of monetary, fiscal and income policies at a given exchange rate environment.

Our theory of bloc floating has revealed ambivalent effects of exchange rate pegging for economic growth: if investment depends on the difference $q - \bar{q}$, then we can reduce $\bar{q}$ by lowering exchange rate volatility. However, this will only produce a temporary investment boom until the capital stock has adjusted and $q - \bar{q} = 0$ at a new level of output and employment. If that level is insufficient, q has to be lowered further, requiring lower real interest rates or a real depreciation or both. However, interest rates are dependent on foreign rates for small countries, and therefore only a reduction in domestic prices or an unsustainable fiscal expansion can generate the required demand.

Can we find any empirical evidence for this reasoning? Given that short-term demand management and long-term growth are rather complex processes, an easy transposition of our model on reality is not possible. Nevertheless, Table 4.2 gives some indication of long-term growth trends of the relevant variables of our model. A correlation among employment, the real effective exchange rate and growing budget deficits for the whole EMS period 1980–97 is not clear. Ireland and Portugal were able to improve employment growth, appreciate their REER and improve their budget position simultaneously. On the other hand, both France and Sweden devalued in real terms and increased their deficits, but employment still grew less

Table 4.2 Growth of macroeconomic variables with respect to Germany

	Employment	Inflation	DM-rate	REER	Budget position
1980–97					
D	0.29	2.83		0.01	−0.52
NL	1.15	−0.85	−0.20	−0.28	0.17
IRL	0.48	1.94	−2.16	0.47	0.81
E	0.26	4.68	−4.25	−0.02	−0.06
POR	0.25	10.39	−7.52	1.46	0.08
AU	0.19	0.63	0.00	0.64	−0.10
GB	0.13	2.17	−2.64	−1.34	−0.18
DEN	−0.08	1.37	−1.26	0.43	0.23
F	−0.09	1.66	−2.16	−0.46	−0.17
I	−0.42	5.22	−4.18	0.20	0.29
SW	−0.69	2.93	−3.90	−0.91	−0.14
1987–92					
D	0.93	3.28		0.16	−0.29
NL	1.43	−1.30	−0.10	−0.96	−0.42
E	0.84	3.53	−0.60	3.40	0.24
AU	0.63	−0.10	0.22	−0.07	−0.38
POR	0.24	9.29	−2.02	5.26	−0.00
IRL	0.19	−0.89	−0.15	−0.34	−1.01
F	−0.32	−0.41	−0.21	−0.59	0.32
I	−0.52	3.34	−4.10	1.00	−0.22
GB	−0.80	2.85	−3.79	2.00	1.06
SW	−1.23	3.10	−3.26	2.68	2.15
DEN	−1.83	−0.14	−0.10	−0.12	1.02
1992–97					
D	−0.64	2.14		1.44	−0.17
IRL	3.75	−0.67	−0.51	−1.19	0.28
NL	2.02	−0.40	−0.02	1.17	0.29
DEN	1.17	−0.38	0.34	0.84	0.61
UK	1.00	0.27	3.96	−3.00	0.66
E	0.76	1.86	−3.45	−3.10	0.18
F	0.75	−0.41	0.42	0.83	0.24
AU	0.36	0.25	−0.04	1.22	−0.21
POR	0.31	2.94	−2.33	−0.01	0.35
SW	−0.07	0.42	−0.14	−3.30	1.55
I	−0.16	1.78	−1.48	−3.90	1.13

Source: OECD and own calculations.

than in Germany. The period of the 'hard' EMS 1987–92 is more in line with our theory. Five countries had employment growth below the German rate of 0.93 per cent and they all either appreciated their Real Effective Exchange Rate (REER) or tightened their fiscal stance. Spain and Portugal, however, did both and still had higher employment growth than Germany. In the post-ERM transition to EMU, most countries fare better than Germany in terms of employment – although at very low growth rates. Compared to the previous period currency, devaluations are significant as are the budgetary consolidation efforts. These figures are no clear evidence for the theory proposed in this chapter. But they indicate at least that deviations from the economic performances of the anchor currency did not go very far.

Our analysis has also shown that the drawbacks of fixed exchange rate regimes are overcome by monetary union: external nominal exchange rate volatility should fall and internal adjustment should become easier. This is a new result. Most of the academic literature has treated EMU in the past as if it were a fixed exchange rate regime. I have shown that this is not correct. The only article that addresses the regime change correctly, although in the different context of monetary transmission mechanisms, are, to my knowledge, Cohen (1989) and Dornbusch *et al*. (1998). However, if EMU changes monetary policy dramatically by making joint decisions with respect to European targets, then we may also have to revalue the costs and benefits of belonging to a particular currency area. Thus, we should also review the propositions of OCA theory.

5 A fresh look at Optimum Currency Area theory

A large body of the economic literature on the European Monetary Union (EMU) has been based on cost–benefit analysis of the desirability of a single currency and under what conditions a country might wish to participate. Little has been written on under what circumstances a country may wish to leave.[1] However, if EMU is meant to last, it might be worthwhile to consider the case of failure in order to avoid it. The decision to join a monetary union is typically addressed in terms of Optimum Currency Area (OCA) models, which focus on static, steady-state alternatives. From this point of view, a country should opt for the euro if the expected benefits of currency unification exceed its costs or disadvantages. Otherwise, it should stay out. However, if the net benefits are not static, the logic of this argument must be inverted: if the costs of being a member of the currency union were to increase beyond the perceived advantages, a country may wish to leave. Some amount of inertia would be provided by the transitional changeover cost of moving back to a national currency, but if the total balance of pros and cons is narrow and uncertain, membership in EMU could become volatile. An example for unstable participation in European institutional arrangements is monetary co-operation in the 1970s: between 1972 and 1978, there were twelve withdrawals and rejoinders to the Basle Agreement, known as 'the snake' (Collignon 1994). This might not qualify as a reference for EMU, given that the degree of institutional commitment between participants was low, and it cannot be compared with the later European Monetary System (EMS), let alone EMU. After all, a monetary union is defined by the institutional substitution of national currencies by a single currency. But from the perspective of OCA analysis, one must explain whether the net balance of advantages from EMU can be stable.

In this chapter we will first take a fresh look at the factors determining costs and benefits of a single currency. In the next chapter we will assess their potential volatility and the implications for the sustainability of EMU. It is commonly argued that the benefits of a single currency are derived from microeconomic efficiency gains resulting from its use over a wider area (Baldwin 1991), while the costs are related to the loss of the exchange rate in stabilisation policies (Willms 1995). The larger use of a common currency provides three distinct advantages: a reduction in transaction costs, welfare gains from more efficient use of reserve assets, and a growth-stimulating reduction of exchange risk. The assessment of costs depends on the structure and flexibility of the economy, the efficiency of exchange-rate variability as an adjustment tool and the nature of potential shocks.

The benefits of using a single currency

When looking at the benefits of monetary union it is useful to refer to the social services money provides. As Brunner and Meltzer (1971) have pointed out, 'by using money, individuals reduce the amount of information they must acquire, process and store . . . . The use of money increases the welfare of each money user by reducing uncertainty, the length of transaction chains and the variance of price ratios and by increasing expected wealth and time available for leisure'. Clearly, a single market with many currencies requires higher costs of acquiring information and transactions than one with a single currency. Therefore, the benefits from using the services of a single currency must be positively related to the size of the currency area. Where do these benefits come from?

First of all, we observe gains from reduced transaction costs. It is clear that abolishing the costs of exchange from one currency to another eliminates inefficiencies and distortions in the single market. These costs are significant. The European Commission (1990) has estimated the total transaction cost savings from a single currency at 0.2–0.5 per cent of EU-GDP per year. This is a rather low although realistic estimate especially when compared to some estimates for the stabilisation benefits of independent currencies (Gosh and Wolf 1994) and given the benchmark of a stable EMS to which the single currency has often been compared. Others have calculated that the foreign exchange management cost amounted to 1 per cent of EU-GDP per annum between 1986 and 1995, of which 0.8 per cent could be saved by a single currency (Dumke *et al.* 1997).

However, aggregate figures do not reflect the barriers to trade that result from the high cost of cross-border payments. The share of cross-border in total payments depends on the degree of integration, that is, the share of intra-community trade. It varies in Europe from a low of 0.5 per cent in Germany to a high of 10 per cent in Greece (CEPS 1994). Costs also vary between wholesale and retail transactions. Since the average charges of transferring an amount of 100 ECU in the late 1990s were 16 per cent of the principal in the European Union (EU), coming down to 0.4 per cent for an amount of 10,000 ECU, only large-value payments are highly efficient and cost-competitive.

The absence of a single currency makes cross-border payments comparable to a distortionary tax in the single market. It discriminates against small transactions and prevents fully integrated consumer markets on the European scale. It reduces welfare unproportionally for small countries. A single currency, although not automatically eliminating all cross-border payment charges, eliminates bid-offer spreads and improves payment technology. Therefore, a single currency creates a clear gain from greater market efficiency. The marginal utility of extending the size of the currency area is larger for small countries with a high degree of integration. Although it is positive for all, it diminishes with the size of the currency area.

In a similar vein, a single currency increases market transparency – which translates into a benefit by reducing the cost of information gathering. To summarise, this first group of advantages resulting from the reduction of transaction costs is related positively to the size of the union and to the degree of integration of the participating countries, although there are diminishing returns to scale.

Secondly, a large currency area has liquidity advantages over a small zone. A single European currency is the second most important international currency for transaction purposes (Hartmann 1996). It will also increase the size of financial markets: for example, the euro area is already the second largest bond market in the world. Even if only a small core group of six countries had formed EMU at first, it would have amounted to half the size of the dollar-bond market – well in excess of the Japanese market. Other markets, including the stock markets, will benefit from overcoming segmentation. The overall effect is better liquidity and price efficiency. This gives the single currency a liquidity-value that increases with the size of the area and exceeds the transactional benefits related to the internal degree of integration. As a consequence, domestic users will benefit from lower financing costs. Furthermore, exporters and importers with the rest of the world will be able to invoice and settle in a currency, which can be bought at low transaction costs in the foreign-exchange market. It will allow economies in holding foreign-exchange reserves by companies, banks and central banks, as is well known from inventory theory (Artis 1994). Additionally, an international currency yields seigniorage revenue when the euro is held by non-EU members. On a political level, if a potential competitor to the US dollar would induce co-operation and greater macroeconomic stability between leading economies in the world, this would reduce potential risk premia.[2] All these benefits come with the depth of financial markets and, therefore, the overall size of EMU,[3] although we would again expect diminishing returns to scale.

However, as McKinnon (1963) has emphasised, the liquidity-value of a currency depends on its internal and external stability. The larger a currency area, the more important price stability becomes in order to give money liquidity-value in the eyes of the inhabitants. A small country can maintain this value by pegging it to an outside currency, that is, by stabilising the exchange rate to a currency with internal stability. Therefore, provided the purchasing power of the single currency is maintained – and this is the 'primary objective' of EMU according to arts. 2, 3a and 105(1) of the Treaty on European Union (TEU) – the total benefits from monetary union will increase with size. In contrast, if price stability is not maintained, this would impose a loss and reduce the (net) benefits. We will deal with this argument in the next section.

Thirdly, a single currency by definition abolishes exchange risk within the single market and this improves allocative efficiency of corporate locations.

Removing exchange-rate uncertainty also reduces risk premia in real interest rates of countries with less than perfect credibility in their exchange-rate peg to the DM. For the union as a whole, this should improve the macroeconomic policy-mix. The consequential reduction in risk and uncertainty in the single market will increase investment and growth as we have seen in Chapter 3. To the degree that this development also raises investment in human capital, a monetary union would lift the permanent growth rate (Mankiw *et al.* 1992). In the long run this advantage should dominate all other considerations, although in the short run it might be overshadowed by stabilisation issues.

We will not discuss these benefits from EMU in detail, as they are well established in the literature. What matters here is that the advantages from EMU increase with the size of the currency area and the degree of integration between participating countries, not in a linear fashion, but with diminishing returns to scale.[4] From an individual (i) country's point of view, the benefits are a function of its own degree of openness (m) and of the size (S) of the monetary union to be joined:

$$B_i = B(S, m_i), \quad B_s > 0, \quad B_m > 0, \quad B_{ss} < 0. \tag{5.1}$$

Table 5.1 gives an indication for some of these variables.

As proxies for size we may take GDP or population.[5] The degree of external openness is an indicator for the benefit derived from the international role of the euro. Given that small European countries are correlated with high degrees of openness, they are likely to be more favourably inclined to join a union than large countries. Inversely, large countries may be less sensitive to arguments about advantages. However, all should have an interest in making EMU a large currency area, unless the size has an impact on the potential disadvantages.

The costs of forming a monetary union

On the cost side, arguments focus on the real costs imposed on a country's economy that may result from giving up the option of devaluing its currency if it is hit by a shock. This is the core of the OCA literature since Mundell's (1961) path-breaking article. It was augmented by McKinnon (1963) who introduced price stability and the degree of openness as a criterion and by Kenen (1969) who insisted that product diversification matters. A currency area is considered optimal if it does not increase its members' vulnerability to shocks or their ability to deal with them (Kenen 1995). Factors which minimise the cost of giving up the exchange rate instrument are: (1) a large degree of openness to trade; (2) factor mobility; (3) wage and price flexibility in both directions; (4) a high degree of product diversification; and (5) the absence of significant asymmetries in shocks or structures (Demertzis *et al.* 1998). However, based on the background of our Chapter 4 it is clear that OCA-theory reasons in terms of fixed exchange rates and

Table 5.1 Size and degree of openness of European Union member states – 1997

	Size		Degree of openness				
	GDP (in bill. of ECU)	Population (in thousands)	Average openness	Imports from the EC as % of GDP	Imports extra EU as % of GDP	Exports to the EC as % of GDP	Exports extra EU as % of GDP
B	213.7	10182	59.9	43.2	14.5	44.1	18.1
DK	143.2	5278	27.2	17.6	8.2	16.8	11.9
D	1853.9	82060	22.6	11.7	9.2	13.7	10.5
GR	105.7	10518	16.0	16.5	6.6	5.7	3.2
E	469.0	39323	20.9	14.8	8.1	13.3	5.7
F	1228.9	58607	19.5	11.3	7.3	12.6	7.8
IRL	66.6	3661	61.7	30.8	23.4	47.1	22.1
I	1011.5	57506	18.9	10.1	7.5	11.2	9.0
L	13.9	421					
NL	318.2	15574	44.1	25.4	16.6	32.7	13.5
A	182.1	8084	28.9	22.1	8.2	15.2	12.3
P	85.2	9876	30.3	26.5	9.7	20.2	4.2
FIN	105.1	5140	30.1	14.6	11.1	17.4	17.1
SW	201.0	8918	31.3	18.2	9.2	19.5	15.8
UK	1134.2	58996	22.5	12.3	11.3	11.6	9.9
EUR 11	5548.2	290434	24.8	14.5	9.2	15.9	10.0
EUR 15	7132.3	374144	25.0	14.5	9.5	15.9	10.1
USA	6896.5	267856	9.9		11.5		8.3
Japan	3708.4	126033	9.6		8.7		10.5

not of monetary unions. The different adjustment and policy transmission channels of a currency union are never discussed.

OCA-literature has established that trade and capital mobility generally favour forming a currency union in Europe, that labour mobility, and wage and price flexibility are low, and the degree of product diversification favours the well-developed countries in Europe's centre. As a consequence, the question of whether Europe is an OCA has concentrated on the discussion of economic shocks. As Demertzis *et al.* (1998) put it, 'A necessary and sufficient condition for low cost is a high positive correlation between the shocks in member regions *and* shocks of similar size'.

According to standard OCA-theory, if disturbances are distributed symme-trically across countries, a common policy response will suffice. But, if the shocks are mainly idiosyncratic or asymmetric, then the case for a single currency is weakened since it may be useful to alter the exchange rate for stabilisation purposes.[6] The asymmetry may be due to shocks (impulses) or economic struc-tures (responses) (Buiter 1997). The cost of not having exchange-rate flexibility available will depend on the size and nature of the shocks, as well as their per-sistence. If they are large, real costs will be high. Structures matter with respect to factor and product markets. In particular, if labour is mobile, a negative shock could be offset by regional labour migrating from unemployment to excess demand areas, so that there is less need for different policy responses to prevent the emergence of regional problems (Eichengreen 1993a). Alternatively, move-ments of goods can substitute for the mobility of labour (and capital) in correcting demand or supply imbalances.

However, several factors work against this simplistic approach. First, a high degree of interdependence reduces the usefulness of the exchange rate as a shock absorber. As we have argued in previous chapters, exchange-rate volatility is likely to dampen growth and therefore reinforces negative demand and supply shocks. Furthermore, as McKinnon (1963) already pointed out, an open economy is more vulnerable to imported inflation. A devaluation translates into price increases, and if workers resist real wage reductions, nominal exchange-rate variability ceases to be an adjustment tool. In the next section, we will give fur-ther attention to this argument. Instead, exchange risks and uncertainty increase with detrimental consequences for investment and growth. Finally, if production structures are highly specialised, a similar effect would take place (Crawford 1996).

Secondly, the nature of shocks is not only relevant with respect to regions, as commonly modelled, but also with respect to the union as a whole. This fact complicates the picture and also opens other avenues to remedy damage. In terms of our discussion on bloc floating in the previous chapter, perfectly symmetric shocks imply $\nu_A = \nu_B$ and perfectly asymmetric shocks $\nu_A = -\nu_B$. Given that $\nu_U = (1 - \eta)\nu_A + \eta\nu_B$, any shock will have consequences for monetary policy in monetary union unless $(1 - \eta)\nu_A = -\eta\nu_B$, for which there is no systematic reason. If the shock is perfectly symmetric, the policy response will be optimal for both regions; otherwise the larger region will dominate it. This does not necessarily imply that small countries are worse off in a monetary union. As we know from Table 4.1 in the last chapter, the impact of shocks is softer in EMU.[7] The consequences of shocks on the union are therefore a priori undetermined. This is all the more true as we know neither how monetary union changes the new central bank's reaction function nor the precise transmission mechanism. Dornbusch *et al.* (1998) have presented evidence that the response of output and inflation to a 1 percentage point increase in interest rates is not uniform: in the UK and Italy it appears to have a strong impact on output, in Spain hardly any. Inflation response is largest in Belgium and Italy and perverse in the UK (because of housing mortgages in the CPI basket). Similarly the output-inflation trade-offs as a reaction to an interest rate increase seem more favourable to small countries than larger ones.

Many studies have tried to assess the empirical size and nature of shocks and asymmetries in Europe and elsewhere.[8] Most conclude that in the EU, shocks are rather uncorrelated and small in size. Given that the relative weight of most countries in total EU-GDP is low (see Table 5.2), the consequences of country-specific shocks for the union as a whole are likely to be minimal.

It also appears from the literature that not all shocks would require exchange-rate flexibility. The negative consequences resulting from financial shocks would be held in check better by fixed rates. The same is true for demand shocks originating in monetary and fiscal policies – provided EMU remains an area with reasonably stable prices. Persistent real shocks, on the other hand, would benefit from exchange-rate adjustments. However, the frequency and probability of such shocks is fairly low in Europe (Ochel 1997). Most studies that attempt to evaluate these shocks empirically use VAR (vector autoregressive)-models in the tradition of Blanchard and Quah (1989). The conclusion is that, in

Table 5.2 Weight in Euro-GDP (%)

	EMU-11	EMU-15
Germany	34.3	27.6
France	22.3	18.0
Italy	17.5	14.1
Spain	8.5	6.8
Netherlands	5.7	4.6
Be-Lux	4.0	3.3
Austria	3.3	2.7
Finland	1.8	1.4
Portugal	1.5	1.2
Ireland	1.0	0.8
UK	–	13.2
Sweden	–	2.9
Denmark	–	2.0
Greece	–	1.4

Source: Economie Européenne 63 (1997).

general, there exists a core of countries where shocks are highly correlated (i.e. symmetrically distributed) and rather similar in size and a periphery where this is much less so. Supply shocks in the centre are more correlated and smaller than in the periphery, but less so than demand shocks. As a consequence, forming a monetary union will have a cost, high for the periphery, low for the centre – at least from a static–comparative point of view (Demertzis *et al.* 1998). It is interesting, that in nearly all studies the core countries are exactly those that have had a tight exchange rate peg with the DM. But it remains an open question as to whether the causality runs from real structures to monetary arrangements or the other way round. Bayoumi and Eichengreen (1993) put their results into a dynamic perspective by concluding: 'Changes on the supply side will make monetary union easier to operate, while those on the demand side will introduce further difficulties'.

These results may be useful for policy making, as they could guide structural reforms in order to reduce the costs. They could also explain whether the short-term perspectives of joining EMU are optimal – an argument that carries some weight in countries with an opt-out from EMU like Denmark and the UK. However, they do not help us to assess the sustainability of EMU. For it is dubious that the empirical estimates of the VAR-models actually estimate what the authors intend. In fact, in order to estimate a VAR-model, strong identifying restrictions need to be imposed on the moving average representation of the system's disturbance terms (Enders 1995). These restrictions are derived from theory and a convenient model is the standard textbook explanation of a downward-sloping aggregate demand curve and an aggregate supply curve that is upward-sloping in the short run, but vertical in the long run. With this structure, all permanent shocks to output can be identified as supply shocks, while temporary or transitory output disturbances are assumed as demand shocks. Changes in the real exchange rate can be attributed to both supply and demand shocks, and changes in inflation are determined by all three shocks. However, as Marston (1998) has pointed out, these strong identifying assumptions in the model are based on the hypothesis that output is fixed in the long run. But if labour supply is sensitive to real wages and real wages refer to a consumption basket including foreign as well as domestic goods, then labour supply is endogenised and aggregate supply is not fixed, but a function of the real exchange rate. A similar argument can be made with respect to intermediate goods. In this case, the identifying restrictions no longer apply and the VAR does not provide information about the relative importance of demand versus supply shocks. Instead, it establishes a distinction between shocks that have permanent effects on output from those that have temporary effects. I will argue in the next chapter that this distinction is more relevant to the issue of sustainability than the decomposition into demand, supply and monetary shocks.

Figure 5.1 shows the importance of transitory and permanent shocks for EU-member states based on Demertzis *et al.* (1998) calculation and Marston's critique.

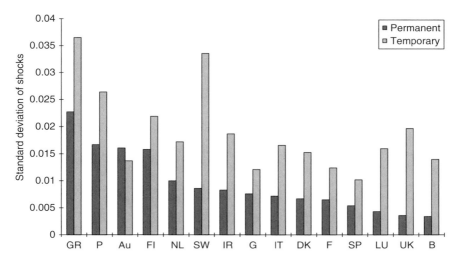

Figure 5.1 Temporary and permanent shocks (1975–95).

On the usefulness of adjusting the nominal exchange rate

Knowledge about the nature of shocks does help to assess the potential for losses from EMU, provided the variation of nominal exchange rates is indeed an adjustment tool. This, however, depends on a specific set of conditions. The ability to achieve a real devaluation by changing the nominal exchange rate can be derived from the following identities:[9]

$$p = (1 - m)p^{\mathrm{d}} + m(p^* + e), \tag{5.2}$$

$$p^{\mathrm{d}} = w - \lambda' + c, \tag{5.3}$$

$$p_{\mathrm{R}} = e + p^* - p^{\mathrm{d}}. \tag{5.4}$$

p^{d} indicates the GDP deflator (the 'domestic' price level), p is the consumer price index – a weighted average of domestic and imported goods prices. w, λ', c are nominal wages, productivity and the mark-up on unit labour costs in log form. As in previous chapters, m is the expenditure share on foreign-produced goods, that is, our indicator for the degree of openness. Equation (5.4) is the real exchange rate. By inserting Equation (5.3) in Equation (5.2) we obtain the real wage

$$\overline{w} = w - p = \lambda' - c - mp_{\mathrm{R}}. \tag{5.5}$$

The real wage increases with productivity, falls with rising profit margins and a real devaluation (a rise in p_R). Therefore, the issue is whether a nominal devaluation will be able to have this effect, that is, if $d\bar{w}/de < 0$.

From the definition of the real wage ($\bar{w} = w - p$) we obtain

$$\frac{d\bar{w}}{de} = \frac{\partial w}{\partial p} \cdot \frac{\partial p}{\partial e} - \frac{\partial p}{\partial e} = \left[\frac{\partial w}{\partial p} - 1\right] \cdot \frac{\partial p}{\partial e} = \left[\frac{\partial w}{\partial p} - 1\right] \cdot m. \tag{5.6}$$

The short-term effect of a nominal devaluation will depend on the degree of openness (m) and on nominal wage flexibility, that is, the expression written in brackets. $\partial w/\partial p$ is the wage-price elasticity by which nominal wages respond to inflation. It corresponds to the nominal inertia coefficient ξ_1 in Equation (1.3) in the first chapter.[10] With unit elasticity, that is, wage indexation of 100 per cent, the term in brackets is zero and the nominal exchange rate variation has no real effect.[11] However, the exchange rate variation always has a price effect: according to Equation (5.2) it raises prices by $\partial p/\partial e = m$. Thus, the larger the degree of openness, the larger the welfare loss is resulting from inflation in response to the nominal exchange rate depreciation, *ceteris paribus*. The alternative case of high or perfect nominal wage rigidity ($\partial w/\partial p) \to 0$ (Keynes's stable money wages) makes the flexible exchange rate an efficient adjustment tool, particularly for very open countries. If the nominal wage is perfectly rigid, the real wage will fall at the rate at which prices increase due to the devaluation, depending on the degree of openness: $(d\bar{w}/de) = -(\partial p/\partial e) = -m$. In this case, the devaluation has the real effect of stabilising output and the nominal effect of imported infla-tion. Finally, if wages were flexible downward $((\partial w/\partial p) < 0)$ the adjustment process would benefit from accommodating negative wage behaviour. Thus, the existence of nominal rigidities is a sufficient condition for making the exchange rate an efficient adjustment tool. However, this efficiency implies that the required variability of the exchange rate is negatively correlated with the degree of openness: large countries need large nominal adjustments, small countries do not.

New classical economics has emphasised that nominal rigidities are hardly compatible with rational behaviour of economic agents in the long run, although this does not exclude short-term effects from policy actions (McCallum 1979). A consistent theory cannot be based on persisting 'money illusion'. However, more recently new Keynesian Economics have produced models in which optimising agents choose to create nominal rigidities (Ball *et al.* 1988). Thus, it is no longer necessary to simply assume nominal rigidities as in the early Keynesian models of the 1970s, but one can also provide sound microeconomic foundations. On the other hand, we have mentioned evidence in Chapter 1 that nominal rigidities are regime-dependent and have a tendency to disappear in an inflationary environ-ment. Thus, the actual value for nominal wage elasticity is an empirical matter.

In Chapter 1, I have quoted evidence from Alogoskoufis and Smith (1991) whereby a dramatic upward shift in the degree of persistence of inflation is quickly reflected in the coefficient of lagged inflation in the Phillips curve, that is, in $\partial w/\partial p$. For the long period between 1857 and 1987, their estimated coefficient is 0.947 for the UK and 0.636 in the USA for 1892–1987. Studies for Europe covering shorter periods indicate values of 0.3 (1977–90) for Germany and 0.07 (1985–91) to 0.6 (1979–84) for France, 0.46 (1972–90) for Spain, 0.58 and 0.48 for Belgium and the Netherlands (1971–90).[12] Muet (1997) has estimated coefficients of 0.68 and 0.70 for the EU15 between 1963 and 1994. Price and wage behaviour after the 1992–3 currency crisis in the EMS indicates that nominal rigidities have increased in line with higher price stability in recent years.[13] Thus, we may safely assume that there are nominal rigidities and a positive adjustment effect, that is, that $\partial w/\partial p - 1 < 0$, when nominal exchange rates are altered in Europe. Hence, by giving up the exchange-rate tool, a country will, indeed, incur a cost.

However, this variable-rate benefit comes at the price of higher inflation. If the authorities of a potential member country are totally committed to price stability (at least at the level expected to prevail under monetary union), then keeping flexible exchange rates does not provide a gain, nor would giving them up constitute a loss. If, however, they are concerned with both price stability and employment, then the utility of the exchange-rate instrument can be described by the authorities' objective function of the form:[14]

$$-\left[\frac{A}{2}(\bar{y}-y)^2 + \frac{\mathrm{d}p^2}{2}\right], \quad \bar{y}-y \geq 0, \tag{5.7}$$

where $\bar{y}$ and y are desired and actual output levels and $\mathrm{d}p$ is the rate of inflation. A is a positive parameter reflecting the authorities' relative preference for output and price stability. The higher the A is, the greater their concern is for keeping output at the desired level. Equation (5.6) shows that there is a short-run trade-off between output and inflation. Hence:

$$y - y_s = \psi(\mathrm{d}p - \mathrm{d}p^e), \quad \psi > 0. \tag{5.8}$$

ψ is here the slope of the Lucas supply curve. It would equal zero with a vertical (long-term) Phillips curve and be high for countries with monetary stability (Lucas 1973). Therefore, a high output-inflation trade-off is equivalent to a flat Phillips curve, and both reflect the benefit of low and stable inflation. y_s is the output level subsequent to the shock, that is, the level that is obtained in the absence of a devaluation. $\mathrm{d}p^e$ is the expected rate of inflation. From Equation (5.2), provided foreign prices remain constant ($\mathrm{d}p* = 0$) we get

$$\mathrm{d}p^e = (1 - m)\mathrm{E}(\mathrm{d}p^d) + m\mathrm{E}(\mathrm{d}e).$$

We will also assume that domestic prices remain constant in the short run ($\mathrm{d}w - \mathrm{d}\lambda + \mathrm{d}z = 0$) so that we get

$$y - y_s = \psi m[\mathrm{d}e - \mathrm{E}(\mathrm{d}e)]. \tag{5.8a}$$

Substituting Equation (5.8a) into Equation (5.7), the objective of the authorities becomes

$$\max_{de} -\left\{\frac{A}{2}[\bar{y} - y_s - \psi m(de - E(de))]^2 + \frac{de^2}{2}\right\}. \tag{5.7a}$$

The first order condition for the maximisation problem in Equation (5.7a) implies

$$de = \frac{A\psi m}{1 + A\psi^2 m^2}(\bar{y} - y_s) + \frac{A\psi^2 m^2}{1 + A\psi^2 m^2}E(de). \tag{5.9}$$

Thus, given that the output objective is higher than the post-shock level (i.e. $\bar{y} > y_s$), the authorities will devalue, even if this measure is not expected. However, under rational expectations we have $E(de) = de$, and we obtain the equilibrium rate of devaluation:

$$de = A\psi m(\bar{y} - y_s) > 0. \tag{5.9a}$$

Thus, the utility of the exchange rate as a potential adjustment instrument depends on the preferences of the authorities for output stabilisation over price stability ($A > 0$), the short-run effect of the devaluation on output ($\psi m > 0$) and the size of the output shock ($\bar{y} - y_s$). At a given price elasticity with respect to output (ψ), the total cost of joining EMU is higher, the larger the concern for stable output is (higher A) and the higher the degree of openness is (m), that is, the smaller a country. Yet, given that this implies $de > 0$ in the steady state,[15] that is, a permanent rate of depreciation, such a situation will cause domestic prices to rise as well, unless nominal rigidities are perfect.

However, ψ is normally higher for countries with price stability. In a Phillips curve world, it is assumed that ψ depends on market structures, wage bargaining, non-wage costs, etc. However, if supply is sensitive to relative prices as in a Lucas-world, the trade-off between output and surprise inflation (surprise devaluation) tends to fade away the more frequently the latter is used (or abused). Therefore, ψ falls for high inflation countries.[16] Thus, there is a negative trade-off between A ('inflation preference') and ψ at least in the medium to long run. This will erode the usefulness of the devaluation option and create a depreciation/inflation bias. We may call this tendency the 'soft currency bias'. Therefore, the marginal cost of giving up the exchange rate as an adjustment tool may be initially high, but it is diminishing with a rising preference for output stability. Over time the gains from joining the monetary union would increase, provided domestic price stability within the union is assured.

Finally, given that a larger import propensity m also implies a larger inflation impact (due to Equation (5.6)), A would normally be negatively correlated with m. As McKinnon (1963) pointed out, this trade-off should prevent the cost of abandoning the exchange rate from growing in a linear fashion. Additionally, a diminishing marginal cost curve in relation to the degree of openness is to be expected. Thus, for a small country with a high degree of openness and a given degree of wage resistance the exchange rate is an efficient adjustment tool. However, this benefit is low because only small adjustments are required, as is the cost of imported inflation at which it is obtained. For small countries, it may therefore be easier to keep the nominal exchange rate stable and to disinflate. For larger countries, the temptation to change the nominal rate is higher, as we have also seen in Chapter 4, because higher real devaluations are needed, but this also increases the inflationary impact. Given that this is likely to develop or increase nominal wage flexibility, the efficiency of adjusting the nominal exchange rate will fall. Ultimately, the cost of giving up the exchange rate tool will tend to be zero.[17] Increasingly, one would have to rely on reducing real wage rigidities in order to move the real wage. Therefore, the ultimate *result* of using the exchange rate instrument frequently to facilitate adjustment is the phenomenon of *labour market rigidity*, that is, a steep Phillips curve.[18]

We may, therefore, conclude that higher the value of the exchange rate as an adjustment tool is the less it is used. Giving it up reflects therefore a dubious cost, at least over the long run. Yet, in the short run, the cost of abandoning the exchange rate instrument in monetary union can be modelled as:

$$C_i = C(A_i, m_i), \quad C_A > 0, \quad C_m > 0, \quad C_{AA} < 0, \quad C_{mm} < 0, \quad C_{Am} < 0.$$
(5.10)

Provided the Phillips curve is not vertical ($\psi \neq 0$), joining a monetary union will impose real costs to a country, if its authorities care for more than only price stability. But the benefits of a devaluation come at the price of higher inflation. Only the net costs are relevant for the decision of joining or leaving a currency area. *Ceteris paribus*, a persistent preference for output stabilisation over price stabilisation will create a 'soft currency bias' (accelerating rates of devaluation and inflation) which sooner or later would turn the cost of joining a low-inflation monetary union into a benefit. Thus, in the long run, steady-state benefits from EMU depend on the commitment to price stability. The short-term decision to join will, however, depend on maximising net benefits by forming an OCA.

Optimising net benefits in the currency area

An OCA needs to optimise something. The obvious variable is net benefits from joining the area. We will first look at steady-state conditions for maximum net benefits. One has to distinguish between an optimum that applies to the monetary union as a whole and an optimum that applies to individual countries. The two are not necessarily identical. The first one implies that any country that wishes to join the union should be admitted as it will add to the total utility of the community. We will call this a Benthamite optimum currency area (BOCA). The second concept implies that only those countries can be accepted as members whose participation does not reduce the net benefits for any other country. We will call this a Pareto Optimal Currency Area (POCA). But first we need to determine the net benefits.

Determining net benefits

The net benefits from joining EMU for country i can be described as:

$$\text{NB}_i = \text{NB}(S, A_i, m_i) = B(S, m_i) - C(A_i, m_i). \tag{5.11}$$

The assessment of net advantages depends on the size of the envisaged currency union, the degree of openness, and the degree of inflation-averseness. Of these, S measures the total size (GDP) of the currency union and dS_i is the marginal contribution to the overall size, that is, the size of an additional country i included into EMU. Although we have seen that reducing exchange risk will improve the permanent growth rate and, therefore, have a positive effect on the net benefits in the long run, we will abstract from this aspect here and focus on the short-term effects of enlarging it by one additional country j (hence: $dS = dS_j$). m_i is given by the economic structure of a country. It is large for small countries as Figure 5.2 shows.

A reflects political preferences for output stabilisation over price stability. Equation (5.11) brings to light an interesting trade-off between the optimal size of EMU and its political orientation. The total differential of Equation (5.11) yields:

$$d\text{NB}_i = B_S dS_j + (B_m - C_m)dm_i - C_A dA_i. \tag{5.11a}$$

The net benefit from a monetary union for country i is maximised when $d\text{NB}_i = 0$.[19] Whether such a maximum is attained or not depends on dS, dm_i and dA_i. The size of the currency area can be increased by including an additional member (j) or by economic growth. The impact from increasing economic integration (m_i) depends on three factors: the balance between marginal benefits from reduced transaction costs, liquidity advantages, and the elimination of exchange risk minus the marginal costs of giving up the exchange rate. As long as $B_m > C_m$, a growing interdependence in the single market would raise net benefits. In view of our previous analysis of benefits and costs, and given a vertical long-run Phillips curve, this condition should hold in general. Observers expect the degree of integration to increase with a single currency, so that net benefits would grow over the long run. In the short run, however, we may take m_i as given and set $dm_i = 0$.[20] That leaves us with the variations of political preferences (dA_i). We will deal here with once-for-all shifts of preferences in a comparative–static approach; in the next chapter we will incorporate reversible and stochastic preference shifts. Provided everything else remains unchanged, a larger preference for output stabilisation over price stability will reduce net benefits in the short run. Over the long run an increase in A_i will, of course, as we have seen, reduce ψ

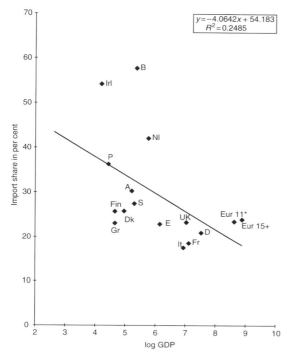

Figure 5.2 Size and import share.

Source: EC Commission and own calculations.

thereby eroding the utility of a devaluation and thereby increase the long-term benefits of the single currency.[21]

From this analysis we derive a first proposition: *if the sustainability of EMU depends on the balance of net benefits, it is the stability of the purchasing power of the new currency,[22] which will be decisive for the union's success.*

However, everything else will not necessarily remain unchanged. In particular, there may be a link between the size of the currency area and political preferences if accepting an additional country would affect monetary stability. In principle, after the start of EMU the European Central Bank (ECB) has taken over responsibility with the 'primary objective of maintaining price stability' (TEU: arts. 2, 3A, and 105). Thus A should be close to zero and the cost of giving up the exchange rate would be minimal, if the additional EMU-members adjust their political pre-ference to the ECB-standard by reducing A, the net benefit would even be aug-mented for such a country. The question is: how will the ECB's A be formed?

In the public debate it is often assumed that A will be an aggregate of national policy preferences. For example, one may think that when Italy – a country with a record of historically high inflation – joins EMU, the ECB's A would be higher than otherwise. Therefore, accepting Italy would lower German welfare, although it would increase the short-term benefits for Italy.[23] But this kind of reasoning is contrary to the TEU. Article 107 of TEU and article 7 of the Statute of the European System of Central Banks (ESCB) and of the ECB define independence in the clearest possible terms:

> When exercising the powers and carrying out the tasks and duties conferred upon them by this Treaty and the Statute of the ESCB, neither the ECB, nor a national central bank, nor any member of their decision-making bodies shall *seek or take instruction* from Community institutions or bodies, from any government of a Member State or from any other body. The Community institutions and bodies and the governments of the Member States undertake to respect this principle and not to seek to influence the members of the decision-making bodies of the ECB or of the national central banks in the performance of their tasks.

Thus, it is the members of the decision-making bodies of the ESCB who will form policy preferences within the general framework of maintaining price stability.

On the other hand, governments may have preferences different from central banks (Rogoff 1985; Cukierman 1994; Eijffinger 1997), or they may reflect different national 'stability cultures' (Jochimsen 1998). We will return to central bank preferences in Chapter 7. Here we are interested in government policies. Given the independence of the central bank, they could only realise these preferences by choosing between being 'in' or 'out' of the common currency.[24] This could make the decision to join or leave EMU a potentially volatile political process. Finally, there exists a third possibility: although politically independent, the members of the Governing Council of the ESCB may culturally reflect the political preferences of their countries of origin.[25] This could lead to a higher A for the union compared to the individual preferences in one individual country. In reality, it is more likely that all central bankers share the same 'stability culture',[26] but for argument's sake let us see what would happen if A reflected national cultures. Admitting country j with the stability commitment $A_j > A_i$ into EMU could lower the net benefit for country i. This is why the convergence criteria in the Maastricht Treaty have gained such a political prominence in the run-up to EMU: convergence to monetary stability (the inflation, interest and exchange rate criteria) without 'excessive deficits' reflects convergence in A-preferences (Jochimson 1998: 81–4). However, Equation (5.11a) shows that there is a potential trade-off between size and 'cultural convergence'. The problem is to decide whether one wishes to optimise the benefits of the union as a whole, or of individual countries.

The Pareto Optimal Currency Area

Admitting members is clearly an improvement for each country i as long as the benefit of one additional country j remains higher than the cost of accepting a higher inflation preference in that country. We can evaluate the impact of admitting country j on net benefits of country i formally by dividing Equation (5.11a) by dS_j:

$$\frac{dNB_i}{dS_j} = B_s - C_A \frac{dA_j}{dS_j} + (B_m - C_m)\frac{dm_i}{dS_j}. \qquad (5.11b)$$

If we assume the degree of integration to remain constant ($dm_i = 0$), which would apply in the short term when EMU-members are selected, the consequences of a larger currency area depend essentially on the preference shift dA_i/dS_j.[27] If preference convergence has been perfect or, we may add, if central bank independence will operate as envisaged in the Treaty, dA_i/dS_j will be zero and country i benefits unambiguously from j joining the currency area ($B_S > 0$). If, however, convergence is imperfect and policy preferences are changed for country i because country j has become a member of EMU, then i's net benefit would be lower – unless this disadvantage is compensated by the gains from a larger currency area. Alternatively, if the stability culture in country j is even higher than in i, net benefits are even greater ($dA_i/dS_j < 0$). The condition for the net benefits of i to remain the same when country j is added would require:[28]

$$\frac{dA_i}{dS_j} = \frac{B_S}{C_A}. \qquad (5.11c)$$

Thus, the ratio of the marginal benefits of size to the marginal costs of abandoning the exchange rate adjustment tool determines the margins of acceptable policy preference diversity in EMU. Consequently, if B_S is higher for small countries than for large countries, the large country would insist on the most restrictive interpretation of admission criteria. On the other hand, the higher the preference convergence between countries, the larger the margins of interpretation are for accepting new members. Yet, if the soft currency bias reduces C_A close to zero over time, then the long-term net benefits and therefore the perspectives of EMU sustainability are higher than expected over the short term.

The trade-off between size of the currency area and policy preferences is illustrated in Figure 5.3.

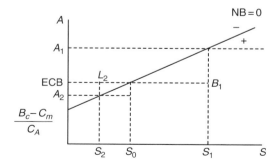

Figure 5.3 Net benefit of a single currency for country i.

The $NB = 0$-line shows the locus of combinations of A and S at which net benefits are zero.[29] Above the line, net benefits are negative and the country i would prefer not to join or to leave the monetary union. Below the line, net benefits are positive. S_0 indicates the size of a currency area where net benefits are equal to zero given the stability preferences of the union. A_1 reflects the loose pre-EMU stability commitment, which would require a large union to compensate for the loss of stability by the economies of scale from a big market, as long as preferences do not change. Yet, if this country's preferences converge to the union standard, its net benefits will be positive at B_1. The opposite applies to the stability prone country with preference A_2. Unless it accepts less price stability, it will incur losses (L_2) at the existing size. However, by increasing the union size to S_0, the disadvantages from a reduced price stability commitment (higher A) are offset by the benefits of a larger currency area.[30] The slope of the $NB = 0$-line is (B_S/C_A).[31] Therefore, any additional member j which increases A_i by less than B_S/C_A creates a net benefit for country i. This is what we may call the Pareto criterion for an OCA:[32] it maximises the aggregate net benefits of its members subject to the condition that no single member's net benefit is reduced by accepting an additional participant.

$$\text{POCA:} \quad \max W = W(\text{NB}_i, \text{NB}_j)$$

subject to the constraint

$$\frac{\mathrm{d}A_j}{\mathrm{d}S_j} \leq \left(\frac{B_S}{C_A}\right)_i. \tag{5.11c'}$$

The Benthamite Optimal Currency Area

Our discussion has so far focused on the net benefit for one isolated country i. This may be relevant for the decision of a specific country to join or leave a currency area, but it does not determine the collective net benefit of the members. An alternative concept of the optimum currency area is a BOCA which maximises the aggregate net benefits of all member countries:

$$\text{BOCA:} \quad \max_{(i=0,1,2,\dots)} \sum \text{NB}_i.$$

What matters here is the sum of all benefits, but this implies the possibility that adding country j may reduce the net benefit in some other country i – although this loss might be more than compensated by the gain of j. In other words, a BOCA may require altruistic behaviour by some countries.[33] This does not exclude some reward or compensating side payments for such behaviour, either in terms of loyalty or of some other policy considerations, such as national security.

A BOCA implies a large monetary union where anyone wishing to join can, as long as the externalised losses for others do not exceed the benefits of the participating country. The selection criteria for such an OCA can be summarised by a statement such as: 'the only real qualification for joining a monetary union is to want to do so and to be willing to accept the rules of the club' (Masson 1996). A POCA is likely to be smaller than the BOCA. *Ceteris paribus*, it would be politically more robust, because the question of 'paying a price for the benefit of others' would not be raised and altruistic behaviour would not be required. Therefore, a POCA is likely to be politically more sustainable than a BOCA.[34] The argument is that monetary union will last as long as net benefits can be reasonably expected to be positive. This implies that what matters are steady-state benefits and not, as we will see in the next section, short-term welfare benefits. A strong definition of sustainability requires that no entrant will ever leave the union so that expected net benefits are always positive for all members. A weaker definition requests that the currency area continues as an effective grouping, even if some withdrawals could occasionally occur. Thus, a priori strong sustainability seems more compatible with a POCA and weak sustainability with a BOCA.

One objection to this line of argument makes a distinction between the conditions for the choice of new members and the conditions for the sustainability of the existing group.[35] A large country may insist on keeping the size of the union small on grounds of concern for price stability. But given that the benefits are then likely to be small as well, it may more easily be tempted to withdraw again. Consequently, the sustainability of the union may be low over time. This argument is valid: if the benefits are low, there is little attraction to stay in the union if things turn sour. The disintegration of the currency union between Malaysia and Singapore in the mid-1960s may provide such an example. The same is probably also true in the case of Czechoslovakia, where the scale-effect of the currency yielded only very low benefits. As we will see in the next section, if the benefits of EMU are subject to stochastic shocks, a 'critical mass of benefits' is required to make a currency union sustainable.

On the other hand, if the government making the decision to join has different preferences from the Treaty commitment, say because its A is high, then its expected net benefits are low or even negative. It may then prefer to remain outside EMU. This may be the case in the UK or Sweden. Similarly, if a country's political preferences changed significantly in this direction during membership, our theory would recommend that the country should leave the monetary union. We will deal with this argument in the next chapter.

Summary and conclusion

This chapter has gone back to the theory of OCA: it has defined an OCA as a union that maximises the net benefits of scale that can be derived from sharing a currency. A large currency area yields significant microeconomic advantages, provided its purchasing power is sustained. The cost of joining the union is dependent on the value given to the short-term advantages of exchange rate manipulation. In the long run the costs tend to zero; therefore, net benefits reflect the time preferences by authorities. This makes it crucial that the preferences of potential participants are sufficiently homogenous to ensure that the particular preferences of one member do not reduce the benefits of any other country (Pareto optimal) or all other countries (BOCA). What matters for the long-run sustainability of the net benefits from the union currency, is the preservation of price stability. If these benefits are maintained, the monetary union should be sustainable.

Our theory of OCAs is different from the traditional approach, built around the insights by Mundell, McKinnon and Kenen. These theories have relatively little predictive power (Goodhart 1995). For example, they contribute little to explaining why monetary separations have usually followed political disunity, like in Central and Eastern Europe in the 1990s. This is because in most models size and political preferences are not explicitly included: they rely simply on the degree of integration. By including our policy variable A, we may explain monetary disruption following a profound political crisis or the choice of some countries, like the UK, to remain outside the euro-area. Still missing, however, is a theory on why monetary unions are not more volatile at the margins. Our analysis shows that the assessment of costs and gains from a single currency is an eminently political question. There is no hard evidence. As we shall see in the next chapter, there are good reasons to believe that if all participating member countries share the same commitment to price stability, EMU will yield significant net benefits. However, politics will remain the Achilles heel. For if the political consensus in one country changed significantly compared to the community consensus, its perceived net benefits could turn negative, and that country might seek to leave the union. This, at least, must be the conclusion from our OCA-theory. As we have seen in the first chapter, such changes in collective intentionality are not unusual. We must now analyse the consequences of such preferences and policy-shifts for the sustainability of a monetary union.

6 Is EMU sustainable?

In the last chapter we argued that a monetary union is sustainable if the aggregate benefits from being in the union exceed the costs of being unable to respond to shocks individually. We implicitly broadened the widely discussed question of who should join a monetary union and asked for the set of conditions under which a country might wish to leave the union. If these conditions were not fulfilled, European Monetary Union (EMU) would be sustainable.

In the literature critical to EMU, it is often argued that Europe is not an Optimum Currency Area (OCA) (Jochimsen 1998) and will, therefore, fail. As Feldstein (1997: 72) put it: '... if countries discover that the shift to a single currency is hurting their economies and that the new political arrangements are also not to their liking, some of them will want to leave'. The assessment that the European Union (EU) does not meet the criteria of an OCA seems to be based on three counts: insufficient labour mobility, insufficient wage/price flexibility, and asymmetries in shocks and structures (Demertzis *et al.* 1998). But even if that were true, which we will question in Chapter 8, it does not imply that EMU does not make sense: that depends on the balance of net benefits. In this respect it is important to distinguish between the structures and shocks in the economy on one hand, and the political preference and response functions on the other. It is only the latter that determines net benefits for the members of the monetary union. This explains why Euro-sceptics like Jochimsen (1998) and Feldstein (1997) discuss in great length the apparent heterogeneity of political preferences in Europe. However, most of their conjectures are based on *attitudes* formed by different national traditions and institutions. They, therefore, miss the point that new institutions create new traditions and ultimately transform attitudes.

The difficulty in assessing political preferences is, of course, part of the larger issues of value theory[1] and the related utility concept. Economic theory has been marred for centuries by attempts to find measures for 'subjective' or 'intrinsic' value judgements. The European debate about 'philosophical convergence' and the solidity of the 'stability culture' is reminiscent of those early writers who tried to attribute utility to *psychological attitudes*: governments or 'countries' are supposed to have preferences for inflation, for interference with monetary policy, etc., as individuals have desires for lipstick or sport cars.[2] The observer tries to guess these preferences by looking into the *cultural attitudes* of individual countries.

However, microeconomic theory has moved on. Consumer behaviour is now understood as choice behaviour. The difference lies in the fact that a preference is an attitude, while a choice is an action. In choice, consumer preferences are constrained by budget constraints. A central assumption in this approach is the (weak) *axiom of revealed preference* that imposes consistency on choices by linking rationality to preferences by imposing constraints. This has the advantage that the theory refers to directly observable objects (*choice behaviour*) rather than to attitudes (*preferences*). Therefore, choice theory avoids the fallacies of introspection and gives decision-making a behavioural foundation (Mas-Colell *et al.* 1995).

The theory of consumer choice is not directly transferable to public choices. The challenge of social or collective choice theory is to find a rule or procedure, which always identifies a collective preference, whatever the variety of separate preferences of the individuals concerned (Hargreaves Heap *et al.* 1992). Such rules may be relevant for institution building in Europe, but they are not the subject here. I would like to argue, however, that the axiom of revealed preference, first developed by Samuelson (1947), can be expanded to a concept of *revealed public preferences*. This requires in a first step that policy preferences are about states and not things, so that policy actions reflect a preference for state x over state y in a frame of accompanying circumstances over a given preference horizon (Von Wright 1990). One sub-set of these circumstances is the institutional constraints imposed on policy actions. In a second step we have to admit that policy choices will display a certain amount of consistency (although not necessarily of time consistency). The (weak) axiom of revealed public preference can then be formulated as follows: if x is ever chosen by public authorities when y is available, then there can be no set of circumstances containing both alternatives for which y is chosen and x is not.[3] For example, if x is price stability and y inflation, the revealed preference axiom states that it is impossible that the authorities have a preference for inflation when price stability is observed.

This statement may appear trivial, but it dispels the *procès d'intention* on which the debate about the presumed 'readiness' of individual countries to join EMU often has been grounded. It also allows us to evaluate policy preferences for price stability by observable inflation rates, in order to estimate net benefits from EMU. Moreover, inflation rates reveal not only policy preferences by authorities, but also the collective preference for price stability (the 'culture'). In this chapter, we will first apply the OCA-concepts of the last chapter to the European economy, and then we will analyse the implications of shocks and volatile policy preferences for the sustainability of EMU. This will lead us to the formulation of some guidelines for a sustainable monetary union.

Is EMU a BOCA or a POCA?

We can now try to evaluate the net benefits of EMU. We will take national inflation rates as a proxy for national inflation preference (dA) and the logarithm of GDP as the marginal increase in size that one country would contribute to the formation of EMU (dS). Taking the log rather than ECU-denominated GDP is justified by the diminishing returns assumptions in the previous chapter, and by the fact that the degree of openness is a log-function of GDP (see Figure 5.2). Of course, directly estimating net benefits would require a formulation for the two functions $B(S_i, m_i)$ and $C(A_i, m_i)$. But instead of making arbitrary assumptions on their form, we proceed by comparing the position of individual countries with the norms set by the convergence criteria regarding inflation in the Maastricht Treaty. The convergence criteria listed in art. 109j derive their sense from making sure that reality reflects 'preference convergence' for price over output stability prior to joining. From this point of view, it is not surprising that the convergence criteria focus on monetary rather than real convergence.[4] Nominal convergence is a necessary and sufficient condition for EMU to start as a Pareto-OCA (POCA). Interpreting the convergence criteria in this way eliminates some of their contradictions and the arbitrariness, which are often cause for criticism (see: Buiter, Corsetti and Roubini 1993). It also establishes a clear hierarchy of the criteria in Treaty on European Union (TEU): art. 109j that should be read as a lexicographic ordering with price stability at the top (Collignon 1996). We, therefore, assume that the inflation target (average of the three best countries plus 1.5 per cent)[5] represents the zero line for acceptable inflation.

We will first simulate the POCA-conditions (5.11c') by comparing (dA_i/dS_i) with the Maastricht norm, assuming that the latter reflects the ratio $(B_S/C_A) = (dA_{EU}/dS_{EU})$. The marginal cost–benefit ratio for each individual country (dA_i/dS_i) is then the ratio of national inflation to the log of GDP, and the European norm is the ratio of the Maastricht inflation target to average EU-GDP in log form. This is shown in Figure 6.1. In order to capture time variances in preferences, we calculated two series, one for 1997 (the reference for EMU-selection) and one for the average inflation 1996–8. It turns out that there are two countries that clearly violate our simulated condition for a POCA: Greece and Luxembourg. With respect to Greece this is not surprising, given that it does not fulfil the convergence criteria (EU-Commission 1998). The case of Luxembourg, however, is explained by its small size, which does not compensate for an inflation record that is only the fifth best. In other words, the four countries with higher price stability (Ireland, France, Austria and Finland) would find that by accepting Luxembourg they would not be compensated by higher benefits for the cost of seeing their own preference for price stability reduced to Luxembourg standards. Curious as this may sound, it reflects the brave new Europe with its new culture of price stability.

Secondly, we may ask how these individual cost–benefit ratios add up to aggregate net benefits from EMU in order to simulate a Benthamite OCA (BOCA). In a first step we have ordered countries according to increasing revealed inflation preference for 1997 and aggregated their marginal cost–benefit ratios. The zero net benefit line of Figure 5.1 in the previous chapter is then proxied by the zero line in Figure 6.2, which assumes that each country must at least meet the Maastricht inflation target. Under this hypothesis, the larger the size of the union is, the larger the potential for positive net benefits will be (given that inflation preference is identical for all members at the norm). The aggregate net benefits of EMU are reflected by adding the marginal cost–benefit ratio of each country to the sum

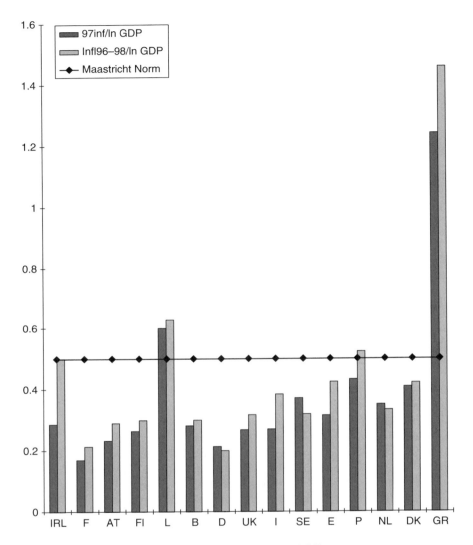

Figure 6.1 Marginal cost–benefit analysis of EMU (Pareto OCA).
Source: Own calculations based on Eurostat.

of the marginal ratios of those countries that have revealed lower inflation. Thus, the first country on the horizontal axis (Ireland) reflects EMU with one member, the last (Greece) EMU at fifteen. Given that fourteen out of fifteen countries meet the inflation target, it is not surprising that net benefits remain positive for Europe. In a second step we maximise this total net benefit. Figure 6.3 gives the difference between the aggregate net benefits and the zero line. Accepting Greece in 1998 would have reduced the net benefit for the union as a whole, but would not

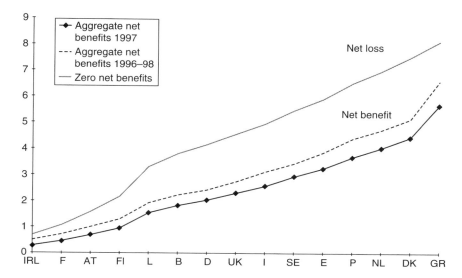

Figure 6.2 Country contribution to aggregate net benefit from EMU (Benthamite OCA).
Source: Own calculations based on Eurostat.

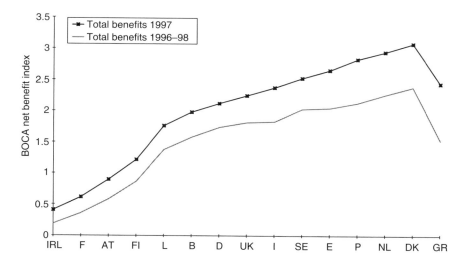

Figure 6.3 Total net benefits in a Benthamite OCA.
Source: Own calculations based on Eurostat.

have turned it into a loss. The Benthamite-optimum was an EMU with fourteen
countries.

Thus, our simulation of OCA criteria yields two results: a BOCA excluded
only Greece in 1997, a POCA would also have rejected Luxembourg. While the

first is in line with the Convergence Reports by the European Commission (1998) and the European Monetary Integration (EMI, 1998), the latter is rather surprising. Of course, it had no bearing on the actual selection of EMU members, which was defined by art. 109j TEU; nobody ever doubted that Luxembourg would be part of EMU. In fact, the selection process is not based on cost–benefit, but on cost-minimising criteria. Furthermore, decision-making in the selection of participants is not strictly compatible with a Pareto-optimum. Moreover, a country's conformity to the necessary conditions was subject to a vote in the European Council with qualified majority. Figure 6.4 shows the weighted votes of each country of the EU.

A qualified majority requires sixty-two votes out of eighty-seven (i.e. 71.3 per cent) (Arrowsmith 1995). Thus, no single country has a blocking majority – not even two large countries.[6] For the selection process this implies that the POCA constraint $(dA_i/dS_j) \leq (B_S/C_A)_i$ must hold at least for three countries 'i', and not only for one. A strict Pareto-optimum would require a veto for each member. Nevertheless, it is likely that the three countries with the highest commitment to price stability have fairly similar preferences, so that EMU resembles more a Pareto-optimal than an unrestricted currency area, even with Luxembourg included. It is, however, interesting to note that the nomination of the members of the Executive Board of the European Central Bank (ECB) are appointed by 'common accord' (TEU: art. 109a) which imposes a higher degree of homogeneity on the executive organ of monetary policy.

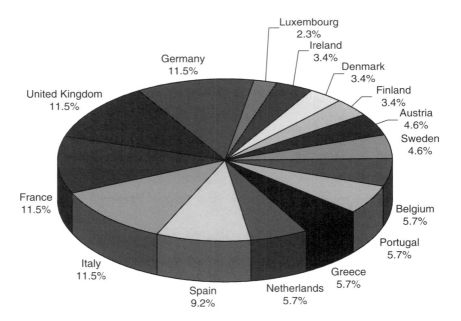

Figure 6.4 Voting weights in the EU.

But if the Treaty does not institutionalise a POCA, it also does not envisage an unconstrained currency area, given that a minority of twenty-six votes (29.9 per cent) can block a potential member. It is really the inflation convergence criteria that define EMU as a BOCA with a small degree of altruistic solidarity. For a country with a revealed preference for inflation higher than the convergence norm, the slope of the net benefit curve in Figure 6.2 will become steeper than the EU-norm, and such country lies to the right of the optimum in Figure 6.3. On the other hand, it is also clear that the selection of the eleven countries forming EMU was not optimal, for the optimum was EU-fourteen. The UK, Denmark and Sweden lie to the left of our optimum and should, therefore, be included.

What is the point of these deliberations? It is not to show that the political judgement in selecting the eleven EMU members was either right or wrong. It is rather to demonstrate that the fresh look on OCA taken in the last chapter can be used for empirical purposes. Our calculations show that at a time when the decision to start stage three of EMU was taken, net benefits were possible for all participants. With respect to the sustainability of EMU, the key question is: are these benefits sufficient to last when the new union is hit by shocks that might alter the preference structure and pressure authorities to change their policy choices?

Transitory instability in net benefits

We have defined an OCA by the net benefits it provides to its members in the steady-state. We will now look at the consequences of variations in net benefits. The principal causes for changes in net benefits are policy preferences and economic shocks that affect the size (or the growth rate) of the monetary union, while the degree of integration might be affected by economic and political disturbances. The literature on OCAs has mainly focused on output shocks and very little on political preference shocks. This is understandable, given the facility of obtaining economic data and the conceptual difficulty to model policy reactions. We can circumvent this dichotomy by asking under what circumstances a member-state might exercise its 'option of defection' from a monetary union. This requires in a first step to compare the potential net present value of future benefits of *not* being part of EMU with those of being a member minus the transitory cost of currency disruption resulting from a change. In a second step, one would consider uncertainty and view adherence to a currency regime as an investment project.

Let us first assert under what conditions a country might find it attractive to leave a monetary union. A look at Equation (5.11a) from the previous chapter reveals immediately an important asymmetry:

$$dNB_i = B_S dS_i + (B_m - C_m)dm_i - C_A dA_i.$$

By joining a monetary union an individual country increases size S_i and over time its degree of openness m_i. If convergence has taken place dA_i is small. Thus, the larger the relative weight of the union compared to the individual country, the more dramatic the improvement. By contrast, when leaving the union, the loss of size would also be significant, given that the relative weight of individual countries in Europe is low and the degree of integration is also likely to fall over time. These losses would have to be offset by the benefit of being able to use the exchange rate as an adjustment tool. Given the importance of the size factor, this requires a very substantial shift in policy preferences.

But why would policy preferences change? Obviously, this may come as a response to shocks in the real economy or – more elusively – because of some political earthquake. Let us first assume that an economic disturbance occurs. A negative output shock would marginally reduce the size of the union and therefore the benefits. As we have seen, if shocks are symmetrical, that is, they hit all members of the union uniformly, then a uniform policy response is adequate to remedy the situation, regardless of their persistence. If shocks are idiosyncratic, regional adjustment is required. The question is then, whether an individual country could be more efficient on its own in finding the right policy response than the union. Essentially, this requires regional policies. Traditional OCA-theory suggests that using the exchange rate could support the required changes in relative prices, although Chapter 5 raised doubts about such theory. Our theory of bloc floating in Chapters 2–4 points in the opposite direction: adjustments may become easier and monetary policy more efficient under EMU.

The US experience with regional shocks also proves that flexible exchange rates are not necessarily indispensable: the transformation of New England from a textile, boot- and shoe-based economy with high unemployment in the 1960s and early 1970s to a centre of high-technology industries with low regional unemployment in the 1980s took place without New England opting for a separate currency (Eichengreen 1993a; Mundell 1998). Thus, other adjustment mechanisms may do a better job.[7] These alternatives must be considered as the 'accompanying circumstances' over the given preference horizon when the exit option from monetary union is evaluated by authorities.

However, one would also have to consider the nature of the shocks independently of these adjustment issues. The uncertainties of the future include also the possibility that temporary disadvantages resulting from EMU (say in case of a negative output shock) might disappear again. This means that changes in policy choices and revealed preferences (dA_i) must respond differently to permanent or temporary shocks. If the output shock were temporary, that is, self-reverting to the original position, an adjustment of the exchange rate would have created a price effect that would have caused output to overshoot the original shocks.[8] If the shocks are persistent or even permanent, then a more fundamental adjustment is required. Figure 5.1 indicates that in Europe such temporary shocks are much more dominant than permanent ones.

Traditional OCA-theory does not take these alternatives sufficiently into account. Here, Hirschman's (1970) critique of the economic profession (as compared to moralists and political scientists) applies: economists mostly pay attention to adverse shifts in supply and demand conditions, while the willingness and ability to maximise benefits remain unchanged, and preferences remain constant. From that perspective, the reversibility of changes in supply and demand conditions must be in doubt: hence, the theory must emphasise the exchange rate tool. If, on the other hand, the regional shock is due to a 'loss of maximising aptitudes or energy'[9] or simply shifts in preferences, then the region's difficulties could eventually be repaired without such an instrument. Obvious candidates for such alternative adjustment channels are relative wages, labour-force participation rates, inter-regional capital mobility and government policy (Eichengreen 1993a). Thus, output shocks might disappear on their own account, or because the necessary efforts to remedy the situation were made. It is this Hirschmanian concept of 'random and more or less easily repairable lapses' which I will call *transitory shocks*.

Secondly, a similar argument can be made with respect to political preference shocks. Let us assume that after the start of EMU the collective preference for output stabilisation changes within one country. Elections may have taken place and the new government follows a different 'economic philosophy' from the community-wide consensus. For example, it might prefer 4 per cent inflation over 4 per cent unemployment,[10] while the community consensus sets 2 per cent equal to price stability. Under a deterministic OCA-model, the new government might be inclined to leave the monetary union as net benefits turn negative with the new preference order. Exit is particularly likely if the slope of the NB = 0-line in Figure 5.1 is flat because the marginal benefit of devaluing is considered high and the economies of scale low (i.e. $(B_S/C_A) \to 0$). In a stochastic model, however, defection is less likely. First of all, if there are some exit costs (sunk costs) involved, they must be deducted from the potential benefits of having a separate currency. This reduces the incentive to get out, for the decision to leave monetary union would require incurring irreversible, sunk costs, while the expected net benefits might revert back. Under these circumstances, it is more likely that 'exit' will be transformed into 'voice', to use Hirschman's (1970) famous model. The new government will complain ('voice') in the hope of improving matters, while continuing as a member country of EMU. This can cause an 'integrative crisis' (Hirschman 1981: 283) that impels members to look for some concerted action. As a consequence, the net gains would increase for the 'voicing' country and the option value of 'exit' would fall. But if this country had abandoned the single currency, it would not only have lost the right to influence the union's decision (which might have some impact on its future development even after quitting), but it would also have lost the intangible capital of benefiting from loyalty among the members of a club. It would be left only with the option of investing again – including the renewed expense of changeover costs – if it wished to rejoin. Thus, an optimal investment or exit policy has to price the two options of 'exit' and 'return' simultaneously.

The 'voice' option is an efficient instrument to influence the choices of others. It contributes to preference homogeneity in the union and helps to return to positive net benefits.[11] The new government can direct its energies to adopt what the group as a whole calls for. In addition, the efforts of obtaining gains through the use of 'voice' will benefit from the fact that the government can threaten to exercise its exit-option as this would reduce size benefits for all. But by actually quitting, the dissatisfied government would lose the benefit of having the exit-option. Thus, keeping the exit-option without using it adds to the net gains of being part of a union, if policy preferences vary.[12] From the days of de Gaulle's 'empty chair' to the British opt-out from the Maastricht Treaty or Germany's hard-nosed poker about the Stability Pact in Dublin 1996, Europe has witnessed the value of an exit-option when bargaining for better political terms of trade.[13]

Of course, the shift in policy actions that may return positive net benefits for one country may lead to a reduction in the benefits of another. The acceptance of this redistribution of benefits is a manifestation of loyalty among union members. As Hirschman (1970: 78) put it: 'Loyalty holds exit at bay and activates voice'. The existence of loyalty is not irrational among members of a monetary union, especially because the decision to leave always has externalities for the others. Therefore, while loyalty postpones exit, its very existence is predicated on the possibility of exit (Hirschman 1970: 82).

What this discussion of political shocks reveals is quite simple: over time most shocks are transitory. Hence, the net benefit from a single currency (or alternatively a flexible exchange rate) cannot be proven with certainty unless the transitory or persisting nature of a shock is clear, and all alternative policy options have been defined. For, if a shock is transitory it will reduce net benefits only temporarily. If a country left EMU, as soon as the balance of net benefits turned negative, it would have lost the advantages from the single currency after the situation has improved again. We must, therefore, establish under what conditions negative net benefits might be compatible with a sustainable monetary union.

Joining or leaving EMU as an investment decision

If we incorporate shocks into the assessment of net benefits, the creation of an OCA becomes a function of the short- and long-term dynamics of expected future benefits. This can best be formalised by viewing participation in EMU not as a simple welfare-maximising operation, but as an investment decision, where investment is defined as the act of incurring an immediate cost in the expectation of future rewards (Dixit and Pindyck 1994). In this respect, the immediate costs are the transitional or changeover costs in moving from one currency to another, while the future rewards are the steady-state net benefits from sharing the single currency. However, investment decisions are made in an environment of uncertainty. The decision to join or leave a currency union is then characterised by three considerations:

1   Transitional costs, once incurred, are irreversible – they are sunk costs. A country that left a currency area and then returned because the balance of expected benefits has changed, would incur such sunk cost twice. Volatility in membership-commitment is expensive.

2   Uncertainty over future rewards. As we have seen, net benefits vary with policy preferences, economic shocks, union size and the degree of integration. In part this explains the large preoccupation with institutional arrangements in the

TEU, for the purpose of institutions is to reduce uncertainty. Yet, the structure of the institutional arrangement determines also partly the size of future rewards.

3   Flexibility about the timing of investment decisions, which allows the gathering of more information about potential rewards. This reduces uncertainty and therefore makes 'waiting' a valuable option.

Thus, the choice of participation in EMU becomes a risky decision in an uncertain environment. By taking uncertainty into account, we can borrow from option theory to assess the decision for or against a single currency.[14] As Dixit and Pindyck (1994) point out, when a firm is exercising an option to invest, it gets a project in place and an option to abandon. The same is true for the decision to join or leave EMU. The value of this exit-option might vary over time, depending on perceived levels of benefits and disadvantages, on the volatility of expectations, and on externalities such as the political fall-out resulting from breaking a contract.[15]

By exercising the option to leave, a country incurs costs that need to be taken into account when assessing the cost–benefit balance. These costs relate to the loss of size and possibly economic integration, as discussed in the last section. They also include the giving up of the exit-option (an option exercised is no longer an 'option', but a 'fact') and the possibility of influencing the other members of the group. Obviously, the larger these costs are, the higher the degree of uncertainty about the future level of net benefits. Consequently, with high uncertainty, the barriers to move to a different currency regime (whether into or out of EMU) are high. High uncertainty includes conservative behaviour, that is, it creates reluctance to join or to leave a monetary union. This may explain why in some of the larger EU member countries the debate about EMU remains so hesitant. The marginal net benefits derived from the single currency are lower for large countries and uncertainty about the future reduces the expected value of net benefits. In smaller countries the benefits are more obvious, given that they would benefit from belonging to a currency area of significantly larger size. This analysis implies that for the two countries with an opt-out, the UK and Denmark, and for Sweden that effectively assumed one, the decision to join EMU will be facilitated by a successful implementation of the euro because this would reduce uncertainty ('seeing is believing').

Thus, in a stochastic world with sunk costs, uncertainty about the future (which includes the possibility that the causes of dissatisfaction might disappear) would have a stabilising effect on the status quo because uncertainty increases the value of waiting. As we know from option theory, the opportunity cost of the in/out decision must be a significant component in the decision itself. Furthermore, the higher the degree of uncertainty of future benefits, the higher the option value of 'waiting', that is, of not changing the existing currency arrangement. But, transitory shocks, as defined before, increase uncertainty and thereby lower the incentive to change. Therefore, they are not a threat to EMU sustainability but a support. On the other hand, this fact explains also that the dissolution of a currency union should only be expected when profound disturbances and systemic malfunctions have undermined the expected steady-state net benefits.

We may summarise these arguments into our second proposition: *if transitional sunk costs of changing currency are high, a country will be reluctant to change in an uncertain environment, unless the expected net benefits from the new currency are high. The higher the uncertainty, the larger the reluctance to change.*

Consequently, any currency area, whether a nation or a monetary union, will exhibit a high degree of inertia. Only when it has become perfectly clear that the existing monetary arrangement yields permanently negative benefits to its members, will they opt for a regime change. Transitory shocks are not sufficient to induce this change. Thus, it would appear that over the last quarter of a century, Europe has come to exactly this conclusion: the old regime was unsustainable.

Long-term cost considerations of currency disruption

Long-term net benefits from monetary union have to take the transitional costs of introducing a new currency into account. The longer EMU lasts, the lower the cost of the changeover will be relative to the gains. At a given degree of uncertainty, the sustainability of EMU will depend on the transitional sunk cost of changing currency and in the long run, steady-state net benefits from the single currency around which rational expectations will oscillate.

First, transitional exit-costs arise from the destruction of information about existing monetary units and the cost of learning about – and adjusting to – the properties of the new currency system (Meltzer 1997). Some of these are simply the mirror image of the changeover to the euro, such as designing, printing and delivering new bank notes, changing monetary laws (including the status of the central bank), altering machines, software, payment systems, etc. Then there are the not insignificant 'menu costs' imposed by new pricing arrangements,[16] although they could be avoided or reduced by starting the new national currency at par with the euro.

More important may be the institutional costs associated with a withdrawal from EMU. Given that Monetary Union is an essential part of the TEU, and given that it makes no provisions for retiring from EMU, re-imposing a national currency would imply a breach of Treaty and cause a loss of 'loyalty'. It is likely that this would happen in a hostile environment. Consequently, other advantages related to being part of the EU, such as free access to the single market, eligibility for structural funds, and subsidies from the Common Agricultural Policy and many other features (Artis and Lee 1994) could be forfeited. This makes the transitional costs of leaving the single currency area much more expensive than those related to joining it. Furthermore, the reduction in the size of the currency area is reducing benefits from widespread currency use for all union members, although the loss would normally be greater for a withdrawing country than for the rest of the union. This natural asymmetry – together with the fact that loyalty from the majority of member countries would come at relatively low cost for them – is a further argument why EMU has good chances to last, once it has started – provided, of course, the steady-state benefits do not deteriorate.

Secondly, because a monetary system is primarily a device for organising information (Goodhart 1995), steady-state changes in net benefits must result from disturbances to monetary information sets, that is, from variations in the internal and external value of money. If the information or liquidity-value of the shared currency diminished permanently, this would lead to a 'disintegrative crisis'. The expected net benefits from EMU would permanently turn negative, and members would be better off by leaving. 'Voice' would be transformed into 'exit'. Individual countries would exercise their option to split and the monetary union would dissolve. For this to happen, the expected long-term benefits from a national currency must exceed the transitory exit-costs related to the break-up. However, given our long list of advantages from size and degree of integration, this would require a serious deterioration in the quality of the currency. Not surprisingly, the latter has frequently occurred when hostilities between regions and/or very high rates of inflation had already undermined the information value of the old currency, as can be seen in the split-up of the Austrian–Hungarian Empire, or more recently of the Soviet Union and Yugoslavia.[17]

For the sustainability of EMU, this second feature is ultimately the most important. Only long-term, steady-state characteristics determine the stability of the system and not transitory shocks, whether symmetric or asymmetric. Short-term volatility of shocks and preferences creates uncertainty and increases the value of the exit option. The cost of giving it up by exercising it would, therefore, also be high ('once you are out, you cannot come back'). Consequently, the lower the volatility of disturbances, the higher the need will be for steady-state advantages from EMU. However, provided that the single currency's value remains stationary over time, low disturbance volatility implies high systematic information stability. In other words, in the long run the benefits from the single currency will be high if price stability is maintained in the union. Therefore, even with variable net benefits our first proposition is confirmed: *Sustainability of the euro ultimately boils down to the question of whether the system of Monetary Union tends to a long-term equilibrium with stable prices, or whether there are endogenous tendencies which would disrupt the stability of the monetary information sets.*

This proposition is somewhat surprising. It implies that monetary stability is a sufficient condition for making EMU sustainable. By contrast, critics have concentrated on real economy arguments against EMU. The most common are lack of flexibility in labour and product markets, low factor mobility, differences in tastes, technology, rates of income growth and domestic institutions (Feldstein 1992). However, these factors reflect different channels to remedy economic disturbances. They are particularly sensitive to the resort of 'voice' in the union. But they do not belong to the domain of monetary policy where the question of the benefits from using a certain currency belongs. Thus, to put things bluntly, a profound economic crisis may destroy the EU as such and EMU with it, but it is impossible that it could destroy EMU and keep the rest alive. We will deal with this 'ultimate' threat to EMU in Chapter 8 where we analyse European unemployment.

The effectiveness of monetary policy under EMU

There is a good theoretical argument for our proposition. If money is neutral, it has no effect on the real economy. The nominal exchange rate is then useless for output stabilisation purposes. In fact, changing the rate may turn out to be destabilising by creating a 'soft currency bias'. But if money is not neutral in the short term, so that there is a 'cost of giving up the exchange rate', then the slope ψ of the short-run trade-off between output and inflation in Equation (5.8) determines the efficiency of monetary policy. Yet, if this slope varies with expected inflation,[18] as Ball *et al.* (1988) have shown, then the efficiency of monetary policy for output stabilisation purposes is dependent on the central banks' success in maintaining price stability. As a consequence, there is a positive relationship between output and inflation variability (Fischer 1994). With higher inflation variance, the efficiency of monetary policy is reduced. Barro (1976: 253) summarised this as follows:

> An increased variance of money makes it more difficult for individuals to react appropriately to the real shifts in the economy. There are two important types of responses to an increased money variance. First, since individuals react by attributing a larger fraction of observed price movements to monetary causes, there is a smaller effect of a given size monetary disturbance on output – that is, the magnitude of the Phillips curve slope is smaller. Second, the associated compounding of individual information problems leads both to a higher variance of output about its full (current) information position and to a reduced predictability of future prices. It also leads to an increase in the variance of relative prices across markets.

This fact is a double-edged sword: as Walsh (1995) points out, a high commitment to price stability increases the cost of inflation reduction, but it also leads to larger output effects of monetary surprises. This can give rise to the paradox that 'both the incentive to inflate and the cost of reducing inflation may increase with greater central bank independence' (Walsh 1995: 33). It could also mean that the instruments of monetary policy (the exchange and interest rate) are sharper in a low inflation environment, so that output stabilisation becomes easier. In other words, the *cost* of disinflation rises in low inflation environments, but the *utility* of disinflation disappears. Therefore, it is not really a cost.[19] By contrast the effectiveness of demand management improves, if price stability is maintained, and this is a potential long-term benefit. Therefore, in a stable monetary union the supposed 'advantage' of flexible exchange rates has been replaced by the much more tangible advantage of more efficient monetary (interest rate) policies. EMU may have greater real effects than previous discussions have suggested.[20] This is an important argument supporting our hypothesis that the Golden Age was brought to an end by the Great Inflation and not by other, structural causes. We will formalise this in Chapter 8.

This theory is quite revisionist in relation to the older Mundell–Flemming literature, which argued that monetary policy is less effective under fixed than under floating exchange rates (see Eichengreen 1993). It is, however, clear that this improved efficiency of stabilisation policies would not only apply to monetary policy, but also to fiscal and wage policies. What matters here is that precisely due to the increased efficiency of monetary policy in a low-inflation monetary environment, it is rational to expect output shock reversals. Therefore, the option of reaping future benefits despite today's output losses increases the utility of being a member of the monetary union. Alternatively, if the union did not maintain price stability, the efficiency of monetary policy for output stabilisation would be lost, and the benefit from staying in the union would gradually disappear. Therefore, there are good reasons why EMU member countries have an incentive to maintain price stability over the long term, once they join.

Summary and conclusion

This chapter has used the conceptual framework of Chapter 5 for the assessment of the sustainability of EMU. It has focused on two propositions:

- If the sustainability of EMU depends on the balance of net benefits derived from a single currency, price stability will be decisive for the new currency's success.
- If the transitional sunk costs of changing currency are high, a country would be reluctant to change in an uncertain environment, unless the expected net benefits from the new currency are high.

Consequently, the sustainability of EMU depends on the long-term steady-state benefits from a large, low inflation currency area. Temporary shocks and policy preference volatility are no threat to the union's sustainability. However, the selection of member countries does have consequences for the political stability of EMU. Our empirical simulation has shown that EMU with eleven countries is neither Pareto nor Benthamite optimal, although it does yield significant net benefits to its members.

Our two propositions lead to a simple recommendation for long-term sustainability of these benefits: maintain price stability! This, of course, is the unambiguous objective of the Maastricht Treaty. Realising this objective requires a high preference for low inflation over output stability, that is, low As in Equation (5.7). In the next chapter we will assert the evidence that this requirement is fulfilled in Europe.

However, our analysis has also highlighted the importance of temporary or transitory versus permanent shocks. While even large transitory disturbances would not threaten the sustainability of EMU, persistent shocks might, if they turned the balance of benefits and costs negative over foreseeable future. However, in a Hirschmanian perspective, the distinction between transitory and persistent shocks can be endogenised: if the monetary union is hit by some exogenous shock, a combination of 'voice' and 'loyalty' can lead to policy choices which will correct the negative consequences of the shock.

This has two implications. First, 'voice' becomes a sustainability guarantee for monetary integration. But this will lead, secondly, to the paradox that EMU will work better, the more conflict about monetary and policies is expressed openly. Yet a high voice-level will make the maintenance of loyalty more difficult. People (and voters) like harmony.[21] Loyalty-promoting institutions like the European Commission – and maybe even the ECB – will not only be interested in stimulating voice at the expense of exit; 'they are', as Hirschman put it, 'often meant to *repress* voice alongside exit.'[22] But such behaviour would endanger the capacity of the union to transform persistent shocks into transitory shocks. Therefore, ensuring the long-term sustainability of EMU will depend on the ability by public authorities to communicate their disagreement not only in a form that helps overcome the disturbances, but also in a way that is comprehensible to the population at large. EMU will need both voice and loyalty.

The best vehicle to foster both elements seems to be a clearly established procedure for the democratic accountability of monetary policy. On one hand, this implies that the ECB will have to report on the monetary policy action used to pursue its clearly defined objectives. Experience shows that a central bank that is not held accountable is more likely to behave in an inconsistent way than an accountable bank (Fischer 1994). On the other hand, such formal accountability may stimulate a union-wide debate on policy objectives. Therefore, this may contribute to rendering policy preference more homogenous and help to maintain the 'stability consensus' in Europe.

Article 109b of the TEU stipulates that the ECB has to report to the European Parliament. This is certainly the right microphone for voice: since its early days, parliament, as representative of the people, has been the focus where dissent and authority, individual interest and collective decision have been brought together (Grant 1987). The European Parliament has the advantage that it is both – a loyalty-promoting institution and the organ of voice. By contrast, national institutions, be they governments, parliaments or the media, have a much more narrow voice-consistency and are therefore closer to exit than voice-activating loyalty.

Finally, we have seen that the balance of net benefits will depend ultimately on the perceived steady-state performance of the union. This has two consequences: if a sentiment of economic crisis pervades, it might not only affect monetary policy preferences, but also the general attitude to being part of a monetary, economic and political union.[23] This raises, in particular, the question of Europe's unemployment. To what degree can monetary policy prevent fundamental disequilibria? Will social tensions undermine the pursuit of price stability? We will return to this question in Chapter 8.

7   Sustaining price stability

In the last two chapters we have emphasised the importance of authorities' relative preference for output and price stability reflected in the policy coefficient A. Knowing the relative importance given to these policy objectives is crucial to the assessment of net benefits which derive from belonging to the monetary union to its members. In this chapter we will look at the commitment to price stability by European authorities from different angles in order to get a clearer view of the relative weight given to these policy objectives. We will first look at the concept of price stability, then at possible inflationary biases in monetary policy objectives and finally, at the European policy frame.

Defining price stability as a policy objective

Maintaining price stability is the primary objective of European Monetary Union (EMU) (Treaty of European Union (TEU) arts. 2, 3a, 105 and Protocol on the Statute of the European System of Central Banks (ESCB) and European Central Bank (ECB)). No doubt this reflects the political consensus that has emerged in Europe around the German model. In the academic field, convictions about the benefits are less unanimous. It is often said we lack an account of the cost of inflation that matches the intensity with which inflation is denounced by policy makers and disliked by the general public (Fischer 1994).

In the 1950–70s orthodox economic theory was built on the Phillips curve trade-off between inflation and output. But after the Great Inflation, these models lost their attraction. As Lucas (1976) put it:

> The inference that permanent inflation will therefore induce a permanent economic high is no doubt (. . .) ancient, yet it is only recently that this notion has undergone the mysterious transformation from obvious fallacy to the cornerstone of the theory of economic policy.

Friedman replaced the simple Phillips curve with the Natural Rate Hypothesis (1968). This eliminated the inflation/output trade-off in the long run but still kept it in the short term. Ultimately, even this was put into question by neo-classical economists who claimed that systematic monetary policy will affect only nominal magnitudes and not real variables like output and employment, even in the short run (Lucas 1972; Sargent 1973; Barro 1976). If the real world is effectively independent from nominal variables, it is not obvious why inflation would represent a cost. Theory has moved from positive to zero benefit from inflation. In the first chapter we have argued that stable money matters in the long run because it sustains the fundamental norms of a market economy. In this chapter we will focus on the short-run policy preferences for output versus inflation stabilisation.

In recent years there seems to have emerged a consensus that the disagreement between Classical economists, Monetarists and Keynesians, rests on differing views about the speed by which markets clear.[1] The answer to this question depends on transaction costs, uncertainty, the nature and cost of information available, the institutional structure of the economy as well as the process of expectations formations (Begg 1982: 134). Consequently, a large part of the literature on the cost of inflation focuses on microeconomic implications.[2]

One important idea about the cost of inflation relates to the information content of money (Goodhart 1989; Brunner and Meltzer 1971). Only if the value of money remains stable over time can the price system signal the innumerable messages on the state of supply and demand for each commodity. These signals will ultimately determine the composition of the output, allocate resources, set the technology of production and divide it among the population. In a well-functioning market economy, competition resolves these tasks efficiently. But if the value of money varies significantly, prices get distorted and the information value of the price system declines. Individual market participants can no longer distinguish between shifts in relative prices and general price level movements. Only 'surprise' inflation would have an impact on output (Lucas 1972). Furthermore, some prices are rigid, and others are flexible, so that the whole price structure changes. This increases uncertainty in the economy and has negative consequences for investment. Another set of inflation-related costs would result from suboptimal real money balances, small menu costs and tax distortions (Bofinger *et al.* 1996). Inflation also has important distributional implications (Riese 1986a). With fixed nominal debt contracts, debtors profit from inflation, creditors from deflation. Given nominal wages contracts, real wages fall during inflation periods and rise in deflation periods. Therefore, both inflation and falling price levels are to be avoided.

Economic theory has produced good arguments as to why price stability is a worthwhile objective to be pursued. But how is price stability to be ensured? The Maastricht Treaty emphasises the institutional arrangements of central bank independence and constraints on budget policies. These are the constitutive rules of EMU. The ESCB is the organisation in charge of maintaining price stability. The TEU also clearly establishes a preference for price stability over other objectives. The ESCB has one of the highest degrees of political independence in the world in order to do so. One should, therefore, expect only a few possible deviations from the constitutive rules of EMU. However, in order to assess the risk that the ECB may not follow its objectives, we may ask two questions:

1   What is the likelihood that the decision-making organs in the ESCB may not *want* to give price stability the overruling preference?
2   Will the ECB be *able* to guarantee price stability even in a hostile environment?

The first question relates to the objectives and motivations of monetary policy. The second takes into account that the ESCB will operate in a real world environment where independent, exogenous – as well as endogenous – shocks require policy makers to respond and act. Economic theory discusses the possibility of monetary authorities having an 'inflationary bias' in their policy actions under the title of 'time inconsistent behaviour'. We will discuss the likelihood of such development in the section on A bias toward price stability in the European policy frame. On the other hand, even if the willingness to fight inflation prevails at the central bank, it is always confronted with two major constraints that may result from unstable wage and cost dynamics and from unsustainable public finances.[3] We will deal with this in the next chapter.

If inflationary pressures from these sources are too high, monetary policy must necessarily become restrictive. If disinflation persisted for a long time, it could lead to social and political instability. This might not put EMU, as such, in doubt, but it could jeopardise European integration in a broader context. Yet, before turning to monetary policy, it is useful to clarify the concept of price stability.

What is price stability?

Over the past 20 years there has been an emerging consensus and commitment among central bankers throughout the world to make price stability the primary policy goal of monetary policy (McDonough 1997). This commitment is expressed in the worldwide reduction in inflation rates over the 1980s into the 1990s. In Europe it can be seen by the significant convergence in price stability and the simultaneous reduction in nominal interest rates (see Figures 7.1 and 7.2).

How well do these indicators measure inflation? Usually, inflation is measured by consumer price indices (CPI), although from a value of money perspective, the GDP-deflator seems more appropriate.[4] There is now an increasing awareness that the CPI overstates the true rate of increase of the cost of living. In the US, this measurement error may attain up to 2 per cent (Shapiro and Wilcox 1996). In Europe, newly constructed Harmonised Indices of Consumer Prices will be available from 1999 that are likely to correct some of these distortions (EMI 1996). However, there seems to be a consensus that recorded inflation rates around 2 per cent are close to price stability, as this figure underlies most of the inflation targets by EU central banks.

From a theoretical point of view, a more appropriate definition of price stability is that 'expected changes in the average price level are small enough and gradual enough that they do not enter business or household decisions' (Pemberton 1992).

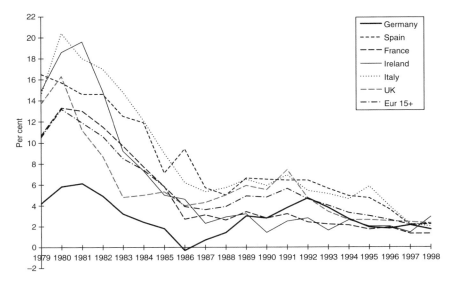

Figure 7.1 Convergence of inflation rates (CPI, annual percentage change).
Source: European Commission.

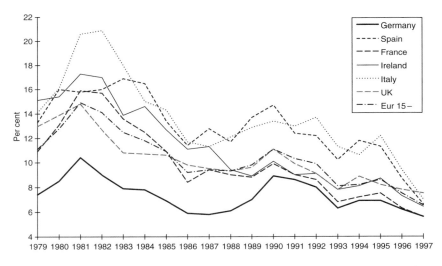

Figure 7.2 Convergence of interest rates (long-term interest rates in per cent per annum).
Source: European Commission.

Therefore, monetary policy is more about containing dynamic price expectations than about eliminating all sources of potential inflationary shocks (McDonough 1997). It also must take a medium-term perspective as it takes time until expectations have entered behaviour or until they have died down. Estimating inflation expectations is a complex task. A range of indicators based on past price movements might be useful, but in any case monetary aggregates and interest rates also contain information.

Our definition of price stability gives some substance to the distinction of will and capacity in central bank behaviour: monetary policy may not be able to control exogenous price level shocks, but it must have the will to bring down inflationary expectations after such shocks. This implies that policy must aim at a low, constant rate of expected inflation and not at a constant price level. However, if expectations are influenced by shocks to the price level, say because agents may not immediately distinguish between permanent and temporary inflation shocks, stabilising expectations requires that authorities reveal the time horizon over which they wish to see inflation return to stability. This can be done by publishing an explicit inflation target.[5] The next question is then: who is responsible for setting the target? If this is done exclusively by the central bank, it is said to have 'goal independence'. If it is set by the government, as in the UK or jointly between government and central bank, as in New Zealand, the central bank is not goal independent, but may still be 'instrument independent'. This means it does not take instructions about how to achieve the goal. The ECB is both goal and instrument independent. This is an important guarantee for ensuring that the ECB will not deviate from its primary objective of maintaining price stability. The precise formulation of ECB independence was quoted in Chapter 5.

Institutional conditions for price stability

Even if the political will to maintain price stability thus defined exists, it is only a necessary and not a sufficient condition for its achievement. Central bank independence is certainly an additional condition for monetary authorities sticking to its objectives without being swayed by other political considerations. Vast literature has developed the idea that delegating monetary policy to an independent central bank may help to overcome the inflationary bias described in the next section. (Rogoff 1985; Cukierman 1992). Empirical evidence from the 1970s and 1980s seems to confirm this theory, at least for industrialised countries (Fischer 1994; De Grauwe 1992). Politically independent central banks seem to produce less inflation than those that have to take orders from the government. The ECB is set up as one of the most independent central banks in the world, not least because its statutes are part of the Maastricht Treaty (TEU) and, therefore, have constitutional quality. This should support long-term price stability in EMU.[6]

The central bank also needs to know how to achieve its objectives. This is not only an argument about technicalities related to the conduct of monetary policy, such as the definition of intermediary targets or the working of the transmission mechanism. Economic theory and knowledge are also crucial. Romer and Romer (1997) insisted that lack of will (dynamic inconsistencies) has been overemphasised in literature as a source of monetary policy failures.[7] Insufficient attention is given to the limits of knowledge about how the economy operates and the obstacle that this provides to good policy. This lack of knowledge at times extends from economists to monetary policy makers, elected leaders and voters. Romer and Romer's (1997) argument deserves consideration. They suggest monetary institutions that would allow the progress of knowledge to be incorporated into policy design as a remedy. In their opinion, the institutional structure of the ECB is very close to their requirements, and they expect that the ECB 'is likely to lead to substantial improvements in policy'.[8] To this structural assessment of the ECB institutions, one may add the extremely solid review of monetary policy instruments and procedures conducted by the European Monetary Institute (EMI 1997). There is probably today no other institution in the world with a higher concentration of sophisticated knowledge about central banking. Of course, policy implementation requires appropriate instruments. Here is not the place to discuss the technicalities of European central banking,[9] but from the various publications of the EMI and ECB, it is clear that the ECB, at least, is familiar with the latest state-of-the-art technology. Certainly, all this accumulated human capital is no guarantee against policy mistakes, but the error margins are reduced. The decisive question then remains about the matter of will. Why would the ECB tolerate inflation?

If inflation carries costs for public welfare or policy makers, it must also allow them to reap benefits. Sustained inflation is possible only if money supply increases in a sustained manner in excess of the growth rate of output. In theory, if the authorities refused to accommodate price increases, inflation would come to a halt. However, society imposes some limits to central banks' ability to resist the expansion of money supply. In the words of Antonio Fazio:

> In large and complex economic systems the level of prices is strongly affected by other variables and circumstances, first of all fiscal policy and labour costs. In such cases the reliance solely on monetary policy to achieve monetary stability can be extremely costly in terms of other objectives.
>
> (Cukierman 1992: 15)

Given that monetary authorities have control over neither exogenous factors such as supply shocks or crises in the financial system, nor social and political instability, appropriate monetary policy might occasionally require a temporary reflation (McDonough 1997). But for the maintenance of price stability what matters most is that monetary policy anchors inflation rates at low levels and thereby locks in low inflation expectations. Consequently, occasions might occur when it would be wrong to request that central bankers give *exclusive* consideration to money supply or price stability, as the social costs of such a policy might become undefendably high. Instead, monetary policy *rules* can help to achieve low expected inflation at low social cost (Meltzer 1997). We will not review here the long debate on 'rules versus discretion', nor the range of rules that have been suggested in the literature. In practice one finds that all major central banks in the world, including the Bundesbank, take real economy influences into account when defining their policy stance (Clarida and Gertler 1997). In the case of EMU the commitment to the 'primary objective to maintain price stability'

(TEU: arts. 3a and 105) implies that monetary policy is geared at eliminating inflationary price expectations; it does not mean that prices may never go up or down.

Following this approach, a hypothesis of un-sustainable EMU would have to explain why the ECB would be inclined to tolerate a persistent expansion of money supply to such a degree that households and firms would anticipate future inflation. In other words, the question is: why and how does monetary policy itself become a source of inflation?

Inflationary biases in monetary policy objectives

Economic literature gives a number of policy motives that can lead to excessive inflation in the context of dynamic inconsistencies. These inconsistencies occur when the best policy planned for some future period is no longer the best when that period arises.[10] Typically, it is assumed that the 'monetary authority' is part of 'government', so that policy objectives set by the government will be pursued by the central bank. It is, however, doubtful that a legally independent, supranational central bank like the ECB will operate in this way. But given that these assumptions dominate the public debate, it is useful to assess the likelihood of possible deviations from price stability-oriented monetary policies under EMU, resulting from dynamic inconsistencies. We may distinguish four motives that could conflict with the price stability objective:[11] (1) the revenue motive, (2) the exchange rate motive, (3) the stability of the financial system and (4) the employment motive. We will try to assess the likelihood that the ESCB will be detracted by these temptations in pursuing the virtue of price stability.

The revenue motive

By printing money, that is, creating a liability that carries no interest, public authorities obtain revenue in the form of central bank profit. This is known as seigniorage. Furthermore, inflation reduces the real value of the outstanding public debt and the related debt service. Therefore, governments may have an interest to inflate, particularly when their tax system is already stretched to the limits. However, if the public is aware of these intentions and expects inflation to rise, the government will reduce the amount of money balances held. This might deter it from inflation, unless it can create 'surprise' inflation. However, persistent surprise inflations would lead to accelerating rates of inflation, as economic agents would incorporate them into their expectations. Therefore, the return on excess inflation is diminishing with longer time horizons, and ultimately disinflation becomes unavoidable.

A straightforward remedy against any kind of dynamic inconsistency is to establish binding rules from which policy cannot depart without costs. EMU has effectively put into place several provisions to prevent such revenue-motivated inflation. First, it has split political and monetary authorities by giving the ECB a statute of independence (TEU: art. 107). The ECB's primary objective of price stability cannot be overruled to follow government revenue motives. Secondly, indirect monetisation is prevented by the prohibition of overdrafts or other credit facilities with the ECB in favour of governments (TEU: art. 104). Third, seigniorage income in EMU will be allocated to national central banks (which are themselves politically independent) in proportion to their paid-up shares in the capital of the ECB (Protocol on the Statute of the ESCB and the ECB: art. 32.5). Consequently, even if it could manifest itself in the ECB council, the revenue motive of one particular government is always diluted to its share in the ECB capital. Only if all member states together, or at least a majority, request higher seigniorage income, will this become a factor of concern for the ECB. The probability of using the inflation tax to reduce government debt is extremely low and seigniorage is negligible in Europe (Collignon and Mundschenk 1999).

The exchange rate motive

Governments may have foreign exchange objectives in order to hold a sufficient amount of foreign reserves when maintaining a fixed exchange rate peg, or for competitiveness purposes when following a mercantilist development strategy.[12] Given that the amount of foreign exchange reserves is a function of the real exchange rate, a situation may arise when a devaluation would help to achieve a given reserve objective. However, as we have seen in Chapter 5, if the real devaluation is resisted by nominal wage increases, prices go up and the government's objective is unattainable. Therefore, authorities need to 'surprise' social partners with an unexpected devaluation that goes even further than expected price increases. This would accelerate the existing inflation rate, when businesses and households adapt their price expectations.

The exchange rate motive is unlikely to have a significant impact on EMU. Although art. 109 (TEU) gives some say to political authorities in the formal arrangements of exchange rate systems for the Euro, it is foreseeable that fixed pegs will only take place in the context of the so-called ERM II, or unilaterally by other countries. The agreements of the Amsterdam European Council stipulate that the ECB could always withdraw from intervention obligations, if the overall objective of price stability were in danger. Furthermore, European national central banks are holding foreign reserves today in order to stabilise their pegs in the EMS. Once their exchange rates are irrevocably fixed, a large part of these reserves will no longer be needed. Initially the reserve holdings will be relatively high with the reserve to import ratio of 2.6 for the EU against 1.0 for the USA, but they would still be below the Japanese ratio (Funke and Kennedy 1997). Thus, there will be little need to accumulate additional foreign reserves. It is more likely that these reserves will slowly be reduced and the balance of payment objective will not be substantial.

On the other hand, most of euroland's external relations will be driven by flexible exchange rates – especially between the US dollar and the Euro. In principle, this should allow a larger degree of autonomy in exchange rate and reserve management. Yet, if such benign neglect destabilises the international monetary relations, as we have pointed out in Chapter 3, then it will be desirable to increase transatlantic cooperation. This could have an impact on the exchange rate objectives of Europe's monetary authorities. But in a larger context of economic cooperation, it should be possible to establish objectives that avoid an inflationary bias (see Bergsten and Henning 1996).

Stability of the financial system

Historically, one function of central banks has been to prevent micro-level banking trouble, crises and panics, from disturbing the macroeconomy (Goodhart 1992). This has led to the emergence of the central bank as a lender of last resort. It is sometimes feared that concern with microbanking stability might divert the central bank's focus from maintaining price stability. Given that interest rates are the principal tool enabling modern central banks to conduct monetary policy, they might face situations in which they would have to raise interest rates aggressively. If the stability of the financial system is fragile, high costs of funds may increase the chances of financial collapse.

The argument has both a short-term and a long-term aspect. It is generally accepted that commercial banks' demands for reserves is virtually inelastic in the short run. Therefore, the central bank has no choice but to accommodate liquidity demand (King 1994). This can lead to an expansion of the money stock beyond levels strictly compatible with price stability, unless the excess liquidity is mopped up in the medium term, that is, when a 'smooth' increase in interest rates starts to reduce commercial banks' demands for reserves. Therefore, the short-term argument of an inflationary bias by the lender of last resort function rests on weak foundations. Only if the financial fragility prevents keeping interest rates at the appropriate level over a longer period of time, will systemic issues interfere with the monetary policy goal of price stability. This may be the case if authorities fear that tight money may lead to widespread default, due to the state of balance sheets, and this may precipitate or worsen a recession via multiplier effects on income. Thus, they may avoid setting interest rates at a level that prevents the emergence of inflationary expectations (Friedman 1990).

To what degree is there evidence that the policy margins of the ECB could be constrained by the financial system and its structures? Since the mid-1960s there have been numerous examples of financial instability in OECD-countries.[13] In the 1990s Sweden, Finland, UK, and less severely, France, experienced financial fragility to some degree, Germany and Italy only very little. Yet, in all those countries significant disinflation has taken place,[14] and everywhere inflation is at historic lows. Thus, despite structural differences in financial markets, monetary performance has converged (Collignon 1998). Clearly then, if there has been no constraint on monetary policy in a period of sometimes aggressive disinflation, why should the ECB find it more difficult to *keep* inflation down?

The only answer possible is that the social costs of a recession are too high in terms of output loss and unemployment. There is evidence that in recent years recessions have tended to be longer in financially fragile economies, reflecting the time taken to reduce the burden of debt by cutting expenditure and rising savings.

The deepest recessions in the early 1990s were in fact in the UK, Sweden and Finland, which also experienced financial crisis symptoms (Davis 1995). However, this implies that the inflationary bias in monetary policy does not result from government objectives or financial instability and systemic risk, but from the employment motive. Furthermore, the revenue and foreign exchange objectives are difficult to pursue in the context of the asymmetric division of power between the ECB and national governments. Meanwhile, the employment motive may have greater impact on the ECB's policy preferences because it may reflect a general public consensus rather than a direct government instruction. It is, therefore, the most serious threat to the ECB's price stability commitment.

The employment motive for inflation

The argument of an inflationary bias resulting from an employment motive is somewhat similar to the exchange rate motive analysed above. It is based on a set of conditions under which short-term neutrality of money does not apply. In the next chapter, I will argue that even in the long run, the neutrality hypothesis needs to be re-interpreted. However, here I concentrate on the short-term trade-off between money and output, as typically represented by a Phillips curve. If the government had the authority over monetary policy, rather than an independent central bank with a price stability objective, it might be tempted to inflate in order to achieve real objectives (Cukierman 1992). If the task is to reduce unemployment, it can do so, provided three conditions hold. First, real wages must stand above the market clearing rate so that employment is constrained by demand for labour. If the latter is a function of real wages, surprise inflation can lower real wages and increase employment. Second, policy makers must have an objective function that gives positive weight to both high price stability and high employment. Third, wage bargainers set nominal wages for a fixed period so that some degree of nominal wage rigidity prevails. As we have seen in Chapters 1 and 5, when setting nominal wages, workers attempt to set real wages by taking inflation expectations into account. Consequently, the authorities can only lower real wages by reneging on their declared price objective in creating surprise inflation. This will then lead to accelerating price increases through the feedback mechanism of inflation expectations in wage bargains (see Chapter 1), while real wage resistance keeps unemployment at its 'natural rate'. Only the unanticipated part of inflation reduces real wages, and consequently only temporary deviations from the natural rate are possible. On the other hand, if the authorities maintain a credible commitment to price stability, forward-looking price and wage-setting will help to reduce inflation-inertia. But if wage bargaining is at least to some degree backward-looking, any disinflation process will raise real wages and increase unemployment. Thus, a possible inflationary bias from employment motives depends on the structures of wage and price-setting[15] and on the policy objectives and preferences of authorities. During disinflations, rising real wages (and unemployment) are the consequence of falling prices, which are incorrectly anticipated by wage bargainers. Therefore, during periods of falling inflation, the credibility of the authorities is crucial.

However, if credibility needs to be 'earned' over time, disinflation is unavoidably associated with some degree of rising unemployment. Several studies have tried to find evidence of a 'credibility' effect linked to low-inflation convergence in the European Monetary System (EMS). Supposedly, governments renounced the option of surprise inflation by committing themselves to keep a fixed exchange rate with the DM. If this commitment had been credible with wage bargainers, they would have adjusted their inflation expectations downwards and the disinflation process would have been less costly in terms of output and unemployment. Anderton *et al.* (1992) studied the structural stability of wage equations in four EU countries. They found neither changes in labour market structures in the UK (despite the Thatcher reforms) nor in France and therefore ascribe the changes in wage behaviour to credibility effects. In Italy, there is evidence of a shift from backward to forward-looking wage behaviour, and this has since been confirmed by the abolition of the *scala mobile*. Other studies are more pessimistic about credibility effects.[16]

The lesson from these experiences is that disinflationary policies in the EMS did not work through the credibility of the exchange rate anchor *alone*, but rather that the exchange rate policy was part of traditional stabilisation packages, focused on income policies and fiscal consolidation. The disinflationary effect of the EMS consisted of increasing the credibility of a range of government policies, rather than on the fixity of the exchange rate, because their disinflation commitment was highly visible. The reputational gain came about only *gradually* due to the policy discipline imposed by ERM membership (Egebo and Englander 1992). Countries seeking credibility had to be prepared, and to prepare their public, to earn their reputation by demonstrating that they were willing to pay a high price in terms of output and job losses for price stability. The 1980s show that convergence in Europe was not possible unless the hard work was done at home (Onofri and Tomasini 1992; Micossi and Padoan 1994). As Artis and Ormerod (1996) conclude: 'The extent of unemployment in Europe is mute witness to the price that has been paid for convergence on the low rates of inflation traditionally enjoyed in Germany'.

Thus, European price stability has been paid for by high social costs. If this is so, why have we not seen more time inconsistent policy behaviour to increase employment? Have Europe's leaders become insensitive to the burden of high unemployment? This seems hardly reasonable. The rising number of jobless is an important factor in run-away public deficits, and the electorate does not seem willing to tolerate a steady deterioration of their living standards. A cynical view sees in the convergence progress to EMU a foreign policy ploy to 'get rid of the Bundesbank'. Thereafter, 'surprise inflations' might reappear in the attempt to remedy unemployment. But this carries the risk, as we have shown, of undermining the sustainability of the single currency. The 'policy ploy' would, therefore, be self-defeating. Thus, the only correct answer must be that *the high costs of disinflation have been paid because policy makers believe in the value of stable money as a policy aim in itself.* They all have converged to a consensus of high price stability. We may conclude that policy preferences for low inflation time consistent behaviour are likely to be high for the ECB, at least higher than they were in Europe over the last quarter of a century. This fact should support the sustainability of EMU. It may also re-pave the way to a new Golden Age, if major policy errors are avoided. We will return to this issue in Chapter 8.

A bias toward price stability in the European policy frame

A commitment to price stability will ultimately increase output stability. Most economic models, and nearly all estimated wage functions, implicitly assume a short-term trade-off between output and inflation, to which monetary policy makers react.[17] If the central bank reveals a high preference for price stability compared to output stability, social partners will learn to take this into account and adjust wages. If they do not, the ECB will be forced to behave in an excessively restrictive manner. Therefore, 'flexibility' in labour markets is to a large extent a matter of the central bank's credibility. The debate about whether labour markets in Europe are not flexible enough to make EMU sustainable is taken up in Chapter 8. From the point of view of monetary policy, it boils down to these questions: are nominal wage developments exogenously set, and can they therefore destabilise the economy, or are they endogenous to a larger set of policy variables? It seems hard to believe that a market economy could survive if wage setting (as any kind of pricing) would take place without regard for the economic environment. There are good reasons to assume that wage bargaining will become endogenised by monetary union (Sievert 1993; Collignon 1994a). If that is so, the crucial issue is: which policy variables matter to wage bargainers? No doubt, the policy stance by the ECB – and in particular, whether it is willing to accommodate wage increases in excess of productivity growth – is crucial. However, the credibility of the central bank's commitment to price stability is essentially determined by the record of past performance, that is, reputation. In the case of the ECB this does not exist. But this does not mean that European monetary authorities are not committed to price stability. Several points can be made:

First of all, the studies of disinflation in the EMS and labour market effects provide us with an important piece of evidence about policy preferences in Europe. Monetary authorities in all low inflation-converging countries clearly have given greater weight to price stability than to output stabilisation since the early 1980s. Sometimes this change in preferences has been gradual and slow, in other cases more determined and rapid, but it is at the basis of the newly regained culture of price stability in Europe.

This conclusion is further supported by some econometric studies estimating parameters for policy preferences directly. Clarida and Gertler (1997) have estimated a Taylor-rule reaction function for the Bundesbank where price stabilisation has 3.5 times the weight of output stability. This is close to Taylor's results for the USA (Taylor 1996). Cukierman *et al.* (1995) have estimated monetary policy reaction functions for seventeen industrial countries from the mid-1970s to the end of the 1980s with wage and foreign inflation, real exchange rates and unemployment as arguments. The results are heterogeneous and often insignificant. Nevertheless, they do allow us to derive some findings about relative emphasis of policy in these countries: if countries show high concern for price stability and/or foreign competitiveness, they will lean against wage inflation by reducing monetary growth in reaction to accelerations in wage inflation. Accommodation of wage inflation is generally weaker in countries with more legally independent central banks. Therefore, given that the ESCB will be even more legally independent than the Bundesbank and politically less vulnerable than national central banks alone (Sievert 1993), we must expect policy preferences in the ESCBs to converge to high preference for price stability over other arguments.

Secondly, the ECB's initial disadvantage of not having a track record is partly offset by the fact that the old established national central banks are members of the system and have a history of convergence to a low inflation. This convergence is supported in its sustainability by what Sievert (1993) called the 'advantage of having money that one cannot create oneself'. While it was the privilege of the Nation-State to print money (and to abuse this sovereign right), under EMU this task is transferred to a community institution, the ESCB, which has the primary objective of maintaining price stability. Consequently the ESCB will be less vulnerable to pressures from different groups in society, be they social partners, financial institutions or governments. The accommodation of inflationary wage settlements will become less likely because the central bank is more removed from social pressures.

Third, a well-known device to sustain low inflation preferences is the appointment of a 'conservative central banker' (Rogoff 1985). According to the Sievert model (1993), the preferences of society matter less to monetary policy due to a natural asymmetry of a centralised European federal institution and decentralised civil societies. However, in the Rogoff model, society can benefit from a central banker who does not share the social objective function and who places 'too large' a weight on inflation-rate stabilisation relative to employment stabilisation. Although the appointment of such a central bank governor reduces the time-consistent rate of inflation, it also suboptimally raises the variance of employment when supply shocks are large. Therefore, there is a trade-off between too much conservativeness and too little. Eijffinger (1997) has tried to estimate the optimal degree of conservativeness in Europe. He finds that conservativeness limits the degree of flexibility (discretion) in monetary policy, so that central banks with high reputation need little 'extra-conservativeness'. The optimal degree of conservativeness depends positively on the natural rate of unemployment, and the slope of the Philips curve. It depends negatively on inflation-averseness of society and the variance of productivity shocks. However, this conservativeness is based on the assumption of a given degree of central bank independence. This will change with the ESCB. In many countries central bank independence has increased in line with the legal convergence requirements (EMI 1998), and consequently the required optimal degree of conservativeness will fall. Figure 7.3 shows the excess of EU-countries over German central bank conservativeness.[18] All countries required a degree of conservativeness substantially higher (up to nearly four times in Spain) than Germany *before* EMU started. This was necessary in order to constrain the discretionary freedom of their monetary policies, but it also increased output volatility. But under EMU, when all member countries benefit from high

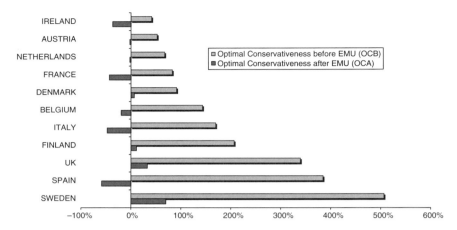

Figure 7.3 Optimal conservativeness before and after EMU as percentage of Germany.

central bank independence, conservativeness can be reduced significantly every-where (except in Germany which serves as a bench mark). In Ireland, Austria, the Netherlands, France, Belgium, Italy and Spain conservativeness can even fall below the German standard, given the economic structure in these countries. Therefore, it is unlikely that the central bank preferences in the council of the ESCB would be bent to an inflationary bias.

Summary and conclusion

This chapter has presented the policy preferences for price stability under EMU. They depend essentially on the policy objectives, given the legal independence of the ECB. The concept of price stability needs to be linked to low inflation expec-tations. Central banking theory has established four motives for why monetary authorities may behave in a time-inconsistent manner. Most of them do not seem to apply to the EMU environment. In fact, it is very likely that the decision-making authorities in the ECB will be strongly committed to low inflation policies. Pro-vided that this determination is met with corresponding behaviour by other eco-nomic actors, and in particular by wage bargainers, monetary policy may contribute to economic growth and employment. In the next chapter we will develop this link between monetary policy and employment.

8 Monetary policy and structural unemployment

Even if the last chapter produced evidence that there is strong political will to maintain price stability in Europe and that it should prevail in European Monetary Union (EMU), the high levels of unemployment in Europe are a matter of concern. The IMF (1997: 68) has warned: 'A failure to address labour market problems would prevent Europe from realising its full growth potential, and could also weaken the credibility of the euro if financial markets perceive that persistent unemployment is eroding support for prudent macroeconomic policies.'[1] In the 1998 World Economic Outlook (IMF 1998: 25) it reiterated its warning: '. . . the broad consensus in favour of policies directed at price stability could be challenged if sufficient progress is not made in reducing structural unemployment; and without such support, even an independent central bank could find it difficult to sustain such policies for long'. Thus, the issue of unemployment is relevant to the sustainability of EMU, although the consequences may be ultimately more far-reaching by undermining not only the currency union, but also the social and political consensus for European integration. On the other hand, by solving its unemployment problem, Europe could re-connect with the economic dynamic of the Golden Age.

Explaining Europe's unemployment is still a major puzzle for macroeconomists (Bean 1994). Theories abound and probably the only consensus is that there must be more than a single cause. One may question whether Europe is really an entity. Viñals and Jimeno (1996) have found that 'most EU countries share a strikingly similar evolution of unemployment since the mid-seventies'. Similarly, Bean (1994) wrote of a 'common experience within the European Community'. The main difference between European Union (EU) countries' performance was due to the different evolution of employment and population groups (public sector, women, youth, etc.). But twelve out of fifteen countries had either high or very high unemployment rates. Increasing European unemployment was associated both with falling inflation from 1975 until 1990 and with stable inflation thereafter. However, despite high unemployment levels, inflation resisted falling – contrary to the trend in the USA. Furthermore, Viñals and Jimeno also found, like Eichengreen (1993a), that the persistence of regional unemployment differentials was not substantially higher in Europe than in the US. During 1971–93, EU-wide unemployment shocks explained almost half the variance of EU-member countries' unemployment rates within one year, increasing to 83 per cent after four years.

Thus, they concluded that a very significant EU-wide component was driving unemployment across Europe. This challenges us to develop a 'European model' behind unemployment.

Probably the most difficult phenomenon to explain has been the high degree of persistence in unemployment. It has become common currency today to blame rigid labour markets for Europe's failure to create more jobs. We will deal with this claim below. It is, however, remarkable that only a decade ago Newell and Symons (1987) came to the radically opposite conclusion: 'The modern US economy produced in the thirty years following the war a higher level of unemployment than the regulated labour markets of Europe'. In the first chapter of this book, I claimed that the end of Bretton Woods and the Golden Age was not so much due to the rigidities in the European social model, but to the persistence of the Great Inflation, which destroyed the social consensus on investment and wage moderation. In the tradition of Newell and Symons (1987) one could reframe the argument: inflation led to the demise of corporatism, defined as 'a set of institutions where the interest organisations of labour and capital are brought together with the state, seeking a high level of employment by limitation of wage demands'. In this chapter I will show that the exclusive focus on wages and labour markets is insufficient for a solution of Europe's job crisis. If employment is demand-constrained – and there are good theoretical reasons to assume that it always is – then the cost of capital and interest rates is logically prior to wages. This means that Europe's high unemployment can be explained by the high level of real interest rates that followed the Great Inflation and by hysteresis related to the adjustment of the capital stock that prevents unemployment from falling. Overcoming Europe's unemployment requires in this case concerted action between social partners and monetary authorities. I will first present some common features of European unemployment, and trace them back to insufficient growth. I will then discuss established theories about equilibrium unemployment or the Non-Accelerating-Inflation Rate of Unemployment (NAIRU). Finally, I will formulate a simple model of unemployment hysteresis based on monetary policy.

Features of European unemployment

Figure 8.1(a) shows the evolution of the European unemployment rate compared to USA and Japan. It has increased from under 2.5 per cent in the 1960s to over 10 per cent. However, rapid growth in unemployment really only started in 1975 and 1980 after the two oil-price shocks, resuming again after German unification and the Gulf War in the early 1990s. Each time this was correlated with falling inflation and a rapid increase and high volatility of real short-term interest rates (see Figures 2.1 and 2.2). In the US the unemployment rate seems to have been stable around 6 per cent over the long term, although a rising trend is evident between the late 1960s and early 1980s, that is, during the period of rising inflation when short-term interest rates became highly volatile (see also Figures 1.4 and 2.2). In Japan the unemployment rate is remarkably stable at a low level, although it seems to have increased marginally during the period of disinflation (cf. Figure 1.2).

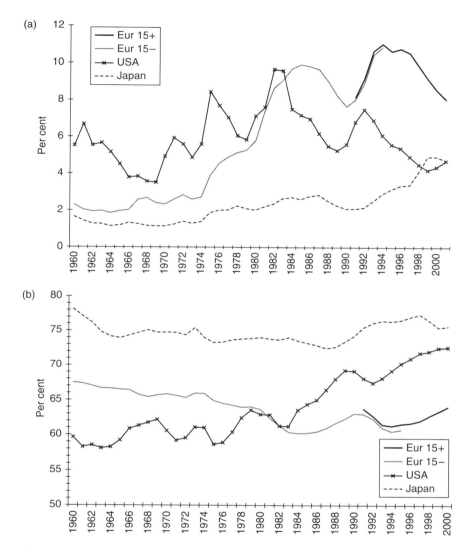

Figure 8.1 (a) Unemployment rates; (b) employment rates.
Source: AMECO (1999).

The traditional approach to explain unemployment is to focus on a simple static equilibrium in the wage-employment space (the 'labour market'). Unemployment occurs because wages are kept above their market-clearing level for a variety of reasons: overly generous social benefits and the relevant tax systems, minimum wage regulations, centralised wage bargaining, rules, laws and norms concerning hiring, firing and the nature of work contracts which discourage the creation of new jobs by limiting an employer's ability to dismiss employees, etc. – in short, rigid labour markets are seen as the root of Europe's unemployment.[2] We will return to these explanations below. However, in a dynamic perspective, it is more appropriate to analyse the balance of flows into and out of the job market. Equilibrium unemployment is then determined by the long-run relation between these flows and the level of unemployment (Greenwald and Stiglitz 1995). Most models explain imbalances by labour-turnover and job search theories, that is, by the determinants of labour supply. In these models, labour demand may depend on costs but rarely on aggregate demand for goods and services. Greenwald and Stiglitz go further by assuming risk-adverse firms that maximise their own market value. In that respect their model could be linked with Tobin's q and rising unemployment would also be determined by insufficient growth.

Empirically, the principal factor behind high unemployment rates in Europe is the low outflow of workers from unemployment to employment (Alogoskoufis *et al*. 1995; Bean 1994). Thus, Europe's ill is the low rate of employment creation.[3] Table 8.1 shows that total employment in the EU has been growing at a significantly lower rate (0.24 per cent p.a.) than in the US (1.76 per cent p.a.) or Japan (0.98 per cent p.a.) over the period 1961–98. These last two countries were *grosso modo* capable of increasing the number of jobs in line with the civilian labour force, so that the trend in unemployment growth was close to zero. In Europe, however, the labour force grew more than twice as fast as employment. European job creation always proceeded at a lower speed, but in the 1960s it was at least close to absorbing the labour force. When this growth accelerated with the arrival of baby-boomers in the 1970s and 1980s, Europe was no longer able to follow with new jobs, despite the fact that employment growth nearly doubled. Hence, the employment rate, that is, the proportion of the population of working age who have work, fell. In the severe recession of the 1990s, European employment levels even shrank. In the USA, by contrast, job creation was faster than labour force growth, so that the employment rate started to rise from the early 1980s (Figure 8.1(b)).

Although cyclical variations in European unemployment are evident, the dominant feature is the rising trend and the high persistence even in times of relative booms. Many observers have concluded that this rise in the mean unemployment rate reflects shifts in the *natural* rate of unemployment or an increase in the NAIRU (Elmeskov 1993 and OECD 1994). The concept of a natural rate of unemployment goes back to Friedman (1968) who used it to explain the breakdown of the Phillips curve trade-off between unemployment and (wage) inflation. If unemployment fell below its natural rate, labour market tightening would push wages (and prices) up. Expected wages would exceed actual wages, and this would lead to an increase of unemployment until wages would come down to their equilibrium level. This equilibrium was supposed to be dependent on structural factors in the labour market. In modern formulations, the natural rate is assimilated to the NAIRU, which is conceptually derived from wage bargaining and rigid labour market structures (Layard *et al*. 1991; Carlin and Soskice 1990). Earlier theories have assumed this rate to be constant with the actual rate oscillating around it. However,

Table 8.1 Aggregate growth rates

	Eur 15−	Eur 15+	USA	Japan	USA/EU	Japan/EU
Civilian labour force						
Average						
1961–98	0.53239308	0.16704559	1.78581092	1.10076969	3.35430905	2.06758828
1967–70	0.2815911		1.72910973	1.3306615	6.14049856	4.72550983
1971–80	0.69504436		2.56190171	0.85288004	3.68595425	1.2270872
1981–90	0.81218256		1.62743329	1.21982661	2.00377768	1.50191184
1991–8		0.16704559	1.08454597	0.97444583	6.49251494	5.83341261
Standard deviation						
1961–98	0.39063897		0.68904536	0.54427996	1.76389302	1.39330687
1961–70	0.29419222		0.65687645	0.45692696	2.23281379	1.55315784
1971–80	0.35874134		0.49086702	0.6410327	1.36830347	1.78689389
1981–90	0.2747754		0.22538026	0.46708973	0.8202345	1.69989648
1991–8		0.33671695	0.34175075	0.53553721	1.01494966	1.59046707
Employment						
Average						
1961–98	0.23868346		1.76385402	0.98046412	7.38992995	4.10780091
1961–70	0.23707379		1.87957497	1.38303441	7.92822748	5.83377177
1971–80	0.33676333		2.04989861	0.74717961	6.08706003	2.21870835
1981–90	0.50456203		1.80682332	0.9137048	3.58097364	1.81088697
1991–8		−0.17462118	1.20793549	0.85230604	−6.91746265	−4.88088579
Standard deviation						
1961–98	0.79256616		1.73062849	0.67070355	2.18357606	0.84624298
1961–70	0.50146154		1.5854725	0.42248565	3.16170308	0.84250857
1971–80	0.6460599		2.22862749	0.74214544	3.44956787	1.14872542
1981–90	1.00343421		1.68927941	0.71508653	1.68349793	0.71263918
1991–8		0.99440996	1.43264501	0.66951868	1.44069858	0.67328235
Unemployment trend growth						
Average						
1961–98	0.29370962		0.0219569	0.12030557	0.07475717	0.40960718
1961–70	0.0445173		−0.15046524	−0.05237291	−3.37992703	−1.17646176
1971–80	0.35828103		0.5120031	0.10570042	1.42905446	0.29502098
1981–90	0.30762054		−0.17939002	0.30612181	−0.58315361	0.99512801
1991–8		0.34166677	−0.12338952	0.12213979	−0.36113996	0.35748222
Standard deviation						
1961–98	0.58914413		1.60391679	0.34991788	2.72245229	0.59394275
1961–70	0.30159306		1.73001546	0.10615258	5.73625745	0.35197287
1971–80	0.47633888		1.84011739	0.3066234	3.86304256	0.64370853
1981–90	0.82612076		1.60001302	0.55761239	1.93677862	0.67497686
1991–8		0.73128327	1.27950402	0.14081258	1.74966947	0.19255545
Growth rates						
Average						
1961–97	3.06216216		2.94324324	5.45675676	0.96116505	1.7819947
1961–70	4.83		3.85	10.47	0.79710145	2.16770186
1971–80	3.01		2.71	4.5	0.90033223	1.49501661
1981–90	2.39		2.71	4.01	1.13389121	1.67782427
1991–7	1.57142857	1.65714286	2.31428571	1.72857143	1.39655172	1.04310345

Table 8.1 Continued

	Eur 15−	Eur 15 +	USA	Japan	USA/EU	Japan/EU
Standard deviation						
1961–97	1.73515151		2.10654279	3.78326289	1.21403969	2.18036458
1961–70	0.87184351		1.92714527	2.17309303	2.21042566	2.49252647
1971–80	1.8095119		2.51062188	2.72315177	1.38745806	1.50490956
1981–90	1.21330586		2.23827811	1.17610468	1.84477647	0.96933899
1991–7	1.11611571	1.23404098	1.43924583	1.57449916	1.1662869	1.27588888
Labour productivity						
Average						
1961–98	2.69600214		1.1158382	4.18094864	0.41388624	1.55079574
1961–70	4.42357824		1.87691011	8.55898641	0.4242968	1.93485589
1971–80	2.56898111		0.60966959	3.61013346	0.23731961	1.40527832
1981–90	1.83133245		0.86006857	3.01022445	0.46964087	1.64373456
1991–8	1.77614541	1.98417141	1.11692113	0.88532566	0.56291564	0.44619414
Standard deviation						
1961–98	1.35468587		1.26034154	3.26999726	0.93035704	2.41384171
1961–70	0.56220717		1.27611046	2.02275949	2.26982244	3.59788986
1971–80	1.34054191		1.66813481	2.1699989	1.24437349	1.61874753
1981–90	0.46756093		0.81318928	1.20051104	1.73921564	2.56760342
1991–8	0.61685645	0.63748571	0.76651454	1.06476625	1.20240271	1.67025902
Total factor productivity						
Average						
1961–98	1.73178095		0.9062171	2.85314881	0.52328622	1.64752293
1961–70	2.98436544		1.55209734	7.37585719	0.52007617	2.47149933
1971–80	1.43055929		0.45411878	1.6780177	0.31744143	1.17298018
1981–90	1.2292053		0.82678056	1.86267033	0.67261389	1.51534518
1991–8	1.17079695	1.07003116	0.76328538	−0.09322465	0.71333005	−0.08712331
Standard deviation						
1961–98	1.19316265		1.29989552	3.27620609	1.08945374	2.74581683
1961–70	0.68129453		1.34578387	1.93722462	1.97533344	2.84344662
1971–80	1.38087579		1.63437775	2.23689078	1.18358056	1.6199073
1981–90	0.65640233		1.14199396	1.15587416	1.73977742	1.76092329
1991–8	0.91163153	0.69916145	0.75589067	1.11417761	1.08113894	1.59359132
Unit labour cost changes						
Average						
1961–98	6.3487347		4.56047759	4.30063031	0.71832858	0.67739959
1961–70	4.71642176		3.32308989	4.94101359	0.70457861	1.04761912
1971–80	11.4910189		7.49033041	9.67986654	0.65184215	0.8423854
1981–90	5.85866755		4.57993143	0.96977555	0.78173602	0.16552835
1991–8	2.57385459	1.98725716	2.42057887	0.93967434	1.21805015	0.4728499
Standard deviation						
1961–98	4.10153962		2.80641429	5.308763	0.68423435	1.2943342
1961–70	1.62518373		2.65332569	1.9422379	1.63263122	1.1950882
1971–80	3.43838437		2.26565926	7.30801591	0.65893135	2.12542146
1981–90	2.54836394		2.09719706	1.52272226	0.82295822	0.59752935
1991–8	1.93986954	1.40162672	0.79977906	1.336852	0.57060774	0.95378604

Table 8.1 Continued

	Eur 15−	Eur 15+	USA	Japan	USA/EU	Japan/EU
GDP deflator						
Average						
1961–97	6.55945946		4.52432432	4.26486486	0.68974042	0.65018541
1961–70	4.4		3.06	5.42	0.69545455	1.23181818
1971–80	10.8		7.47	7.89	0.69166667	0.73055556
1981–90	6.68		4.53	1.92	0.67814371	0.28742515
1991–7	3.41428571	3.41428571	2.4	0.78571429	0.70292887	0.23012552
Standard deviation						
1961–97	3.40681176		2.5230499	3.94195497	0.74058976	1.15708036
1961–70	0.98092926		1.65475745	1.05071404	1.68692842	1.0711415
1971–80	2.39304548		1.68328383	5.24583433	0.70340653	2.19211644
1981–90	2.4234044		2.044532	1.06854002	0.84366109	0.44092518
1991–7	1.21987509	1.21987509	0.51639778	1.08386434	0.42332021	0.88850436
Inflation (CPI)						
Average						
1961–98	6.26809211		4.39736842	4.50526316	0.70154815	0.71876148
1961–70	3.86		2.61	5.63	0.6761658	1.45854922
1971–80	10.67		7.19	8.82	0.67385192	0.82661668
1981–90	6.53		4.75	1.88	0.72741194	0.28790199
1991–8	3.4484375	3.4859375	2.7	0.9875	0.77454056	0.28328104
Standard deviation						
1961–98	3.608357		2.48449101	4.12349546	0.68853803	1.14276261
1961–70	0.6328068		1.34532111	1.37763888	2.12595869	2.17702921
1971–80	2.87365427		2.29804265	4.96001792	0.7996935	1.72603154
1981–90	2.95599203		1.77404121	1.394274	0.60015088	0.47167719
1991–8	1.14244779	1.18478425	0.53718845	0.95534212	0.45340613	0.80634269
Profit margin trend growth						
Average						
1961–97	0.07577018		−0.08919452	−0.11292317	−1.17717173	−1.49033786
1961–70	−0.31642176		−0.26308989	0.47898641	0.83145324	−1.51375942
1971–80	−0.69101889		−0.02033041	−1.78986654	0.02942092	2.59018467
1981–90	0.82133245		−0.04993143	0.95022445	−0.06079321	1.15693036
1991–7	0.66636839	0.97410255	0.00476005	−0.08165721	0.0048866	−0.08382814
Standard deviation						
1961–97	1.33314694		1.0229694	2.27143042	0.76733432	1.703811
1961–70	0.87764534		1.12667476	2.30455781	1.28374722	2.6258418
1971–80	1.73456398		1.12465679	2.94294509	0.64838011	1.69664834
1981–90	0.97942686		1.19534808	1.03542555	1.2204567	1.05717495
1991–7	0.99329236	0.84945411	0.51280436	1.11111523	0.60368694	1.30803444
Nominal wage						
Average						
1961–97	10.1903226		5.67631579	8.48157895	0.55703004	0.83231702
1961–70	9.14		5.2	13.5	0.56892779	1.47702407
1971–80	14.06		8.1	13.29	0.57610242	0.94523471
1981–90	7.69		5.44	3.98	0.70741222	0.51755527
1991–7	7.3	3.97142857	3.78888889	2.23333333	0.95403677	0.56235012

Table 8.1 Continued

	Eur 15−	Eur 15 +	USA	Japan	USA/EU	Japan/EU
Standard deviation						
1961–97	3.45353489		2.13939044	6.28906624	0.61947845	1.82105189
1961–70	1.58057655		1.6693312	1.70228604	1.05615334	1.07700323
1971–80	2.48515593		0.95102284	6.43090628	0.38268136	2.58772747
1981–90	2.26737734		1.87569246	1.26121634	0.82725201	0.55624457
1991–7	0.42426407	1.36956719	1.16452184	1.68300327	0.85028456	1.22885776
Real product wage						
Average						
1961–97	2.64324324		1.2027027	4.38108108	0.45501022	1.65746421
1961–70	4.74		2.14	8.08	0.45147679	1.70464135
1971–80	3.26		0.63	5.4	0.19325153	1.65644172
1981–90	1.01		0.91	2.06	0.9009901	2.03960396
1991–7	1.1	1.03333333	1.1	0.95714286	1.06451613	0.92626728
Standard deviation						
1961–97	1.83991856		1.04069594	3.4133592	0.56562066	1.85516863
1961–70	0.82219219		0.64325561	1.94696345	0.78236648	2.36801501
1971–80	1.40095206		1.07398531	3.11876044	0.76661104	2.22617214
1981–90	0.65903971		0.89498603	1.02869929	1.35801535	1.56090639
1991–7	0.71879529	0.76332606	0.88317609	0.92350265	1.15701027	1.20984033
Real CPI wage						
Average						
1961–98	2.7664474		1.27894737	3.97631579	0.46060893	1.43205781
1961–70	5.28		2.59	7.87	0.4905303	1.4905303
1971–80	3.39		0.91	4.47	0.26843658	1.31858407
1981–90	1.16		0.69	2.1	0.59482759	1.81034483
1991–8	0.9015625	0.8640625	0.8375	0.8375	0.96925859	0.96925859
Standard deviation						
1961–98	2.15813577		1.30594439	3.41201646	0.60512615	1.58100176
1961–70	1.20627986		0.58395205	1.91546339	0.48409334	1.58790961
1971–80	1.65358197		1.66563301	3.46443839	1.00728784	2.09511137
1981–90	1.01456066		0.91220124	1.21472448	0.89910962	1.19729113
1991–8	0.8165746	0.77526457	0.75581082	1.0927521	0.97490695	1.40952152

Eur 15− reflects data based on Germany excluding the former GDR.
Eur 15+ reflects data based on Germany including the new states of East Germany.

over the years this idea has increasingly been discredited. As Blanchard and Jimeno (1995) put it: 'The natural rate of unemployment is all but natural, and all but constant'. Table 8.2 shows some estimates by different studies that support this claim.

It appears that a wide range of NAIRUs is consistent with empirical evidence (see also Staiger *et al.* 1997). High and low estimates vary by a range of 28 to over 100 per cent. Galbraith (1997) has called this 'an embarrassment to the profession of economists: What is the practical usefulness of such an imprecise concept?' In

Table 8.2 A comparison of NAIRU estimates from cross-country studies

		USA	*Canada*	*UK*	*Germany*	*France*
Layard *et al.* (1991)	1969–79	6.0	7.0	5.2	1.9	3.9
	1980–8	6.4	8.1	7.9	4.0	7.8
Adams *et al.* (1987)	1981–3	7.3	7.0	8.4	5.3	8.1
Jaeger and Parkinson (1994)	1991	6.4	9.2	7.0	6.8	–
Turner and Rauffet (1994)	1990–2	5–6.5	–	7–9	5.5	9.0
Barell *et al.* (1993)	1993	–	–	7–8	5.5–7	5.5–7
Barell *et al.* (1995)	1968–93	6.4	8.1	6.1	5.2	6.7
	1981–93	6.6	9.4	8.7	8.1	9.3
Gordon (1996)	1955–96	5.7–6.4	–	–	–	–

Source: Barell *et al.* (1995): 20; Gordon (1996).

fact, it seems that the estimated NAIRUs sluggishly track the actual unemployment rate. As Galbraith observed:

> When unemployment rises, analysts tend to discover that the demographic characteristics of workers are deteriorating, or that the job-wage and wage-price dynamic has become unsustainable (Gordon 1988). And then the unemployment rate drifts down again, those flaws mysteriously begin to disappear and a lower NAIRU is estimated. Recent empirical studies like Eisner (1996) and Fair (1996) have confirmed this instability, both across time and in transnational comparisons.
>
> (1997: 101)

But if the natural rate is frequently shifting, this has far-reaching consequences for theory and policy. Where would the level of unemployment be consistent with price stability? In Chapter 3 we have used the NAIRU concept to establish targets for internal balance. But if the NAIRU is volatile, policy targets would shift frequently, increasing the volatility of the fundamental equilibrium exchange rate (see Chapter 3). The question then is: what determines the (shifting) level of equilibrium unemployment?

Ball (1997) has shown that the increase in the natural rate in Europe is strongly related to disinflation and to actual unemployment. This is evidence for hysteresis theories, which are still not well understood. Theories explaining hysteresis have built on the level of unemployment benefits, the length of joblessness and its impact on qualification, skills, etc. and on the insider–outsider dynamics in wage bargaining. However, if last year's unemployment rate determines this year's in the absence of new shocks, it is difficult to see how the NAIRU can be an equilibrium that attracts deviations back to the natural rate. Thus we would have to redefine the concept of equilibrium unemployment in hysteresis models. I will present a simple model below which is based on capital stock adjustment. Nevertheless, the issue of labour market rigidities is so dominant in all work on unemployment that first we must take a close look at this phenomenon.

The issue of labour market flexibility

The concept of labour market flexibility is a difficult one, as only controversial definitions exist. In fact, 'flexibility' has become a weasel word which increasingly has overtaken the abuse of the adjective 'social' about which Hayek (1988: 14) wrote that it had 'probably become the most confusing expression in our entire moral and political vocabulary . . . and now increasingly supplants the word "good" as a designation of what is morally right'. In order to address this confusion, it is useful to separate two different processes. The first is long-term labour market flexibility related to the dynamic process through which workers adjust to changes caused by new products, services, technologies, etc. Policy measures aimed to overcome this kind of rigidity focus on skills, qualification and training, that is, on enabling workers to respond to demand by firms. This aspect is the least controversial and stood at the centre of the European employment summit in Luxembourg 1997. The second is the short-term concept of labour market flexibility that refers to the ease by which one can adjust labour inputs to changes in the level of demand. This process is at the centre of our explanation in this chapter. It can take the channel of flexibility of prices, wages and costs, that is, nominal rigidities. Alternatively, one may concentrate on the variability of quantities (numbers of staff, hours of work, etc.). Usually, however, the concept of labour market flexibility is used to describe the trade-off between nominal and real variables.

Empirical evidence in Table 8.1 reveals that European labour markets are flexible on the first account, rigid on the second, and the concept of linking nominal and real variables through a trade-off *à la* Phillips yields surprising results in the case of Japan, as we will see in the next section. The variability of employment, measured by the standard deviation of the growth rate in Table 8.1, was significantly higher in the USA than in Europe or Japan. Thus, in terms of real magnitudes, labour was most flexible in America and least flexible in Japan (except during the 1970s). This is also reflected in the variation of unemployment or in studies on labour migration. By contrast, price and wage flexibility is higher in Europe than in America. The standard deviations of European price and wage inflation exceed those in the USA since the 1970s and those in Japan since the 1980s. Of course, these figures reflect the well-known positive correlation of mean inflation with its variance (Taylor 1981). But it is interesting to note that nominal unit labour costs reveal the same pattern of distinct variability, although GDP inflation trends are more similar in the three countries. Thus, it is not unreasonable to conclude that higher European price and wage flexibility may have compensated for some lack in employment flexibility.[4] Riese (1997) has put his distinction into the paradigm of a spot market economy where wages are more stable than output fluctuations and a contract-market economy, which stabilises output. We will provide a theoretical explanation below.

Yet, if price and wage flexibility is higher in Europe, why does unemployment continue to grow? A crucial factor is insufficient economic growth in Europe.

Growth and unemployment

There is little doubt that economic growth is important for the evolution of unemployment rates. Even in the four European countries often mentioned as examples for labour market reforms and the successful reduction of unemployment, growth has been significant.

Table 8.3 suggests that the remarkable increase in the average growth rate of these four countries from 1989–93 to 1994–8 has been correlated with reduced unemployment in the UK, Ireland and Denmark. However, in the Netherlands, where growth has been stagnant or even falling, unemployment rose. In the large low-growth countries this is even more obvious. The IMF (1997) explains this by 'cyclical' factors, but I will show that demand management can also have long-term effects. This does not exclude a role for long-term labour market reforms, but it provides a second angle for attacking unemployment.

The connection between economic growth and employment is simple: new jobs are only created if, and only if, output increases more than labour productivity. This is shown in Figure 8.2.

It reveals three cases: high growth in GDP and productivity and low unemployment in Japan; low rates on all three accounts in the USA; low economic but high productivity growth and high unemployment in Europe. In all three major world economies, both economic growth and productivity growth fell significantly in the 1970s. But while labour productivity advances have remained fairly stable thereafter, GDP growth has been more uncertain. Productivity trends have stabilised around 1 per cent in the USA, just below 2 per cent in the EU and 3 per cent in Japan, at least before the 1990s (Table 8.1). The volatility of productivity growth was normally higher in Japan and the US. Difficulties in European job creation result from insufficient GDP growth. During the two severe recessions in the early 1980s and 1990s, Europe destroyed jobs massively, something that has happened neither in the USA nor in Japan. In the boom of the late 1980s, European economic growth rose well above productivity so that new jobs were created and unemployment fell again. But in the subsequent recession, five million jobs disappeared again (Morley 1998). This is

Table 8.3 Economic growth and unemployment (%)

	Average growth rate			Average unemployment		
	1989–93	*1994–8*	*Difference*	*1989–93*	*1994–8*	*Difference*
UK	0.68	3.02	2.34	8.0	7.16	−0.8
Ireland	4.56	7.64	3.08	14.9	11.62	−3.3
Denmark	0.94	3.04	2.1	10.5	9.28	−1.2
Netherlands	2.78	3.06	0.28	7.1	7.46	0.3
Germany	3.08	2.26	−0.82	7.0	10.36	3.4
France	1.5	2.28	0.78	9.9	12.24	2.3
Italy	1.12	1.82	0.7	11.0	11.9	0.9

Source: IMF (1997).

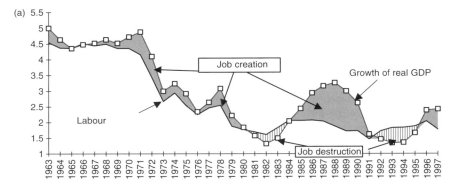

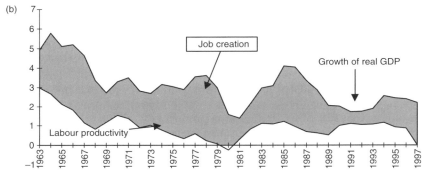

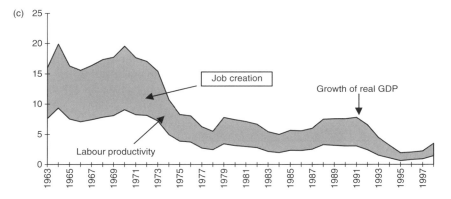

Figure 8.2 Job creating growth (5-year moving average) in (a) Europe; (b) USA; (c) Japan.
Source: European Commission.

a different story from the US, where productivity growth has been much lower, and economic growth has created many more jobs. In Japan, on the other hand, the remarkable correlation between GDP and labour productivity growth may explain why Japan is the only OECD country to have maintained low rates of unemployment (well below 5 per cent) throughout the post-war period (OECD 1994: part I, 38).

The Japanese labour market experience is worth a study of its own.[5] But the pattern of Figure 8.2(c) shows a possible explanation by the labour-hoarding behaviour of Japanese firms that is also reflected in the high stability of employment growth in Table 8.1. Until the early 1990s, changes in output reflect changes in labour productivity. This conclusion is also supported by Figure 8.3(b) which shows that during the recessions of the early 1970s (oil shock) and 1990s (bubble burst), Japan's total factor productivity fell in absolute terms.

This explanation is interesting with respect to conventional explanations of unemployment resulting from 'rigid labour markets'. As we will show below, one measure for nominal wage rigidity is the sacrifice ratio. Yet, by definition, labour hoarding would lead to low sacrifice ratios, so that we obtain the odd result that a labour-hoarding economy, like Japan, has a 'flexible labour market'.[6] It should remind us to use this concept with great care. The other lesson from Japan is that high productivity increases are compatible with high employment rates. Therefore, what really matters is GDP growth.

Assuming that the Japanese labour market is a world of its own, the difference in developments between the EU and the USA still demands an explanation. According to Table 8.1, average labour productivity growth in the EU has stabilised around an annual rate of 1.8 per cent since the early 1980s. Assuming that the labour force will continue to grow with the long-term trend of 0.5 per cent, economic growth must exceed 2.3 per cent in order to create new jobs. The European Commission (1998a) has calculated that a significant reduction of unemployment would require growth rates of 3–3.5 per cent p.a. in order to mobilise Europe's employment potential fully over the medium-term. However, the effective output growth reached these levels only between 1986 and 1990, while it stood at 2.0 per cent in the decade before and at 1.57 per cent in the 1990s (see Table 8.1). Thus, Europe's unemployment has its roots in insufficient GDP growth.

One may object that the US proves the contrary. Here, economic growth has exceeded 2.5 per cent over the last quarter of a century, somewhat higher than in Europe, but not dramatically so. If unemployment did not rise, it was because labour productivity grew by only 0.6–1.1 per cent in the USA in the 1970s and 1980s, and the labour force with 1 per cent p.a. This left room for job-creating effects of economic growth. Thus, over the long term, the essential difference between US and EU performance has not been the difference in GDP growth, but the difference in labour productivity growth, which has been nearly twice the US rate in Europe. The conclusion must be that Europe suffers either from too low a growth or too rapid a productivity increase. If we want to understand the difference in European, American and Japanese employment creation, we have to look at the differences in growth performance.

Growth accounting

We may use a simple Solow growth accounting model to highlight the specifics of European and American growth experiences. We assume aggregate output as being produced using two inputs, capital (K) and labour (L) at a given technology τ:

$$y = \tau F(K, L). \tag{8.1}$$

If we divide output by labour we get labour productivity as a function of capital intensity:

$$\lambda = \tau f(k), \qquad f'(k) > 0, \qquad f''(k) < 0 \tag{8.2}$$

with $\lambda = y/L$ and $k = K/L$. $f'(k)$ is the marginal product of capital per unit of labour. We also assume diminishing returns to each factor. If we assume the specific form of a Cobb–Douglas production function

$$y = \tau \cdot K^{\alpha} L^{1-\alpha}, \tag{8.1a}$$

the growth rate of productivity becomes

$$\dot{\lambda} = \frac{d\tau}{\tau} + \alpha \frac{dk}{k}. \tag{8.3}$$

The first element on the RHS in Equation (8.3) describes the increase in total factor productivity or technological progress, the second indicates the contribution of the increase in capital stock per worker employed, that is, the capital–labour ratio. The growth of technological progress is an increase in output with the same amount and proportion of factor inputs. Therefore, if total factor productivity (TFP) rises, capital intensity (K/L) remains constant. The simultaneous increase in labour and capital productivity also implies that the capital–output ratio (K/y) falls. This is called Hicks-neutral progress. The other factor in rising labour productivity is the increase in capital intensity. If the elasticity of output with respect to capital is approximately one-third and this reflects the (relatively) constant technological factor share of capital in a Cobb–Douglas production function, then the increase of labour-productivity over and above TFP is due to the contribution of the growth rate of the capital stock per person employed.

The European Commission (e.g. 1997), in line with standard neoclassical textbooks (i.e. Rose 1973) calls this second effect 'capital–labour substitution'. This is correct insofar as an increase in labour productivity allows the production of a given output with less labour input; if productivity increases due to higher capital, labour is substituted by capital. However, if output is not constant but growing, we may well see that both capital and labour increase, although not at the same rate. It would then seem misleading to call the effect of capital accumulation per worker employed 'labour–capital substitution'. This distinction is all the more important as the reference to the substitution of factors of production implies in a neoclassical context that it is caused by relative shifts in factor prices. But as I will show below, this 'substitution' can also be caused by a deviation of relative income shares of labour and capital from their technological shares in the production function.

Neoclassical growth theory has established that permanent increases in the capital–labour ratio are unsustainable due to diminishing returns to capital. Therefore, a *permanent* increase in the savings (or investment) rate produces a *temporary* increase in the *growth rate* of output per workers, and a permanent increase in the *level* of labour productivity. Only changes in technological progress have sustainable growth effects (Romer 1996). Thus, in theory, a country should not deviate durably from its balanced growth path. However, this is exactly what we observe in Europe: since the 1970s labour productivity has been improving con-sistently at a higher rate than in the USA due to more rapid accumulation of capital per person employed.

Let us look at the facts. Technology change has progressed most rapidly in the 1960s and early 1970s as demonstrated by Figure 8.3. Since the mid-1970s it has slowed down worldwide – a puzzle that still awaits convincing explanation by economists, given the microchip revolution. Since the late 1970s total factor productivity has increased fairly constantly with a trend of 1.2–1.4 per cent in Europe and 0.8 in the USA. In Japan it used to be higher than in Europe, but it has become unstable in recent years (see also Table 8.1). However, technological progress accounted for only two-thirds of total labour productivity increases in Europe and Japan, while it explains 80 per cent in the US over the 1960–98 period. In the 1970s, the share of TFP in labour productivity fell everywhere (nearly three-quarters in the US, one-half in the EU, less in Japan). But in the 1980s, TFP explained nearly all of American labour productivity and returned to its usual relation of two-thirds in Europe and Japan. Thus, in Europe and Japan the accumulation of capital per worker has played a much more important role. Figure 8.4 shows that since 1960, capital intensity (K/L) remained nearly unchanged in the USA, rose dramatically in Japan, and occupied a middle position in Europe.

Thus, technological progress is essentially Hicks-neutral in America, but not in the two other economies. As a consequence, labour productivity due to capital accumulation per worker grew rapidly in Japan and Europe. Since the technological factor share of capital in Japan (29.6 per cent) is lower than in Europe (31.4 per cent) and the US (33.3 per cent), the increase in capital intensity raises labour productivity somewhat less in Japan.

Thus, we have again three different cases: low labour productivity growth, constant capital intensity and low unemployment in the USA; high productivity growth, very rapid accumulation of capital per worker and low unemployment in Japan; high productivity gains, rising capital intensity and high unemployment in Europe. Hence, Europe's unemployment problems cannot be explained by its high productivity growth or 'capital–labour substitution' alone, because on both accounts Japan implemented higher rates of change without significant

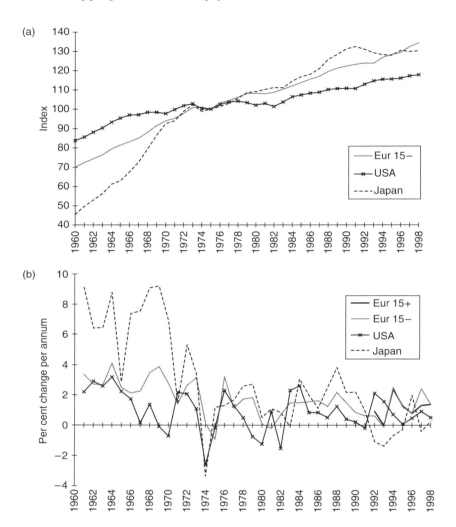

Figure 8.3 (a) Total factor productivity (Index 1975 = 100); (b) total factor productivity change (technological progress).

Source: European Commission.

unemployment. On the other hand, trend in GDP growth was fairly similar in the US and Europe. But higher capital accumulation per worker in the EU pushed the employment threshold up and therefore lowered the job-creating effect of economic growth. If Europe wants to overcome its unemployment crisis, it must increase growth or lower capital accumulation per worker, or do both.

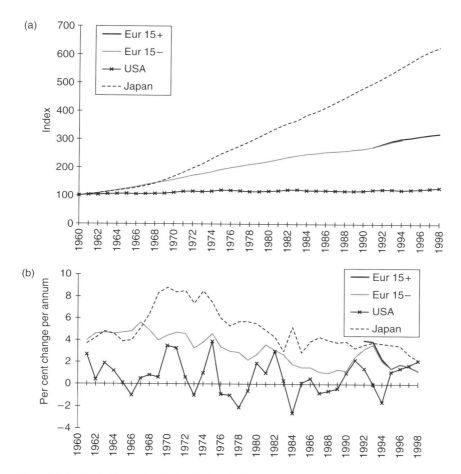

Figure 8.4 (a) Capital intensity (Index 1960 = 100); (b) annual variation in capital intensity.
Source: European Commission.

Explaining Europe's low employment creation

The riddle to be explained can be put into two questions: why is Europe's economic growth so low, despite its high increases in productivity? This question allows Keynesian explanations of unemployment. The alternative, neoclassical question is: why is European capital intensity rising so much faster than in the USA, while growth cannot be improved?[7] Before we look at the answer provided by the two theoretical approaches, we must first determine the growth dynamics of employment.

Determining the unemployment rate

According to neoclassical theory, the economy is on a balanced growth path when actual investment equals the (net) increase of the capital stock required to keep the labour force and technological progress growing at their natural rates. In this case, output and capital grow at the same rate, and this rate is equal to the growth of the labour force plus technological progress. The capital–labour ratio is constant in this case. Hence in the steady state:

$$\dot{y} = \frac{I}{P_0 K} = \bar{n} + \frac{\mathrm{d}\tau}{\tau}, \tag{8.4}$$

where $\dot{y}$ is the GDP growth rate and $\bar{n}$ the rate of growth of the labour force. I is the value of investment (capital equipment purchases) and $P_0 K$ is the capital stock valued at replacement costs. In order to keep things simple, we will henceforth assume that $(\mathrm{d}\tau/\tau) = 0$. Economic growth depends on capital accumulation and investment. We, therefore, return to our model for investment behaviour expressed in Equations (2.2)–(2.4) in Chapter 2. We will focus here on the rate of growth of the capital stock. We therefore divide Equation (2.4) by the value of the capital stock $(P_0 K)$ and get:

$$\frac{I}{P_0 K} = a_0 + \varphi[q(i) - \bar{q}], \tag{8.5}$$

where $\bar{q}$ is the 'normal' value of Tobin's q, with $\varphi(+) = +$, $\varphi(0) = 0$, $\varphi(-) = -$ and a_0 the autonomous or natural rate of capital accumulation. We also know that $q_i = (\partial q/\partial i) < 0$. Growth equilibrium occurs when the savings out of net income support net investment, so that:

$$a_0 + \varphi[(q(i) - \bar{q})] = s\frac{Py}{P_0 K} = s\frac{f'(k)}{k} \tag{8.6}$$

with s as savings rate and Py as net income.[8] If $q = \bar{q}$ our system is in equilibrium and the capital–output ratio adjusts to savings and the natural growth rate of investment:

$$\frac{K}{y} = \frac{s}{a_0}. \tag{8.6'}$$

It should be clear from Chapter 2 that q represents profits as entrepreneurial quasi-rents which tend to disappear over time if monetary policy[9] remains stable (i constant) since investment will adjust to profitable opportunities. Once it has adjusted, $q(i) = \bar{q}$ and the prevailing interest is the 'natural rate of interest' in the Wicksell-sense.[10] The speed of this arbitrage depends on the cost of adjustment: if these costs were zero, q would instantaneously jump to $\bar{q}$. Therefore, as long as adjustment costs are positive, short-term monetary policy measures can have real effects by lifting or lowering q, thereby inducing an adjustment process in the capital stock. Thus, transitory disequilibria could become long-lasting.[11]

To keep unemployment constant, the capital stock will have to grow at the rate of the labour force plus the increase in the capital–labour ratio (dk/k). The real rate of employment growth (n) is constrained by the rate of accumulation:

$$\frac{I}{P_0 K} = \frac{dk}{k} + n. \tag{8.7}$$

Given that our simplified model abstracts from technological progress ($d\tau/\tau = 0$),[12] an increase in the capital intensity k is the only way to increase productivity. This can be derived from Equation (8.2) which is a monotonically increasing function. Therefore, its inverse $k = f^{-1}(\lambda)$ exists with the derivative

$$\frac{dk}{d\lambda} = \frac{\tau}{f'(k)}. \tag{8.8}$$

Hence, the rise in capital intensity depends on the increase in productivity:

$$dk = \frac{\tau}{f'(k)} \cdot d\lambda. \tag{8.8'}$$

If productivity remains constant ($d\lambda = 0$), we have balanced growth and the rate of growth of the capital stock will be identical with employment growth (as in Equation (8.4)). As we have seen, higher employment requires more rapid growth of the capital stock or lower productivity or both. We now substitute Equation (8.8') into Equations (8.7) and (8.5) and obtain the dynamic labour demand function:

$$n = a_0 + \varphi(q - \bar{q}) - \frac{\tau}{f'(k)} \cdot \frac{d\lambda}{k}. \tag{8.9}$$

We also assume that labour supply is growing at the same rate as the labour force $\bar{n}$. In the steady-state equilibrium labour demand and supply are in balance ($n = \bar{n}$), investment equals saving $q(i) = \bar{q}(i^*)$ and the capital–labour ratio remains constant, so that $d\lambda = 0$. Hence $\bar{n} = a_0$.[13]

This implies that labour market flow disequilibria are caused by discrepancies in savings and investment or by changes in the capital–labour ratio:

$$n - \bar{n} = \varphi(q - \bar{q}) - \frac{\tau}{f'(k)} \cdot \frac{d\lambda}{k}. \tag{8.9a}$$

Next, we look at the evolution of stocks. We know that the labour force grows at the natural rate:

$$N_t = N_0(1 + \bar{n})^t, \tag{8.10a}$$

and the employment level at

$$L_t = L_0(1 + n)^t,$$ (8.10b)

Thus, the employment rate is

$$\frac{L_t}{N_t} \approx \frac{L_0}{N_0}(1 + n - \bar{n})^t,$$ (8.10c)

and the rate of unemployment

$$U_t = 1 - \frac{L_0}{N_0}(1 + n - \bar{n})^t,$$ (8.10d)

where L_0 and N_0 are initial values. Obviously, if employment grows at a rate faster than the labour force, the employment rate increases and unemployment falls. But from Equation (8.9) we know that a deviation of employment growth from its natural rate is only possible if productivity changes due to a change in the capital intensity (e.g. $d\lambda > 0$) or because planned investment deviates from saving $q \neq \bar{q}$.

This allows an interesting insight. We remember from Chapter 2 that q is a function of i which is set by the central bank.[14] Let i_0 be the initial rate of interest at which $q(i_0) = \bar{q}(i^*)$. The economy is now in equilibrium with $n = \bar{n}$ and $i = i^*$. Thus, we may call the related initial rate of unemployment a natural rate. Next, assume that authorities raise interest rates.[15] Thus: $q(i) < \bar{q}(i_0)$ for $i > i_0$ and because of Equation (8.7) employment grows less than the labour force ($n < a_0 = \bar{n}$). Hence, unemployment increases above the natural rate. However, the capital stock will adjust to the new conditions of profitability. Disinvestment will take place until the marginal return on capital equals the higher interest rate. Because q are temporary quasi-rents which disappear over time, q will return to $\bar{q}(i^*)$, even if $i_0 < i_t = i^*$ and n will return to $\bar{n}$. Thus, Wicksell's new natural rate i^* is higher than the previous equilibrium rate i_0, and the level of equilibrium unemployment is also higher. In this model partial adjustment is due to the speed by which the capital stock changes. Hence, a variation of the interest rate will only cause a temporary deviation of the rate of employment *growth* from its natural level. However, this temporary deviation will cause a permanent shift in the employment *level*: while the unemployment rate rises above its natural level as long as $q < \bar{q}$, it will stabilise at a higher natural rate when $q = \bar{q}$. The inverse logic applies to a cut in interest rates. Consequently, the natural rate of unemployment is a function of the interest rate.

This result is obtained by incorporating Tobin's investment theory into a neoclassical Solow growth model. It allows us to explain why the natural rate of unemployment is closely related to the actual rate, as many hysteresis models claim. This implies, of course, that there are multiple equilibria for the natural rate of unemployment. We could, however, have obtained the same result if instead of using the investment rate as a function of *q*, we had used the neoclassical formula-tion and had made the savings ratio dependent on interest rates. As we know, a change in the savings rate has a *level* effect and not a *growth* effect. Thus, the equili-brium unemployment rate would shift with savings/investment shocks and then remain stable.

Equation (8.9a) describes a model which allows us to explain unemployment from a Keynesian and neoclassical perspective: Keynesian (un)employment growth is determined by the dynamics of $q - \bar{q}$. A neoclassical interpretation assumes investment equal saving ($q = \bar{q}$), but focuses on rising capital intensity $dk/k > 0$. We will deal with the latter first.

The neoclassical explanation: capital–labour substitution

We have seen that in a neoclassical world with balanced growth, the capital–labour ratio is stable. Therefore, if $dk > 0$, the equilibrium must be disturbed. The cause for the disturbance may be seen in rigid labour markets that distort relative factor prices. An enormous amount of empirical literature tries to assess the specific factors for these assumed labour market distortions. The argument asserts that Europe's (real) wages are too high due to 'competition-restraining institutions and anti-competitive practises in the labour markets' (OECD 1994: Vol. II, 52). The theoretical thinking behind this claim can be derived from the micro-behaviour of firms who either minimise their input costs of labour and capital at a given level of output, or who need to maintain their international competitiveness by rising productivity. In the first case, firms substitute expensive labour by cheaper capital. In the second, they seek to improve productivity in order to reduce unit labour costs.

The substitution argument can be demonstrated by using a production func-tion like Equation (8.1) or Equation (8.1a). *K* and *L* are the amounts of input which have to be hired by the firm at the user costs *r* and the real wage $\bar{w}$. Thus, the cost function is

$$C = rK + \bar{w}L. \tag{8.11}$$

For a given level of output, and using the production function Equation (8.1a), the first order condition for a cost minimum yields:

$$\frac{r}{\bar{w}} = \frac{F_K}{F_L} = \frac{\alpha L}{(1 - \alpha)K}. \tag{8.11a}$$

As is well known, the input–price ratio must be equal to the ratio of the marginal products of capital and labour, which is a measure for the marginal rate of capital substitution for labour. Under perfect competition, this condition is always fulfilled. The least-cost combination of capital and labour required to produce varying levels of output determines the optimal capital–labour ratio as

$$k^* \equiv \frac{K}{L} = \frac{\alpha}{1-\alpha} \cdot \frac{\overline{w}}{r}. \qquad (8.12)$$

Given that α is the technically determined elasticity of output to capital, and r and w are supposed to be exogenously given, k^* reflects the optimal input ratio. If, however, k is not constant, as we observed in Europe (see Figure 8.4), then this must result from a change in the factor–price ratio $(\overline{w}/r)$. Now, if the real rate of interest r is taken as fixed, it follows that a push in real wages will increase the capital–labour ratio, and the employment rate n will fall below its natural level due to Equation (8.9a). If the marginal product of capital diminishes after a rise in the capital–labour ratio, and this is reflected by lower real interest rates, the process may even accelerate. Hence, excessive wage pressure appears to be responsible for rising unemployment.[16]

This argument is usually supported by comparisons of real wages. According to the IMF (1996), real compensation per worker in Europe increased by almost 2 per cent p.a. over the past twenty-five years compared to 0.5 per cent annual growth in the US real earnings. However, these data deviate somewhat from those published by the European Commission (see Table 8.1). Here, the real product wage has increased since 1961 by 2.6 per cent p.a. in the EU and by 1.2 per cent in the US.[17] Yet, in Japan – which has the lowest rate of unemployment in the OECD – the real product wage increased by 4.4 per cent. If we take the real consumer wage,[18] the figures are 1.3 per cent for the USA, 2.8 per cent for Europe and 4 per cent for Japan.[19] Furthermore, increases in real wages have converged between the EU and the USA since the 1980s. In the 1990s, Japan also lowered real wage increases to this level, but unemployment started to rise. Thus, real wage increases are not always linked to rising unemployment. However, increases in the real product wage are equal to labour productivity growth and the change in the wage share.[20] The change in the wage share is the real wage position, calculated as the difference between increases in the real product wage and labour productivity, shown in Figure 8.5(a). Since the mid-1970s real wages have increased less than labour productivity, thereby increasing the aggregate profit margin (Figure 8.5(b)).

However, one may argue that productivity increased because of the underlying wage pressure.[21] Hence the neoclassical thesis that excessive wage costs lead to capital–labour substitution and unemployment, hinges on the assumption that wage pressure has *caused* increases in labour productivity over and above the level of total factor productivity advances. This is a testable hypothesis. We will define real wage pressure as the difference between the rise in real wages and total factor productivity. According to theory, a positive difference would lead to capital–labour substitution and push the capital–labour ratio up, lowering employment. Figure 8.5(c) shows that real wage pressure has not been dramatically different from the real wage position. It was high in Europe and Japan in the 1960s. After the first oil price shock, wage pressure has been absent in Europe except for the short period after the second oil shock and after German unification. Therefore, it seems

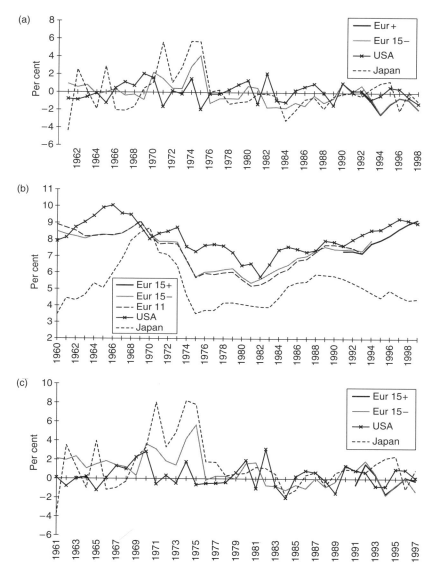

Figure 8.5 (a) Real wage position (real wage – productivity; annual change); (b) profitability; (c) real wage pressure (real wage – total factor productivity; annual change).

Source: European Commission and own calculation.

counter-intuitive to conclude that high wage pressure caused Europe's high increase in capital intensity and unemployment.

Econometric tests support the intuition (see Annexure). Time series analysis for 1961–99 reveals that Europe's rate of capital accumulation per worker seems to be

trend-stationary with a structural break at German unification. The trend is negative, that is, the increases in the K/L-ratio are diminishing. By contrast, in the USA
the null hypothesis that capital intensity contains a unit root is strongly rejected and
the series must be stationary. Similarly, wage pressure is stationary in both economies yet follows a negative trend in Europe. Over the whole period, wage pressure
was less than half a per cent in the USA and below 1 per cent in the EU 11 and in
Germany.[22] These data would allow us to regress the growth rate of capital intensity
on wage pressure in the USA, and the deviations from the capital intensity trend on
the deviations of wage pressure for Europe. Both models yield disappointing
results: the R^2-values are low and heteroscedasticity distorts the t-values. Since the
coefficients are generally lower for Europe than the US, this could indicate that the
neoclassical model works better in America than in Europe. However, the overall
conclusion must be that the simple hypothesis of wage pressure causing capital–
labour substitution is a misspecified model. Other factors must contribute to the
rise in Europe's capital–labour ratio and unemployment.

One factor seems to be technological catch-up growth that Europe needed to
undertake to reach American standards of living. This would explain the negative
trend in capital accumulation per worker. Figure 8.6 shows that over 80 per cent
of the European increase in capital intensity can be explained by the gap of relative
GDP per capita[23] compared to the US in 1960.

A ten percentage point reduction in the income gap with America lowers the
annual increase of capital intensity by half a percentage point on average. Thus,
the greater the real convergence within Europe, and between Europe and the US,

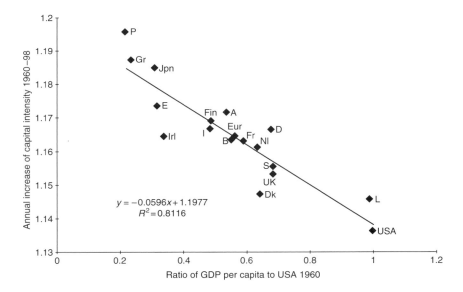

Figure 8.6 Convergence of capital intensity.

Source: European Commission.

the more likely it is that Europe will display Hicks-neutral technological progress instead of so-called labour–capital substitution.[24] The rapid increases in European capital–labour ratios appear to have more to do with its level of economic development than with labour market distortions. But this implies that Europe must have a significantly higher growth potential than has actually been achieved in the last quarter of a century. Unemployment is not due to 'bad' productivity increases, but to insufficient growth.

The Keynesian explanation: insufficient investment

Given the empirical ambiguity of the neoclassical explanation, we may now focus on the investment function in our employment Equation (8.9a). In the steady state, the capital stock should grow at the same rate as the labour force plus technological progress. If the actual growth rate falls below (rises above) this required rate, unemployment rises (falls) to a new, higher (lower) equilibrium level. Therefore, persistently high unemployment may be caused by periods of low capital accumulation that are followed by periods of insufficiently high investment to bring people back into work.

One indicator of this case in Europe might be the relative number of years with positive or negative output gaps. Table 8.4 gives some selected country coefficients for the pre- and post-1981-disinflation periods.

The balance of positive to negative years has seriously deteriorated in all EU-countries, except perhaps in Portugal. While excess demand used to be five times as frequent in the EU before 1981, this trend reversed thereafter, when negative output gaps were three to four times more frequent. Thus, effective demand must have had a role in rising unemployment. Even the OECD (1994) has acknowledged 'a deficiency of demand ... reflected in significant output gaps' (OECD 1994: 66).

The lack of demand may be correlated with the rate of investment as a percentage of GDP. This feature is apparent from Figure 8.7(a).

During the Golden Age, the investment share in the EU 15 was high (between 22 and 24 per cent), and unemployment low (2 per cent). When the investment share fell after the first oil price shock, unemployment exploded. But during the period from 1985–90, when the European economy grew at 3–3.5 per cent, the

Table 8.4 Ratio of number of years with positive to negative output gaps

	1960–81	*1982–97*
EU 15	5.0	0.38
Germany	2.0	0.23
France	1.0	0.54
Netherlands	2.0	0.31
Belgium	1.3	0.31
Spain	1.4	0.45
Portugal	0.8	0.78

Source: European Commission.

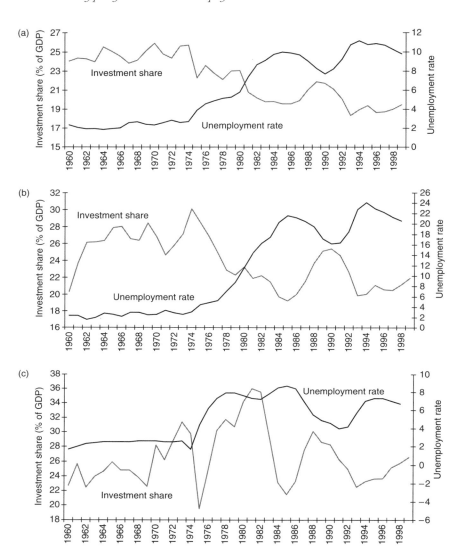

Figure 8.7 Investment share and unemployment rate: (a) EU 15; (b) Spain; (c) Portugal.
Source: European Commission.

investment share rose back up to 20 per cent. Thus, unemployment can nearly be seen as the mirror image of the investment share (Morley 1998). This explanation of European unemployment is surprisingly simple. In order to check its robustness, I looked at Spain and Portugal. Blanchard and Jimeno (1995) called it 'the biggest empirical challenge' to explain the dramatic difference in unemployment rates of these two countries. They found that there is no simple mapping from observable labour market characteristics (rules and institutions) to structural unemployment. Spain and Portugal are more similar in this respect than any other pair of EU countries, and yet their unemployment rates vary by 15 per cent. Can investment shares provide a better explanation? Figures 8.7(b) and (c) show the result: Spain's pattern is remarkably similar to the EU 15, but Portugal is different. While in Spain and Europe the investment share fell continuously after the end of the Golden Age, it continued to rise in Portugal until the early 1980s and stayed high even thereafter. It never fell to the low rates of Spain or Europe. Thus, even if a fall in the investment ratio in the mid-1970s pushed unemployment rates up, these developments were much less harmful in Portugal than elsewhere.

How can low investment be explained? Two avenues for research are open: one derives from a demand-accelerator approach. New-Keynesians look at price and wage rigidities usually in the context of imperfect markets that prevent higher demand and investment from being created by lower prices. They have incorporated previous criticism from new classical economics about the micro-foundations of a macro-theory and the assumption of rational expectations, and they have focused on the microeconomic conditions needed for nominal stickiness to arise. Systemic real rigidities due to asymmetric information and co-ordination failures take a prominent role in these models (Benassi *et al.* 1994: 18). Although the logic of their models is different from the classical approach, they often come to similar conclusions: the need for product and labour market reforms. The other avenue derives from monetary-Keynesians who argue that the cause for persistent high unemployment is found in excessively high real interest rates (Tomann 1997). However, this hypothesis requires an explanation for high real interest rates, just as the new-Keynesians needed to develop theories for wage and price rigidities.

In our model, we have used Tobin's investment function. Although it is difficult to verify q empirically (see Chapter 2), it is useful for analytical purposes. In previous chapters we have argued that $\bar{q}$ is likely to rise with financial uncertainty, such as interest and exchange rate volatility. Such increased uncertainty has been a major factor in the post-Bretton Woods era. A consequence of higher $\bar{q}$ would be lower investment rates. Now it is evident from Figure 8.7 that the investment share fell at the same time when exchange and interest rates became more volatile after Bretton Woods. Secondly, the expected profitability of investment projects, as expressed by Tobin's marginal q, would have to be higher, when $\bar{q}$ rises. Thus, it is not obvious that the observed increase in profitability (see Figure 8.5 and Table 8.1) would necessarily have translated into higher investment. This would require expected profits to exceed the required minimum profit rate. But this expected profitability depends also on monetary policy, that is, interest and exchange levels. We have summarised these factors in the function $q(i)$ and will return to this below. However, it is well known that interest rates have been unusually high since the early 1980 (see Figures 2.1 and 2.2 and Ciocca and Nardozzi 1996). While they have come down in both nominal and real terms in the US in the early 1990s, real rates have remained high for Europe.[25] Given that $q(i) - \bar{q}$ always tends toward zero, this implies that Europe's equilibrium unemployment must be high, because the interest rate increases have not been matched by symmetric rate reductions. Why that is so requires an explanation.

In the literature we find mainly three causes for Europe's high interest rate. The most common is the crowding-out hypothesis of public finance. However, in Collignon (1996) and Collignon and Mundschenk (1999), I have argued that the link is the opposite:[26] public debt and deficits have risen because real interest rates rose over and above the rate of growth. I will therefore not pursue this line of argument here. Secondly, one may explain high real interest rates by 'conventions' that agents in financial markets establish when their expectations are governed by a 'prevailing view' as to what the interest rate is expected to be (Ciocca and Nardozzi 1996). Although this raises the important question of how expectations are formed,[27] I will focus on the particular aspect of monetary policy and develop a model below that explains persistent unemployment as a result of inconsistent wage and monetary policies. Thirdly, Phelps (1994, 1995) has constructed models in which wage increases have a similar crowding-out effect as public deficits. However, this logic requires fixed or tight money supply. It therefore seems to me more convincing to follow Modigliani (1997) whereby Europe's high real interest rates reflect tight money, which may have caused persistent lack of demand.

Thus, the answer why Europe's growth is so low can be found in high interest rates. But this leads to a new puzzle: why has Europe's monetary policy been so tight? Is it due to policy errors, or are there structural causes? We are interested here in the long-run implications of monetary policies on growth and employment. This is not to deny that labour market institutions may have an impact on employment. But from our point of view, what matters for the sustainability of EMU is monetary policy. Yet, before we build our model, the proposition that money may have long-term consequences for real variables needs further development.[28]

The neutrality proposition of money and unemployment

In the section on *A bias toward price stability in the European policy frame*, in Chapter 7 we discussed the employment motive as a potential inflationary bias in monetary policy. This was a short-term argument for time-inconsistent policies. It is generally assumed that in the long run nominal rigidities are overcome and prices adjust fully, so that monetary policy has no long-term effect on the real economy. Only cyclical variations and transitory deviations can be affected by money. Macroeconomic policy is 'relatively impotent in dealing with unemployment resulting from structural causes' (OECD 1994: 66). This is the neutrality proposition. Monetary neutrality means that nominal variables have nominal effects, but they do not alter real quantities. However, as most theories would readily concede, monetary policy and interest rates determine to some degree the level of investment. To the extent that capital accumulation contributes to long-term growth, monetary policy might have an impact on employment that goes beyond the transitory shocks of time-inconsistent policies. The question was first raised by Tobin (1965) in the context of portfolio choice. He found that the growth of money can have long-run effects on the real rate of interest, capital intensity, output and welfare. Since then, other models have yielded different answers (Orphanides and Solow 1990: 256). But if transitory, that is, 'neutral', monetary shocks can have persistent effects, then the neutrality proposition must be re-interpreted.

The differences in analysis and policy emphasis reflect the theoretical debate between (new or neo-) classical and Keynesian economists about the adjustment mechanism in financial, goods and labour markets. As we have seen, the former believe that all markets, including the labour market, clear either perpetually or at least in the long run through the adjustment mechanism of prices, unless institutional impediments distort them. Institutional reforms are then required to resolve them. On the other hand, Keynesians believe that market economies can suffer from chronic and persistent demand failures, even when markets are in equilibrium because the adjustment mechanism goes from price to quantities. This statement does not imply that prices are fixed, but simply that price adjustment is not instantaneous. Thus, the debate seems to hinge on the *speed of market clearing*. New Keynesians have built on asymmetric information and co-ordination failure to explain nominal price and wage stickiness. An alternative approach is derived from *relative* speed of adjustment in market hierarchy models (Tomann 1997: 20). At the top of the hierarchy are fast adjusting markets, such as money and capital markets, while at the bottom slow adjustment is reflected in persistent disequilibria. According to this theory, labour markets are slow adjusters. However, in this form, the theory has the disadvantage that unemployment is a disequilibrium phenomenon; it cannot explain the rise in *equilibrium* unemployment.

In systems of 'finite price velocities' (Leijonhufvud 1967) or of incomplete nominal adjustment (Romer 1996) it is possible that prices at which trading takes place deviate from Walrasian equilibrium prices, so that desired transactions are not always met and quantities are adjusted. Labour market equilibrium is then not defined by the coincidence of supply and demand of labour units, as neoclassical theory would have it, but as a situation in which wages have ceased to adjust (Modigliani 1997: 252). Consequently, with the given (equilibrium) price for labour, quantities (employment) adjust to effective demand, which is determined by the monetary mechanism. It is this mechanism that can explain how monetary policy can influence employment and growth.[29]

There are two versions of describing the monetary mechanism. Under the classical-monetarist assumption of perfect price flexibility, aggregate real output is always maintained at the full-employment level. The money market will clear because an excess demand for money should cause a decline in the price level until real money supply matches demand. The labour market will clear if wages are sufficiently flexible. This is the so-called classical dichotomy: the specification of the real economy model determines the equilibrium values of the real variables of the system while the specification of the monetary framework determines the equilibrium of the monetary variables (Patinkin 1989). From this point of view, Europe's persistent unemployment would be the consequence of a (partial) disequilibrium resulting from certain market imperfections such as trade union power, social benefits, minimum or efficiency wages, insider/outsider dynamics, etc. Stimulating output and employment requires in this model that money supply expands first, so that the public finds itself with more money than it wishes to hold and responds by spending it on goods. However, the unsolved question is why and how should the public have acquired money it did not wish to hold? (Modigliani and Papademos 1980: 9). If prices and quantities are simultaneously determined, as they are in a Walrasian world, there is no cause and no effect.

Under Keynesian assumptions there is a logical chain from financial to goods to labour markets that follows from what Riese (1994) calls 'the monetary foundation of interest rates'. In a strictly Keynesian logic, he derives the interest rate as the (scarcity) price for money as the *primum* and quantity adjustments as *secundum*. However, this requires the recognition of a fundamental asymmetry between the money market and other markets.

Money and markets

The money market is the market where cash (reserve assets) is traded. Its primary role is the redistribution of reserves within the banking system, stemming from the role of banks as providers of liquidity and payment services. In general equilibrium models with different markets, Walras' Law says that the sum of net market demands, valued at whatever prices generating those demands, must be exactly zero. This means that the aggregate positive excess demand in one market must be exactly offset by the negative excess demand (i.e. the excess supply) in other markets. In a monetary economy this Law must also apply to money, product and labour markets. Yet, as every central banker knows[30] (but unfortunately only few economists), the purpose of monetary policy is to create a permanent and structural shortage of central bank reserves in the money market, for this allows the monetary authority to set and steer interest rates. This means that it is the function of a central bank to create a 'disequilibrium' in the sense that the aggregate demand for reserve assets (cash) in the banking system permanently exceeds the supply of liquidity by *private* financial institutions in the money market.[31] In other words, the money market has to be a seller's market if the Central Bank is to have any impact. If money demand by banks exceeds supply by banks *ex ante*, the composition of asset portfolios is readjusted by banks selling financial assets to the central bank. Schnadt (1994: 40) rightly insists that it is the fact of the existence of net demand for reserves, that is, the shortage, and not the magnitude of demand, that allows the central bank to determine the level of interest rates.[32] The central bank is therefore the marginal supplier of reserves, which cannot be provided by the banking system in the event of an aggregate market shortage.[33] *Ex post*, the money market is of course always in equilibrium because at a given interest rate the central bank provides all the required reserve assets.

This implies that the structural excess demand for money creates as its mirror image an excess supply of resources. The transmission process goes via the capital market and investment to the goods and labour market. In the product markets, the 'scarcity of money' gives rise to the buyer's markets, which are characteristic for monetary market economies. But in the labour market, it causes a structural surplus of labour supply (Riese 1990). Of course, *ex post*, all markets, including the labour market, are 'in equilibrium' because all prices (including wages) are consistent with the level of interest rates set by the central bank. Obviously, the larger the *ex ante* excess demand for money, that is, the tighter monetary policy, the higher the excess supply in other markets. Modigliani (1997: 252) summarised this logic in the statement: 'The essence of the Keynesian revolution is that the money market is cleared not through an imaginary high flexibility of wages, but, despite wage rigidity, through movements in unemployment and interest rates'. By adjusting the employment of economic resources to effective demand, the goods market can indeed exhibit a tendency to return to a market clearing equilibrium. Yet, this will necessarily cause a structural surplus in the labour market as a counterpart to the structural shortage in the money market, although the degree of (un)employment of labour will vary. Thus, equilibrium in the labour market designates simply a state or path along which expectations are correct (Phelps 1994). Guaranteeing the survival of the unemployed part of the labour force by paying transfers and social benefits may then be a matter of social charity or justice, possibly also for x-efficiency, but it does not necessarily distort the proper functioning of a market economy and would not cause unemployment.[34]

These considerations are important for the understanding of the role of monetary policy in the long-term evolution of Europe's employment performance. The claim, of course, is not that the central bank is almighty. It is not, for it is only one – albeit an important – player in the money market. Its policy actions set the refinance conditions in the capital market, which is also, influenced by other factors, such as risk and uncertainty. If the tightness of the monetary policy stance determines the degree of (labour) resource utilisation via investor's portfolio equilibrium, then monetary policy cannot be without effect on employment. This is a matter of general or structural equilibrium of the economy and not a short-term trade-off between inflation and unemployment. The question is, therefore, under what conditions does the long-term neutrality of money not apply?[35] If monetary policy, by setting the nominal rate, can affect short-term real interest rate (because in the short term the inflation rate is fixed), and if this has long-run nominal effects on the rate of inflation, (as well as real effects on investment, growth and employment), then the neutrality hypothesis would only hold if all these real effects were short-lived. Thus, to prove that money is not neutral, we need to clarify under what conditions short-term shocks can have permanent effects. If a temporary disturbance had more than transitory effects so that the whole history of disturbances, that is, the actual time path, becomes relevant, then the system would not necessarily return to its 'natural rate' equilibrium, but would evolve along a random walk.

This feature is caught in hysteresis models.[36] The most well known is the insider–outsider model of wage bargaining in which the evolution of wages and employment depends critically upon whether an insider who becomes unemployed retains influence on the wage bargain. However, strong empirical evidence supporting this model is still lacking. The facts for Europe suggest that

European countries may have a problem in the persistence of real wage aspirations rather than with hysteresis problems stemming from insider membership (Adnett 1996: 217). In other words, perhaps *it is not so much the institutional structure of labour markets that has determined wage settlements, but rather the level of inflation.* We have formalised this idea in Chapter 1. However, if monetary policy can (and must) control inflation, it will also have effects on the real economy. In order to explain the consequences for employment, we must therefore look for the long-term consequences of short-term monetary policy actions. The following simple model aims at explaining a possible link between monetary policy and unemployment hysteresis.

A monetary model of the NAIRU

We will proceed in three steps. First, we will restate the traditional explanation of the NAIRU as a result of price and wage setting. Then, we will introduce the interest rate as an argument of price and wage setting. Finally, we will explain the interest rate as a function of wage developments in the next section.

Defining the NAIRU

The fundamental intuition of a natural rate of unemployment or a NAIRU is that there exists a rate of unemployment at which wages and prices (or inflation) remain constant. If authorities tried to push actual unemployment below this natural rate, they accelerate inflation. This logic is well established by the Layard, Nickell, Jackman (LNJ) model (1991, 1994) of the NAIRU. As it is useful to our own explanation of the dependency of natural unemployment on monetary policy, we will reproduce its basic structure here.

The LNJ-model assumes imperfect competition in goods and labour markets and explains the development of wage–price spirals by inconsistent wage and price claims. Only if the real wage desired by wage setters is the same as that considered feasible by price setters, will inflation be stable. The variable that brings about this consistency in the LNJ-model is the level of unemployment. In its very simplified version the model consists of two equations:

$$p - w^e = c_{10} - c_{11}u - c_{12}\Delta\pi - \lambda', \quad c_{11} \geq 0 \text{ (Price setting)}, \quad (8.13a)$$

$$w - p^e = c_{20} - c_{21}u - c_{22}\Delta\pi + \lambda'^e + \mathbf{z}, \quad c_{21} > 0 \text{ (Wage setting)}, \quad (8.13b)$$

where p, w, λ' and u are the price level, wages, productivity and unemployment in logs and the superscript indicates expectations. Prices are set by firms as a mark-up on expected wages[37] and wages as a mark-up on expected prices and productivity.[38] The price setting equation is often interpreted as a labour demand and the wage setting as a labour supply function.

From Equation (8.13a) one can derive the Price-determined or feasible Real Wage (PRW), while Equation (8.13b) sets the Bargained Real Wage (BRW),[39] as shown in Figure 8.8. Under assumptions of rational expectations, $\Delta\pi$ is the same as price surprises, and the coefficients c_{12} and c_{22} indicate the levels of nominal inertia with high values standing for high Nominal Wage Rigidity (NWR).[40] The mark-up tends to rise with the level of activity and expected demand although this is not necessary for the logic of the model.[41] When $c_{11} = 0$ and $c_{12} = 0$, we have 'normal-cost' pricing with a fixed mark-up over nominal unit labour costs. $p - (w - \lambda') = c_{10}$ and the PRW, $w - p = \lambda' - c_{10}$ becomes a horizontal line.[42] We will, however, see that there are strong macroeconomic reasons why the price mark-up may not be constant but correlated with activity. Empirical studies indicate that there seems to be a small response of the mark-up over wages to activity so that the PRW-line is fairly flat. Traditionally, the size of the price mark-up is assumed to reflect the degree of monopoly power of the firm in the goods markets that depends on the inverse of the elasticity of demand. However, later we will develop a model where the mark-up reflects macroeconomic quasi-rents, described by Keynes (1930).

The BRW is positively sloped. c_{20} can be interpreted as a full employment reservation wage in real terms. c_{21} is always assumed positive because the wage mark-up is supposed to increase as employment rises and the labour market tightens. The higher c_{21} is, that is, the steeper the BRW-line, the higher real wage flexibility is.[43] Empirical evidence reports that estimates for c_{21} are usually low for USA (0.28), medium for EU (1.6) and very high for Japan (41.0) (Bean 1994). Thus, it is interesting that American labour markets appear less flexible than Europes'. z is a vector measuring autonomous wage pressure depending on structural factors such as trade union power, the generosity of unemployment benefits or the mismatch between labour supply and demand.

In equilibrium actual wages are at their expected values, and inflation surprises are excluded. Therefore, the equilibrium unemployment rate or NAIRU

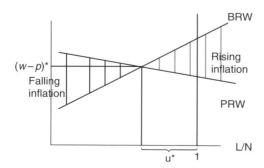

Figure 8.8 NAIRU as labour market equilibrium.

is determined as

$$u^* = \frac{c_{10} + c_{20} + z}{c_{11} + c_{21}}. \tag{8.14}$$

The determination of the natural rate depends on four structural and one policy parameter, and it is independent of productivity. LNJ (1994) have incorporated z into c_{20}, so that $c_{20} = z_0 + z_t$ (unions, benefits, etc.); they call c_{10} an exogenous price push although the notion of a profit push would be more exact and c_{20} an exogenous wage push. For reasons that will become clear below, I prefer the explicit formulation of the wage Equation (8.13b), taking c_{20} as a random exogenous wage push and z as the structural variable. c_{21} is called an indicator for real wage flexibility and c_{11} for price flexibility.[44] The important result from Equation (8.14) is that an exogenous wage push c_{20} increases equilibrium unemployment and an increase in flexibility c_{21} lowers it. Increases in trade union power, higher social benefits and other 'structural' changes z_t all shift the NAIRU up. But an autonomous profit push c_{10} also increases equilibrium unemployment and more flexible product markets lower it.

We may now also restate formally the concepts of the Phillips curve and the sacrifice ratio, which we have used occasionally in previous chapters. We have the Phillips curve as:

$$\Delta\pi = -\frac{c_{11} + c_{21}}{c_{12} + c_{22}} \left(u - \frac{c_{10} + c_{20} + z}{c_{11} + c_{21}} \right) \text{ (Phillips curve).} \tag{8.15}$$

The LNJ-definition for Real Wage Rigidity (RWR) is the inverse of real wage and price flexibility $(c_{11} + c_{21})$, that is, inverse of the degree to which extra unemployment reduces the gap between the target and the feasible real wage:

$$\text{RWR} = \frac{1}{c_{11} + c_{21}}.$$

Nominal inertia or nominal wage and price flexibility are

$$\text{NI} = c_{12} + c_{22},$$

and the measure for NWR is the sacrifice ratio that determines the cost of disin-flation in terms of unemployment increases:

$$\frac{\Delta u}{\Delta\pi} = \text{NWR} = \text{RWR}^*\text{NI} = \frac{c_{12} + c_{22}}{c_{11} + c_{21}} \text{ (Sacrifice ratio).} \tag{8.16}$$

The question is, of course: what determines these coefficients? We have argued in Chapter 5 that a flat Phillips curve or a high output-inflation trade-off reflects the benefit of low and stable inflation. Therefore, the slope of the Phillips curve is in the long run a function of the inflation mean. We can now give the following explanation for this fact: in a low inflation regime the degree of wage indexation (which was symbolised by ξ_1 in Equation (1.3)) would be low. Nominal contract length would increase and so would nominal inertia.[45] Consequently, the slope of the Phillips curve becomes flat and the sacrifice ratio rises. A small decrease in inflation would require large increases in unemployment. This would also imply that disinflation to very low rates of inflation becomes increasingly costly and that monetary policy becomes increasingly efficient.[46]

Consensus has it that a price push (c_{10}) or wage push (c_{20}) is exogenous, while the other factors (z) depend on structural or institutional arrangements such as the benefit system, trade union power, etc. Given that these structural issues have received widespread attention, and although economists have been largely unsuccessful in isolating robust relations between the increase in unemployment over time and shifts in exogenous factors (Blanchard in a comment to Ball, 1997), I wish to focus on the two exogenous parameters c_{10} and c_{20}. Assuming that capital intensity and productivity remain constant at the normalised level, that no nominal rigidity exists ($c_{12} = c_{22} = 0$) because firms apply 'normal cost' pricing, and that wage bargainers have rational expectations, we obtain:

$$p = c_{10} + w^e - \lambda' \tag{8.13a'}$$

with a fixed mark-up c_{10} over unit labour cost and a horizontal PRW line in Figure 8.9. The PRW is identical with productivity multiplied by the labour share.[47] An exogenous push on c_{10} implies that firms desire higher profit margins or lower real wages. According to Equation (8.14) this would increase natural

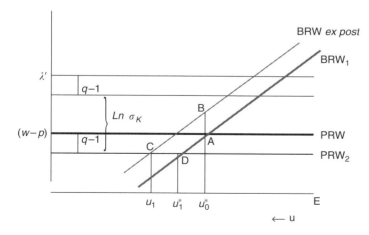

Figure 8.9 The effect of an interest rate increase in a contract economy.

unemployment. Thus, *rising equilibrium unemployment can result from higher desired reservation wages or from higher required profit margins*.

If the nominal wage negotiated by labour is higher than the feasible wage (w^f), firms will seek to increase prices in order to obtain the required profit mark-up, and the real wage will fall. But, if trade unions target a higher real wage, they will bargain for higher nominal wages and a cost-price spiral develops. If prices are to remain stable, profit margins are too low and unemployment has to increase in order to lower the real wage. The opposite happens if the targeted nominal wage is below the level expected by price setters, with falling prices and higher profits, production, employment and wages increase, until the real wage is consistent with stable prices and employment. As LNJ (1994: 27) put it: 'The problem is not that real wages are too high, but that too high real wages are desired at given unemployment.' However, their statement is tautologically identical with the following: 'The problem is not that real wages are too high, but that profit margins are too low at given levels of employment.'

The LNJ model does not provide us with an elaborate theory for the 'feasible' profit margin. Standard explanations focus on market power and demand elasticities under imperfect competition or on bounded rationality leading to normal cost pricing (Carlin and Soskice 1990). However, these theories suffer from ad-hocism. More serious is the objection that such price setting models arrive at the macro level by simply aggregating micro prices. They therefore assume that relative prices are independent of the absolute price level. This reflects an invalid dichotomy of the pricing process (Patinkin 1989: 174). To be fair, LNJ (1991) introduce IS-LM equations into their model to determine aggregate demand, but their approach is open to criticism of the classical dichotomy discussed above. Not surprisingly, the theory has focused on the determination of real wages by so-called 'real' factors z, without much monetary theory to explain the determination of the absolute price level. This asymmetry is apparent from Equation (8.13b) which incorporates the vector z for which an equivalent in Equation (8.13a) is missing. However, it is clear from Equation (8.13a$'$) that an exogenous shock to the required profit margin, say increasing c_{10}, would require a lower real wage. As a consequence, the price-setting line in Figure 8.6 would shift down and equilibrium unemployment increases. In this case, a rise in the NAIRU is not caused by labour market developments, but by developments in the goods markets. LNJ derive the price-setting equation from micro-behaviour on the level of the firm. However, if the price level is determined at the macroeconomic level, say by monetary policy, we need to link the micro-behaviour of the firm to policy actions. We will do that in the next section. Here we may simply mention the micro response at firm level if profit margins are 'too low'. If the representative firm cannot influence ('set') prices in aggregate because they are determined at the macro level by policy,[48] there are exactly three options for how it can increase profit margins: lowering nominal wages, increasing productivity, or eliminating unprofitable companies. At the same time, capital intensity will appear to rise. If nominal wages are rigid, only the last two options remain. However, Equation (8.14) has shown that equilibrium unemployment is independent of productivity. Therefore, productivity shocks may lead to *dis*equilibrium unemployment but not to a higher natural rate. The increase in the NAIRU must be a consequence of reduced employment due to insufficient growth, as we saw above and the only explanation for the low growth rate can be found in the low profit margin. The LNR-conclusion (1994: 27–8), 'the ultimate cause of both unemployment and higher real wages is the wage pressure', can be inverted into 'the *ultimate cause of both unemployment and higher real wages is the low price level relative to wages*'. Thus, unemployment is related to the price level, but this link is not of the empirical *ad hoc* nature of the Phillips curve. In order to explain this phenomenon, we require a theory for determining the price level and (dis)inflation. Elements of such theory can be derived from Keynes's *Treatise on Money* (1930) and have been developed by Riese (1986, 1994).

Interest rates and the price mark-up

The link between the price level and profitability has been shown by Keynes's (1930) fundamental equation. It can be reformulated in the form (see Collignon 1997):

$$P = \frac{W}{\lambda} + i_0 \cdot q \cdot b. \tag{8.17}$$

The aggregate mark-up is now no longer an arbitrary empirical value.[49] Instead it will cover the (rental) cost of net capital ($i_0 b$) plus entrepreneurial profits $q - \bar{q}$, that is, the quasi-rent which Keynes (1930) called Q-profits.[50] We assume for simplicity that all capital goods are financed by bonds B for which the nominal interest rate i_0 is to be paid. b is therefore the ratio of outstanding bonds (B) which are equal to (historic) value of capital per unit of output (y). q could also be interpreted as the shadow price of capital.

What matters for price setting is the nominal rate of interest, as firms stand under contractual obligations to service their debt in money terms. However, what matters for the determination of the required mark-up is the real interest rate plus inflation surprises.[51] If decelerating inflation rates are not correctly anticipated, so that realised inflation in the next period is lower than what was expected by financial markets, the mark-up will rise and the labour share will fall during disinflation periods – which is precisely what Figure 8.5(a) shows.

If $q(i_0) = \bar{q}(i^*) = 1$, the market value of the investment project is equal to its replacement costs and its net present value is zero. This reflects, therefore, the 'normal' capacity utilisation of the firm, at which the mark-up is just sufficient to cover the cost of capital[52] or the debt service $i_0 b$. Thus, when $q(i_0) = \bar{q}(i^*) = 1$, we have the equilibrium price level determined by unit labour costs (W/λ) and the normal (rental) cost of capital per output. This implies prices are indeed set as a mark-up on wages (unit labour costs) on the microlevel, and that the size of the mark-up does not depend on market power, but on capital cost which are dependent on monetary policy.[53] In order to stimulate new investment, profits must be higher than capital costs. This implies $q(i) > 1$ which would require a cut in interest rates ($i < i^*$). q-profits would then be positive until the capital stock has adjusted to the new equilibrium ($q = \overline{q} = 1$).[54] Therefore, Equation (8.17) implies that the price and profit margin levels rise in the early phase of an economic boom because $q > 1$, but, *ceteris paribus*, fall subsequently.[55] Inversely, real wages first fall and then rise. Thus, it would be justified – and is borne out by LNJ's evidence – to assume that prices are correlated with economic activity, so that the mark-up on labour cost is not constant, but declines as output rises. Our theory also implies that the mark-up has to rise at first in order to start the boom.[56] Thus, our price equation provides a macro-explanation for time-varying mark-ups that is different from traditional micro-models (see Carlin and Soskice 1990: 422).

Our theory of the price level shows the short-term impact of monetary policy: interest rates[57] affect simultaneously prices (via q and i_0) and quantities (via investment and demand) – but only until q has returned to the level of $\overline{q}$. Consistent with Equations (8.9) and (8.17), the quantity effect of interest rates permanently shifts income and employment levels, but not growth rates. The price effect has a temporary component related to the adjustment from one income level to another and a persistent element related to the cost structure of the firm. As we will see below, this may explain Sims' famous price puzzle.[58] In terms of the LNJ-model, the debt service $i_0 b$ determines the parameter c_{10} as cost push, while $q(i)$ would explain why c_{11} is positive. Together they explain the required profit share, and that determines the feasible real wage for the economy as a whole.

Equations (8.13a and b) and (8.17) are static descriptions of the price level and real wage. They are not directly comparable with the dynamic systems of Equations (8.9) and (8.14). However, with some auxiliary assumptions we can work out how a one-off interest rate shift affects unemployment. Where our theory deviates from traditional NAIRU-models is that the central bank cares about price stability and adjusts interest rates in pursuit of this objective. This has important consequences for the mark-up and for unemployment. We may distinguish two polar cases: a *spot market economy* where the interest rate i_0 varies each time in the exact proportion as the money market rate, and a contract economy where interest rates and capital costs are fixed until the end of the capital goods's life (Riese 1997).

We will at first assume a *contract economy*. Here, a variation in interest rates has only consequences for demand, not for capital costs.[59] Assume that we increase i. This would lower $q(i)$ and also push realised prices below the anticipated 'normal' level. Thus the *ex post* mark-up is less than what is required to service the nominal debt of firms. As a consequence, real wages should fall to PRW_2 in Figure 8.9. However, the demand-induced fall in prices increases the *ex post* real wage to B. Thus, realised and required mark-ups diverge. As some firms will go into liquidation, unemployment will increase up to the point u_1 and real wages will fall to C, that is, the level A originally bargained. At the actual rate of unemployment u_1 the real wage has been reduced to the level required by firms to service their debt, despite the lower price level. Yet, this is *not* an equilibrium position, and leads to decelerating inflation due to falling labour costs. However, given that credit contracts carry fixed nominal interest rates, real interest rates will rise with falling inflation. As a consequence, the required mark-up will increase.[60] However, the adjustment through the elimination of the least competitive firms implies a reduction in the aggregate capital stock, so that q is slowly returning to its equilibrium level $\overline{q}$ (assumed to equal 1). As profitability (the marginal product of capital) improves, the mark-up will rise, but feasible real wages will not improve. The price setting line will remain at PRW_2. On the other hand, workers realise that they have obtained higher (*ex post*) real wages than they would have expected at the prevailing level of unemployment. They will therefore continue to bargain along the BRW_1-line, keeping real wages constant.[61] Actual unemployment is reduced to the new equilibrium level at u_1^* which is higher than the previous equilibrium level u_0^*. The real wage stabilises at D, and the mark-up has increased in order to service the higher *real* interest rate, although the nominal interest rate has not changed. *Here we obtain the result that a falling labour share is correlated with rising equilibrium unemployment*.

This explanation is in line with hysteresis models. The logic here is that wage bargaining is about income shares: firms will agree to workers's wage claims as long as it allows them to realise a profit margin sufficient to cover the cost of capital. But if nominal interest rates and hence the debt service are fixed while inflation falls, a lower real wage is required. Unemployment is then the consequence of a real adjustment to monetary policy. A reduction of equilibrium unemployment requires a nominal interest rate cut below the natural level, when the whole logic works the other way round.

So far, our model of the NAIRU has assumed that only demand was affected by the interest rate increase. However, some structural changes cannot be excluded. If firms respond to the profit squeeze by increasing productivity, or if less productive firms are liquidated, and labour does not fully recuperate this increase in wages (say, because the utility of outsiders enters the wage bargaining function at least to some degree), then the λ' and the PRW_1-line will rise and structural unemployment falls.

Next, we move to a *spot market economy*. The increase in money market interest rates now has two consequences: first, it will reduce effective demand and the *ex post* price level, as before; secondly, it will also affect the 'structural' price setting equation because the debt service (for the liabilities incurred when the capital stock was purchased) is rising with interest rates. Thus, the cost of capital increases and real wages have to fall below the PRW_2-line in Figure 8.9. Thus, the *required* mark-up will rise even more than in the contract economy, but the logic is the same. As a consequence, unemployment is more volatile in a spot-market economy than in a contract economy. We have seen this to be a feature of US performance and it may be at the root of the perception of the American labour market as being 'more flexible', despite econometric evidence to the contrary.

We may conclude that monetary policy does have an impact not only on short-term employment by creating price surprises, but also on the natural rate of unemployment by shocking the relative price structure of capital and labour. In a neoclassical framework, the relative income shares of labour and capital reflect their respective marginal products. But in a monetary–Keynesian perspective, when interest rates are exogenously determined by monetary policy and capital market uncertainty (liquidity preference), factor proportions adjust to relative prices and not the inverse. As nominal liabilities incurred have to be honoured, adjustment can only take place through variations of employment and not through reductions in capital (except for bankruptcies). This gives the impression that labour is substituted by capital. But this 'substitution' is not caused by labour market rigidities or wage pressure, but by nominal rigidities in the capital market. More flexible labour markets might reduce the amplitude of unemployment variations (making the BRW-line steeper), but they would not overcome the fact that the equilibrium real wage and the corresponding unemployment are a function of the level of (real) interest rates. The question then, of course, remains: what determines the interest rate level? We will provide an explanation in the next section. In our simplified model we continue to abstract from uncertainty in capital markets and will impute the level of interest rates to the central bank. If the central bank's objective is to maintain price stability, we have to take into account the interdependence between monetary policy and wage/employment dynamics.

Monetary policy and wage dynamics

Inflationary dynamics can be separated into demand or (transitory) profit inflation,[62] when q increases after a cut in interest rates, and into wage cost push inflation (wage inflation), when nominal wages increase more than productivity (Riese 1986a). Again we will distinguish between a contract and a spot market economy.

From Equation (8.17) we can derive, after some manipulation, the inflation rate for the contract economy as:

$$\pi = (\dot{w} - \dot{\lambda})\sigma_w + q_i \frac{i_0 b}{P} \cdot \Delta i, \tag{8.18}$$

where π the inflation rate, $\dot{w}$ and $\dot{\lambda}$ the proportional rates of increase in nominal wages and productivity, σ_w the labour share in (net) national income, b/P the capital–output ratio or the ratio of real corporate debt to turnover (because $b = (P_0 K)/y = (B/y)$). Therefore $i_0(b/P)$ is the real capital cost per unit of output.[63] Δi is the variation of interest rates undertaken by the central bank and q_i is the partial derivative of q with respect to i, that is, the elasticity by which profits respond to interest rates. Its value can be derived from the definition of q in Equations (2.3), (2.3a), (2.3b):

$$q = \frac{1 + i_N}{1 + i} = \frac{1 + i_N - E(\pi)}{1 + i - \pi} \approx \frac{R}{r}, \tag{8.19}$$

where R is the expected rate of return on new investment. Taking the total differential we obtain:

$$dq = \frac{1}{r}dR - \frac{R}{r^2}dr. \tag{8.19a}$$

In the short run the inflation rate is fixed so that $dr = di$. In equilibrium $q = (1 + \rho)$ and therefore $R = (1 + \rho)r$. Inserting into Equation (8.19a) and dividing by di yields:

$$\frac{dq}{di} := q_i = \frac{1}{r} \left[R_i - (1 + \rho) \right]. \tag{8.19b}$$

q_i reflects the impact that a variation in the nominal interest rate will have on Tobin's q. R_i measures the degree by which expectations on the return on capital are affected by variations in interest rates. Normally, its value would be negative. In a strictly neoclassical world, where R reflects the marginal product of capital and no risk prevails ($R_i = \rho = 0$), $q_i = -(1/r)$. *This implies that monetary policy is only effective if real interest rates are positive.* When the expected rate of return is negatively influenced by monetary policy ($R_i < 0$) and risk and uncertainty prevails in capital markets ($\rho > 1$), q_i would be smaller than the factor $-(1/r)$. Thus, in general, q_i is negative and its absolute value rather large.

Equation (8.18) shows that inflation is determined by monetary policy and unit labour costs. If monetary policy is to maintain price stability, its efficiency depends on the transmission mechanism of interest rate changes on prices. This mechanism works differently in contract and spot economies. We will look at the two polar cases and then solutions in between.

1. In a contract economy, monetary policy has a direct impact on profit inflation but not on capital cost: a rise in interest rates (Δi) lowers π because lower effective demand will reduce profits and prices ($q_i < 0$). But the effectiveness of monetary price stabilisation depends largely on labour cost developments. If the wage share in the economy (σ_w) is high, and nominal wages increase more rapidly than labour productivity, monetary tightening is unlikely to reduce inflation expectations immediately to zero. The central bank will then have to maintain a tight monetary stance until wage increases fall to the level of productivity increases. Unemployment will rise because of Equations (8.13a) and (8.14). We define a tight monetary stance as an interest rate that yields $q(i) < \bar{q}(i^*)$. However, given that the effect of i on q is only transitory, repeated interest rate increases may be required until unit labour costs and inflation are stabilised. We can formalise this by deriving the following *monetary policy rule for the pure contract economy* from Equation (8.18):

$$\Delta i = \frac{1}{\beta} \left[\sigma_w (\dot{w} - \dot{\lambda}) - \pi_m \right], \tag{8.20}$$

where $\beta = -q_i i_0 (b/P) > 0$ and π_m is the inflation target of the central bank. The extent to which the monetary authorities raise interest rates over time is determined by the structural parameter β and the increase in unit labour cost, weighted at the labour share, minus the acceptable rate of inflation (π_m). Obviously, the lower the inflation target is, the sharper or longer drawn out the interest rate increase will be as a response to given wage cost development. The parameter β depends on the debt structure in the economy. It reflects the cost ratio of debt service to income multiplied with the (negative) interest elasticity of Q-profits. Under very simplified assumptions

$$\left(R_i = \rho = 0, \left(\frac{B}{Py}\right) = \left(\frac{K}{y}\right)\right), \quad \text{we get:} \quad \beta = \left(\frac{i}{r}\right) \cdot \left(\frac{K}{y}\right).$$

In general, we can assume that β is positive and that the coefficient before the bracket in Equation (8.20) is higher, the lower the debt ratio in the economy and the lower the contracted interest rate on the outstanding debt and the higher the real interest rate. The intuition behind this is clear: the lower the capital intensity, the stronger the shifts in capital cost must be in order to affect investment decisions.

2. In a *perfect spot market economy*, the picture is more complicated. Equation (8.18) then becomes

$$\pi = (\dot{w} - \dot{\lambda})\sigma_w + \left(q_i \frac{ib}{P} + q\frac{b}{P}\right)\Delta i, \tag{8.18a}$$

and the coefficient β in (8.20) changes to: $\beta = -(q_i i + q)b/p$. Given that we have seen q_i to be negative and rather large, while q is positive around 1, β should normally be positive. Therefore, monetary policy can always stabilise inflation by rising interest rates. However, Equation (8.18a) reveals an interesting feature that might explain Sims (1992) 'price puzzle', according to which an increase in interest rate might first accelerate inflation and only later reduce it. In a spot market economy, any increase in interest rates has a cost-push element ($q(b/P) \cdot \Delta i$). If it takes time for the demand effect ($q_i(ib/P)$) to trickle down, then prices will first rise and then fall. This is what the VAR-models observe.[64]

3. Finally, we can abandon the polar economy model and assume that our economy finances the purchases of capital goods by a mix of fixed and flexible interest rates. If we design ϕ to the share of fixed interest bonds, then β becomes

$$\beta = -[\phi q_i i_0 + (1 - \phi)(q_i i_t + q)]\frac{b}{P}, \tag{8.21}$$

where i_0 stands for the fixed and i_t for the flexible interest rate. Again, the stability condition

$$[\phi i_0 + (1 - \phi)i_t]q_i + (1 - \phi)q < 0$$

is normally fulfilled under our simplifying assumptions.[65]

Thus, our analysis yields the result that under normal circumstances, monetary policy is always capable of reducing or stabilising inflation by increasing interest rates. However, the speed and effectiveness of the stabilisation policy, and therefore also of the social cost involved, will depend on the link between profit and wage inflation. This can be modelled either by some kind of Friedmanian Phillips curve dynamic where nominal wages rise when $q > 0$ due to a tightening of the labour market. Consequently, an increase in interest rates would then lower $q(i)$ below equilibrium and reduce price inflation (π) via demand, wage inflation ($\dot{w}$) and unit labour costs. Alternatively, the same result can be obtained if wage bargaining is not (or only a little) influenced by labour market conditions and it focuses on the distribution of income shares (the 'justice' motive). This leads to the cumulative process of profit (q) and income inflation ($\dot{w} - \dot{\lambda}$) described by Riese (1986a). If the increase in interest rates lowers the profit share via a demand reduction, and wage bargainers aim to keep income shares constant, then unit labour costs will have to fall. Although this fits with the idea that in the long run income shares of labour and capital are constant, it does not explain why the labour share has been shrinking in the European economy since the mid-1970s (Figure 8.5(a)) at the expense of the profit share. However, as we have seen in the previous section, if interest rates had been rising, then the profit share had to increase in order to cover the increased debt service. Therefore, the deteriorating real wage position is entirely consistent with the period of high real interest rates and disinflation after 1980. If the capital–labour ratio has been increasing despite the falling wage pressure, it would have been a reaction by firms to the interest rate-induced fall in q-profits and the need to lower the labour share (and real wages) in order to service rising corporate debt.[66] Given NWR (downward stickiness) and a restrictive monetary policy stance, the lower labour share would have been achieved by rising labour productivity over and above total factor productivity. This explains Europe's rising unemployment. In conclusion, in our model, it is the interaction of monetary policy, corporate finance and wage bargaining that determine the outcome of the employment level.

A fully accommodating monetary policy would keep interest rates constant and adjust its inflation target to the wage cost developments, such that in Equation (8.16) the expression in brackets equals zero. But if monetary policy is committed to price stability, it would set π_m close to zero and raise interest rates aggressively to fight inflation. Thus, it is not surprising that real interest rates have been rising in the period of disinflation since the early 1980s[67] (Ciocca and Nardozzi 1996). Therefore, both monetary and wage policies must have direct consequences for employment. We will now establish the conditions under which the right policy mix will contribute to job creation.

The monetary policy reaction function

Let us assume that employment stands at the initial level E_0 and that the economy is in equilibrium with $q = \bar{q} = 1$ and $d\lambda = 0$. Next, the central bank lowers interest rates, say because it pursues a time-inconsistent policy objective. As a consequence, q will rise, investment will be stimulated beyond planned savings and quasi-rents appear. This disequilibrium translates in an upward move of the price level according to Equations (8.17) and (8.18). If we assume that unit labour costs do not change, then this is a transitory price level movement reflecting higher profit margins. Investment and employment increase until the diminishing returns from the increased capital stock have reduced q back to 1, and competition has reduced prices back to the equilibrium level. But during the adjustment process, real variables have changed: the new employment level E_t is higher than E_0, while interest rates are lower and prices are stable. The natural rate of unemployment has fallen.

However, this is an unlikely story. Wages will respond to the move in prices, either because wage bargainers cannot distinguish between transitory price adjustments and continued inflation, or because workers tend to resist the new distribution of income in favour of profits, or simply according to a Phillips curve trade-off where wages increase with employment. We can model the wage reaction to price by taking up our price and wage equations from the first chapter. By inserting Equation (1.1a) into Equation (1.3) we get:

$$\dot{w}_t = \xi_1[\pi^*(1-\theta) + \theta\pi_{t-1}] + \xi_2 x_t + \varepsilon_t, \tag{8.22}$$

where ξ_1 is the coefficient for nominal wage indexation equal to 1 under rational expectations. π^* is the forward-looking steady-state inflation rate and x_t is a vector of arguments that influence wage bargaining other than inflation.[68] If $\theta = 0$, wage bargaining is exclusively forward-looking and prices are perfectly flexible. In the inverse case, $\theta = 1$, inflation is perfectly persistent and wages are rationally set in a backward-looking fashion. As we have seen in Chapter 1, θ is regime-dependant. We assume rational expectations $\xi_1 = 1$, $E(\varepsilon_t) = 0$ and for simplicity $\xi_2 = 0$.[69] Substituting Equation (8.22) into Equation (8.20):

$$i_t = i_{t-1} + \frac{1}{\beta}\left[\sigma_w\left((1-\theta)\pi^* + \theta\pi_{t-1} - \dot{\lambda}_t\right) - \pi_m\right]. \tag{8.20a}$$

This equation gives the monetary policy rule at which the interest rate should be set, if the authorities pursue an inflation target. Interest rates will remain constant at a natural rate $(i_{t-1} = i^*)$, if the expression in the squared bracket is zero. They can fall, however, if its value is negative. For a given policy objective, this will depend on price expectations and labour productivity. If inflationary wage dynamics exceed productivity growth, so that unit labour costs rise, interest rates must be increased. However, if unit labour costs fall, interest rates should be cut. If the central bank has a credible reputation to maintain price stability, we have $\pi_m = \pi^* = 0$ and (8.20a) becomes:

$$i_t = i_{t-1} + \frac{\sigma_w}{\beta}\left(\theta\pi_{t-1} - \dot{\lambda}_t\right). \tag{8.20b}$$

Thus, moderate inflation is compatible with expectations of steady-state price stability under two conditions: if backward indexing (θ) is low and if labour productivity increases sufficiently to keep unit labour costs stable. This is what we have observed in the Golden Age of Bretton Woods.[70] As we have seen, after the regime shift to flexible exchange rates and high inflation, θ increased and inflation expectations became quasi-permanently high. This is our explanation for Europe's high unemployment. What will change under the new regime shift to the euro? Under EMU a new regime of price stability should be expected, so that interest rates could come down. In general, wage cost inflation pressures are higher when the central bank has a low reputation (i.e. when θ is high). Therefore, monetary policy would have to become more restrictive (the required increase in interest rates would be higher) than if the central bank's credibility is high.[71] This has also been observed by Sievert (1993). From this point of view, the European Central Bank (ECB) is likely to benefit from the clear commitment to price stability, and its high degree of independence, but it will also need to earn its reputation in practice.

However, if the central bank's credibility is low, so that unit labour costs increase, unemployment is a likely consequence. First, the central bank will sooner or later have to raise interest rates above the previous natural rate according to Equation (8.20) in order to fight inflation (Equation 8.18) and this implies that $q(i_t) < 0$. As we have seen, *ex post* profit margins available in the prevailing macroeconomic environment are now too low, or real wages are 'too high'. Secondly, firms will react to cost pressures by increasing productivity ($\mathrm{d}\lambda > 0$). This will further lower employment growth according to Equation (8.13a). From this point of view, wage pressure does seem to explain the high rate of capital accumulation per worker that is prevalent in Europe. Hence, unemployment would appear to have both a Keynesian and a Neoclassical cause. However, it is clear that the apparent wage pressure and the related increase in capital intensity will only arise in the context of restrictive monetary policies. If authorities accommodated the wage pressure, prices would increase proportionately and firms would not have to restore profit margins by increasing productivity over and above technological progress. Nobody would notice any 'labour market rigidities'.

The restrictive phase of monetary policy will only come to a halt when the growth in unit labour costs stops, so that $\dot{w} - \lambda - \xi_1[\pi^*(1 - \theta) + \theta\pi_{t-1}] + \xi_2 x_t - \lambda_t = 0$. At that point we will reach a new level of the natural rate of unemployment or NAIRU, which is higher than the previous one. This increase in equilibrium unemployment results from the disinflation process because price-wage dynamics forced the central bank to raise interest rates.

What can be done to raise employment? If the central bank simply lowered interest rates, little would be gained, for it would re-ignite the vicious circle of rising inflation followed by disinflation with still higher structural unemployment. This phenomenon has been referred to as 'speed limits' on the rate of reduction in unemployment (OECD 1994: 69). The only way to stimulate economic growth and employment without inflation is obtained from Equation (8.16) as the condition:

$$\Delta i = \frac{\sigma_w}{\beta}(\dot{w} - \dot{\lambda}). \tag{8.18''}$$

That is to say, a non-inflationary reduction in interest rates requires a *fall* in unit labour costs.[72] In this case, q would rise above equilibrium *without* causing an upward shift in the price level. Higher profit margins would then stimulate investment and growth. There are, however, some important constraints to this strategy.

First, if nominal wages are rigid, a fall in unit labour costs can only come from an increase in productivity. In our simplified model, this increase must result from a higher rate of capital accumulation per worker and this reduces the employment-creating effect of economic growth. If, however, we incorporate the Hicks-neutral technological progress into our model, the margins for interest rate reductions are increased. Second, sustainable employment growth is only possible in an environment of low inflation, otherwise wage increases will be higher than productivity increases and interest rates have to be raised, not lowered. Third, wage restraint alone, without supporting cuts in interest rates, will not create new jobs. For if $q = 1$ and $\Delta i = 0$ and $(\dot{w} - \dot{\lambda}) < 0$, the price level will simply fall (see Equations (8.17) and (8.18)) without renewed growth. Wage restraint then simply causes a deflation. The wage share $\sigma_w = 1 - (W/\lambda P)$ will not fall, the profit margin will not increase and investment and growth will not be forthcoming.

Summary and conclusion

We may now summarise our model.

1   With given technology, the level of employment is determined by the level of the capital stock.
2   The variation in employment and, therefore, the change in unemployment are determined by (net) investment and the change in labour productivity.
3   Changes in labour productivity over and above technological progress may result from catch-up growth and cost pressure. Empirical evidence for Europe indicates that a rising capital–labour ratio results less from wage pressure but more from catch-up growth and repeated interest rate increases.
4   Investment depends on profit expectations and, therefore, on the deviation of interest rates from their equilibrium level. In equilibrium, interest rates determine the level of the capital stock and therefore the level of employment. The adjustment of the disequilibrium goes from interest rates (the independent variable) to investment (the dependent variable).
5   Interest rates are set by the central banks in response to inflation expectations. The higher the increase in unit labour cost, the higher the interest rate increase required to maintain price stability. Also, the lower the central bank's credibility to fight inflation, the higher the interest rate rise.
6   Stable unit labour costs imply constancy in the interest rate level and thus of the equilibrium capital stock. Therefore, employment only remains stable when nominal wages increase in line with productivity.
7   Non-inflationary employment growth is possible if, and only if, both unit labour costs and interest rates fall together, so that the price level stays constant and the profit margin increases. A reduction in unit labour costs without an

interest rate cut would lead to deflation, not to price stability nor employment growth.

8 Hysteresis effects on (un)employment levels are derived from interest rate dynamics. Persistence of *rising* unemployment levels is a consequence of inflation persistence in combination with restrictive monetary policies. Both together explain the upward shifts in the equilibrium unemployment rate and the slow downward adjustment and not, or only marginally, labour market structures.

What evidence do we have that our model describes reality correctly? We stand at the frontier of research. It would be desirable to put at least some of our propositions into testable hypotheses. Nevertheless, some elements have been established in the literature: unemployment displays hysteresis effects and seems to be correlated with disinflation (Ball 1997; Belke 1996). Investment and growth provide reasonable explanations for Europe's high rates of unemployment (Morley 1998; Economie Européenne 1997). Interest rates matter for employment. Although the mechanisms are still rather unexplored, most studies focus on real interest rates (Newel and Symons 1987; Phelps 1994, 1995; Atkinson *et al.* 1993; Barrell *et al.* 1997). However, in our model nominal short-term rates are crucial. Granger-causality tests indicate that in the USA both nominal and real rates unequivocally Granger-cause changes in unemployment. In Germany, by contrast, there is no evidence for real interest rates Granger-causing employment, but weak evidence for nominal rates. This might be further evidence that the USA works as a spot economy and Germany as a contract economy. Further research and specification of a testable model are required. With respect to monetary policy, the link between money and labour markets is less orthodox. Some studies have tried to find feedback effects from exchange rate regimes to wage formation (Barrell and Whitley 1992; Horn and Zwiener 1992; Artis and Ormerod 1994). But they found little evidence that the wage formation process has become very similar across Europe despite convergence in inflation. In fact, insofar as the ERM was instrumental for this purpose, price stability was imported, while in Germany disinflation came about by the Bundesbank's commitment to price stability and not by exchange rate policies. It is widely believed that German wage restraint is related to the credibility of the Bundesbank to threaten and implement interest rate increases if nominal wage bargains are considered to be 'excessive' (Streeck 1994). In fact, the Bundesbank has explicitly acknowledged that an important purpose of its money supply targeting is 'to make the aims of monetary policy clearer to labour and management, whose co-operation is essential if inflation is to be brought under control without detrimental effects to employment'.[73] This strategy seems to have worked, for wage behaviour is such that over the long run wages rise in line with productivity in the long run (Horn and Zwiener 1992).

The challenge for sustainable EMU will be the reproduction of a wage regime that keeps unit labour costs under control and allows low (real) interest rates. This was the foundation of the Golden Age under Bretton Woods; it has also been at the root of the successful performance of the US economy after 1992. How to bring unit labour cost under control requires further research.

Our assumption in this book was that inflation matters more than labour market 'rigidities'. But tax policies can also become a source of disturbance. Daveri and Tabellini (1997) have claimed that in Europe, increases in unemployment and the slowdown of growth are related because they both stem from excessively high cost of labour. This has diminished the incentives to invest into capacity enlargement and has increased incentives to substitute capital for labour. As one of the main causes for high labour costs, they identify high taxes on labour. Furthermore, a high tax rate on capital income is correlated with low unemployment rates. This is consistent with the story of labour being substituted by capital: low taxes on capital increase the net (after tax) return on capital, while high labour taxes reduce the net return on labour. This distorts factor incomes. This hypothesis requires further research as it may be one missing factor in our model of rising capital–labour ratios in Europe. European Commission data (1997a) show that the implicit tax rate on labour has risen from 34.9 per cent in 1981 to 42 per cent in 1995, while taxation on capital and other production factors fell 10 percentage points from 45.5 to 35.0 per cent. Consumer taxes remained nearly constant between 13 and 14 per cent. This implies a relative price shift of nearly 50 per cent. If wage bargainers take income distribution and equity considerations into account when negotiating, or if trade unions defend the net real wage, then a rise in labour taxes will increase labour costs.[74] However, the direction of causality is not clear. The increases of effective tax rates on labour income from the period 1981–5 to 1986–91 also correspond to the intensity of disinflation.[75] Countries with high disinflation have stronger increases in the tax burden on labour than those with little reductions in inflation. Thus, it would appear that the social consequences of disinflation (output and employment losses) are shifted more to labour and less to capital. A more equal share of the tax burden could help to reduce unit labour cost and might contribute to less unemployment.[76] It also means that a more equitable distribution of the tax burden would make stability-oriented policies easier for the ECB, since unit labour costs are less likely to rise. However, price stability ultimately depends on the central bank's determination to eradicate inflationary expectations. Thus, we return to the proposition that in the end it is monetary policy that guarantees the sustainability of EMU by maintaining price stability. This is the task of the European System of Central Banks (ESCB).

Annexure
(written with the help of Susanne Mundschenk)

The intention in this annex is to analyse the well-known hypothesis that wage pressure causes capital intensity and, therefore, causes capital labour substitution to increase. We tried to find support for this hypothesis by linear regression modelling with autoregressive variables for the EU and the US.

However, the EU is an aggregate of fifteen countries with different experiences over the examined period, the results might be misguiding. We, therefore, also included EMU-countries (EU 11) and Germany in our analysis.

The Data series are the growth rates of capital intensity and wage pressure defined as the difference of real wages minus total factor productivity. The first step is to examine the dynamic behaviour of the series, that is, if stationarity of the series is assured and if the variables are integrated of the same order. Classical regression with series of different integration order would produce spurious results, that is, have economic sense (see Granger and Newbold 1974). We will explore the order of integration using the Augmented Dickey–Fuller and the Phillips–Perron (1988) Test given in Table 8.A1.

Regardless of whether a trend is included or not, the null hypothesis that the series are non-stationary cannot be rejected for the capital intensity in Europe and Germany whereas the US series non-stationarity is strongly rejected. The unit root tests for the wage pressure of Europe and Germany, however, reject the unit root at least at a 5 per cent level. The trends were found to be significant. Therefore, classical regression analysis seems inappropriate.

Table 8.A1 Unit root tests

Variable	Without trend		With trend	
	ADF	PP	ADF	PP
Panel 1				
CIEU15	−1.33	−1.35	−2.65	−2.76
CIEU11	−1.38	−1.32	−2.71	−2.81
CID	−1.75	−2.35	−1.78	−2.84
CIUS	−3.51**	−4.18	−3.78*	−4.21
Panel 2				
WPEU15	−3.04328*	−3.27701	−4.15047*	−4.15799
WPEU11	−2.66191	−3.00185	−3.77961*	−4.16411
WPD	−3.18253*	−3.60568	−4.65725**	−4.69947
WPUS	−4.45694**	−5.96800	−4.41857*	−5.89844
Panel 3				
Δ CIEU15	−5.81**			
Δ CIEU11	−6.31**			
Δ CID	−6.1**			
Critical values				
5%	−2.95		−3.55	
1%	−3.64		−4.26	

Panel 1: Dickey–Fuller and Phillips–Perron Test equations contain three lags of the dependent variable.
Panel 2: Dickey–Fuller and Phillips–Perron Test equations contain one lagged dependent variable.
Panel 3: Dickey–Fuller Test and Phillips–Perron Test equations contain one lagged dependent variable.
Source: Critical values are based on MacKinnon (1991).
*Significant at 5 per cent level.
**Significant at 1 per cent level.

Visual inspection of the time series suggests a structural break after German Reunification in 1989. Unit root tests are biased towards accepting the null of a unit root in the presence of structural breaks. As a consequence, we want to test whether the unit root specification can be rejected if the structural break is filtered out. In the first step, the series are detrended by regressing the variable on an intercept, a time trend and a level dummy:

$$CapI^i = a_0 c + a_1 t + a_3 \text{dum},$$

where $CapI^i$ stands for the growth rate of capital intensity for country i, c is an intercept, t a time trend and dum a dummy variable with c_{10} for $t \le 1989$ and zero otherwise. The residuals of this regression are the filtered series. In the second step, a unit root test on the filtered series is performed (Table 8.A2).

The filtered series do not seem to contain a unit root. Thus, if we want to test an appropriate regression model we could regress the detrended capital intensity on the detrended wage pressure, as both series seem to follow different trends.

The result of a trend is contrary to the hypothesis of wage pressure causing capital intensity to rise. However, a deterministic long run downward trend of capital intensity growth is in line with the assumption of a catch up process in Europe developed in Chapter 8 (see Figure 8.6). Furthermore, a deterministic trend of falling wage pressure is also contrary to the assumption of high wage pressure causing unemployment in the 1980s and 1990s. It seems more convincing to assume reverse causality. We must, therefore, reformulate the hypothesis: can higher or lower wage pressure (relative to the trend) explain the deviation of the capital intensity growth rate from its trend?

To reach a parsimonious model we start with regressing Capital Intensity (CI) on two Autoregressive terms (AR) and the Wage Pressure (WP) with two lags. For Europe and Germany the filtered series of capital intensity (res^i) and the detrended series of Wage Pressure (resWP) are used. We present the regression results for the USA, Europe 15 and Germany (Figure 8.A1). The regression for Europe led to similar results with no additional information. For comparison

Table 8.A2 Unit root test in presence of a structural break in 1989

Variable	
res(CIEU15)	− 4.17*
res(CIEU11)	− 4.05*
res(CID)	− 3.94*
Critical values	
57%	− 3.77
1%	− 4.39

Source: Critical values are based on Perron (1989).
*Significant at 5 per cent level.

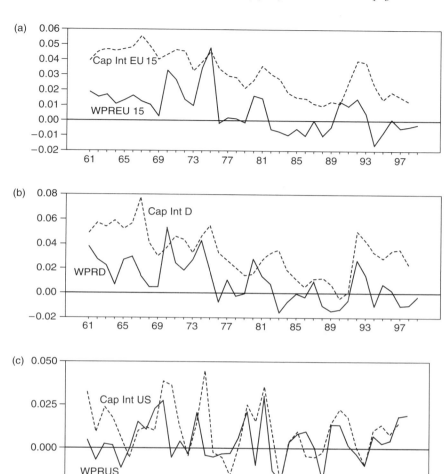

Figure 8.A1 Wage pressure and cap intensity: (a) EU 15; (b) Germany; (c) USA.

reasons we regressed the US series on a constant obtaining a variable for the deviation of its mean (Table 8.A3).

These results are disappointing as the R^2 is low and additional tests revealed the presence of heteroscedasticity. The model seems to be misspecified. The driving force behind the diminishing growth rate of capital intensity (K/L) and its deviation must be explained by influences other than wage pressure. Further research is required (Table 8.A3).

Table 8.A3 Regression results (observations: 33)

	Detrended regression		
	US	Eur 15	Germany
Dependent variable	resUS	resEU	resD
Constant	−0.00038538	0.00050838	−0.000196
t-values	−0.210	0.529	−0.107
AR{1}	0.23241	0.48987	0.35096
t-values	1.582	2.578	2.221
AR{2}		−0.21624	
t-values		−1.264	
resWP	0.68274	0.20422	0.28319
t-values	4.365	2.187	1.879
resWP{1}	0.44556	0.10476	0.43202
t-values	2.519	1.004	2.997
R^2	0.498821	0.462458	0.473065

Notes

1 Why stable money matters or 'the loss of paradise'

1 Searle (1995: 24–6) defines collective intentionality as making the statement 'we intend' which is 'I-intentionality plus something else'.
2 Eichengreen and Kenen (1994: 4–5) have made the distinction orthographically: Institutions with a capital 'I' are *organisations* that shape and condition the behaviour of governments and serve as conservators of the rules, conventions and understandings that structure economic relations. Institutions with a small 'i' mean *the rules and understandings themselves*, whether articulated formally or acknowledged implicitly.
3 See TEU: arts. 2, 3a.2, 105.
4 For a description see Bini-Smaghi *et al.* (1994).
5 Modern economic theory easily forgets that, in the origin, economics was a Moral Philosophy. See Schumpeter (1954).
6 An example is given by Jean Monnet's speech in Strasbourg, on 30 November 1954:

> Un marché commun ne peut être réalisé en un jour, et les mesures de libération des échanges ou convertibilité des monnaies n'y suffisent pas. Les avantages que chacun peut retirer de l'établissement du marché commun ne peuvent être pleinement développés que s'il apparaît définitif. Aucun pays ne peut renoncer à ses protections s'il n'a la garantie que les autres Etats renoncent pareillement aux protections et aux discriminations. Il fait donc que des règles communes soient établies, dont le respect soit assuré.
>
> (Jean Monnet 1996: 92)

7 In fact, critics of European Monetary Union (EMU) have often thought the heterogeneousness of attitudes as the main obstacle to a sustainable euro (Jochimsen 1998).
8 In fact the disintegration of a democratic system in Germany did not begin with the *Weltwirtschaftskrise*, but earlier, in the aftermath of the inflation and stabilisation crisis of the mid-1920s. See Childers (1982).
9 The frequently heard proposition that 'EMU is a political and not an economic project' therefore falls short of its fundamental normative character. It is 'political' only in the sense that politics is about collective intentionality.
10 See Chapter 5.
11 See footnote 14.
12 These figures might give a slightly distorted picture because of the Balassa-effect. McKinnon (1973, 1991) has argued that the wholesale price index is more appropriate to capture the real return on assets.
13 Some of the rapid recorded nominal price and wage increases were due to the Balassa-effect. See Obstfeld (1993).

14 The regressions are:

Levine–Renelt model to account for changes in European growth of output per head

	1923–38	*1950–73*	*1973–89*
Constant	2.01	2.01	2.01
Initial GDP/head	−2.43	−2.49	−3.55
Investment/GDP	1.42	2.22	2.06
Secondary enrolment	0.16	0.68	0.79
Primary enrolment	1.90	1.99	1.79
Government/GDP	−0.62	−0.87	−1.27
Forecast	2.44	3.54	1.83
Actual	2.12	3.84	2.14

15 By coincidence it turns out that Europe's rich countries also were part of the exchange rate mechanism of the European Monetary System (EMS) over a significant part of the analysed period and pursued more restrictive stabilisation policies than other European countries.

16 If the oil supply shock of 1974 was a response to the previous demand shock of US-macro management in the late 1960s, then it becomes difficult to take them as indicators for the stability of the environment versus the destabilising influence of demand management, as Bayoumi and Eichengreen (1993) suggest following the aggregate demand–aggregate supply framework of VAR-models.

17 Neoclassical growth models imply that inflation would only affect the level of output, but not the steady-state growth rate. However, new growth theory could generate a growth effect of inflation (Fischer 1994). We will develop a formal model linking growth and price stability in Chapter 8.

18 Real wage growth is: $\dot{w}_t - \pi_t = (\xi_1 - 1)\pi_t + \xi_2 x_t$. If the degree of indexation is not perfect, inflation does have an impact on real wages.

19 This would be particularly true if we modelled the error terms in our price and wage setting equations not as white noise, but as a moving average. Under those circumstances, past price surprises influence the mean wage inflation. This implies that in a period of disinflation the mean decrease of wage inflation is lower than the deceleration in price inflation. We will return to this argument in Chapter 8.

20 See also Chapters 5 and 8.

21 By setting ξ_1 and $\theta = 1$ and $\xi_2 = 0$, we have assumed the most rigid structure possible in goods and labour market.

22 See also footnote 69 in Chapter 8.

23 In fact this may – together with low price persistence θ – explain Japan's remarkable experience after the oil price shocks.

24 Ideally, with high institutional credibility $\theta = 0$ and $\pi^* = 0$ in Equation (1.3), so that we get even with perfect real wage rigidities ($\xi_2 - 0$): $w_t = \eta_t$ which is a white noise process.

25 For a discussion of competing hypotheses of how US money growth and inflation spread to the rest of the world, including evidence see Bordo (1993).

26 Until 1967 inflation convergence in the fixed rate system of Bretton Woods was similar to that observed later under the EMS. In 1968, 1969 and 1970 devaluations and revaluations occurred and the fixity did not remain in place. See De Grauwe (1996).

2 After Bretton Woods: the world of bloc floating

1 See also Chapter 8.

2 For a detailed description of the EMS and its mechanisms see Collignon (1994).

3 For Bénassy-Quéré (1999) the criterion is a quarter of the volatility compared to the other two world currencies.

4 For methodological reasons we assume stationarity in real exchange rates and focus on exchange volatility.

5 Under perfect foresight, nominal and real q's are identical; under rational expectations the difference is a white noise process.

6 If we divide both CF_{Nt} and I_{N0} by the price index at period zero and by the relevant future inflation rates, we obtain $\sum_{t=1}^{n} \Delta y_t / \Delta K = F_K$.

7 It may be helpful to think about a period in this model as the time between an interest rate change, which rises (or lowers) q and the adjustment in investment, which brings q back to equilibrium.

8 In the General Theory, Keynes (1936: Chapter 18) made great efforts to prove that r_N was independent from r_A. If all agents had absolute perfect foresight, including the timing of interest rate increases, then r_N would indeed be independent of r_A. We will return to the question of profit margins in Chapter 8. On the other hand, it is also clear that in the case of exports, the cash flow in foreign currency is (as a rule) not affected by domestic monetary policy.

9 Empirical studies show that lagged q's work well in explaining investment behaviour (Sensenbrenner 1991). For simplicity, we formulate the investment function without lags.

10 Be reminded that i_B does *not* stand for the return on *monetary assets* in B but for the nominal return on real capital. Therefore, there is no automatic equivalence of i_A and i_B if investment requires adjustment costs.

11 For a more comprehensive model see Dornbusch (1983).

12 Nominal exchange rate dynamics are given by: $[e_t = e_{t-1}(1 + \delta)]$, so that a positive δ_1 implies an appreciation of A's currency and a devaluation of B's currency. The real exchange rate is determined by the relative price relations:

$$P_1 = \frac{P_B}{P_A e_{A/B}}, \qquad P_2 = \frac{P_C}{P_A e_{A/C}}, \qquad P_3 = \frac{P_1}{P_2},$$

where P_A, P_B, P_C are national price indices and $e_{A/B}$ is the nominal exchange rate defined as the price of foreign currency B in terms of A's domestic currency. P_3 results from cross exchange rates. The rate of real depreciation is equivalent to the first difference of the logs of P_i, that is $[\mathrm{d}p_i = (\partial P_i/\partial t) \cdot (1/P_i), \ i = 1, 2, 3]$. Therefore, a depreciation of A's currency implies, *ceteris paribus*, a fall in e ($\delta < 0$) and an increase in p_i that is ($\mathrm{d}p_1 > 0$).

13 We have taken i_A as exogenously given. If we assumed A to be small with respect to B, so that $i_A = i^* - \delta$, with i^* the monetary interest rate in B, then Equation (2.3a) would imply *ex post* that $q = 1$ if $i_B - \pi_A = i^* - \pi_B$. This means that the real return on trading with B must be higher than the real interest rate on monetary assets in B, for otherwise it would be recommendable to place funds in B's securities and if $i_B = i_A$ this is equivalent to placing them in domestic securities. Consequently the real return, which is an incentive for investment into tradables is only possible with a 'competitive', that is, undervalued, exchange rate.

14 For a formal demonstration see Collignon (1999).

15 Effective labour defines the number of workers at a given state of technology. As long as a country is not working at the production-possibility frontier and still has scope for catch-up growth, it also has free capacities of effective labour.

16 See Chapter 1. In second-generation tigers, like Thailand, growth started after the devaluations in the early 1980s.

17 For Europe, see Boltho 1996. How to measure a real appreciation is a different matter. The Balassa–Samuelson effect implies that productivity differentials between tradable and non-tradable sectors lead to divergences in real exchange levels among countries. McKinnon (1973: 96–7) argues that the WPI is the better deflator and has been remarkably stable between the mid-1950s and 1960s.

18 Because of our simplifying assumptions $q - \bar{q}$ would reduce to Equation (2.6b), if adjustment were instantaneous. However, with partial adjustment, σ_1^2 is not constant and $q - \bar{q}$ is not white noise.

19 In reality there are, of course, also other risk factors: relative prices, inflation, and interest rate volatility or policy risk.

20 For simplicity we assume identical coefficients of risk aversion. Political risk may lead to differentiated ϑs.

21 See Chapter 5.

22 Of course, a real devaluation would also help by shifting the marginal efficiency of capital and increasing the range of profitable investment opportunities. But in the long run this strategy implies a permanent distortion of relative prices.

23 Assuming all partial trade balances initially to be zero, trade weights can be represented by import shares and the real effective exchange rate index is: $P = P_1^{\alpha_1} \cdot P_2^{\alpha_2}$ where the import shares are the weights for the respective bilateral real exchange rates and also the elasticity by which the effective exchange rate responds to a change in the bilateral relative prices. Taking logarithms gives: $p = \alpha_1 p_1 + \alpha_2 p_2$ where p, p_1, p_2 are all logs. In a three-country world it follows that $p_3 = p_1 - p_2$. The variance of the effective exchange rate is:

$$\sigma_A^2 = \mathrm{var}(p) = \alpha_1^2 \mathrm{var}(p_1) + \alpha_2^2 \mathrm{var}(p_2) + 2\alpha_1\alpha_2 \mathrm{cov}(p_1, p_2)$$
$$= \alpha_1^2\sigma_1^2 + \alpha_2^2\sigma_2^2 + 2\alpha_2\sigma_{1,2}.$$

24 In fact we saw that this already applied to the 'snake in the tunnel', but the institutional set-up was insufficient.

25 If authorities reduced the volatility of both P_1 and P_2 we return to Bretton Woods.

26 Bénassy-Quéré (1999) assumes $\sigma_1 = 0.25\sigma_2$ as a significant criterion.

27 From Equation (2.8b) it is clear that bloc floating also reduces the variance of the real effective exchange rate. See Collignon (1999).

28 σ_3^2 in Table 2.3 refers to the variance of P_3, the real exchange rate between B and C.

29 Of course, the *level* of the exchange rate can create a competitive bias for one country.

30 Under perfect bloc floating autonomous investment is the sum of I_n and I_B when $\bar{q}_N = \bar{q}_B = 1$.

31 We will analyse the implications of this fact, in depth, in Chapter 4.

32 See Collignon (1999). Whether it also rises in absolute terms depends on the impact on p_3. In the next section it will be shown that a fall in α_2 will in any case increase the volatility in the fundamental equilibrium exchange rate between A and C.

3 International consequences of bloc floating

1 This chapter is based on Collignon (1999).

2 Given that in $p_A = \alpha_1 p_1 + \alpha_2 p_2$, we have $\partial p_2/\partial p_A = 1/\alpha_2$.

3 Given that the price elasticity for A's exports ($\varepsilon_{C/A}$) to and imports ($\varepsilon_{A/C}$) from C are

$$\varepsilon_{C/A} = \frac{\partial AC}{\partial P_1} \cdot \frac{P_1}{AC} = AC_P \cdot \frac{P_1}{AC} \quad \text{and} \quad \varepsilon_{A/C} = \frac{\partial CA}{\partial P_1} \cdot \frac{P_1}{CA} = AC_P \cdot \frac{P_1}{CA}$$

and assuming initial trade balance $AC = P_2 CA$, the equation can be written in terms of the Marshall–Lerner condition (see Dornbusch 1980: 67).

4 s is the marginal propensity to save in the form of net foreign investment. In equilibrium $T^* = 0$ implies $s = 0$. This is different from the savings rate in Chapter 8.

5 See Chapter 2.

6 The Fundamental Equilibrium Exchange Rate (FEER) is actually the real effective exchange rate at which equilibrium is achieved, that is, $\bar{P}_A = \alpha_1 p_1 + \alpha_2 p_2$. Given that we treat p_1 as parametric in the bloc floating regime, we can assimilate $\bar{P}_2$ to the FEER.

7 The usual text book classification of assigning exchange rate policies (demand management) to internal balance requires that the slope of the internal balance curve is steeper than for external balance (see Kenen 1985). This implies, due to Equations (3.4a) and (3.5a), that $1\text{-}s\text{-}m > m$. In other words, if the intended trade balance is zero, so that foreign investment and the marginal savings rate are also zero, then the assignment rule is only stable if the degree of openness is below 50 per cent. However, bloc floating does not affect *this* stability condition.

8 We have excluded terms-of-trade shocks in this model by assuming relative domestic prices to be constant.

9 Williamson (1994: 190) points out that for very high trade elasticities and flat EB- and IB-curves, there may be an empirical case for PPP (although this is not borne out by the facts for manufactured goods). Our model shows that in a world with bloc floating, PPP is even less likely to occur.

10 In anticipation of the next chapter, we see here that this adjustment process is only possible for the anchor currency, because it alone controls the flexible exchange rate. The periphery could only achieve adjustment to equilibrium by reducing its domestic price level relative to the anchor, that is, by 'competitive disinflation'.

11 As we assume P_1 as fixed, only α_2 is relevant.

12 If net foreign investment is zero ($s = 0$), the impact translates $1 : 1$.

13 If the currency bloc increases, $\partial \alpha_2 < 0$.

14 By dividing Equation (3.10) by $\overline{P}_2$ we get the equilibrium rate of appreciation:

$$\frac{\mathrm{d}\overline{P}_2}{\overline{P}_2} = \frac{b_1}{\alpha_2} \cdot \frac{\mathrm{d}T^*}{\overline{P}_2} + \frac{b_2}{\alpha_2} \cdot \frac{\mathrm{d}Y^*}{\overline{P}_2} \tag{3.10$'$}$$

where $\mathrm{d}T^*/\overline{P}_2$ and $\mathrm{d}Y^*/\overline{P}_2$ are the policy objectives in real foreign currency terms. To keep things simple, we will proceed with Equation (3.10). Our explanation of fundamental equilibrium volatility in this section ties in with our discussion of exchange risk and required excess returns in the previous chapter (Equations (2.5a)–(2.6b)).

15 In the context of our NAIRU-model in Chapter 8, ΔY^* reflects the GDP growth n that is required for a specific employment target.

16 Under certain restrictive assumptions (perfectly determinate real returns and one period forecast) Equation (3.13) can be transformed into Equation (2.6b).

17 This feature provides a logical explanation for the increase in intra-European trade and the diminishing share of trade with the rest of the world (see Table 3.2). We could verify the evidence by a formal test where the extra-European trade share of Germany (the anchor currency) or the EU as a whole, is regressed on the relative volatility of the DM/$ and the DM/ECU exchange rate and some other structural parameters. However, this remains as research work for the future.

18 For an explanation of why the yen did not become an anchor currency, see Bayoumi and Eichengreen (1999).

19 An exception is Frankel and Wei (1995), who use a gravity model.

20 Charles Goodhart suggested this to me.

21 For an analysis of 'how the independent actions of individuals will produce an order which is not part of their intentions', see Hayek (1979).

22 By a structural reduction in interest rates, I mean that both peaks and bottoms and the mean interest rate over the interest cycle are lower than in the previous regime.

4 The instability of the bloc floating regime

1 See footnote 8 in Chapter 2.

2 For an analysis of the French experience, see Fitoussi *et al.* (1993).

3 Small letters indicate logs.

4 A zero growth rate for A's income can also be interpreted as the normalised growth rate in the system.

5 ν reflects both demand and supply disturbances. In the literature on Optimum Currency Areas (OCAs), it has become common practice to distinguish between supply shocks with permanent effects on the level of output and demand shocks that have only temporary effects (both have permanent effects on prices, although in opposite directions). However, these disturbances are an artificial construct resulting from the strong identifying assumptions in the estimated VAR-models, where supply is fixed in the long run. If, however, supply is a function of relative prices, the distinction breaks down (see Marston 1998). Thus, it seems justifiable to use one disturbance term for amalgamated supply and demand shocks.

6 Of course, we could include supply shocks into the model but they would add nothing to the logic we wish to demonstrate.

7 There has been a significant amount of debate on whether the EMS has effectively worked in such an asymmetric manner (see Gros and Thygesen (1992) for a review). But even if Germany may sometimes have taken into account concerns by other ERM-members, there can be little doubt that the system works with the described structural features. Indeed, this was one of the motivating forces for non-German EU-members to join EMU.

8 In a monetarist model where $\pi_C = \mu_C$, the rate of appreciation is dependent on the money supply in C.

9 In fact, it also caused the appreciation of all other currencies in the DM-bloc, such as the FFR, the ATS, NLG, etc.

10 If we take Equation (4.11a) and apply the policy rule B we get:

$$\delta_1 = \pi_B + \frac{\alpha_2}{\alpha_1}(\pi_C - \delta_2) - \frac{1}{\alpha_2}\pi_A + \frac{a_{13}}{\alpha_1\alpha_{12}}\Delta g_A = 0.$$

If the anchor country keeps its international competitiveness constant ($\pi_C - \delta_2 = 0$) and does not change its fiscal policy, we get $\pi_B = (1/\alpha_2)\pi_A$.

11 It is, therefore, not surprising that France was preoccupied with the dollar exchange rate in the early 1990s when German unification led to a fiscal expansion and Germany's nominal and real exchange rate appreciated. Nor is it surprising that German authorities had difficulties in understanding the argument, given that they reasoned from the point of view of the anchor country.

12 As we have seen in the previous chapter, pegging to A would improve trade and investment between A and B. However, if A is large with respect to B, the likely outcome is high β_1 and low α_1.

13 Based on the data in Table 5.1 the relation is $\beta_1 = 38.784 - 3.651$ Ln (GDP) with $R^2 = 0.248$.

14 In fact, it is a typical Hayekian result of unintended consequences from intended behaviour. See Hayek (1979).

15 This is in line with the TEU which sets price stability as the policy constraints (art. 105) but formulates 'sustainable and non-inflationary growth' and a 'high level of employment', etc. as a general policy objectives (art. 2). Therefore, monetary policy must be seen as an optimisation process.

16 If money demand behaviour does not change after monetary union, the coefficients in Equation (4.2c) would be weighted averages as in Equation (4.1c). However, it is not necessary to impose this condition, as long as the changes remain small.

17 An increase ($\delta_U > 0$) reflects an appreciation.

18 Dornbusch *et al.* (1998) come to a similar conclusion in the somewhat different framework of monetary policy with a Taylor-rule.

19 Comparing Equations (4.11a) and (4.11c), given that $\pi_B = \pi_A = \pi_U = 0$ and $\delta_1 = 0$, $\Delta g_A = \Delta g_B = 0$, $\gamma_A = 0$ yields: $\delta_2 = \pi_C > \delta_U = \pi_C - (\eta/u_{12})\gamma_B$. If π_C is also zero, the

equilibrium exchange rate would devalue if $\bar{\gamma}_B > 0$, in order to yield the demand required to absorb the growing production potential.

20 This throws an interesting light on the Franco-German monetary policy debate. In France, the argument is often heard that the Euro must not become 'as strong as the DM'. In Germany, the reply is that 'a strong currency does no harm'. The French line of thought is marked by the deflationary experience of bloc floating; the German view reflects the confidence of an anchor country that has full control over its monetary policy.

21 Obviously, the argument can be inverted to show that bloc floating causes an inflationary bias for slow-growth countries. This might well explain why Germany had an interest to leave the Bretton Woods System.

22 Under Bretton Woods, government transfers and aid were also important.

23 This theoretical controversy is reminiscent of the famous debate between Keynes and Ohlin about the transfer problem. But while Keynes used the classical argument to attack the Versailles Treaty for lowering living standards in Germany, Riese turned the argument around by pointing at the long-term welfare gains from economic growth. His approach has, of course, a more general validity than Keynes's post-war reparation context revealed.

5 A fresh look at Optimum Currency Area theory

1 An exception is Goodhart (1995).

2 For arguments in favour of more stability see Chapter 3. For the opposite view see Feldstein (1997).

3 For a comprehensive assessment see Funke and Kennedy (1997).

4 Textbook economics on EMU usually show benefits from a monetary union as a rising linear function of the degree of openness. See de Grauwe (1992), Meltzer (1997).

5 It is clear that these proxies have certain weaknesses. They do not fully take into account short- or long-term capital flows, nor internal linkages related to the diversification of trade and production. However, the intuitive argument can be made with reference to GDP. We return to this question at the end of the chapter.

6 Although the argument derives from Mundell's 1961 paper, he does not agree with the usual interpretation given to this analysis. On 24 March 1998 he wrote in the *Wall Street Journal Europe*:

> But if the critics of monetary union are right in asserting that a monetary union cannot insulate a region from shocks to demand, they are wrong in thinking that exchange rates can do any better. There is no exchange rate policy that can insulate an economy from the changes in real income arising from real shocks. I suppose I bear part of the blame for the argument because it figured prominently in my exposition of the theory of optimum currency areas in my 1961 article introducing the subject. [. . .] I had no intention, of course, of proposing anything as silly as a redistribution of monetary areas in North America. My point was rather to show that if the argument for flexible exchange rates is valid at all, it is only valid for single region countries.

I would surmise that Mundell is actually closer to understanding the difference between fixed exchange rates and currency unions than most of the OCA literature.

7 Estimates for IS-LM equations are surprisingly rare. I only found Gosh and Masson (1991) with figures for the US economy and the rest of the world. Taking their coefficients and German GDP-weights and applying them to our Table 4.1, a 1 per cent positive demand shock in Germany would increase prices by 0.58 per cent in the Union and appreciate the exchange rate by 0.45 per cent. If prices were kept perfectly stable so that output adjusts endogenously, then the exchange rate would appreciate by only 0.35 percentage points and output in the Union would fall by 0.25 per cent. These figures are certainly not negligible,

but they are not important enough to justify the re-introduction of the exchange rate instrument between the individual regions of EMU in case of some adverse shock.

8 The classic references are Melitz (1991); De Grauwe and Vanhaverbeke (1991); Masson and Taylor (1992); Krugman (1993); Eichengreen (1990a,b); Bayoumi and Eichengreen (1993); Bayoumi (1995); von Hagen and Hammond (1995) and Muet (1995/95a).

9 We will introduce behavioural equations in Chapter 8.

10 A slightly more complex formulation is given in Chapter 8, Equation (8.9).

11 This corresponds to the case of perfect rational expectations. Under the neutrality of money hypothesis $\partial w/\partial p$ would always converge to one. Although this might be true in the long run, the use of the exchange rate as an adjustment tool implies that nominal wage elasticity is less than one in the short term. The case of 'sticky wages', that is, the absence of downward nominal wage flexibility, is of greater relevance for countries with appreciating currencies. Given that our analysis focuses on negative output shocks, we can neglect this phenomenon here.

12 See different chapters in P. de Grauwe *et al.* (1996).

13 These estimates are in line with Lucas 1973 and our model in Chapter 1. See also Chapter 8.

14 We follow Cukierman (1992).

15 d$e > 0$ is a policy rule and not a policy action. See McCallum (1979).

16 For a discussion see Lucas (1973) and Ball *et al.* (1988). For empirical evidence in Europe, see Artis and Ormerod (1994).

17 In discussions with the author, Peter Bofinger has pointed out that it is wrong to assume that monetary authorities have stable preferences for inflation (or output stability) like consumers have preferences for spaghetti. Their policy decisions depend on time preferences. This is true. However, our analysis does not assume a stable A. It changes over time and with structural factors in the economy. But with a given time horizon, our argument remains valid. We will return to this in the next chapter.

18 The *cause* was the insufficient credibility of the price stability commitment by monetary authorities.

19 In fact, if we assume m_i to remain stable, the second order condition for Equation (11) to be a maximum is:

$$B_{SS}\mathrm{d}S^2 - 2B_{SA}\mathrm{d}A\mathrm{d}S - C_{AA}\mathrm{d}A^2 < 0$$

Provided that the returns from larger size or larger concern about output stability are diminishing (B_{SS}, $C_{AA} < 0$), a maximum is always guaranteed if the cross-partial derivative $B_{SA} = C_{AS} \leq 0$. However, this latter condition is exactly the case if adding one member reduces (or at least leaves unaltered) the cost of giving up the exchange rate tool because it reinforces the price stability preference of the union. We will call this a Pareto optimising currency area.

20 This procedure is especially justified if we take the log of GDP as proxy for size, for the benefits from size will then increase at a diminishing rate which reflects the lower degree of openness for large countries. One notable exception relates to the selection of union members. If a large country with low m joins small countries with high ms, this affects their average degree of integration, which might fall. However, for each individual country it will increase. This is relevant in the hypothetical case of a large country withdrawing from the union (d$S < 0$), possibly increasing the degree of integration (d$m > 0$) for the remaining countries.

21 Obviously, this argument is based on the assumption of domestic price stability in the currency area, that is, d$p^{\mathrm{d}} = 0$. If imported inflation accelerates domestic inflation, then the advantages of the exchange rate tool are even more short-lived.

22 In reality what matters is stability relative to the value of alternative forms of liquidity.

23 A clear description of these concerns is given by Jochimsen (1998: 167–72).

24 As the example of the French insistence on employment policies in parallel to monetary policy shows, there are also other ways of establishing a safety valve than opting-out of

EMU: coordination of structural policies, including labour market policies. We return to this in the next chapter.

25 The idea that national central bank governors might implement orders from their governments, despite formal independence, has been rejected by Sievert (1997) who referred to peer-pressure within the central bank's Governing Council as the mechanism by which philosophical convergence takes place.

26 For evidence read the Round Table Discussion between leading central bankers reprinted in Capie *et al*. (1994).

27 We assume for simplicity that A_i reflects the average preference of monetary union, that is, all members have perfectly converged in their preferences, except country j.

28 As footnote 19 showed, Equation (5.11c) fulfils the second order condition for a maximum of net benefits in country i.

29 For clarity, the figure was drawn with the assumption of fixed marginal cost and benefits. The NB = 0-line is then:

$$A = \frac{B_S}{C_A} S + \frac{(B_m - C_m)}{C_A} m.$$

30 German obsession with the question: 'Will the euro be as hard as the DM?' was therefore short-sighted, because it overlooked the benefits from size.

31 Changes in the degree of integration and openness (m) are considered as a shift parameter.

32 Strictly speaking Pareto-improving currency area. Note that in the very long term, when C_A tends to zero, any currency area is Pareto-improving, because inflation-reducing.

33 In the critical language of Jochimson (1998: 172) this is called 'compromises at the expense of others'.

34 However, one must not completely discard the consequences for a country j that is rejected on POCA grounds. If such a rejection affected the POCA-countries via m or C_A, it might actually reduce the net benefits from monetary union for its members. In such cases the critical country may be accepted on grounds of loyalty. See Hirschman (1970: 98–105) who discusses the concept of 'Loyalty and the Difficult Exit from Public Goods (and Evils)'.

35 I thank Charles Goodhart for raising this point with me.

6 Is EMU sustainable?

1 Von Wright (1990) considers the concept of preference as the 'common conceptual root of the three main types of evaluative discourse, namely, aesthetic, economic and moral'.

2 See Chapter 5, footnote 17.

3 This definition is derived from Mas-Collel *et al*. (1995: 10).

4 For a discussion of these concepts see Brittan and Mayes (1992), and Collignon (1996).

5 See EMI (1998).

6 It appears that this arrangement resulted from the need to avoid that one country (the UK at the time) block the project, because it had a 'consistently negative' attitude, responding 'with a centuries-old, political reflex of fear and aversion' (Bini-Smaghi *et al*. 1994).

7 Large and persistent fiscal transfers are not an efficient adjustment tool, as the experience in Germany's East and Italy's South indicate.

8 If the exchange rate were fully flexible and not a one-off adjustment, exchange rate overshooting *à la* Dornbusch would take the place of output volatility.

9 Hirschman (1970: 1).

10 This was a famous formula employed by the German Chancellor H. Schmidt in the 1970s. It proves that even in a stability-prone country, output considerations are not always absent.

11 Obviously, in the case of *temporary* economic shocks with little inertia, not even the voice option is required.

12 Alternatively, we may say that the uncertainty about future benefits lowers the value of the expected national currency benefits.
13 However, the UK-opt-out to EMU did not really modify actions by other EU-member states. But this is because the 'opt-out' was understood to be in reality a non-participation with an option to join.
14 With the Maastricht Treaty, EU-member states effectively signed a forward contract for the delivery of a single currency, while the UK and later Denmark took a call option. Therefore, for thirteen EU-countries, the decision to join EMU can no longer be viewed as an 'option' (more precisely, it is a combination of European style put-call option which is equivalent to a forward contract) – it is an obligation, although the value of this forward contract may be subject for debate. However, the decision not to honour the commitment, either by not joining or by leaving EMU always remains a possibility, even if it is a costly one.
15 These potential externalities are clearly described by Feldstein (1997) who refers to the American experience with secession of the South. However, it is one thing to treat them as a contingent liability which enters cost considerations of an investment project and quite another to present them as if EMU would make the world a less safe place, as Feldstein asserts.
16 For theoretical proof that small menu costs can have significant impact see Mankiw (1985), and Akerlof and Yellen (1985).
17 The case of Czechoslovakia is less obvious.
18 Strictly speaking, the slope varies with the mean of the inflation rate.
19 The same applies, of course, to the utility of devaluations. Thus, in the long run with stable prices in the monetary union the margin expressed by Equation (5.11c) tends to become very large and the selection of EMU-members depends on the time horizon applied to the selection procedure.
20 Walsh 1995. This was also to be the conclusion from Ball *et al.* (1988):

> our finding that average inflation affects the short-run output-inflation trade-off is important for policy . . . . It is likely that the trade-off facing policy-makers in the United States have changed as a consequence of disinflation in the 1980s. Our estimates imply that a reduction in average inflation from 10 to 5 per cent substantially alters the short-run impact of aggregate demand.

21 This could be seen very clearly after the difficult process of appointing the first president of the European Central Bank (ECB).
22 Interestingly, this is exactly what Feldstein (1997: 65) observed twenty-seven years after Hirschman wrote his book:

> At present, individual European governments (especially in France and Germany) are suppressing their disagreement about the control of monetary policy to minimise the risk of political disapproval of EMU in their respective countries. But if EMU proceeds, the independence of the ECB and the goals of monetary policy will become a source of serious conflicts among member countries.

23 The debate about whether EMU needs political union is of bottomless emptiness. Monetary union *is* a form of political union.

7 Sustaining price stability

1 We will return to this in the next chapter.
2 For an excellent overview see Fischer (1994).
3 A third dimension is related to terms of trade shocks. Given that they are outside the control of domestic agents, we will not discuss them here.
4 For a discussion of different indicators see Bofinger *et al.* (1996: 12–14).

5 For the experience of major economies, see Leiderman and Svenson (1995). Only USA and Japan do not follow this practice (Bofinger *et al*. 1996: 21).

6 For the opposite argument, see also De Grauwe (1997) with further literature.

7 Eucken (1952), one of the inventors of German's 'Ordnungspolitik', already anticipated this idea, when he wrote (252):

> ... die Erfahrung zeigt, daß eine Währungsverfassung, die den Leitern der Geldpolitik freie Hand läßt, diesen mehr zutraut, als ihnen im allgemeinen zugetraut werden kann. Unkenntnis, Schwäche gegenüber Interessensgruppen und der öffentlichen Meinung, falsche Theorien, alles das beeinflußt diese Leiter sehr zum Schaden der ihnen anvertrauten Aufgabe.

8 See Romer and Romer (1997: 399).

9 For an overview, see Bofinger (1998).

10 How to respond to dynamic inconsistency is, of course, the essence of a moral problem. By assuming that authorities can (or should) renege on commitments, the theory claims that what is wrong for individuals is right for policy. This way of thinking may trace its roots back to N. Machiavelli, but I would maintain that no society can survive (i.e. be sustained) if lying, cheating and breaking one's word becomes the rule. Taylor (1983) has observed that many governments overcome dynamic inconsistency problems without the classical arrangements proposed by theory. Maybe the reason is that the sense of ethics among policy makers is more prevalent than theory supposes (See also Romer and Romer 1997: 315).

11 We follow Cukierman (1992) in the subsequent argument.

12 The following does not apply to a mercantilist strategy that uses competitive disinflation rather than nominal devaluations. Only the first is sustainable in the long run. See Riese (1986) and (1986a).

13 Some notable events are: the UK secondary banking crisis in 1973, the Herstatt collapse in Germany 1974, the LDC debt crisis in August 1982, the stock market crash in October 1987, the US-thrifts crisis in the 1980s, the banking crises in Finland, Sweden and Japan in the 1990s and the ECU bond market in 1992. See Davis (1995).

14 It can be argued that UK's exit from the ERM was accelerated by financial fragility, given the intolerably high interest rates necessary to defend the DM-peg. However, the depth of the recession in UK indicates that the exchange rate level of the peg was simply wrong.

15 Long lasting nominal wage contracts are useful for low inflation, if the central bank gives high priority to price stability, but they can also be a temptation for surprise inflations. Short-term nominal wage contracts are useful in disinflations as they prevent lasting overvaluations in real wages and therefore reduce the 'sacrifice ratio' (on this point see Ball 1994). But they also make monetary policy less efficient with respect to real effects (see Chapter 8).

16 See Collignon (1994) for references and an overview.

17 In the next chapter we will look at the long-term relation of monetary policy and economic growth.

18 Germany is taken as the reference as many believe that the Bundesbank's reputation is the standard for the future ECB.

8 Monetary policy and structural unemployment

1 We may add to this that unemployment also has become an onerous charge for public finance. The European Commission (1993) has calculated the total cost of unemployment in 1993 to be 210,000 million ECU; Layard and Philpott (1991) have calculated that each unemployed person in the UK cost the Exchequer over £8,000 a year. See also Adnett (1996: 201). In Germany, estimates by the IAB reckons that the cost of unemployment is DM 158.9 bn or DM 40075 per person (Süddeutsche Zeitung Nr. 277/1997).

2   Policy makers seem to converge on the same conclusions about labour market imperfec-
    tions (OECD 1994; IMF 1997). An exception is the European Commission where at least
    some credit is given to the idea that 'the origins of Europe's unemployment problems are
    macroeconomic rather than microeconomic – rooted much more in past failures of eco-
    nomic policy than in weaknesses of labour market policy' (Morley 1998: 17).

3   In the language of Phelps (1994) the problem is the hiring rate.

4   This possibility was also recognised by Eichengreen (1993a), who wrote:

> 'Though the evidence on this question is not clear-cut, it appears that, when disturbances
> cause regional unemployment rates within European countries to diverge, other
> mechanisms, perhaps including relative wage adjustments, labour-force participation
> rates, inter-regional capital mobility, and government policy, substitute adequately for
> Europe's limited labour mobility in order to bring them back into line' (Eichengreen
> 1993a: 124).

5   See for example Dore *et al.* (1989).

6   In fact it seems that the 'flexibility' of the Japanese labour market which is reflected in high
    x-efficiency (high effort, willingness to cooperate, etc.) is due precisely to its rigidity with
    respect to employment levels. Part of this x-efficiency is also expressed in the greater var-
    iance in annual wage increases. See Dore *et al.* (1989).

7   It is interesting that in the European Union, increases in the capital intensity and labour
    productivity seem to have preceded increases in the growth rate in the 1960s and 1970s,
    while they moved in opposite directions in the 1980s and the early 1990s. We will explain
    this phenomenon in the context of our model (see footnote 56).

8   We also assume that the GDP-deflator is the same as the capital cost deflator, that is, $P = P_0$.

9   This is a very simplified model of the transmission mechanism. I am aware that in reality,
    risk and uncertainty as well as structure in the banking system and financial markets
    trouble the link between monetary policy instruments and capital costs significantly.
    However, as we will see below, short-term money market rates have an important systemic
    role in our system. Our simplifying assumptions allow us to focus on these features. For
    a study of how short-term affect long-term interest rates in Europe, see Gebauer, Müller
    et al. (1994).

10 The advantage of using q is that we do not have to distinguish between nominal or real
    interest rates and can, therefore, track down investment to monetary policy.

11 If $q = \bar{q}$, planned investment is equal to planned savings and in aggregate no quasi-rents
    accrue to entrepreneurs (Collignon 1997). Therefore, the condition of equilibrium reflects
    an 'IS'-locus in the (q, I)-space (Tobin and Brainard 1977). This implies also that profitable
    investment opportunities require a (temporary) deviation from IS-equilibrium.

12 If $d\tau/\tau > 0$, Equation (8.7) becomes:

$$\frac{I}{P_0 K} = n + \frac{dk}{k} + \frac{d\tau}{\tau}.$$

13 This reflects a 'Golden Age' (Robinson 1965: 99) or Harrod-equilibrium with Equation
    (8.2') as $(K/P_y) = (s/\bar{n})$ and Wicksell's natural rate of interest as i^*.

14 Over the long run when the inflation rate changes, it is more useful for comparative pur-
    poses to use the real short-term rate as in Figure 2.2.

15 If we accounted for risk considerations in capital markets and changes in liquidity pre-
    ferences, these factors could cause similar effects. Within certain limits, monetary policy
    might be able to compensate for those effects, but not necessarily in all cases.

16 Be reminded that we have set technological progress equal to zero. If it is positive, real
    wages could (and should) increase in the same proportion in order to keep the capital–
    labour ratio constant. In other words 'excessive' wage pressure implies real wage increases
    over and above TFP increases.

17 The real product wage increase was calculated as the ratio of nominal wage compensation to GDP-deflator in Table 8.1.

18 The real consumer wage is the ratio of nominal wage compensation to CPI increases.

19 The discrepancies between these figures may in part be explained by the fact that the IMF calculated the European Union without Greece, Luxembourg and Portugal, using ppp-based weights. In the Eurostat data, these three countries are included and the aggregates are based on the European System of Integrated Accounts, while those for the US and Japan are taken from the OECD national accounting system. The Eurostat data should, therefore, be more homogenous and pertinent for Europe.

20 See footnote 47.

21 See DIW (1998).

22 In Japan, which we did not analyse, it was higher with just 1 per cent.

23 Estimated at purchasing power standards.

24 This is why I prefer not to speak of capital–labour substitution but of capital accumulation per worker.

25 In the next section we will show that high real interest rates implied high profit mark-ups and low real wages. Thus, the deteriorating real wage position in Figure 8.5(a) might simply reflect the high level in capital costs.

26 At best there may be an effect on world interest rate levels.

27 We have touched on some factors related to the monetary regime in previous chapters.

28 For example Phelps (1995) claims that 'it is questionable whether monetary policy can engineer a permanently elevated real interest rate'.

29 Modigliani and Papademos (1980) define the monetary mechanism as 'the mechanism through which the monetary authority by controlling certain financial variables achieves (more or less) effective control over national income'.

30 EMI 1997: 14.

> Decisions on (monetary policy instruments) will have to be made by the ECB with a view to the functions the set of instruments is expected to fulfil and, *inter alia*, against the background of considerations such as the link between the monetary policy strategy and the instrument, the structural liquidity deficit or surplus of the banking sector at that time and the likely volatility of autonomous liquidity factors.

31 As the structural shortage is a permanent feature, the central bank has to provide additional liquidity through the 'open discount window'. Therefore, the money market is in 'expectational' equilibrium in the sense that market participant's expectations are correct. The 'open discount window' guarantees this expectational equilibrium.

32 Thus, the money market works as a Keynesian market with prices as exogenous and quantities as endogenous variables. Modigliani's description of the monetary mechanism is sometimes confusing because he does not clearly make the distinction between the direction of the adjustment. He, therefore, believes that if banks are selling assets to the central bank, interest rates rise – which is only the case if the central bank is *not* buying enough.

33 Schnadt (1994: 40) shows that alternative procedures of creating a net surplus of reserves would lead to the same result whereby the central bank can set interest rates.

34 The correlation between benefit regimes and unemployment observed by many studies may well be spurious.

35 Blanchard (1990) reminds us that the long-run neutrality hypothesis is imposed on models out of theoretical considerations and is a matter of faith rather than empirical evidence.

36 Hysteresis occurs when a system does not return to its previous state after the disturbance that has caused its deviation is removed. Thus, a temporary cause has a lasting effect. It is not enough to restore the original state in order to restore the original environment. Hysteresis proper occurs only when a dynamic system of difference equations possesses

one or more unit roots (Benassi *et al.* 1994). High persistence reflects high autoregressive coefficients for less than 1.

37 Strictly, prices are a mark-up on expected unit labour costs ($w^e - \lambda'$).

38 In fact, this so-called wage mark-up is equivalent to the labour income share. Multiplying labour productivity by this labour share yields the real wage. Realistically, the wage setting equation explains the real consumption wage after tax as a mark-up over the reservation wage. The latter ($c_{20} + \lambda'$) depends on the value of unemployment benefits, the value of leisure, per capita income, productivity, etc. In an open economy with imported consumer goods, the real consumption wage is necessarily different from the real product wage (Bean 1994). Since the subtleties of these specifications are not relevant to the logic of our model, we assume the real consumption and the real product wage to be identical. We also abstract from tax issues here.

39 This is the formulation by Carlin and Soskice (1990).

40 The coefficients c_{12} and c_{22} can be approximated with the expression ($\xi_1 - 1$) derived from Equation (1.3) in Chapter 1. There we have defined ξ_1 as the degree of nominal wage indexation. At perfect indexation $\xi_1 = 1$, nominal wages are flexible and c_{22} or c_{12} tend to zero. If indexation falls, nominal wage rigidity increases. See also Walsh (1995).

41 LNJ (1994: 19 and 1991: Chapter 8).

42 Therefore c_{10} is the logarithmic approximation of the mark-up. If we write the price level as $P = (W/\lambda)(1 + \mu)$ and take logs, we get $p = w - \lambda' + \ln(1 + \mu)$, hence $\ln(1 + ?) = c_{10}$ and the real wage is the log of productivity minus the log of the profit margin.

43 In our wage Equation (1.3) we set the coefficient vector $\xi_2 = 0$ which would imply $c_{21} = 0$ and therefore perfect wage rigidity and a horizontal BRW-line.

44 The formulation of price flexibility is slightly different here from the Alogoskoufis and Smith (1991) or Obstfeld (1993) approach that we used in Chapter 1. In Equation (1.1a) a high value for θ indicate inflation persistence and $\theta = 0$ perfect price flexibility with respect to long run equilibrium. Only if unemployment were related to price expectations (π^*) could we find a relation between these two coefficients of 'price flexibility'.

45 This argument does not only apply to wage contracts, but also to credit contracts, as we will see later.

46 Fischer (1994) noted the positive correlation between a flat Phillips curve, high sacrifice ratios and central bank independence and called it puzzling. However the puzzle disappears when one interprets the sacrifice ratio as an indicator for monetary policy effectiveness as I have done.

47 The mark-up from footnote 42 can also be written as $\sigma_k = (\mu/1 + \mu)$, so that $P = (W/\lambda \cdot 1/(1 - \sigma_k))$ and in logs: $p = w - \lambda' - \ln(1 - \sigma_k) \approx w - \lambda' - c_{10}$. However, $1 - \sigma_k = \sigma_w$, that is, profit and labour shares equal 1, so that the real wage can also be written as $W/P = \lambda \cdot \sigma_L$ or $w - p = \lambda' + \ln(\sigma_w)$. See also Carlin and Soskice (1990: 140–3); Collignon (1997).

48 That implies firms can only set *relative* prices in accordance with their respective market power, but not the absolute price level. This means prices are weighting-claims on income.

49 In terms of footnotes 42 and 47 the aggregate mark-up is

$$\frac{i_0 q b}{W/\lambda} = 1 + \mu = \frac{1}{1 - \sigma_k} = \frac{1}{\sigma_w}.$$

In log form we have according to Equation (8.9a'): $c_{10} = \ln i_0 q b$.

50 The concept is also found in Myrdal (1933) and links neatly with Tobin's q, although he was apparently not aware of this fact. See Tobin and Golub (1998: 150); Schmidt (1995); Collignon (1997).

51 Dividing Equation (8.13) by P yields

$$\sigma_{K_t} = 1 - \frac{W}{P\lambda} = [r_t + E(\pi)]\frac{b_t}{P_t}q.$$

Assuming the capital–output ratio b/q and q constant, the variation of the profit share $\Delta\sigma_K$ is

$$\Delta\sigma_K \approx [\Delta r + E(\pi) - \pi]\frac{b}{P}q.$$

52 For simplicity we assume average equal marginal costs.

53 In a neoclassical model, the cost of capital would match the marginal product of capital. Q-profits can then be interpreted as a kind of macroeconomic producer surplus that can be positive or negative. In models with imperfect competition, the price mark-up is added to total marginal cost, so that the mark-up would vary with $q(i)$. In our definition, the mark-up covers the cost of capital plus q-profits. The reason is that in a Keynesian framework, quantities adjust to prices, so that the price of capital (= credit) is the independent variable and the stock of capital (including its marginal product) adjusts. National income shares are not identical with technical factor shares.

54 We abstract here from risk considerations that raise $\bar{q}$ above one$(\bar{q} = 1 + \rho)$.

55 For evidence on time-varying mark-ups see Forsman *et al.* (1997), and Martins *et al.* (1996).

56 This could explain why increases in capital intensity and productivity have preceded increases in growth rates in the 1960s and 1970s: they improved the mark-up when nominal wages were sticky. In the 1980s and 1990s with tight monetary policy (lower growth), productivity increases might have been the answer to the monetary profit squeeze. This hypothesis deserves further research.

57 In more complex models the argument can be extended to exchange rates and fiscal policy.

58 Eichenbaum in a comment to Sims' (1992) price-puzzle stated: 'I know of no business cycle theory which is consistent with the notion that monetary contractions lead to prolonged periods of inflation'. Keynes' (1930) theory would not imply exactly this; but as we will see later, in a spot market economy the cost-push effect of an interest increase can exceed the demand contraction effect for some considerable span of time.

59 The transmission mechanism for such a miracle might be credit rationing: the central bank raises money market rates which flattens or inverts the yield curve and thereby reduces the profit margins of financial intermediaries. Therefore, capital market rates may remain fixed, but lower credit supply reduces effective demand. The logic is less convincing in the case of interest cuts: higher profit margins would only increase domestic credit if demand was rationed before. However, we could also construct the model so that *new* investment depends on lower interests, and old investment carries the higher old rate.

60 See footnote 51.

61 This could be interpreted as insider behaviour, while it actually only reflects stable wage preferences.

62 Given that q can also be interpreted as the shadow price of capital, the profit inflation can also be seen, under certain conditions, as an asset inflation.

63 If $P = P_0(1 + \pi)$ and $i_0 = r + \pi$ then $i_0 b/P \approx r K/y$.

64 For European evidence of the price puzzle, see Barran *et al.* (1997).

65 Assuming $i = i_0 = i_t$ and $q_i = -(1/r)$, we get $(1 - \phi)q < 1 + \pi/r$.

66 For a role of public debt, see Collignon and Mundschenk (1999).

67 What is, however, surprising is that they have not come down more, after price stability was obtained.

68 If wage setting responded to interest rates and/or monetary policy, this would be an argument in the factor x_t.

69 Empirical estimates of wage equations show that ξ_2 is normally much lower than ξ_1. See De Grauwe *et al.* (1996). Allowing for Phillips curve dynamics would add nothing to the logic of our model, although it might lower the persistence effect.

70 At least if we take unit labour cost for tradables. See McKinnon (1973: 96–7).

71 Goodhart (1997) has noticed that German monetary policy has adjusted interest rates less aggressively than countries with less successful price stability records. To this, Issing (1997) has answered:

> Features of the transmission process may slow the build-up of inflationary momentum and expectations following a shock. The reputation of the Bundesbank, backed by the consensus in German society giving priority to stability, may reinforce this tendency. Therefore, the Bundesbank may be able to afford to act 'less' and 'later' and still achieve a better record in controlling its ultimate targets.

72 If π_m is larger than zero, say 2 per cent, obviously unit labour costs could increase accordingly.

73 The passage is quoted by Clarida and Gertler (1997) with reference to a Bundesbank publication dated 1989. A more recent version has purified and neutralised the passage:

> ... daß es nützlich wäre, allen Verantwortlichen durch ein quantifiziertes Geldmengenziel den monetären Rahmen für das nominale gesamtwirtschaftliche Ausgabenwachstum ausdrücklich vorzugeben. Dies geschah in der Hoffnung, durch ein Geldmengenziel die Anpassung an die von der Geldpolitik verfolgte stabilitätsorientierte Linie zu fördern, mögliche Zweifel an der Ernsthaftigkeit der monetären Stabilisierungsbemühungen der Notenbank auszuräumen und eine widerspruchsfreie Abstimmung der einzelnen Teilbereiche der Wirtschaftspolitik zu erleichtern. Damit sollte gleichzeitig auch das Risiko vermindert werden, vermeidbar erscheinenden Fehlentwicklungen später durch schmerzhafte Restriktionsmaßnahmen entgegenwirken zu müssen. Möglich geworden war eine Geldmengenstrategie durch den Zusammenbruch des Systems von Bretton Woods im Jahre 1973 und den Übergang zu flexiblen Wechselkursen, wodurch die Bundesbank die Kontrolle über die heimische Geldmenge zurückgewonnen hatte.
>
> (Deutsche Bundesbank 1995: 51)

74 For details of labour cost responses to changes in tax rates, see OECD (1994: Vol. II, 246).

75 Calculated as the difference of average inflation rates between 1981–5 and 1986–91.

76 This is also a tentative conclusion in OECD (1994).

Bibliography

Adnett, N. (1996) *European Labour Markets, Analysis and Policy*, London and New York: Longman.

Akerlof, G. and Yellen, I. (1985) 'Can Small Deviations from Rationality Make Significant Differences to Economic Equilibria?', *The American Economic Review* 75(4): 708–20.

Alogoskoufis, G. and Smith, R. (1991) 'The Phillips Curve, The Persistence of Inflation, and the Lucas Critique: Evidence from Exchange-Rate Regimes', *The American Economic Review* 81(5): 1254–75.

Alogoskoufis, G., Bean, Ch., Bertola, G., Cohen, D., Dolado, J. and Saint-Paul, G. (1995) 'Unemployment: Choices for Europe', *Monitoring European Integration* 5, London: CEPR.

Anderton, B., Barrell, R. and in't Veld, J. W. (1992) 'Forward Looking Wages and the Analysis of Monetary Union', in R. Barrell and J. Whitley (eds), *Macroeconomic Policy Co-ordination, the ERM and Monetary Union*, London: Sage.

Argy, V. (1990) 'Choice of Exchange Rate Regime for a Smaller Economy: A Survey of Some Key Issues', in V. Argy and De Grauwe (eds), Washington, DC: IMF.

Arrowsmith, J. (1995) 'Opting out of Stage 3: Life in the Lower Tier of EMU', Occasional Papers 49, London: National Institute of Economic and Social Research.

Artis, M. (1994) 'European Monetary Union', in M. Artis and N. Lee (eds) *The Economics of the European Union: Policy and Analysis*, Oxford: Oxford University Press.

Artis, M. and Lee, N. (eds) (1994) The Economics of the European Union: Policy and Analysis, Oxford: Oxford University Press.

Artis, M. and Ormerod, P. (1994) 'Is There an "EMS-Effect" in European Labour Markets?', in C. Johnson and S. Collignon (eds) *The Monetary Economics of Europe: Causes of the EMS Crisis*, London: Pinter.

Artis, M. and Ormerod, P. (1996) 'Another look at the "EMS-Effect" in European Labour Markets', in P. De Grauwe, S. Micossi and G. Tullio (eds) *Inflation and Wage Behaviour in Europe*, Oxford: Clarendon Press.

Atkinson, A., Blanchard, O., Fitoussi, J.-P., Flemming, J., Malinvaud, E., Phelps, E. and Solow, R. (1993) 'Taux d'intérêt et chômage', References/OFCE, Paris: Presse de la Fondation Nationale des Sciences Politiques.

Baldwin, R. (1991) 'On the Microeconomics of the European Monetary Union', in *European Economy*, special edition no. 1.

Ball, L. (1994) 'What determines the sacrifice ratio?', in N. G. Mankiw (ed.) (1994) *Monetary Policy*, Chicago: The University of Chicago Press.

—— (1997) 'Disinflation and the NAIRU' in C. P. Romer and D. H. Romer (eds) *Reducing Inflation. Motivation and Strategy*, Chicago: The University of Chicago Press.

Ball, L., Mankiw, N. G. and Romer, D. (1988) 'The New Keynesian Economics and the Out put – Inflation trade-off', in *Brookings Papers on Economic Activity* 1: 1–65.

Bank of England (1997) *Quarterly Bulletin* 37 (February).

Barran, F., Coudert, V. and Mojon, B. (1997) 'The Transmission of Monetary Policy in the European Countries', in S. Collignon (ed.) *European Monetary Policy*, AMUE, London: Pinter.

Barrell, R. and Whitley, J. (1992) 'Macroeconomic Policy Co-ordination, the ERM and Monetary Union', London: Sage.

Barrell, R., Morgan, J. and Pain, N. (1995) 'Employment, Inequality and Flexibility – A Comparative Study of Labour Markets in North America and Europe', National Institute of Economic and Social Research (July), mimeo.

Barrell, R., Anderton, B., Lansbury, M. and Sefton, J. (1998) 'FEERs for the NIEs: Exchange Rate Policies and Development Strategies in Taiwan, Korea, Singapore and Thailand', in S. Collignon, Y. C. Park and J. Pisani-Ferry (eds) *Exchange Rate Policies in Emerging Asian Countries: Domestic and International Aspects*, Studies in the Growth Economies of Asia no. 13, London: Routledge.

Barro, R. J. (1976) 'Rational Expectations and the Role of Monetary Policy', in E. Lucas and T. J. Sargent (eds)(1981) *Rational Expectations and Econometric practice*, London: George Allan and Unwin.

Bayoumi, T. (1994) 'A Formal Model of Optimum Currency Areas', in Discussion Paper no. 968, CEPR.

Bayoumi, T. (1995) 'Who Needs Bands? Exchange Rate Policy before EMU', in Discussion Paper no. 1188, CEPR.

Bayoumi, T. and Eichengreen, B. (1993) 'Shocking Aspects of European Monetary Unification', in F. Giavazzi and F. Torres (eds) *Adjustment and Growth in the European monetary Union*, New York: Cambridge University Press. Reprinted in Eichengreen (1997).

Bayoumi, T. and Eichengreen, B. (1999) 'Is Asia an Optimum Currency Area? Can it become one? Regional, Global and Historical Perspectives on Asian Monetary Relations', in S. Collignon, Y. C. Park and J. Pisani-Ferry (eds) *Exchange Rate Policies in Emerging Asian Countries*, Studies in the Growth Economies of Asia no. 13, London: Routledge.

Bean, Ch. (1994) 'European Unemployment: A Survey', *Journal of Economic Literature* 32(2): 573–619.

Begg, D. K. H. (1982) *The Rational Expectations Revolution in Macroeconomics – Theories and Evidences*, Oxford: Philip Allan.

Belke, A. (1996) 'Testing for Unit Roots in West German and US Unemployment Rates: Do "Great Crashes" Cause Trend Breaks?', *Konjunkturpolitik* 4: 327–60.

Belke, A. and Gros, D. (1997) 'Evidence on the Cost of Intra-European Exchange Rate Variability', Institut für Europäische Wirtschaft, Ruhr-Universität Bochum, Diskussionsbeiträge 13.

Benassi, C., Chirco, A. and Colombo, C. (1994) *The New Keynesian Economics*, Oxford and Cambridge, MA: Blackwell.

Bénassy-Quéré, A. (1995) 'Ni Change Fixe, Ni Change Flexible', in *La lettre du CEPII* 133, (March).

—— (1997) 'Optimal Pegs for Asian Currencies', mimeo.

—— (1999) 'Exchange Rate Regimes and Policies: An Empirical Analysis', in S. Collignon, Y. C. Park and J. Pisani-Ferry (eds) *Exchange Rate Policies in Emerging Asian Countries*, Studies in the Growth Economies of Asia no. 13, London: Routledge.

Bercusson, S., Deakin, P., Koistinen, Y., Kravaritou, U., Mückenberger, A., Supiot, A. and Veneziani, B. (1996) Soziales Europa – ein Manifest, rororo aktuell, Hamburg.

Bergsten, C. F. and Henning, C. R. (1996) *Global Economic Leadership and the Group of Seven*, Washington, DC: Institute for International Economics.

Bernholz, P. (1989) 'Ordo-liberals and the Control of the Money Supply', in A. Peacock and H. Willgerodt (eds) *German Neo-Liberals and the Social Market Economy*, Trade Policy Research Center, London: Macmillan.

Bilson, J. F. O. (1979) 'Recent Developments in Monetary Models of Exchange Rate determination', *IMF Staff Papers* 26.

Bini-Smaghi, L., Padoa-Schioppa, T. and Papadia, F. (1994) 'The Transition to EMU in the Maastricht Treaty', Essays in *International Finance* 194, Princeton: Princeton University Press.

Blanchard, O. (1979) 'Speculative Bubbles, Crashes and Rational Expectations', *Economics Letters* 3: 387–9.

—— (1990) 'Why does Money Affect Output?', in B. Friedman and F. H. Hahn (eds) *Handbook of Monetary Economics*, vol. 2, Handbook in Economics 8, Amsterdam: Elsevier Science.

Blanchard, O. and Fischer, S. (1989) Lectures on Macroeconomics, Cambridge, MA: MIT Press.

Blanchard, O. and Jimeno, J. F. (1995) 'Structural Unemployment: Spain versus Portugal', *The American Economic Review* 85(2): 212–18.

Blanchard, O. and Quah, D. (1989) 'The Dynamic Effects of Aggregate Demand and Supply Disturbances', *The American Economic Review* 79: 655–73.

Bofinger, P. (1998) 'The Monetary Policy of the European Central Bank', Paper prepared for the SimCorp Conference 'The Financial Challenge of the EMU', April 1–2, Industriens Hus, Copenhagen, mimeo.

Bofinger, P., Reischle, I. and Schächter, A. (1996) *Geldpolitik. Ziele, Institutionen, Strategien und Instrumente*, Verlag Vahlen, München.

Boltho, A. (1996) 'Convergence, Competitiveness and the Exchange Rate', in N. Crafts and G. Toniolo (eds) *Economic Growth in Europe since 1945*, CEPR, Cambridge: Cambridge University Press.

Bordo, M. D. (1993) 'The Bretton Woods International Monetary System: A Historical Overview', in M. D. Bordo and B. Eichengreen (eds) *A Retrospective on the Bretton Woods System – Lessons for International Monetary Reforms*, NBER, Chicago: The University of Chicago Press.

Bordo, M. D. and Eichengreen, B. (1993) *A Retrospective on the Bretton Woods System – Lessons for International Monetary Reforms*, NBER, Chicago: The University of Chicago Press.

Boyer, R. (1988) 'Wage/Labour Relations, Growth, and Crisis: A Hidden Dialectic', in R. Boyer (ed.) *The Search for Labour Market Flexibility: The European Economies in Transition*, Oxford: Clarendon Press.

Breuer, J. B. (1994) 'An Assessment of the Evidence on Purchasing Power Parity', in J. Williamson (ed.) *Estimating Equilibrium Exchange Rates*, Washington, DC: Institute for International Economics.

Brittan, A. and Mayes, D. (1992) *Achieving Monetary Union in Europe*, London: Sage.

Brunner, K. and Meltzer, A. H. (1971) 'The Uses of Money: Money in the Theory of an Exchange Economy', *The American Economic Review* 61(5): 784–805.

Buiter, W. (1997) 'The Economic Case for Monetary Union in the European Union', Cambridge University, mimeo.

Buiter, W., Corsetti, G. and Roubini, N. (1993) 'Excessive Deficits: Sense and Nonsense in the Treaty of Maastricht', *Economic Policy* 16: 221–44.

Capie, F., Goodhart, C., Fisher, S. and Schnadt, N. (1994) 'The Future of Central Banking – Tercentenary Symposium of the Bank of England', Cambridge: Cambridge University Press.

Card, D. and Hyslop, D. (1997) 'Does Inflation Grease the Wheels of the Labour Market?', in C. Romer and D. Romer (eds) *Reducing Inflation. Motivation and Strategy*, Chicago: The University of Chicago Press.

Carlin, W. and Soskice, D. (1990) *Macroeconomics and the Wage Bargain – A Modern Approach to Employment, Inflation and the Exchange Rate*, New York: Oxford University Press.

CEPS (1994) 'European Payments Systems and EMU', working party report 11, Brussels.

Childers, T. (1982) 'Inflation, Stabilization, and Political Realignment in Germany 1924 to 1928', in G. Feldman, C.-L. Holtfrerich, G. Ritter, P.-C. Witt (eds) (Veröffentlichungen der Historischen Kommission zu Berlin) *The German Inflation reconsidered – A preliminary balance*, pp. 409–31, Berlin and New York: Walter de Gruyter.

Ciocca, P. and Nardozzi, G. (1996) *The High Price of Money. An Interpretation of World Interest Rates*, Oxford: Clarendon Press.

Clarida, R. and Gertler, M. (1997) 'How the Bundesbank Conducts Monetary Policy', in C. Romer and D. Romer (eds) *Reducing Inflation. Motivation and Strategy*, Chicago: The University of Chicago Press.

Cohen, D. (1989) 'The Costs and Benefits of a European Currency', in M. de Cecco and A. Giovannini (eds) *A European Central Bank? Perspectives on monetary unification after ten years of the EMS*, Cambridge: Cambridge University Press.

Collignon, S. (1994) *Europe's Monetary Future*, London: Pinter.

——(1994a) 'Über den Zusammenhang von Wettbewerbsfähigkeit und Wechselkursen' in U. Jens, Langfristige Strukturprobleme der deutschen Wirtschaft, Baden-Baden: Nomos Verlagsgesellschaft. (English translation: 'The Link between Competitiveness and Exchange Rates' in *De Pecunia* VII, 1 March 1995): pp. 55–82.

——(1995) 'Droits de l'homme, investissement et développement africain', in P. Hugon, G. Pourcet and S. Quiers-Valette (CERED-Forum) *L'Afrique des incertitudes*, coll. Tiers Monde – IEDES, Paris: Presses Universitaires de France.

——(1996) *Geldwertstabilität für Europa – Die Währungsunion auf dem Prüfstand*, Gütersloh: Verlag Bertelsmann Stiftung.

——(1997) 'Unemployment and Monetary Policy in the Single Market: A Dialogue with Franco Modigliani', in S. Collignon (ed.) *European Monetary Policy*, London: Pinter.

——(1998) 'Monetary Integration between Economies with Differential Structures', in S. W. Black and M. Moersch (eds) *Competion and Convergence in Financial Markets – The German and Anglo-American Models*, Amsterdam: Elsevier Science.

——(1999) 'Bloc Floating and Exchange Rate Volatility: The Causes and Consequences of Currency Blocs', in S. Collignon, Y. C. Park and J. Pisani-Ferry (eds) *Exchange Rate Policies in Emerging Asian Countries*, Studies in the Growth Economies of Asia no. 13, London: Routledge.

Collignon, S. and Mundschenk, S. (1999) 'The Sustainability of Public Debt in Europe', *Economia Internazionale* LII, 1: 101–59, Paris: AMUE.

Collignon, S., Park, Y. C. and Pisani-Ferry, J. (eds)(1999) *Exchange Rate Policies in Emerging Asian Countries*, Studies in the Growth Economies of Asia no. 13, London: Routledge.

Congdon, T. (1997) 'Why the Euro Will Fail', in P. Temperton (ed.) *The Euro*, Chichester: John Wiley and Sons.

Cooper, R. (1968) *The Economics of Interdependence: Economic Policy in the Atlantic Community*, New York: McGraw Hill.

Crafts, N. and Toniolo, G. (1996) 'Postwar Growth: An Overview', in N. Crafts and G. Toniolo (eds) *Economic Growth in Europe since 1945*, CEPR, Cambridge: Cambridge University Press.

Crawford, M. (1996) *One Money for Europe? The Economics and Politics of EMU*, London: Macmillan.

Cukierman, A. (1992) *Central Bank Strategy, Credibility and Independence. Theory and Evidence*, Cambridge, MA: MIT Press.

Cukierman, A., Rodrigez, P. and Webb, S. (1995) *Central Bank Autonomy and Exchange Rate Regimes – Their Effects on Monetary Accommodation and Activism*, April, mimeo.

Daveri, F. and Tabellini, G. (1997) 'Unemployment, Growth and Taxation in Industrial Countries', in Discussion Paper no. 1681, CEPR.

Davis, Ph. (1995) *Debt, Financial Fragility and Systemic Risk*, Oxford: Clarendon Press.

De Grauwe, P. (1989) *International Money. Postwar Trends and Theories*, Oxford: Oxford University Press.

—— (1992) *The Economics of Monetary Integration* (1st edition), Oxford: Oxford University Press.

—— (1997) *The Economics of Monetary Integration* (3rd edition), Oxford: Oxford University Press.

—— (1996) 'Inflation Convergence during the Transition to EMU', in P. De Grauwe, S. Micossi and G. Tullio (eds) *Inflation and Wage Behaviour in Europe*, Oxford and New York: Clarendon Press.

De Grauwe, P. and Vanhaverbeke, W. (1991) 'Is Europe an Optimum Currency Area? Evidence from Regional Data', in Discussion Paper no. 555, CEPR.

De Grauwe, P., Micossi, S. and Tullio, G. (eds) (1996) *Inflation and Wage Behaviour in Europe*, Oxford: Clarendon Press.

Demertzis, M., Hughes Hallett, A. and Rummel, O. (1998) 'Is a 2-speed System in Europe the Answer to the Conflict Between the German and the Anglo-Saxon Models of Monetary Control?' in S. W. Black and M. Moersch (eds) *Competition and Convergence in Financial Markets. The German and Anglo-American Models*, Amsterdam: Elsevier Science.

Deutsche Bundesbank (1995) Die Geldpolitik der Bundesbank, Frankfurt am Main, October.

DIW (1997) Die Lage der Weltwirtschaft und der deutschen Wirtschaft im Herbst 1997, Wochenbericht 44/97 (October), Berlin.

—— (1998) Die Lage der Weltwirtschaft und der deutschen Wirtschaft im Frühjahr 1998, Wochenbericht 20/98 (May), Berlin.

Dixit, A. and Pindyck, R. (1994) *Investment under Uncertainty*, Princeton: Princeton University Press.

Dominquez, K. and Frankel, J. A. (1993) 'Does Foreign Exchange Intervention Work?' (September), Washington, DC: Institute for International Economics.

Dore, R., Bounine-Cabalé, J. and Tapiola, K. (1989) *Japan at Work: Markets, Managements and Flexibility*, Paris: OCDE.

Dornbusch, R. (1976) 'Expectations and Exchange Rate Dynamics', *Journal of Political Economy* 84(6): 1161–76.

—— (1980) *Open Economy Macroeconomics*, New York: Harper International, Basic Books.

—— (1982) 'Equilibrium and Disequilibrium Exchange Rates' in *Zeitschrift für Wirtschafts- und Sozialwissenschaften*, mimeo.

—— (1983) 'Exchange Rate Risk and the Macroeconomics of Exchange Rate Determination'. Reprinted in R. Dornbusch (ed.) (1988) *Exchange Rate and Inflation*, Cambridge, MA: MIT Press.

Dornbusch, R., Favero, C. A. and Giavazzi, F. (1998) 'A Red Letter Day?', in *Discussion Paper Series* no. 1804, London: CEPR.

Dornbusch, R. and Frankel, J. A. (1988) 'The Flexible Exchange Rate System: Experience and Alternatives'. Reprinted in J. A. Frankel (1995) *On Exchange Rates*, Cambridge, MA: MIT Press.

Driffil, I. and Miller, M. (1992) 'Is the Road to Monetary Union Paved with Recession?' in R. Barrell and I. Whitley (eds) *Macroeconomic Policy Co-ordination in Europe. The ERM and Monetary Union*, National Institute of Economic and Social Research, London: Sage.

Duffie, D. (1990) 'Money in General Equilibrium Theory', in B. M. Friedman and F. H. Hahn (eds) *Handbook of Monetary Economics 1*, Handbook in Economics 8, Amsterdam: Elsevier Science.

Dumke, R. H., Hermann, A., Juchems, A. and Sherman, H. (1997) Währungsvielfalt behindert Vollendung des Europäischen Binnenmarkts in: *ifo Schnelldienst* 9/97.

Economie Européenne (1994) 'Concurrence et Integration – Politique Communautaire de Contrôle des Concentrations' 57, Brussels: Commission Européenne.

—— (1997) Rapport Economique Annuel 1997, no. 63, Brussels: Commission Européenne.

Egebo, T. and Englander, S. (1992) 'Institutional Commitments and Policy Credibility: A Critical Survey and Empirical Evidence from the ERM', *OECD Economic Studies* 18: 45–84.

Eichengreen, B. (1990a) 'One Money for Europe? Lessons from the US Currency Union', *Economic Policy* 10: 117–87.

—— (1990b) 'Is Europe an Optimum Currency Area?', in Discussion Paper no. 478, CEPR.

—— (1990c) *Essays in the History of International Finance, 1919–1939*, Cambridge: Cambridge University Press.

—— (1993) 'Epilogue: Three Perspectives on the Bretton Woods System', in M. Bordo and B. Eichengreen (eds) *A Retrospective on the Bretton Woods System – Lessons for International Monetary Reforms*, NBER, Chicago: The University of Chicago Press.

—— (1993a) 'Labour Markets and European Monetary Unification', in P. R. Masson and M. P. Taylor (eds) *Policy Issues in the Operation of Currency Unions*, Cambridge: Cambridge University Press. Reprinted in Eichengreen (1997).

—— (1996) 'Institutions and Economic Growth: Europe After World War II', in N. Crafts and G. Toniolo (eds) *Economic Growth in Europe since 1945*, CEPR, Cambridge: Cambridge University Press.

—— (1997) *European Monetary Unification – Theory, Practice, and Analysis*, Cambridge, MA: MIT Press.

—— (1997a) 'The Bretton Woods System: Paradise Lost?', in B. Eichengreen and M. Flandreau (eds) *The Gold Standard in Theory and History*, London: Routledge.

Eichengreen, B. and Kenen, P. B. (1994) 'Managing the World Economy under the Bretton Woods System: An Overview', in P. B. Kennen (ed.) *Managing the World Economy – Fifty Years after the Bretton Woods*, Washington, DC: Institute for International Economics.

Eichengreen, B. and Ch. Wyplosz (1990) The Economic Consequences of the Franc Poincaré, in: B. Eichengreen (ed.) *Elusive Stability – Essays in the History of International Finance, 1919–1939*, Cambridge: Cambridge University Press.

Eichengreen, B. and Wyplosz, Ch. (1993) 'The Unstable EMS', in *Brookings Papers in Economy Activity* 1. Reprinted in Eichengreen (1997).

Eijffinger, S. C.W. (1997) 'The Credibility of the European Central Bank', in S. Collignon (ed.) *European Monetary Policy*, London: Pinter.

Eisner, R. (1996) 'A New View of the NAIRU', Northwestern University, mimeo.

Elmeskov, I. (1993) 'High and Persistent Unemployment: Assessment of the Problem and its Causes', OECD Economics Department, working paper no. 132, Paris.

Enders,W. (1995) 'Applied Econometric Time Series', New York: John Wiley and Sons.

Eucken,W. (1952) *Grundsätze der Wirtschaftspolitik* (new edition), J. C. B. Mohr (Paul Siebeck), Tübingen, 1990.

—— (1989) *Die Grundlagen der Nationalökonomie* (9th edition), Berlin: Springer-Verlag.

European Commission (1990) 'One Market, One Money', *European Economy* 44, Brussels.

—— (1993) 'Growth, Competitiveness, Employment. The Challenges and Ways Forward to the 21st Century', in *Bulletin of the European Communities*, Supplement 6/93.

—— (1997) Rapport économique annuel, 1997, in *Economie Européenne* 63, Brussels.

—— (1997a) 'Vers une stratégie fiscale pour l'Union Européenne', Brussels, mimeo.

—— (1998) Convergence Report 1998, 25 March 1998, Luxembourg: Office for Official Publications of the European Communities.

European Monetary Institute (EMI) (1996) Annual Report 1995 (April), Frankfurt.

—— (1997) 'The Single Monetary Policy in Stage Three. Specification of the Operational Framework' (January), Frankfurt.

—— (1998) Convergence Report (March), Frankfurt.

Fair, R. (1996) 'Testing, the Standard View of the Long-Run Unemployment-Inflation Relationship', (April), Yale University, mimeo.

Feldstein, M. (1992) 'Does European Monetary Union have a Future?', CEPR Conference la Coruña 11/12, December 1992, mimeo.

Feldstein, M. (1997) 'EMU and Internal Conflict', *Foreign Affairs* 76(6): 60–73.

Feinstein, C. H., Temin, P. and Toniolo, G. (1997) 'The European Economy Between the Wars', New York: Oxford University Press.

Fischer, S. (1977) 'Long-term Contracts, Rational Expectations, and the Optimal Money Supply Rule', in *Journal of Political Economy* 85(1): 191–205.

—— (1993) 'The Role of Macroeconomic Factors in Growth', *Journal of Monetary Economics* 32(3): 485–512.

—— (1994) 'Modern Central Banking', in F. Cappie, C. Goodhart, S. Fisher and N. Schnadt (eds) *The Future of Central Banking – The Tercentenary Symposium of the Bank of England*, Cambridge: Cambridge University Press.

Fitoussi, J.-P., Atkinson, A. B., Blanchard, O. E., Flemming, J. S., Malinvaud, E., Phelps, E. S. and Solow, R. M. (1993) 'Competitive disinflation – The Mark and Budgetary Politics in Europe', OFCE, New York: Oxford University Press.

Flassbeck, H. (1994) 'The Implications of Different Labour Market Regimes in Europe and the Lessons from the German Unification for the EMS and EMU', in C. Johnson and S. Collignon (1994) *The Monetary Economics of Europe. Causes of the EMS Crisis*, London: Pinter.

Flood, R. P. and Mussa, M. (1994) 'Issues Concerning Nominal Anchors for Monetary Policy', in T. J. T. Baliño and Cottarelli (eds) *Frameworks for Monetary Stability – Policy Issues and Country Experiences*, Washington, DC: IMF.

Forsman, P., Saarenheimo, T. and Terviö, M. (1997) 'Time-Varying Markups. Empirical Analysis of Markups in Finnish Industries', Bank of Finland, *Discussion Papers* 16/97, Economics Department.

Frankel, J. (1993) *On Exchange Rates*, Cambridge, MA: MIT Press.

Frankel, J. and Wei, S.-J. (1992) 'Yen Bloc or Dollar Bloc? Exchange Rate Policies in the East Asian Economies', in T. Ito and A. Krueger (eds) *Macroeconomic Linkage*, Chicago: The University of Chicago Press.

—— (1993) 'Trade Blocs and Currency Blocs', in CEPR, The Monetary Future of Europe, Conference papers La Coruña 11/12, December 1992.

—— (1995) 'European Integration and the Regionalization of World Trade and Currencies: The Economics and the Politics', in B. Eichengreen, J. Frieden and J. von Hagen (eds) *Monetary and Fiscal Policy in an Integrated Europe*, Heidelberg: Springer.

Frankel, J. and Razin, A. with Chi Wa Yuen (1996) *Fiscal Policies and Growth in the World Economy* (3rd edition), Cambridge, MA: MIT Press.

Friedman, B. (1990) 'Implications of Corporate Indebtedness for Monetary Policy', *NBER* working paper no. 3266.

Friedman, B. and Hahn, F. H. (eds) (1990) *Handbook of Monetary Economics 1*, Handbook in Economics 8, Amsterdam: Elsevier Science.

Friedman, M. (1953) 'The Methodology of Positive Economics', *Essays in Positive Economics*, Chicago: The University of Chicago Press.

—— (1953a) 'The Case for Flexible Exchange Rates', *Essays in Positive Economics*, Chicago: The University of Chicago Press.

—— (1968) 'The Role of Monetary Policy', *The American Economic Review* 58(1): 1–17.

Friedman, M. and Schwartz, A. J. (1982) 'Monetary Trends in the United States and the United Kingdom – Their Relation to Income, Prices, and Interest Rates, 1867–1975', NBER, Chicago: The University of Chicago Press.

Funke, N. and Kennedy, M. (1997) International Implications of European Economic and Monetary Union, OECD working paper no. 174 (Economic Department).

Galbraith, J. K. (1997) 'Time to Ditch the NAIRU', *Journal of Economic Perspectives* 11(1): 93–108.

Gebauer, W., Müller, M., Schmidt, K. J.W., Thiel, M. and Worms, A. (1994) 'Determinants of Long-Term Interest Rates in Selected Countries: Towards a European Central Bank Policy Design', in C. Johnson and S. Collignon (1994) *The Monetary Economics of Europe. Causes of the EMS Crisis*, London: Pinter.

Gebauer, W., Schmidt, K. J. W. and Veestraten, D. (1994) 'Kapitalmarktindikatoren und Investitionen in Sachkapital – Eine empirische Analyse', working paper no. 37 (November), Geld–Währung–Kapitalmarkt, Frankfurt: J.W. Goethe Universität.

Giavazzi, F. and Giovannini, A. (1989) *Limiting Exchange Rate Flexibility. The European Monetary System*, Cambridge, MA: MIT Press.

Giavazzi, F. and Pagano, M. (1988) 'The Advantage of Tying One's Hand: EMS Discipline and Central Bank Credibility', *European Economic Review* 32, 1055–75.

Gilbert, M. (1997) 'The Gold-Dollar System: Conditions of Equilibrium and the Price of Gold', in B. Eichengreen and M. Flandreau (eds) *The Gold Standard in Theory and History*, London: Routledge.

Goldstein, M. and Mussa, M. (1993) 'The Integration of World Capital Markets', WP/93/95, Washington, DC: IMF.

Goodhart, C. (1989) *Money, Information and Uncertainty* (2nd edition), Basingstoke: Macmillan.

—— (1992) 'The Objectives for, and Conduct of, Monetary Policy in the 1990s'. Reprinted in C. Goodhart (1995) *The Central Bank and the Dynamic System*, Basingstoke: Macmillan.

—— (1995) 'The Political Economy of Monetary Union', in P. Kenen (ed.) *Understanding Interdependence. The Macroeconomics of the Open Economy*, Princeton: Princeton University Press.

—— (1997) 'Why Do the Monetary Authorities Smooth Interest Rates?', in S. Collignon (ed.) *European Monetary Policy*, London: Pinter.

Gordon, D. M. (1988) 'The Un-Natural Rate of Unemployment: An Econometric Critique of the NAIRU hypothesis', *The American Economic Review* 78(2): 117–123.

Gordon, R. J. (1996) 'The Time-varying NAIRU and its Implication for Economic Policy', *Discussion Paper series* no. 1492, CEPR.

Gosh, A. R. and Masson, P. R. (1991) 'Model Uncertainty, Learning and the Gains from Coordination', *The American Economic Review* 81(3): 465–79.

Gosh, A. R. and Wolf, H. (1994) 'How many moneys? A Genetic Approach to Finding Optimum Currency Areas', *NBER* working paper no. 4805.

Grandmont, J.-M. (1983) 'Money and Value – A Reconsideration of Classical and Neoclassical Monetary Theory', Cambridge, New York and Paris: Maison des Sciences de l'Homme, Cambridge University Press.

Granger, C. and Newbold, P. (1974) 'Spurious Regressions in Econometrics', *Journal of Econometrics* 2: 111–20.

Grant, R. (1987) *John Locke's Liberalism*, Chicago and London: The University of Chicago Press.

Greenwald, B. C. and Stiglitz, J. E. (1995) 'Labor-Market Adjustments and the Persistence of Unemployment', *The American Economic Review* 85(2): 219–25.

Gros, D. (1996) 'Germany's Stake in Exchange Rate Stability', in *CEPS Review* 1 (May).

Gros, D. and Thygesen, N. (1992) *European Monetary Integration. From the European Monetary System to the European Monetary Union*, London: St. Martin's Press, Longman.

Hargreaves Heap, S., Hollis, M., Lyons, B., Sugden, R. and Weale, A. (1992) *The Theory of Choice – A Critical Guide*, Cambridge, MA: Blackwell.

Hartmann, Ph. (1996) 'The Future of the Euro: A Transactions Perspective', CEPS Research Report no. 20.

Hayek, F. A. (1979) *The Counterrevolution of Science. Studies on the Abuse of Reason*, Indianapolis: Liberty Press.

—— (1988) *The Fatal Conceit. The Errors of Socialism*, London: Routledge.

Herr, H. (1992) Geld, Währungswettbewerb und Währungssysteme – Theorische und Historische der internationalen Geldwirtschaft, Frankfurt: Campus Verlag.

Hirschman, A. O. (1970) *Exit, Voice and Loyalty*, Cambridge, MA: Harvard University Press.

—— (1981) 'Three Uses of Political Economy in Analysing European Integration', in A. O. Hirschman, *Essays in Trespassing. Economics to Politics and Beyond*, Cambridge: Cambridge University Press.

Hirschman, O. (1982) *Shifting Involvements. Private Interest and Public Action*, Oxford: Basil Blackwell.

Hobsbawm, E. (1994) *Age of Extremes. The Short Twentieth Century 1914–1991*, London: Penguin.

Horn, G. A. and Zwiener, R. (1992) 'Wage Regimes in a United Europe. A Simulation Study on QUEST', in R. Barrel and J. Whitley (1992) *Macroeconomic Policy Co-ordination in Europe, the ERM and Monetary Union*, London: Sage.

Hörngren, L. and Vredin, A. (1989) 'Exchange Risk Premia in a Currency Basket System', in *Weltwirtschaftliches Archiv* 125 (2), 310–325.

Huh, C. G. and Trehan, B. (1995) 'Modeling the Time-Series Behavior of the Aggregate Wage Rate', *FRBSF Economic Review* 1: 3–13.

Hughes, M. (1982) 'Economic Interest, Social Attitudes and Creditor Ideology: Popular Responses to Inflation', in G. Feldman, C.-L. Holtfrerich, G. Ritter and P.-C. Witt (eds) (Veröffentlichungen der Historischen Kommission zu Berlin), *The German Inflation reconsidered – A preliminary balance*: 385–408, Berlin and New York: Walter de Gruyter.

Huizinga, J. (1994) 'Exchange Rate Volatility, Uncertainty and Investment: An Empirical Investigation', in L. Leidermann and A. Razin (eds) *Capital Mobility: The impact on Consumption, Investment and Growth*, Cambridge: Cambridge University Press.

Hume, D. (1740) *A Treatise on Human Nature*, vol. III (ed.) (1918) Oxford: Oxford University Press.

International Monetary Fund (1996) *World Economic Outlook* (October), Washington, DC.

—— (1997) *World Economic Outlook* (October), Washington, DC.

—— (1998) *World Economic Outlook* (April), Washington, DC.

Issing, O. (1997) Comment on Chapter 8, in S. Collignon (ed.) *European Monetary Policy*, London: Pinter.

James, H. (1996) *International Monetary Cooperation Since Bretton Woods*, Oxford: Oxford University Press.

Jochimsen, R. (1998) *Perspektiven der europäischen Wirtschaft- und Währungsunion*, Baden-Baden: Nomos Verlagsgesellschaft.

Johnson, C. and Collignon, S. (1994) *The Monetary Economics of Europe: Causes of the EMS Crisis*, London: Pinter.

Kenen, P. B. (1969) 'The Theory of Optimum Currency Areas: An Eclectic View', in R. A. Mundell and A. K. Swoboda (eds) *Monetary Problems of the International Economy*, Chicago: The University of Chicago Press.

—— (1985) 'Macroeconomic Theory and Policy: How the Closed Economy was Opened', in R. W. Jones and P. B. Kenen (eds) *Handbook of International Economics*, vol. II, coll. Handbook in Economics, Amsterdam: Elsevier Science.

—— (ed.) (1994) *Managing the World Economy – Fifty Years after the Bretton Woods*, Washington: Institute for International Economics.

—— (1995) *Economic and Monetary Union in Europe. Moving beyond Maastricht*, Cambridge: Cambridge University Press.

Kenen, P. and Rodrik (1986) 'Measuring and Analyzing the Effects of short-term Volatility in Real Exchange Rates', *Review of Economics and Statistics* 68(2): 311–15.

Keynes, J. M. (1930) *A Treatise on Money*, London: Macmillan.

—— (1936) *The General Theory of Employment Interest and Money*, London: Macmillan.

—— (1938) 'My Early Beliefs', in *Essays in Biography, Collected Writings*, vol. X, London: Macmillan.

King, M. (1994) 'The UK experience with Monetary Policy Instruments', *Bank of England Quarterly Bulletin* (August).

Knappe, E. and Funk, L. (1997) 'Irritationen über den Zusammenhang zwischen Arbeitsproduktivität und Beschäftigung', in *List Forum für Wirtschaft- und Finanzpolitik* 23: 65–81.

Krugman, P. (1993) 'Lessons of Massachussets for EMU', in F. Torres and F. Giavazzi (eds) *Adjustments and Growth in the European Monetary Union*, Cambridge: Cambridge University Press.

Lascelles, D. (1997) *The Crash of 2003*, London: Centre for the Study of Financial Innovation.

Layard, R. and Philpott, J. (1991) *Stopping Unemployment*, London: Employment Institute.

Layard, R., Nickell, S. and Jackman, R. (1991) *Unemployment – Macroeconomic Performance and the Labour Market*, New York: Oxford University Press.

—— (1994) *The Unemployment Crisis*, New York: Oxford University Press.

Leijonhufvud, A. (1967) 'Keynes and the Keynesians: a suggested interpretation', *The American Economic Review* 57: 401–10.

Leiderman, L. and Svensson, L. E. O. (eds) (1995) *Inflation Targets*, London: CEPR and Opera, Italy: IGIER.

Levine, R. and Renelt, D. (1992) 'A Sensitivity Analysis of Cross-country Growth Regressions', *The American Economic Review* 82: 942–63.

Little, I. M. D., Cooper, R. N., Corden, W. M. and Rajapatirana, S. (1993) *Boom, Crisis, and Adjustment – The Macroeconomic Experience of Developing Countries*, The International Bank for Reconstruction and Development, New York: Oxford University Press.

Lucas, R. (1972) 'Expectations and the Neutrality of Money', *Journal of Economic Theory* 4.

—— (1973) 'Some International Evidence on Output-Inflation Trade-Offs', *The American Economic Review* 68: 473–91.

—— (1976) 'Econometric Policy Evaluations: A Critique', in K. Brunner and A. Meltzer (eds) *The Phillips Curve and Labour Markets*, Amsterdam: North Holland.

MacKinnon, J. G. (1991) 'Critical values for cointegration tests', in R. F. Engle and C. W. J. Granger (eds) *Long Run Economic Relationships*, pp. 267–76, Oxford: Oxford University Press.

Mankiw, N. G. (1985) 'Small Menu Costs and Large Business Cycles: A Macroeconomic Model of Monopoly', *Quarterly Journal of Economics* 100: 529–39.

Mankiw, N. G., Romer, D. and Weil, D. (1992) 'A Contribution to the Empirics of Economic Growth', *Quarterly Journal of Economics* 107: 407–37.

Marston, R. C. (1998) Comment (on A. Demertzis *et al.*), in S. W. Black and M. Moersch (eds) *Competition and Convergence in Financial Markets – The German and Anglo-Saxon Models*, Amsterdam: Elsevier Science.

Martins, J. O., Scarpetta, S. and Pilat, D. (1996) 'Markup Pricing, Market Structure and the Business Cycle', *OECD Economic Studies* 27, 1996/II.

Mas-Collel, A., Whinston, M. D. and Green, J. R. (1995) *Microeconomic Theory*, New York: Oxford University Press.

Masson, P. R. (1996) *Fiscal Dimensions of EMU*, IMF PPAA/96/7 (June), Washington: IMF.

Masson, P. R. and Taylor, M. P. (1992) 'Common Currency Areas and Currency Unions: an Analysis of the Issues', in Discussion Paper no. 44, CEPR.

——(eds) (1993) *Policy Issues in the Operation of Currency Unions*, Cambridge: Cambridge University Press.

McCallum, B. (1979) 'The Current State of the Policy-Ineffectiveness Debate', *The American Economic Review*, Papers and Proceedings 69, 2.

——(1989) *Monetary Economics, Theory and Policy*, New York and London: Macmillan.

——(1996) *International Monetary Economics*, Oxford: Oxford University Press.

McDonough, W. (1997) 'A Framework for the Pursuit of Price Stability', in *FRBNY Economic Policy Review* (August).

McKinnon, R. (1963) 'Optimum Currency Areas', *The American Economic Review* 53: 717–25.

——(1973) 'Money and Capital in Economic Development', Washington, DC: The Brookings Institution.

——(1991) *The Order of Economic Liberalization. Financial Control in the Transition to a Market Economy*, Baltimore and London: Johns Hopkins University Press.

——(1996) *The Rules of the Game – International Money and Exchange Rates*, Cambridge, MA: MIT Press.

McNamara, K. R. (1998) *The Currency of Ideas – Monetary Politics in the European Union*, New York: Cornell University Press.

Melitz, J. (1991) 'A Suggested Reformulation of the Theory of Optimal Currency Areas', in Discussion Paper no. 590, CEPR.

Meltzer, A. (1997) 'Money and the European Union', in S. Collignon (ed.) *European Monetary Policy*, London: Pinter.

Menger, K. (1892) 'On the Origin of Money', *The Economic Journal* 2: 239–55.

Micossi, S. and Padoan, P. C. (1994) 'Italy in the EMS: After Crisis, Salvation?', in Ch. Johnson and S. Collignon (1994) *The Monetary Economics of Europe. Causes of the EMS Crisis*, London: Pinter.

Minford, P. (1992) *Rational Expectations Macroeconomics*, Oxford: Blackwell.

Mizen, P. and Pentecost, E. J. (1996) 'Currency Substitution in Theory and Practice', in P. Mizen and E. J. Pentecost (eds) *The Macroeconomics of International Currencies – Theory, Policy and Evidence*: Edward Elgar Publishing.

Modigliani, F. (1997) 'The Shameful Rate of Unemployment in the EMS: Causes and Cures', in S. Collignon (ed.) *European Monetary Policy*, London: Pinter.

Modigliani, F. and Papademos, L. (1980) 'The Structure of Financial Markets and the Monetary Mechanism'. Reprinted in S. Johnson (ed.) *The Collected Papers of*

Franco Modigliani, vol. 4, *Monetary Theory and Stabilization Policies*, Cambridge, MA: MIT Press.

Molle,W. and Morsink, R. (1990) 'Direct Investments and Monetary Integration', in *European Economy*, mimeo.

Monnet, J. (1996) *Repères pour une méthode – Propos sur l'Europe à faire*, Fayard.

Morley, J. (1998) 'Unemployment in the EU – an American or a European Solution?', in J. Morley and A. Storm with O. Cullman and M. White, 'Unemployment in Europe – The Policy Change', in Discussion Paper 73, London: The Royal Institute of International Affairs.

Muet, P. A. (1995) 'Ajustements macroéconomiques et coordination en Union Monetaire', Paper presented at the Journées AFSE 1995, Nantes, 8–9 June 1995.

—— (1995a) 'Croissance, emploi et chômage dans les années quatre-vingt', *Revue de l'OFCE* no. 35.

—— (1997) *Déficit de croissance et chômage: le coût de la non-cooperation*, Fondation Notre Europe, Etude no. 1 (January).

Mundell, R. (1961) 'A Theory of Optimum Currency Areas', *The American Economic Review* 51: 657–65.

—— (1998) 'Great Expectations for the Euro', in *Wall Street Journal Europe* (24 and 25 March).

Myrdal, G. (1933) 'Der Gleichgewichtsbegriff als Instrument der geldtheoretischen Analyse', in F. A. von Hayek (ed.) *Beiträge zur Geldtheorie*, Vienna: Springer.

Newell, A. and Symons, J. S. V. (1987) 'Corporatism, Laissez-Faire and the Rise in Unemployment', *European Economic Review* 31: 567–614.

Nitsch, M. (1995) 'Geld und Unterentwicklung: Der Fall Lateinamerika', in W. Schelkle and M. Nitsch (eds) *Rätsel Geld – Annäherungen aus ökonomischer, soziologischer und historischer Sicht*: pp. 77–105, Marburg: Metropolis Verlag.

North, D. C. (1993) 'Institutions and Credible Commitment', *Journal of Institutional and Theorical Economics*, 149: 11–23.

Nurkse, R. (1944) *International Currency Experience*, Geneva: League of Nations.

Obstfeld, M. (1993) 'The Adjustment Mechanism', in M. D. Bordo and B. Eichengreen (eds) *A Retrospective on the Bretton Woods System – Lessons for International Monetary Reforms*, NBER, Chicago and London: The University of Chicago Press.

Ochel, W. (1997) Europäische Wirtschafts- und Währungsunion und Beschäftigung, *ifo Schnelldienst* 15/97.

OECD (1994) 'The OECD Jobs Study: Evidence and Explanations', Paris.

Olson, M. (1996) 'The Varieties of Eurosclerosis: The Rise and Decline of Nations Since 1982', in N. Crafts and G. Toniolo (eds), *Economic growth in Europe since 1945*, CEPR, Cambridge: Cambridge University Press.

Onofri, P. and Tomasini, S. (1992) 'France and Italy: A Tale of Two Adjustments', in R. Barrell/ AMUE (1992) *Economic Convergence and Monetary Union in Europe*, London: Sage.

Orphanides, A. and Solow, R. M. (1990) 'Money, Inflation and Growth', in B. M. Friedman and F. H. Hahn (eds) *Handbook of Monetary Economics 1*, Handbook in Economics, Amsterdam: Elsevier Science.

Padoan, P. C. and Fantacone, S. (1997) 'Who's Afraid of Italy's Adjustment? Sustainability of EMU as seen from an Undisciplined Country', Rome: University of Rome 'La Sapienza' and CER.

Padoa-Schioppa, T. (1992) 'L'europa verso l'unione monetaria', *Economia* 231, Torino: Einaudi.

Padoa-Schioppa, T. and Saccomanni, F. (1994) 'Managing a Market-Led Global Financial System', in P. B. Kenen (ed.) *Managing the World Economy – Fifty Years after the Bretton Woods*, Washington DC: Institute for International Economics.

Patinkin, D. (1989) *Money, Interest, and Prices*, Cambridge, MA: MIT Press.

Pemberton, R. L.– now Lord Kingston – (1992) LSE Lecture II (November), London, mimeo.

Perron, P. (1989) 'The Great Crash, The Oil Price Shock, and the Unit Root Hypothesis', *Econometrica* 57: 1361–401.

Phelps, E. (1994) *Structural Slumps*, Cambridge, MA and London: Harvard University Press.

—— (1995) 'The Structuralist Theory of Employment', *The American Economic Review* 85, 2.

Phillips, P. and Perron, P. (1988) 'Testing for a Unit Root in Time Series Regression', *Biometrica* 75: 335 –46.

Rana, R. (1981) ASEAN Exchange Rates: Policies and Trade Effects, Singapore: Institute of Southeast Asian Studies.

Riese, H. (1986) 'Entwicklungsstrategie und ökonomische Theorie – Anmerkungen zu einem vernachlässigten Thema', in *Ökonomie und Gesellschaft*, Jahrbuch 4: Entwicklungs-länder und Weltmarkt, Frankfurt: Campus Verlag.

—— (1986a) *Theorie der Inflation*, J. C. B. Mohr Tübingen.

—— (1990) *Geld im Sozialismus*, Regensburg: Transfer Verlag.

—— (1994) *Keynes, Sraffa und die monetäre Theorie der Produktion*, mimeo.

—— (1995) 'Geld – das letzte Rätsel der Nationalökonomie', in W. Schelkle and M. Nietsch (eds) *Rätsel Geld – Annäherungen aus ökonomischer, soziologischer und historischer Sicht*: pp. 45–62, Marburg: Metropolis Verlag.

—— (1997) Comment on Chapter 16, in S. Collignon (ed.) *European Monetary Policy*, London and Washington, DC: Pinter.

Robinson, J. (1965) *The Accumulation of Capital* (2nd edition), Macmillan.

Rogoff, K. (1985) 'The Optimal Degree of Commitment to an Intermediate Monetary target', *Quarterly Journal of Economics* 100: 1169–89.

Romer, D. (1996) *Advanced Macroeconomics*, McGraw-Hill advanced series in economy, New York: McGraw-Hill.

Romer, C. D. and Romer, D. H. (1997) 'Institutions for Monetary Stability', in C. D. Romer and D. H. Romer (eds) *Reducing Inflation. Motivation and Strategy*, Chicago: The University of Chicago Press.

Röpke, W. (1951) 'Interdependence of Domestic and International Economic Systems', reprint in A. Peacock and H. Willgerodt (eds) (1989) *Germany's Social Market Economy: Origins and Evolution*, Trade Policy Research Centre, London: Macmillan.

Rose, K. (1973) *Grundlagen der Wachstumstheorie*, UTB 22, Göttingen.

Ryle, G. (1949) (reprinted in 1990) *The Concept of the Mind*, London: Penguin.

Samuelson, P. A. (1947) 'Foundation of Economic Analysis', *Harvard Economic Studies* 80, Cambridge, MA: Harvard University Press.

Sargent, T. (1973) 'Rational Expectations, the Real Rate of Interest, and the Natural Rate of Unemployment'. Reprinted in R. Lucas and T. Sargent (eds) (1981) *Rational Expectations and Econometric Practice*, London: George Allan and Unwin.

Schmidt, K. J. W. (1995) 'Tobins q ? Myrdals Q ? Ein Fallbeispiel für den Wert von Fremd-sprachenkenntnissen', *Credit und Capital* 28: 175–200.

Schnadt, N. (1994) 'The Domestic Money Markets of the UK, France, Germany and the US', The City Research Project, London: London Business School.

Schumpeter, J. A. (1954) *History of Economic Analysis*, revised in 1982 by Marion L. Severn, Oxford: Oxford University Press.

Searle, J. R. (1969) 'How to derive "ought" from "is"', in W. D. Hudson (1969) *The Is/Ought Question: a Collection of Papers on the Central Problem of Moral Philosophy*, London: Macmillan.

Searle, J. R. (1995) *The Construction of Social Reality*, Harmondsworth: Penguin.

Sensebrenner, S. G. (1991) 'Aggregate Investment, the Stock Market, and the Q-Model: Robust Results for Six OECD countries', *European Economic Review* 35: 769–825.

Shapiro, M. D. and Wilcox, D. W. (1996) 'Mismanagement in the Consumer Price Index: An Evaluation', *NBER Macroeconomics Annual* 1996.

Sievert, O. (1993) 'Geld, das man nicht selbst herstellen kann – Ein ordnungspolitisches Plädoyer für die Europäische Währungsunion', in P. Bofinger, S. Collignon and E. M. Lipp (1993) *Währungsunion oder Währungschaos – Was kommt nach der D-Mark?*, Wiesbaden: Gabler Verlag.

—— (1997) Zur Europäischen Währungsunion – das Eigentliche und der Unrat auf dem Wege dahin. Vortrag bei der Hamburger Sparkasse 13 (August), mimeo.

Sims, C. A. (1992) 'Interpreting the Macroeconomic Time Series Facts – The Effects of Monetary Policy', *European Economic Review* 36: 975–1011.

Smith, V. C. (1936) (reprinted in 1990) 'The Rationale of Central Banking and the Free Banking Alternative', Indianapolis: Liberty Press.

Staiger, D., Stock, J. H. and Watson, M. W. (1997) 'How Precise Are Estimates of the Natural Rate of Unemployment?', in C. D. Romer and D. H. Romer (eds) *Reducing Inflation – Motivation and Strategy*, NBER, Studies in Business Cycle 30, Chicago and London: The University of Chicago Press.

Stockman, A. (1987) 'The Equilibrium Approach to Exchange Rates, in Federal Reserve Bank of Richmond', *Economic Review*, pp. 12–30.

Streeck, W. (1994) 'Pay Restraint Without Incomes Policy: Institutionalized Monetarism and Industrial Unionism in Germany', in R. Dore, R. Boyer and Z. Mars (eds) *The Return to Incomes Policy, Social Change in Western Europe*, London: Pinter.

Taylor, J. (1979) 'Staggered Wage Setting in a Macro Model', *The American Economic Review* 69: 108–13.

—— (1981) 'On the relation between the variability of inflation and the average inflation rate', in K. Brunner and A. Meltzer (eds) 'The costs and consequences of inflation', *Carnegie-Rochester conference series on Public Policy*, 15: 57–85.

—— (1983) Comments, *Journal of Monetary Economics* 12.

—— (1996) 'Stabilisation Policy and Long-term Growth', in R. Landau, T. Taylor and G. Wright (eds) *The Mosaic of Economic Growth*, Stanford: Stanford University Press.

Tietmeyer, H. (1995) 'Ökonomische und politische Konvergenz als Grundlage einer Europäischen Währungsunion', in R. Hummel (ed.) *Ein Markt – eine Währung. Countdown für die Eurowährung?*, Vienna: Signum Verlag.

Tobin, J. (1965) 'Money and Economic Growth', *Econometria* 33: 671–84.

Tobin, J. and Brainard, W. (1977) 'Asset Markets and the Cost of Capital', in J. Tobin (1982) *Essays in Economics: Theory and Policy* 3, Cambridge, MA: MIT Press.

Tobin, J. and Golub, S. (1998) *Money, Credit and Capital*, New York: Mc Graw-Hill.

Tomann, H. (1997) *Stabilitätspolitik – Theorie, Strategie und europäische Perspektive*, Berlin: Springer-Verlag.

Treaty on European Union (1992) *Official Journal of the European Communities* 35, 31, C224.

Viñals, J. and Jimeno, J. F. (1996) European Unemployment and Monetary Union, mimeo.

Von Hagen, J. and Hammond, G. W. (1995) 'Regional Insurance Against Asymmetric Shocks: An Empirical Study for the European Community', in Discussion Paper no. 1170, CEPR.

Von Wright, G. H. (1990) 'Preferences', in J. Eatwell, M. Milgate and P. Newman (eds) *Utility and Probability*, London: Macmillan.

Walsh, C. E. (1995) 'Central Bank Independence and the Short-Run Output-Inflation Trade-Off in the European Community', in B. J. Eichengreen, Frieden and J. von Hagen (eds) *Monetary and Fiscal Policy in an Integrated Europe*, Berlin: Springer-Verlag.

Williamson, J. (1983) *The Open Economy and the World Economy*, New York: Harper International, Basic Books.

—— (1991) 'FEERs and the ERM', *National Institute Economic Review* 137, August, pp. 45–50.

—— (1994) 'Estimating Equilibrium Exchange Rates', Washington, DC: Institute for International Economics.

Willms, M. (1995) *Internationale Währungspolitik*, Munich: Verlag Franz Vahlen.

Index

1998 World Economic Outlook 143

aggregate investment function 41
Alogoskoufis, G. 20, 23, 102
American labour market 181
Amsterdam European Council 136
anchor currency 37; versus basket peg 47
Anderton, B. 139
appreciation of currency 42
Artis, M. 139
Asian tiger countries 54
Augmented Dickey–Fuller Test 191

balanced growth path 160
balance of payment disequilibria 55
Balassa effect 10
Ball, L. 126
Bargained Real Wage (BRW) 175
Barro, R. J. 126
basket pegs 49
Basle Agreement of 1973 16, 93
Bayoumi, T. 100
Benassy-Quéré, A. 36
Benthamite optimum currency area (BOCA) 105,
    110–11; total net benefits in 117; *see* Pareto
    optimum currency area (POCA); *see also*
    Optimum currency area (OCA)
bilateral pegging 49
Blanchard, O. 99, 150, 168
bloc floating 47, 52; credibility shocks under 89;
    divided into four phases of monetary
    development 53–4; 'enlarging effect' 56;
    fiscal policy 80; impact of 58; as an
    international monetary system 34–9;
    logic of, in steady state 83; modelling 57;
    steady-state dynamics under 79–83;
    theory of 73; *see also* exchange rate
    volatility
bloc floating world, three-country model 57;
    empirical evidence for 68; external balance
    in 57–60; internal balance in 60; trade
    matrix of 57
Bordo, M. D. 19
Brainard, W. 40–1

Bretton Woods Agreement 7, 9, 11; Golden Age
    of 186; for monetary stability 9
Bretton Woods System 10, 19, 27;
    breakdown of 15
Brunner, K. 94
bubble burst 155

capital intensity: annual variation 159; and
    wage pressure, growth rates 191
capital–labour substitution 163
'category mistake' 19
central bank: 'goal independence' 133;
    independence of 133; 'instrument independent'
    133; as lender of the last resort 137
choice behaviour 114
Ciocca, P. 169
Clarida, R. 140
Classical economists 130
classical gold standard adjustment
    mechanism 90
Cobb–Douglas production function 156
Cohen, D. 92
collective intentionality, structure of 5
Common Agricultural Policy 124
common currency: benefits of 94–105; use of 93
'competitive disinflation' 81
'conservative central banker' 141
consumer price indices (CPI) 131
contract economy 180, 183
Convergence Reports by the European
    Commission (1998) 118
Cooper, R. 10
Crafts, N. 12, 18
cross-border payments 94
Cukierman, A. 140
currency area, optimising net benefits
    of 105
currency blocs 56; emergence of 49;
    investment function in 39; model 39–51;
    regional 27; with two anchor currencies 51
currency disruption, long-term considerations
    of 124
currency substitution models 2
currency zones, share in world exports 37

Daveri, F. 190
deflationary bias 81
De Grauwe, P. 67
demand shocks 100
Demertzis, M. 98, 100
Denmark 59, 123
depreciation, equilibrium rate of 65
Deutschmark (DM), as an alternative reserve
    asset 15
'disintegrative crisis' 125
Dixit, A. 123
DM bloc 34, 36
DM currency zone 33, 37
DM–dollar rate, behaviour of 66
dollar: overvaluation 10; zone 36–7
dollar-bond market 95
Dornbusch, R. 55, 64, 75, 92, 99
Dutch employment miracle 81
dynamic labour demand function 161

economic shocks, discussion of 98; impact of 99
effective exchange rate, intra-bloc 68
Eichengreen, B. 8, 11, 13, 18, 21, 98, 100, 143
Eijffinger, S. C. W. 141
employment: Europe's low creation of 159;
    growth dynamics of 159; motive for
    inflation 138–40; sustainable 188
equilibrium exchange rate, behaviour 66
ERM-II 136
ERM crisis 36, 72
EU-11 73; investment share and employment
    rate 1960–98 168; wage pressure and capital
    intensity 193
euro/dollar: market 32; rate 74
Euro-exchange rate 74
Euro-GDP, relative weight of countries in 99;
    capital–labour ratio 166; convergence of
    capital intensity 166; economic growth and
    unemployment 153; employment rates
    1960–2000 145; job creating growth 154;
    policy preferences 140; rate of capital
    accumulation per worker 165; unemployment
    rates 1960–2000 145; unification of
    monetary institutions 26
European Central Bank (ECB) 83, 107, 128–9;
    Executive Board 118
European Commission (1990) 94, 155–6; data 190
European currency bloc 73
European employment summit 152
European growth 1890–1992 8; sources 13;
    inflation and wages, formal model 20
European Monetary Institute 134
European Monetary Integration (EMI) 8, 118
European monetary stability, search for 8
European Monetary System (EMS) 20, 28, 47, 66,
    68, 82, 93, 139; disinflationary policies 139; as a
    European response 33
European Monetary Union (EMU) 1, 7, 34,
    73, 113, 120, 129–30, 143; as a BOCA
    or a POCA 114; country contribution to

aggregate net benefit from 117; joining or
    leaving as an investment decision 122–4;
    membership, determining net benefits
    of 106; optimal conservativeness before
    and after 142; (Pareto OCA) marginal
    cost–benefit analysis 116; sustainability 1, 123,
    125, 127; trade-off between optimal size and
    political orientati on 106
European Parliament 128
European policy frame 140
European social model 14; three pillars of 15
European System of Central Banks (ESCB) 3,
    129–30, 190; Article 7 of Statute 108; Governing
    Council 108
European unemployment 143, 146, 155, 168, 187
European Union (EU): member states, size and
    degree of openness (1997) 97
Eurosceptics 113; warnings 1
'Eurosclerosis' 18
exchange rate regimes: and volatility 51; of IMF
    members 36
exchange rate system: fixed 27; 'fixed but
    adjustable' 34
exchange rate: dynamics 56, 64–8; effects of 42;
    instrument, cost of giving up 96; flexible 18, 27;
    management, and orientation of trade in 1991
    38; motive 136
exchange rate volatility 33, 52; shock-induced 74;
    under bloc floating and basket pegs 48
exchange risk 41–5; measurement 45
exit-option from EMU 121

Fazio, A. 134
Feldstein, M. 113
financial markets, microstructure 32
financial system, stability of 137
Finland 138
'finite price velocities' 171
'flexible labour market' 155
France 81; foreign exchange reserve variation in 35;
    inflation differential to USA 1955–97 24–5;
    interest rates 1957–99 30; marginal q of 53
'Franc fort' policy 29
Frankel, J. 36, 68
Friedman, M. 15, 28, 129, 168
Friedmanian–Phillips curve dynamic 185
Friedman's theory 55
fundamental equilibrium exchange rate (FEER)
    61–4, 151

Galbraith, J. K. 150–1
GARCH model 65; of the REER for Germany,
    USA and Japan 73
GATT 14
Gebauer, W. 52
Germany: competitiveness 71; foreign exchange
    reserve variation 35; growth of macroeconomic
    variables 91; hyperinflation 7; inflation
    differential to USA 1955–97 24–5; interest rates
    1957–99 30; marginal q of 53; NEER, volatility

of 72; post-war economic model 6; re-unification 54; unification shock 82; wage pressure and capital intensity 193
Gertler, M. 140
global capital market, emerging 29
gold, as a reserve asset 10
gold–dollar exchange standard 10
Golden Age 126, 167, 169
Gold Standard 28
Golub, S. 41
Granger-causality tests 189
Great Depression 9
Great Inflation 20, 23, 29, 126, 129, 144
Greece 115–6
Greenwald, B. C. 146
growth accounting 156–9
growth rate, permanent 96

Harmonised Indices of Consumer Prices 131
Hayek, F. A. 152
Hirschman, A. O. 3, 120, 122
Hirschmanian concept 121, 127
Hume, D. 4
hysteresis models 173, 181

IMF 52, 143, 153, 164
implicit tax rate on labour 190
import shares 60
income level, equilibrium 61
inflation: convergence, recessive dynamics of 86; GNP-weighted 19; and growth rate 17; rates, convergence of 132; and unemployment 17
'inflationary bias' 131
inflationary shocks 26
'inflation preference' 104
institutional 'stability conditions' 6
institutions: constitutive and regulative rules, interdependence 6; motivational and imperative credibility 5; sustaining 6
'instrumental rationality', neoclassical postulate of 7
interest rates: changes in 183; convergence of 132; Europe's high 170; increase in a contract economy, effect of 177; and price mark-up 179; real short-term 31
international reserves, multilateral management 32
inventory theory 95
investment: decision under risk 49; and portfolio allocation 45
investment-saving relation 89
Ireland 116
IS-elasticities, national 89
IS-LM model, standard 76; three-polar world 78
isolationist strategy 47
Italy: inflation differential to USA 1955–97 24–5

Japan: BRW 175; employment rates 1960–2000 145; GDP and labour productivity growth 155;

inflation differential to USA 1955–97 24–5; job creating growth 155; unemployment rates 144–5, 164
Japanese labour market 155
Japanese Yen 37
Jimeno, J. F. 143, 146, 168
job search theories 146
Jochimsen, R. 113

Kenen, P. 68, 96, 112
Keynes, J. M. 11–12; fundamental equation of 179; General Theory of 10–11, 28; and Ohlin debate 90; stable money wages of 102; *Treatise on Money* of 179
Keynesian Economics 102
Keynesian (un)employment growth 163
Keynesian explanations of unemployment 159
Keynesian revolution 173
Keynesians 130

labour market 146
'labour market rigidities' 187
labour markets: characteristics 169; flexibility 152; flow disequilibria 161; rigidity 105; turnover 146
lagged inflation, coefficient 103
Layard, Nickell, Jackman (LNJ) model 174, 176, 178
Levine, R. 13, 18
liquidity expansion 33
Little, M. D. 32
Louvre Agreement (1987) 54, 69
'loyalty' 128
loyalty promoting institutions 128
Lucas, R. 23, 57, 129
Lucas supply curve 103
Lucas world 104
Luxembourg 115, 118, 152

Maastricht norm 115
Maastricht Treaty 4, 54, 85, 127, 130, 133; *see* Treaty on European Union (TEU)
McCallum, B. 76
McKinnon, R. 95–6, 98, 104, 112
marginal efficiency of capital 40
market clearing, speed of 171
Marshall–Lerner condition 58–9
Marshall Plan 10, 14
Marston, R. C. 100
mean-variance portfolio model 39
Meltzer, A. H. 94
misery indices 16–17
models with 'bubble' characteristics 55
Modigliani, F. 170, 173
Monetarists 130
monetary anchor, three types 28
monetary arrangements, institutional norms 3
monetary blocs, emergence 36
monetary hierarchy, models 2

monetary institutions, sustainability 1
monetary-Keynesian perspective 181
monetary mechanism descriptions, classical
   dichotomy 171
monetary neutrality 170
monetary policy: democratic accountability 128;
   objectives, inflationary biases in 135; reaction
   function of 185; role in Europe's employment
   performance 173; under EMU, effectiveness of
   126; and wage dynamics 182–8
monetary system, international 33
monetary union: costs of forming 96; regime shift
   consequences 79; steady state in 83
monetary variables, response to shocks 88
money: functions of 2; information content of
   130; as an institution 3; institution of 2;
   long-run effects of stability of 7; and markets
   172–4; and unemployment, neutrality
   proposition 170
money-demand behaviour, shocks to 89
multi-currency reserve system 32
Mundell, R. 96, 112
Mundell–Flemming literature 127
Mundschenk, S. 170

NAIRU-compatible income level 62–3
Nardozzi, G. 169
Natural Rate Hypothesis 129
'natural rate of interest' 160
neoclassical and Keynesian economists,
   theoretical debate between 171
neoclassical economics 7
Neoclassical growth theory 157
New Dark Age 16–18
Newell, A. 144
New England 120
New Keynesians 169
Nominal Effective Exchange Rates (NEERs)
   69; Germany 71; volatility (USA versus
   Germany) 70
nominal exchange rate, usefulness of
   adjusting 101–5
nominal unit labour costs, relative to 19
   countries 11
non-accelerating-inflation rate of unemployment
   (NAIRU) 60, 144; comparison from cross-country
   studies 151; defining 174; as labour market
   equilibrium 175; monetary model of 174–82
North, D. C. 5
Nurkse, R. 7, 9, 12
NWR: downward stickiness 185; Nominal
   wage rigidity 175

Obstfeld, M. 20–1
OECD-countries: financial stability of 137;
   rate of unemployment in 164
oil shock 16, 18, 155
Olson, M. 18
OPEC 29

Optimum currency area (OCA): literature 96,
   98; models 93; predictive power of theory
   of 112; selection criteria for 111; theory 75,
   92, 98; traditional theory 120; transitory
   instability in net benefits of 119–22;
   see Benthamite optimum currency area
   (BOCA) and Pareto optimum currency
   area (POCA)
opt-out 123
Ormerod, P. 139
output gaps 167

Pareto optimum currency area (POCA) 106,
   108–10; *see* Benthamite optimum currency area
   (BOCA); *see also* Optimum currency area (OCA)
Pareto criterion 109
Pareto optimum 118; instability, macroeconomic 16
Phelps, E. 170
Phillips curve 7, 19, 22, 103, 105, 129, 141, 176–7
Phillips curve world 104
Phillips–Perron Test 191
Pindyck, R. 123
Plaza (1985) 54, 66
policy-mix, macroeconomic 96
political preference shocks 121
Portugal 167, 169; investment share and
   employment rate 1960–98 168
post-Bretton Woods era 169
Price-determined or feasible Real Wage (PRW)
   175, 177
price level, theory of 180
price stability: bias toward 140; case for 18;
   defining as a policy objective 129;
   definition 131–3; institutional conditions
   for 133; objective 135;
   policy preferences for 142

Q-profits 179, 183
Quah, D. 99

Rana, R. 68
random shocks, three types of models 86
Real effective exchange rate (REER) 77, 91;
   Germany 71; index 46–7, 56
real exchange rate, movements 55
real wage pressure 165
Real wage rigidity (RWR) 176
Renelt, D. 13, 18
revealed preference, axiom of 114
revenue motive 135
Riese, H. 2, 152, 179, 185
risk premia: and portfolio shares 50; under
   pegging regimes 48
risk premium, intra-bloc 67
Rogoff model 141
Romer, C. D. 133–4
Romer, D. H. 133–4
Röpke, W. 6
Ryle, G. 19

Samuelson, P. A. 114
scala mobile 139
Schnadt, N. 172
Searle, J. R. 5
shocks, short-term dynamics 86–90
Sievert, O. 141
Sim's price puzzle 180
single currency: factors determining costs and benefits of 93; purchasing power of 95
Single Market Programme 18
Smith, R. 20, 23, 102
Smithsonian Agreement of 1971 16, 27
'snake in the tunnel' 16
'soft currency bias' 104
Solow growth model 162
Spain 169; investment share and employment rate 1960–98 168
spot market economy 180–1, 183–4
'stability culture' 113
Stability Pact, Dublin 1996 12
standard open economy 76–9
Stiglitz, J. E. 146
stocks, evolution of 161
supply shocks 100
Sweden 138
Symons, J. S. 144

Tabellini, G. 190
tax policies 190
Taylor-rule reaction function 140
technology change 157
temporary and permanent shocks (1975–95) 101
theory of consumer choice 114
'the snake' 93
three-country world, model 39
'time inconsistent behaviour' 131
Tobin, J. 40–1, 170
Tobin's investment function 169
Tobin's investment theory 162
Tobin's *q* 40, 45, 76, 90, 160
Toniolo, G. 12, 18
total factor productivity 157–8; change 158
trade balance, variations 58

transitory shocks 121; versus permanent shocks 127
Treaty on European Union (TEU) 1, 95, 124, 129–30; Article 107 108; Article 109b 128; *see* Maastricht treaty

UK 123; deepest recession 138; inflation differential to USA 1955–97 24–5
unemployment: 'European model', behind 144; features of European 144; hysteresis effects on levels of 189; Keynesian explanation of 167–70; neoclassical explanation of 163; problems of Europe 157; rate, determining 160–3; rate of reduction in 187; shocks 143
unit labour cost 14
unit root test 191
US dollar/DM exchange rate 69
USA: BRW 175; employment rates 1960–2000 145; foreign exchange reserve variation 35; inflation rate, 1955–97 24–5; interest rates 1957–99 30; job creating growth 155; unemployment rates 1960–2000 145; wage pressure and capital intensity 193

value theory 113
vector-autoregressive (VAR) models 99–100
Viñals, J. 143
'voice' 128; option 121
voting weights in the EU 118

wage bargainers 186; BRW 175
wage bargaining: insider–outsider model of 173
wage inflation 46, 141
wage pressure 164
wage-price elasticity 102
wage-price flexibility 75
wage reaction to price 186
Walras' Law 172
Wei, S.-J. 36, 68
Western Europe: Dark Age 8–9; economic growth 43; essential characteristics of 13; Golden Age 8–9, 23; Golden Age versus Dark Age 12
Williamson, J. 62, 64